One might think the title of this book is
that is there to catch one's interest and g
it is sensational, but it is also a very seri
(especially Reformed) theological assum
is a powerful presentation of the Holy Spirit's important
history of redemption—a subject that has been "domesticated" in most Reformed circles. This will be an especially challenging book for those on 'my side of the aisle.' Thank you Dr. Ruthven!

—Raymond W. Clark
Professor of Biblical Studies (retired)
Covenant College
Lookout Mountain, GA.

Dr. Jon Ruthven's book is a gold mine of insight into the serious problems facing western theological education and Christian discipleship in general. I found the insights into the difference between a radical reading of the New Testament and traditional Reformation denominations' interpretation of key Christian concepts, especially faith, to be very challenging and very enlightening. I believe *What's Wrong with Protestant Theology?* potentially to have the same affect upon the theological landscape today as Karl Barth's Commentary on Romans had in the early years of the 20th century. It has the potential to cause an earthquake on the theological scene. But, that which truly is of God will not be shaken. I believe every Christian leader should read it. I was personally very enriched, and excited by *What's Wrong With Protestant Theology?*

—Randy Clark
Founder, Global Awakening Ministries
Author with Bill Johnson, *The Essential Guide to Healing*

Dr. Jon Ruthven has written, or has helped to write, a half dozen important Pentecostal/charismatic works, perhaps the best known being *On the Cessation of the Charismata,* which is the classic rejoinder to the theology of cessationism. *What's Wrong with Protestant Theology?* will undoubtedly become a classic too. The theme of this new work, meticulously documented with Scripture, is that God always intended his children to be prophets: that is, to hear his voice directly and proceed infac obedience. This intent is the obvious (and often-ignored) cornerstone of Paul's writings, expressed especially 1 Corinthians 14; but Ruthven shows how this theme is also expressed in both the Old and New Testaments.

—William De Arteaga

Author, *Quenching the Spirit: Examining Centuries of Opposition to the Moving of the Holy Spirit*

Jon Ruthven's recent revision of *On the Cessation of the Charismata* (Word & Spirit Press), made me anxious for this latest provocative work. Those of us working with the burgeoning overseas churches of charismatic experience submit: "And why not shake up the troops?" This section of the church, though diverse and sometimes immature, has seen growth in a little over one hundred years from almost nothing to over seven hundred million (one forth of Christianity) and continues with growth that far outstrips other Protestants! So why shouldn't Dr. Ruthven give the reasons why this phenomenon, though still beneath the radar of the secular and some religious media, see the light of day? Traditional Protestant theology came to its fork in the road at its Kadesh-barnea (the Reformation). It rejected God's plan of risk and faith, took the wrong fork, and has been wandering in the wilderness of an Enlightenment worldview ever since. Though still God's children, such have been eating monotonous "manna" instead of the milk and honey of Canaan, which Ruthven calls "the continuing prophetic Spirit of the New Covenant." This limiting of the Holy Spirit's activity was a terrible mistake of Protestant theology, because the goal of Scripture itself is this central spiritual dynamic between God and mankind. Walking by faith means living in risk, a divine requisite that Scripture expresses in both Testaments.

—Del Tarr

Missionary to Africa and former President of Assemblies of God Theological Seminary.

Author, *The Foolishness of God: A Linguist Looks at the Mystery of Tongues*

WHAT'S WRONG WITH PROTESTANT THEOLOGY

TRADITION VS. BIBLICAL EMPHASIS

JON MARK RUTHVEN

Christos

What's Wrong with Protestant Theology?
Tradition vs. Biblical Emphasis
Second Edition

Christos Publishing
P.O. Box 1333
Lee's Summit, MO 64063
http://TheResurgenceStore.com

Christos Publishing produces superbly researched Christian books informed by a Spirit-led worldview.

Abbreviations

Ancient Biblical and Judaic Texts

Gen	Genesis
Exo	Exodus
Lev	Leviticus
Num	Numbers
Deut	Deuteronomy
Josh	Joshua
Jdg	Judges
Ruth	—
1,2 Sam	1,2 Samuel
1,2 Kng	1,2 Kings
1,2 Chr	1,2 Chronicles
Ezra	—
Neh	Nehemiah
Est	Esther
Job	—
Psa	Psalms
Prov	Proverbs
Ecc	Ecclesiastes
Song	Song of Solomon
Isa	Isaiah
Jer	Jeremiah
Lam	Lamentations
Ezek	Ezekiel
Dan	Daniel
Hos	Hosea
Joel	—
Amos	—
Oba	Obadiah
Jon	Jonah
Mic	Micah
Nah	Nahum
Hab	Habakkuk
Zeph	Zephaniah
Hag	Haggai
Zech	Zechariah
Mal	Malachi
Matt	Matthew
Mark	—
Luke	—
John	—
Acts	—
Rom	Romans
1, 2 Cor	1,2 Corinthians
Gal	Galatians
Eph	Ephesians
Phil	Philippians
Col	Colossians
1,2 Thes	1,2 Thessa-lonians
1,2 Tim	1,2 Timothy
Tit	Titus
Phlm	Philemon
Heb	Hebrews
Jas	James
1,2 Pet	1,2 Peter
1,2,3 Jhn	1,2,3 John
Jude	—
Rev	Revelation
Ber.	*Berakhot*
Shab	*Shabbat*
S 'Olam Rab	*Seder Olam Rabbah*

Others

ABD	*Anchor Bible Dictionary*
AGTS	Assemblies of God Theological Seminary
ANF	*Ante-Nicene Fathers*
ATLA	American Theological Library Association
ATS	Association of Theological Schools
BAG	Bauer, Arndt, Gingrich, *A Greek Lexicon of the New Testament and Early Christian Literature*
BETL	*Bibliotheca Ephemeridem Theologicarum Louvaiencium*
BibSac	*Bibliotheca Sacra*
CBQ	*Catholic Biblical Quarterly*
CT	*Christianity Today*
HNTC	Harper New Testament Commentary
HTR	*Harvard Theological Review*
IVP	*Inter Varsity Press*
JBL	*Journal of Biblical Literature*
JETS	*Journal of the Evangelical Theological Society*
JPT	*Journal of Pentecostal Theology*
JSNT	*Journal for the Study of the New Testament*
NICNT	New International Commentary on the New Testament
NIDNTT	*New International Dictionary of New Testament Theology*

NIDOTE	*New International Dictionary of Old Testament Exegesis*	SBL	Society of Biblical Literature
par(s)	parallel(s)	SPCK	Society for the Promotion of Christian Knowledge
PL	*Patrologiae cursus completes: Series latina*	*TDNT*	*Theological Dictionary of the New Testament,* G. Kittel, ed.
PNF	*Post-Nicene Fathers*	*TWOT*	*Theological Wordbook of the Old Testament*
RGG	*Religion im Geschichte und Gegenwart*	v, vv	verse, verses

SUMMARY

REVEALING A GOD WHO SPEAKS AND EMPOWERS TODAY

The conflict between the message of Jesus and the doctrine of the religious leaders of his time (and our time) focused on the central issue of how (or if) one hears from God today. Indeed, Scripture shows that this is the central issue for all of humanity! Put another way, the difference between the message of the Bible and the message of traditional (human) religion is the emphasis on two different kinds of knowing: the biblical "knowing," that is, the experience of God, vs. merely knowing information about him.

Traditional human religion avoids the emphasis of Scripture which is to communicate directly and obediently with God. This experience fulfills the promise of both the Old Covenant that is so tragically rejected (Exo 20:18–19; Heb 12), and the New Covenant, which seeks to place the Spirit of God directly upon us, put his prophetic words of power in our mouth (Isa 59:21 > Acts 2:39), and place his instructions (Jer 31:33 > 2 Cor 3; Heb 8—12) or voice "today" (Heb 3:7, 15; 4:7; 12:25) directly into our heart.

To avoid this "speaking God," the teachers of the Law in normative Judaism had decided that the Torah (teaching) of God was "not in heaven" (Deut 30:12) but was given exclusively to human teachers of the Law to decide on how it was to be understood and applied (*halakah*).

In case of a dispute over *halakah*, the only recourse was to appeal to the majority of scholars (Exo 23:2).

Apparently against the Christian emphasis, Jewish scholars were not to appeal to any intervention by God—his miracles or even his direct word—to decide on applying His Torah (since, to their thinking, they had probably ceased anyway). This position is very close to that of traditional Protestant theological education, which is all about endless information from scholars, preachers, and Sunday school teachers. Thus Protestantism focuses on "repent and be baptized" (preparation) and very little on encounter with God's prophetic voice: "and you will receive the gift of the Holy Spirit" (the goal of the preparation) in Acts 2:38–39, a text that fulfills John's description of Jesus' mission as bestowing the Spirit (Matt 3:11; Mark 1:8; Luke 3:16; John 1:33).

Against this scribal position (learning and obeying a document), apparently well-established by his time, Jesus' main criticism of these scribes (teachers of the Law) went directly against their normative, definitive approach to understanding and applying God's will for their lives:

> [37] You have never heard his voice nor seen his form, [38] nor does his word dwell in you, for you do not believe the one he sent. [39] You diligently study the Scriptures because you think that by them you possess eternal life. These are the Scriptures that testify about me, [40] yet you refuse to come to me to have life. [46] If you believed Moses, you would believe me, for he wrote about me. (John 5:37–40, 46 NIV)

Jesus, against traditional religion of all ages, faithfully follows the emphasis of the Bible, which is to promote the central mandate of mankind: to hear and heed God's voice and to imitate Jesus, who modeled this perfectly. This "word of the Lord" draws us into intimacy with Him, while directing us to confront evil, even at great cost and pain, because it opposes God's life and rule. But following a characteristically human tendency to avoid God's voice, the Protestant tradition, following rabbinic Judaism explicitly, focused on an important but less-than-central issue—the exposition of Scripture—which resulted in de-emphasizing the central mission Scripture proclaims. This central mission is not only intimacy and communication with God but also acknowledging God's work prophetically and asserting His authority over the created order to guard it against the serpent and destroyer (Gen 1:26–28; 2:15; Mark 3:14; Luke 10:17–21). Christians live by a messianic epistemology based on immediate revelation by the Holy Spirit as its ideal—even central—characteristic, as Isaiah 11:2–3 shows. Is not this prophecy of the Messiah also an example to be followed?

> [2] The Spirit of the LORD will rest on him—the Spirit of wisdom and of understanding, the Spirit of counsel and of power, the Spirit of knowledge and of the fear of the LORD— [3] and he will delight in the fear of the LORD. He will not judge by what he sees with his eyes, or decide by what he hears with his ears. (NIV)

The mandate, then, is to hear God's immediate voice, which usually commands the hearer to live out an experience of God's mighty working against opposition and testing. Scripture describes this process as faith.

By contrast, the Protestant tradition has focused on the preparation for the life of faith. The Protestant central focus was born of a specific conflict over a fairly simple question: "How much does it cost to go to heaven?" Against the greed of a decaying church, which was offering passes out of Purgatory for a price, the Reformers came up with an answer: "It's free, and here's why." This answer centered subsequent theology on the atonement of Christ for sin as the New Covenant. To support this new doctrinal emphasis, the Reformers' theology stripped the authority of the pope and church tradition by placing it on the "apostles' doctrine" in the Holy Scriptures as expressed in the creeds. The Reformation generally defended their emphasis on scriptural authority by denying any "miracles" or revelatory spiritual gifts which might be used to accredit or form new doctrine (whether Catholic or Radical Reformation). To a large extent, scholastic Protestantism followed the creedal tradition of the church by explicitly substituting an intellectual knowledge of doctrine for a knowledge of God by immediate revelation in, or to, the human heart. This issue was central when Jesus confronted the scribes, "His voice you have never heard, his form you have never seen" (John 5:37). This doctrine of "It is not in heaven," excluded the voice of God (or his miracle power) from influencing the conduct of one's life.

In this move, Protestants took a wrong turn in that the scriptural authority they sought to defend emphasized the very miracles and especially the immediate, ongoing revelatory voice of God that they denied (the point of John 5:43–47). Their emphasis upon "salvation" from sin by repentance and baptism expresses a "gospel of preparation," which is contrary to the emphasis of Scripture itself, namely, the gospel of the kingdom of God, or of the Spirit, or of the New Covenant. This gospel Jesus himself introduced (Isa 61:1–2 > Luke 4:18); modeled in his earthly ministry of kingdom power; ratified in his blood; vindicated by his resurrection; and now bestows from heaven. He even becomes the New Covenant by his very presence in our lives.

Jesus' mission was to introduce and mediate the kingdom of God, the Spirit of God, and the New Covenant (the three phrases overlap greatly but retain distinct senses). The goal of his mission is expressed in the call to action within the charter message of Christianity: the Pentecost address of Acts 2. There, vv. 38–39 allude to a rarely noticed promise of the Spirit of prophecy in Isaiah 59:19–21. This promised Spirit is the essence of "My covenant with them" (Isa 59:21). The revelatory-prophetic nature of this covenant comports with the more familiar New Covenant passage from Jeremiah 31:31–34, where the knowledge of the Lord is described as immediate, written in the heart, not taught by tradition.

This book establishes this thesis after outlining the key features of Protestant theology, by showing that the central emphasis of Scripture involves the process of the prophetic word of God coming to mankind, directly and immediately into individual hearts.

This emphasis of Scripture is proven by . . .

- the recurring, central plot line of biblical narratives

- the central temptation to mankind (Gen 3; Matt 4 || Luke 4)
- the essence of the New Covenant, and
- the central, explicit mission of Jesus: to bestow the prophetic Spirit.

The work then specifies this biblical emphasis through a concluding chapter showing Protestant distortions of discipleship—how the essential nature of the gospel is vitiated by traditional, anti-biblical methods of transmitting God's message—and experiential reality—to the next generations.

PART ONE

HOW WE GOT OUR PROTESTANT THEOLOGY AND WHY IT MATTERS

1
INTRODUCTION

Tucked away in the fine print, or at least in the oral law, of my job description as a theology professor, was the expectation that we would entertain prospective students who periodically visited to check out our seminary. Part of this recruiting effort (a dangerous part!) was to introduce the faculty. Since I was the resident loose cannon, the deans, tentatively, sometimes with knuckles white, would introduce me as the professor of theology.

I always had some standard icebreakers: "They say that if you laid all the theologians in the world end-to-end, they'd never reach a conclusion." Or, "If you don't want to get nauseous, there are three things you never want to see made: laws, sausage, and theology!" The history of theology isn't as holy as we might think—especially in the last five centuries. It's a human tendency to glorify past religious heroes as a way of avoiding present, painful truth (Matt 23:30). After all, theology came up with such winners as the "gap" theory of Gen 1:2, Noah cursed the black race, the assumption that Mussolini was the Antichrist, and the belief that God stopped all miracles when he inspired the last sentence of the Book of Revelation (against Jer 32:20 and Rom 11:29). But just because theology generates some crazy stuff doesn't mean we can't try to get it right—the purpose of this book.

I sometimes went on to explain that I said all this to say that there's a right way and a wrong way to express one's Christian faith and that perhaps it would be nice if we started with the message of the Bible rather than mining it for supporting quotes after our theology was formulated. Trouble is, at the time, I wasn't entirely sure what a theology would look like if I actually did that myself. Now I think I'm closer.

Continuing my introduction to potential students, I would then usually offer a short homily on how seminary can mess up your life if you don't keep your spiritual vision and calling a priority. "Even seminaries," I intoned, "which were founded to enhance your spiritual vision and calling, can subtly substitute an alien value system, betrayed by such terms as grades, degrees, higher education, preeminence, outstanding student, graduation, magna cum laude and the like. These are really comparison terms, but comparing what to what—which dude could memorize the most information about the prophet Haggai? Or write the cleverest paper on supralapsarianism?

"This core vocabulary of the educational establishment," I opined, "reveals its core value system: intellectual competition and pride. Don't be seduced by this system."

"The devil himself," I ranted, "could graduate, with a high degree, with excellence, even *summa cum laude* (with highest praise) from a seminary, simply because he knows more theology, Greek, Hebrew, and what have you, than anyone else! But the devil's knowledge is a detached intellectualism, not the biblical knowledge of faith: revelation, persistence, and intimacy with God."

It seems that many a jest is made in earnest, which is why I usually reserved these last two declarations for my classes—after the students were safely enrolled and had paid their tuition! My kidding around was perhaps my way of dealing with the frustration and pain in my double-minded career. Despite working with lovely, nurturing Christian colleagues (though some administrators were appalled when I expressed my dismay at seminary education), I had the growing, sick feeling that something was terribly wrong with this educational system and with what I was trying to do as a theology professor.

Over the years the fog I was in gradually dissipated enough for me perceive three problems:

1. I was definitely caught up in an intellectual focus of the academy. The emphasis in the faculty handbook was essentially reduced to our inside joke: "publish or parish"—you keep your job by writing profound scholarship that would impress other scholars. (Seventy percent of academic journal articles are never cited in anyone else's work, so you have to wonder if they were ever even read! This didn't matter though: if your articles were published in a serious peer-reviewed journal, it was definite job insurance!) Even though I was publishing more than most, I often wondered what all my writing had to do with the kingdom of God. I liked to think that some of it was helpful, but I had doubts about my motives.

The other part of the intellectual focus was about the competitive race to the top—that is, producing outstanding students who could remember a lot of stuff or argue brilliantly and graduate at the top of their class. It was also about whether or not our great degrees would impress the academic world and the accrediting associations (more on this later). Who were these people that needed impressing, and why were we even seeking their approval? Such questions plagued me, especially when I often wondered what God's accreditation would look like, and why we didn't seem to be interested in finding out.

2. I claimed (at least in the school catalogue) to produce graduates who were effective in ministry and ethically and theologically aware, but the actual courses did not necessarily reflect the ideal Christian worker based on biblical emphases (one who loves God, is Spirit-gifted, a prayer warrior, spiritually aware, effective in evangelism and discipling, etc.). The curriculum simply did not (and perhaps could not) clearly and systematically develop the type of disciple that Jesus and his disciples seemed to train (e.g., Mark 6; Luke 9 and 10). The feedback from surveys of seminary graduates told us that only 20–30% of what they had learned in seminary was useful in ministry. (More to come on this in Section V.)

3. Despite teaching in a fairly large evangelical seminary (we were told that we should stress that we were evangelical, not charismatic), I

found a serious disconnect between my perception of what the Bible was emphasizing and my traditional Protestant theology.

So, I began to wonder, perhaps my problems with theology extended back beyond my own seminary days. After all, they were only doing their job: working hard at being a seminary.

SO WHAT WENT WRONG? AND HOW DO WE KNOW IT?

As with academic politics, also with theology: I was not a fast learner. Frequently, I would stumble over the truth but manage to recover quickly, dust myself off, and continue on my way. But a big question always haunted me: How do I know what is true about God? How do I know that I'm getting it right about my Christian theology? There are so many theologies, after all—a predicament that goes all the way back to the Garden of Eden, but for my tradition (Protestantism), about 500 years.

MY FOUNDATION ON THE ROCK?

Way back when I was in my first year of Bible college, I remember sitting in the bright sunshine on a large rock overlooking a lake. I was reading the speeches in the Book of Acts. I became agitated and wailed to myself: "This isn't the gospel!" I was genuinely upset that Peter and Paul "just didn't get it" when they had their first big chance to present the true Christian message. I didn't expect the "Four Spiritual Laws" exactly, but where was the message of the cross and the sacrifice of Christ for the payment of our sins through his substitutionary atonement? True, there was usually a call for repentance, but only as preparation to receive the Spirit—which I knew was fairly optional, and at the wrong end of the *ordo salutis* (sequence, or steps, of salvation) in which I was raised. You needed the Spirit up front for conviction of sin—to be converted—but not so much later on except that you needed the Spirit to keep on convicting you of sins as part of your sanctification (that is, if you wanted to make it to heaven). True, you needed the Spirit as power for service, but that seemed mostly for professional clergy, for which I was in training. But those sermons in Acts, especially the first one in Acts 2, were theologically off center for sure. I believed then (and now) in the full authority, inspiration, and inerrancy of Scripture—so how could I arrive at such strenuous conclusions about the nature of the gospel, even to the point of wanting to rewrite the sermons of Acts to get them theologically correct?

WHY THE POWER OF THE SPIRIT MAKES EVANGELICALS NERVOUS

There was a reason why the original Protestant Reformers (whom evangelicals today claim as their own) were uneasy about the Acts sermons, especially the punch line about the Holy Spirit[1]—which is so closely associated in the Bible with miracles, revelation, prophecy, and divine authority. This fear came about through a bit of a process.

The Reformers were literally fighting for their new theology—and their lives—against those who claimed the authority of the Holy Spirit and his miraculous and prophetic power. On one side, entrenched in power for more than a thousand years, was the Roman church, supported by claims to miracles and revelations as proof of their legitimacy and by its nasty habit of torturing, burning, or hanging those who disagreed. On the other side, it was the more contemporaneous Radical Reformation that broke not only from the Romanists, but also from the Reformers by rejecting not only the authority of the pope and the writings of the Church Fathers, but also, some Radicals rejected the Bible as well. They claimed that these writings were man-made and therefore they rejected their authority, because the only authority for this group of Radicals was the "inner light" of the divine Spirit.

At this point, Martin Luther, who was the leader of the mainstream Reformation (or Protestanism) scoffed that one of the Radical leaders, Thomas Müntzer, had "swallowed the Holy Spirit, feathers and all!" He went on to say, "No yokel is so rude but when he has dreams and fancies: he thinks himself inspired by the Holy Ghost and must be a prophet." One of Luther's friends Heinrich Zwingli agreed: "There is not an individual, however clownish he may be, who does not claim to be inspired by the Holy Ghost, and who does not put forth as prophecies his ravings and dreams." Sounds like a kind of charismatic movement was afoot. And the Reformers weren't happy that they lost control.

Granted, these were not sensitive, inclusive, ecumenical times—particularly for developing a consensus about the various workings of the Holy Spirit. For these mainstream Protestants such as Luther, Zwingli, and later Calvin, miracles and prophecies had only one (completed) function, that is, to establish true doctrine. Therefore, the miraculous was thereafter forbidden, as such Protestants believed that no new doctrine could develop after the New Testament. Their formula was this: "No more New Testament additions (from the pope or from church traditions); therefore, no new miracles to accredit them," and vice versa.

So why were they saying this? Mainly because they were in this life-and-death fight with the papists (the Catholics).

THE BIG QUESTION THAT SHAPED PROTESTANT THEOLOGY: HOW MUCH DOES IT COST TO GO TO HEAVEN?

The really big concern during the time of the Reformation was how to avoid hell (or purgatory) and make it to heaven. A massive Catholic media blitz throughout Europe, complete with thunderous, smoke-and-mirrors staged dramas of hell, demons, screaming sinners, and the Last Judgment by an angry God, made church fundraising a little easier. It wasn't exactly "Avatar" or "Jurassic Park," but for the 16th century, the special effects got the job done. Especially if you explained to the terrified audience that for a few bucks (or whatever the market would bear), they could not only escape such a horrible fate, but for only a few more easy payments could get their dead relatives out, too!

Against this theological terrorism, the offer of avoiding hell looked a lot easier merely by going on pilgrimages, doing charity work, praying the rosary—a lot of times—cleaning up around the cathedral, or whatever. If you didn't have much money, you could in this way pile up enough good works to make the heavenly cut. Fear of the fires of hell definitely kept people busy—and broke. All this business, of course, was reinforced by the pope, whose pastoral letters (encyclicals) sent all over Europe, represented the total authority of God himself. If a local group didn't shell out enough support for the church, the pope had the authority to cut off eternal salvation to a whole country! The pope, after all, was seen as the last in an unbroken succession of apostles, beginning with St. Peter. So you didn't mess with the pope![2]

The Reformers, relatively thoughtful, godly, and reasonable men, were more than a little put off by this "pay to play" theology, feeling it was greedy and just plain wrong.[3] They felt compelled to protest against this nonsense, hence the name Protestant. So how do you convince people to protest against the pope when priests and congregations alike were quaking in fear? The Catholics were big on church discipline in those days, what with the burnings, hangings, thumbscrews, iron maidens, and all.

Obviously, this wasn't going to be easy. The Reformers had to come up with a highly credible response to all this—a theology that would provide godly truth and comfort to the afflicted, while also persuading the local royalty to protect them when the papal police came in retaliation for getting between the pope and his money.

The Reformers had to show enough people that the pope expressed illegitimate authority and that his methods of gaining salvation (avoiding purgatory or hell) were bogus. People wavered: how could they trust these radical new ideas against the church that had survived for 1,500 years? Yes, they could see that the pope was greedy and corrupt, but didn't it make sense to listen to him if he was the last apostle; and why shouldn't God expect a reasonable trade of good works for a shot at heaven? If the pope could be bought off, why not God?

THE PROTESTANT STRATEGY

Luther and others had their work cut out for them. If they were to live long, they had to quickly stake out their authority and clarify their message. At first, as a good Doctor of Theology, Luther challenged the Romanists to a debate that would cover 95 points of doctrine.

This was going to be a long, drawn out debate. You could spend hours on just one point! And Luther might not survive it.

So to keep it simple, Luther came up with a catchy slogan for his theology: three (or four) "*solas*":

1. *sola scriptura,* by Scripture alone
2. *sola gratia,* by grace alone
3. *sola fide,* by faith alone
4. *sola Christi,* by Christ alone—not by the pope or by church tradition (this slogan was sometimes added, though always assumed).

The first three *solas* were narrowly focused on this huge church fight over how much it cost to go to heaven–or at least to get out of purgatory. At any rate, these three key ideas of the Reformation were essentially answers to the questions, "By what authority can we go toe-to-toe with the pope," and "How much does it really cost to go to heaven?"

Sola scriptura was a sound bite that dealt first with the question of authority. It described the Reformation's inspired return to the Bible as the ultimate source of religious authority for theology, rather than the piled up traditions and papal pronouncements of the church. This had the effect of cutting the authority of the papacy off at its knees, forcing Romanists to debate doctrines on biblical grounds rather than on the basis of their accumulated traditions and alleged papal revelations. In other words, to answer the second question, a true doctrine of salvation must be supported by Scripture alone. For the Reformers, Church Fathers and theologians might comment or give an opinion on a doctrine, and certainly the creeds were valued, but doctrine itself can be proven only by a single authority: Scripture alone.

But, it turns out, the Protestant idea of *sola scriptura* had some loopholes when doing doctrine.[4] *Sola scriptura* really meant that you came up with a theological argument, idea, or doctrine first, and then you rummaged around in Scripture for some verses to support it.[5] If Scripture was to be involved in theologizing at all, in any era, that has been pretty much the procedure. Even today biblical scholars (and an occasional theologian) complain that biblical scholarship and theology are disconnected—a problem I hope partially to correct in this book's sequel. Theologians generally don't seem to be all that interested in bridging the gap between biblical and systematic theology, unless it's to put a novel spin on Scripture to protect their theology. Nor do they expect theology to be generated, typically, by reading the Bible, but rather by their attempts to cope with new philosophical ideas or to win in church fights over doctrine (a sport for which Protestants are famous)—and to get and keep tenure in a seminary! I've never seen the reverse of these steps (Scripture first, then theology), much less any attempt to discover the emphasis of the Bible before deciding on a theological outline. Biblical emphasis that gives rise to theology is what this book tries to do.

Sola gratia (salvation by grace alone) was the next slogan. It contrasted the free forgiveness of sins against the payments to priests for liberation from purgatory, as well as the practice of tapping into the surplus merit piled up by really, really good, pious saints to cover the sins of the average Joe.

The Reformers simply tweaked this surplus-merit-from-saints idea into another "*sola*": *sola Christi*—Christ alone (not the saints) provides saving merit. Hence, the Reformers defined "grace" as "un-merited favor" from God due to the only source of merits, that is, the sacrifice of Christ for our sins. The merit that Jesus generated by his work on the cross—the merit that could then be applied to an undeserving sinner—was an unassailable core insight of Protestantism. This creation of merit happened once and for all; there was no need for a Romanist mass, which repeated the sacrifice of Christ every week in church.

Sola fide (the Protestant doctrine of salvation by faith alone) emerged in case one was tempted to generate one's own merit for salvation. "By faith alone" was contrasted with the Romanist emphasis upon works or penance that involved a kind of earning one's salvation and forgiveness through certain activities, such as confessing to a priest (and paying him), fasting, doing good deeds, saying specific prayers a number of times, or visiting shrines. (Even today in the Philippines some penitents get themselves crucified every Easter to accrue merit.)

The Reformers insisted that all of this activity took the focus off the supreme sacrifice of Jesus on the cross and His free (gracious) gift of salvation. One had only to receive by faith (not works) this free gift for salvation to take effect. The Reformers generally agreed that this faith was somehow initiated and/or enhanced by the Holy Spirit (without Catholic spectacular, hellish sound-and-light shows in the town square to get the same effect). After the Spirit worked to get the convicted "saved" and perhaps "sanctified" (being good), the Holy Spirit didn't have too much else to do. Where the Spirit used to work through spiritual gifts and miracles, he stopped roughly at the end of the New Testament era—at least according to this radical new Protestant theology.

While these simple *solas* marginally corrected some abuses of the Romanist church, they didn't necessarily, therefore, express the emphases of Scripture—God's revealed message to mankind. Now, let's backtrack a bit.

SOLA SCRIPTURA: SCRIPTURE ALONE?

It turns out that despite all the Reformation zeal to return to the principle of *sola scriptura*, the Reformers' theologies weren't all that hooked up with Scripture either. So because of the Reformation theology in the fight between the old and new churches, I needn't have worried about the Acts sermons I was reading back then on that rock. I learned later that these speeches weren't too important anyway for making Protestant theology, since from Luther onward, Acts was to be considered, as he said, so much history and miracles. Therefore, Acts, along with the Gospels, was excluded from the "true and noblest books" of the New Testament.[6] Luther's noblest books were mostly Paul's epistles, whence came reliable doctrine, that is, the religious facts expressed in creeds. Thus, Luther set the negative Protestant attitude toward sixty percent of the New Testament: the Gospels and Acts. Luther allowed, however, that perhaps the Gospel of John was the least objectionable of these books. For this exception he offered only a single reason: The Gospel of John contained "the fewest miracles"! Seriously. Luther actually said that!

So, ever after, Protestantism taught that you get your theology from the teaching bits of the New Testament (the epistles), rather than from the miracle-filled history of the Gospels and Acts (too many miracles contaminated good doctrine). Luther wasn't too crazy about the Books of James and Revelation either. James hinted that true faith resulted in good works, while Revelation was not very useful, except maybe to identify the Romish church with the "great whore of Babylon" that was supported and inspired by the beast, who was Satan. More interesting theology! Though given the rotten state of the church at that time, it was an easy sell!

So for the Reformers, e.g., Luther, Calvin and increasingly among their followers, miracles (including spiritual gifts like prophecy) had a bad rap. Why? The Catholics were constantly appealing to their miracles to prove the validity of their doctrine against the "Protestant Revolt"—which never could seem to come up with any (well, they did, but they didn't want to publicize them).[7] How, after all, could Protestants compete against such Catholic miracles as a statue of the Blessed Virgin weeping real tears? Or a blind man suddenly being healed after touching a relic box holding hairs from the beard of St. Bartholomew? With all his reported recent apparitions (the latest at a Burger King in Nebraska), Elvis's sideburns couldn't even come close to that!

On top of all this, the Catholics had their ace-in-the-hole—the pope, who, after all, was the last apostle, and as such, could issue newly-revealed doctrine pretty much any time he felt so moved. Since the pope's revelations had essentially the same authority as Scripture, and since Catholics didn't do much Scripture reading anyway in those days, these papal encyclicals held the added aura of fresh doctrine hot off the press from God. Who needed ancient Scripture when you could have constant updates from the current apostle? One of the most recent doctrines from the pope is (surprise!) the infallibility of the pope! On the issue of miracles and revelations, the Protestants found themselves empty-handed, out-maneuvered, and frustrated.[8]

So after much Reformation skeptical badmouthing of the Catholics' miracles and revelations, with limited effect, John Calvin came up with an argument that was truly inspired—except Calvin didn't believe (too much) in that kind of popish revelation, so we'll call it a clever, if flawed, idea. He managed to turn a serious disadvantage (no miracles to accredit the Reformation) into a convincing virtue. Their absence of miracles proved the Protestants had the right doctrine after all! So how does he pull this off? He writes:

> In demanding miracles of us they act dishonestly. For we are not forging some new gospel, but are retaining that very gospel whose truth all the miracles that Jesus Christ and his disciples ever wrought serve to confirm. But, compared with us, they have strange power: even to this day they can confirm their faith by continual miracles. Instead they allege miracles, which can disturb a mind, otherwise at rest. They are so foolish and ridiculous, so vain and false! (*Institutes,* Prefatory Address 3).

Hmmm. Clever! By agreeing with their Catholic opponents that miracles existed only to prove doctrine and glorify saints, instead of being a normal part of the gifting of the church, Calvin managed to throw the baby out with the bath water. He consigned true miracles to the New Testament era, while dismissing Catholic claims as lying wonders, empowered by the Antichrist. Calvin sure knew how to enhance ecumenical dialogue! So despite their own experience with gifts of healing and revelation,[9] the Reformers resurrected an ancient doctrine first developed by anti-Christian Greek pagans, Jews, and a series of Christian heretics.[10] This cessationism was later seized upon by some Christian bureaucrats who felt threatened by the charismatic experiences of their own parishioners. For Protestants, then, modern miracles were an oxymoron—and completely off the table.[11] They just didn't happen anymore. Or, rather, theologically, they couldn't happen anymore. However, God didn't seem to get the memo, so somehow they kept happening anyway.[12]

WATER INTO WINE: APOSTLES INTO POPES

The Reformers also developed another clever counter-argument to cope with the pope, the last apostle. Instead of allowing contemporary miracles to prove doctrine and instead of the pope's writing encyclicals to lay out new doctrine, the Reformers simply moved the notion of a sixteenth-century pope-as-last-apostle, with all his confirming miracles and his ability to write new doctrine, back into the New Testament era.[13] They turned apostles into popes! (Or is it vice versa?)

Did you ever wonder why, of all the gifts of the Holy Spirit, almost no Protestants today—not even most Pentecostals—think the gift of apostleship continued? Now you know. The Protestants simply didn't want any more popes running around trying to boss the church, dictate their doctrines, and write new Scripture, so they quarantined them in the Apostolic Age.[14] See how theology is made? Like sausage: they grab whatever is at hand and throw it in the mix. There is a tendency to think that if they solved the big problem confronting them at the time, then they've solved everything! Not much sense of the big picture, that is, of the emphasis of Scripture—God's message.

So to the Protestants, the pope was, therefore, not the last apostle. The last apostle was, well, the last apostle of Jesus in the New Testament—one of Jesus' eleven, excluding Judas Iscariot, or twelve, if you count Matthias. Or thirteen, if you count Paul; or nineteen if you count some others who seem to be called apostles (including [gasp!] a woman—Rom 16:7),[15] or maybe even 89, if you count the 70 (or 72) "others" "sent out" (literally, "apostled") to do apostle-type things in Luke 10.[16] For Protestants, all these apostles (popes) were all cleverly imprisoned in the first-century Bible times.

So who cares, really, that the apostles became popes in Protestant theology? Well, by raising the apostles to the glittering status of popes who appealed to miracles and to revelation to accredit their doctrine, the Protestant notion of the "priesthood of all believers" was undercut. The

Reformers again under-reacted to their Catholic heritage, which was now their opposition. It was a given to Catholics that "saints" were accredited by miracles, which in turn accredited the Catholic doctrines. The Reformers continued to cling to this notion of spiritual superstars (special saints) whose status was unattainable by the average Christian, except that instead of traditional Catholic saints only the New Testament apostles could be accredited with miracles. All the miracles performed by these New Testament apostles, up to around AD 90 or so, were for one purpose: to accredit the doctrine that the apostles would write.

Protestants make much of 2 Corinthians 12:12, "signs of a true apostle" are "signs, wonders and miracles." Or, if Jesus did the miracles, they were to prove that he was God. Actually, Jesus' miracles ("signs" or "works") were to show that God his Father was at work, because Jesus actually said, "The Son can do nothing of his own accord" (John 5:19)! So, in the Protestant concept of miracles which accredited only Jesus or apostles, if you claimed that through prayer Uncle Ed was suddenly healed of cancer, you raised dark (and unbiblical) suspicions: "You're saying you are Jesus or God, or you are now qualified to add a few chapters to the Bible?"

This exclusivism directly opposes the New Testament, whose mission is to see the power of the Spirit spread as broadly as possible, not jealously guarded by a hierarchy (e.g., Num 11:29; Acts 2:17, 39; 1 Cor 14:1). Nevertheless, this Protestant attitude toward apostles-as-popes contributed significantly to the doctrine of cessationism that would dominate Protestantism for almost four more centuries. Even today there are theologians and movements that teach that signs and wonders apply only to the original apostles, not to contemporary believers.[17] But the New Testament itself totally disagrees: it has Paul insisting, "Imitate me exactly as (*kathōs*) I imitate Christ" (1 Cor 11:1, cf. 4:16; 1 Thess 1:6; 2:4, etc.). (Another case of Luther and the Reformers ignoring *sola scriptura*?)

The appearing of the spiritual gift of prophecy was similarly denied. The Reformation logic was this: since prophecy is a gift of the Spirit that miraculously foretells the future, and since the Scripture was revealed like prophecy, then prophecy is a miracle. Moreover, since the Pope claimed he could speak with the authority of God to create new doctrine (Scripture?), this sounded exactly like a claim to the prophetic gift of the New Testament. This was intolerable, therefore the doctrine of cessation could be applied here, as well.

So, to both Catholics and Protestants, miracles and revelation had only one function: to prove the truth of "doctrine" (a creed-like collection of Christian facts) or the authority of the ones dispensing the doctrine, rather like Romanist saints who did miracles to demonstrate their piety. But with Protestants, we couldn't very well have people running around today performing miracles, especially giving out prophecies, because if they did, they would be necessarily adding to Scripture. If so, then when sister Clara was instantly and convincingly healed of severe halitosis after someone in the Spirit predicted it by faith, we could expect, at very least, a second chapter popping up in the Book of Jude! Not much different than the Catholics and the way they "proved" their new doctrines—except they thought a miracle could happen; for Protestants, it officially couldn't.

Accordingly for the Reformers, apostles (in the role of first-century popes) wrote their encyclicals: the documents of the New Testament. Somehow it didn't seem to occur to the Reformers that Scripture itself claims that only three[18] of the 12, or 13, or 19, or 90 or more apostles (popes) actually wrote any part of the New Testament, and of that, only 45.8% by volume! Non-apostles, in fact, wrote most of the New Testament! Oh well, let's not get picky about the Protestant idea of "apostle."[19] We do, after all, have the concept of the "apostles' doctrine" (Acts 2:42) which became the Protestant equivalent of the collected early popes' encyclicals—the New Testament writings (or at least some of them) that derived from the authority of the apostles (the last and only popes). So the connection of the New Testament and the apostles is a little shakier than the Protestant arguments assumed.[20] Indeed, the idea of miracles "proving" the New Testament becomes even shakier. And yet this is the theology of the Protestant founding fathers, one that is not too prudent to think deeply about—rather like examining sausage.

But let's bravely think about it a little more.

We've seen how the doctrine of the cessation of miracles was resurrected by Protestants—I say "resurrected," because this doctrine was invented a few centuries before by pagan Greeks and Jews who hassled each other and especially Christians over reports of miracles among them. This doctrine of cessationism paradoxically co-existed with reports of all kinds of miracles and prophecies throughout church history up through the Reformation era. Why? Well, if you are defending your doctrines, the last thing you want to do is concede miracle-working among your opponents. It makes you look bad. This happened over and over when some Christians took the New Testament seriously and started praying for sick people or receiving revelatory dreams or messages: jealous church officials typically banned the practice. Or if they did it themselves, then it was cool. Saints Augustine, Gregory VI, and even some writers of the Westminster Confession both denied and affirmed revelation and miracles! (Sigh! More sausage.)

We've talked about how doctrine is made and defended, let's talk now about the Protestant idea of doctrine itself.

PROTESTANT "DOCTRINE" AND ITS DISCONTENTS

It seems the very concept of doctrine has its problems too. Besides having odd notions about miracles and spiritual gifts, Reformers also imported another notion into the New Testament—that is, that doctrine is like a list of propositions, or facts, about Christianity. They got this idea from the Catholics, who after all, many of the earlier Reformers had been before they started thinking about the theology they learned in the all-Catholic universities of the time. The Reformer's doctrine was based on the post-biblical development of the creeds, that is, a handy, pocket sized list of "right answers" to wrong teaching which every Christian was supposed to memorize.

The early creeds (official lists of correct doctrines) responded to controversies over philosophy and theology, so it was no surprise that the creeds answered some questions that the Bible never raised or certainly never emphasized. The more answers the creeds provided, the more debate they inspired, until we ended up with multi-volume systematic theologies like St Thomas Aquinas's *Summa theologiae.*[21] Subtly then, the creeds and the resulting theologies shaped the thinking and rewrote the vocabulary of Christians. For example:

Faith (a revelatory gift of the Holy Spirit) became "the Faith"—the (supposed) core ideas of Christianity. The very word "creed" comes from the Latin, *credere*, "to believe." We get our word, "credit" from this, as in: "You believe or have faith I'll pay back the 50 bucks you loaned me!" So, "to believe/have faith" came to mean a mental approval of and giving allegiance to a list of religious ideas we now call doctrines. (We'll discuss this problem in a projected sequel to this book, tentatively titled *How Protestants Rewrote the Bible*).

Correct doctrine (the right creed) became the test of orthodoxy, that is, maintaining religiously correct teaching or right opinion. The result was a Christian defined as one who could check off agreement with the list of right opinions. The history of the church was one of conflicts over who was right in their opinion. For a while, Christians were killing each other over whether the Holy Spirit proceeded from the Father or from the Father and the Son—in Christian love, of course! So correct doctrine (that is, getting your religious facts straight) became a big deal. In the Catholic university setting, whence sprang the Reformation, debate over theology was as big a sport as football is to American universities. So getting your doctrine straight, logical, defensible, and profound could get you on the All-American team (well, All-European team) with a lot of prestige and offers to join the big leagues as a professor.

This intellectualizing of Christianity shaped all future generations of Protestants where right belief became subtly, but greatly, more important than biblically-defined faith itself (hearing God via the Spirit and obeying). The following observation will doubtless draw the ire of traditionalists: this preoccupation with "doctrine" expressed nothing less than the ancient attraction of Eve to the apple. We see the temptation when considering that theology is usually described as "faith seeking understanding," which opposes the biblical goal of growing "from faith into faith"—with faith being an experience of revelation directly from God which is then obeyed.

The Catholic university education of the Reformers shaped a parallel theme that was central to the Reformation, especially to Lutheran theology, that is, their concept of "the Word." Protestantism was centrally a verbal phenomenon with preaching the focus of the church service: one educated guy up front uttered "the word" and everybody else, lined up row on row, listened. Even Luther was a little jealous of his authority to preach the word: "Noblemen, townsmen, peasant classes understand the Evangelium [gospel theology] better than I or St. Paul; they are now wise and think themselves more learned than all the ministers" (Luther, in Walch XIV, 1360). Luther could take that "priesthood of all believers" thing he taught only so far! The preaching of the gospel was the word of God going forth. Jesus himself was the word in that the verbal (creedal) message he presented as well as what was written about him was crucial to understand to attain salvation. It is reasonable, then, that the Scriptures became the "word of God," since they clearly were a collection of words. So then, if you believed the right words about Jesus, you could go to heaven, in much the same way as Christians believed that if they understood and affirmed the words of their creed, they would be "right believing" Christians. We still have that emphasis today—people buy "red letter" Bibles that highlight the words of Jesus, while the deeds of Jesus remain subtly in the background. The Gospel of Luke (24:19), however, says that Jesus was mighty in (note the word order) "deed and word."[22] "Miracle and prophetic utterance" was the way the contemporary Jews and Christians understood that phrase!

Trouble is, even though this is the Reformation view of "the word," it isn't God's idea of "the word"—at least insofar as the Bible presents it. (I'll leave that as a teaser to the section on "word" in the sequel to this book.)

Appealing to Scripture to support the doctrines they developed instead of developing creed-like statements mostly from the authority of the pope, the Reformers made their big breakthrough for Protestantism. As we have seen, even though the New Testament was all equally divinely inspired, to Protestants some parts of the New Testament carried more weight depending upon literary form (history vs. doctrine) or references (or rather, lack of references) to miracles.

As theologians did throughout all of church history, the Reformation process of formulating doctrine was to first cobble up the doctrine—usually clever answers in a theological debate—and then check it against Scripture. This process is called "proof-texting" or mining Scripture for right phrases and verses to support the theology already developed. It is exemplified by the Westminster Confession of Faith (ca. 1640s) when a suspicious Parliament forced them to add supporting Scripture references to prove biblical grounding for each paragraph of a theology already written![23]

One can only wonder how these scholars took this insult by laymen to their authority to write theology![24]

This same proof-texting approach is used semi-consciously by college students who mine serious journal articles and books for quotes that seem to support points in term papers—all without much awareness of, or interest in the larger academic argument of the article or book. The out-of-context quotations only serve the illusion that the student's point is somehow academically validated by the scholar cited. Used to drive me crazy when I graded their papers...but then I was convicted of my own not so distant past!

So then, much theology was written by already deciding the message of Christianity—without first stepping back to apply the crucial standard one would expect from a *sola scriptura* slogan: It is not what the Bible says that is important (a slick theologian can make it say anything); but rather, what is the Bible trying to emphasize? To my knowledge, theologians rarely, if ever, asked this question before beginning to theologize. Even the 20th-century Biblical Theology Movement, which aimed to let the Bible speak with its own voice, was influenced by preconceived themes from traditional theology rather than by the emphases of Scripture.

No, theologians usually theologize to get in their two cents' worth during church fights, that is, in response to what they regard as errors or heresies. (Of course, that's what I am doing here, but I hope my appeal to Scripture to promote its emphases will justify my efforts.) The other reason for theologizing is the burning desire to clarify the truth (with part of the truth being, for professors, the need to publish to get promotion, tenure, and respect of one's peers, 2 Cor 10:12–18).

SUMMARY

Protestant theology, by its very name, is a protest and therefore reactive in its struggle with some admittedly bad abuses in the church. Despite our tendency to idealize our founders (speaking as a Protestant fellow-traveler), it is time to admit that their theology was far from perfect.[25] We must recognize that they both over and under-reacted in ways that greatly distorted or even denied biblical truth. On some issues they both over and under-reacted when compared to the teaching of Scripture.

In their theological debates the Reformers could have learned some lessons from Jesus. Instead of reacting directly to his opponents' questions, Jesus almost always got behind the question to examine its premises. Whenever he was challenged to choose one of two options, as in the question about taxation, he properly broke down the question and then answered it (Mark 12:14–17).[26] Jesus follows the puzzling instruction in Proverbs 26:4–5, that is, to answer or not answer a fool (one who does not get wisdom from God) according to his foolishness. In other words, go to the underlying premise of the question before responding. It seems the Reformers didn't often do that: like the formulators of the creeds, they lived in the same intellectual traditions as their opponents. So no wonder they uncritically shared their premises and pursued a highly-evolved defensive vocabulary. It's clear what's wrong with Protestant theology is that they did not consult the testimonium of Scripture[27] thoroughly enough before formulating their answers (theology).[28]

Some examples:

Salvation to Protestants involved paying for sin, avoiding hell, and being good in the meantime. Certainly there is nothing wrong with that. This theme is central to Reformation theology, but it is nonetheless an under-reaction to Catholic dogma. Similarly, when the Reformers developed this doctrine of salvation with supporting themes, such as covenant, grace, and faith, they were adapting those terms to a Catholic vocabulary but not recovering their New Testament (NT) meanings. Salvation still meant, essentially, "escape from hell" (not that there's anything wrong with that). However, aside from behaving ethically, what to do in the meantime was not spelled out by theologians according to the emphasis of Scripture. In any case, salvation, at least in the Gospels, almost always refers first to physical healing or exorcism!

The New Covenant, closely related to the doctrine of salvation, was used by Protestants to describe the sacrifice of Jesus on the cross to replace the Old Testament animal sacrifices which took away sins. This understanding is what most people have in mind during communion when the verse is read: "This is the New Covenant in my blood." The following chapters will show that the Reformers missed it—Jesus' death was not the New Covenant itself, rather it ratified the New Covenant in the same way the animal sacrifices in the Old Testament ratified, re-signed, or renewed the Old Covenant contract. The sacrifices "paid" for sins in the sense that the actions (sins) which broke the contract/covenant were made null and void because a new or renewed covenant was established. This is where Catholics condone a problem when they redo the sacrifice of Christ in the mass each Sunday. Can't do that Scripture affirms (Heb 6:6)! The very reason Jesus came was to introduce, model, ratify, vindicate, commission, and bestow the New Covenant. The New Covenant itself is the Holy Spirit which enables us to communicate directly with God. (Don't throw this book in the trash just yet; keep reading and for my plentiful supply of scriptural evidence!)

Grace is another doctrine related to salvation usually defined by Protestants as "unmerited favor" expressed in the "merits of the shed blood of Christ." This "merits" concept is borrowed from the Catholic notion that saints can pile up a surplus of merits (like funds in a bank) that can be transferred to anyone who prays to them to cover the cost of salvation. By contrast to both Catholic and Protestant concept of grace as merit, the New Testament emphasizes grace as generous spiritual empowering in a charismatic sense. We get our term, charismata—spiritual gifts, from the usual New Testament word for grace (*charis*).

Faith for salvation to a Protestant is usually more than giving mental assent to the fact that Jesus died for one's sins. But not much more. It's akin to the old practice of believing in a creed that establishes you as a Christian. A hint of this is that Protestants often distinguish "saving faith" from "miraculous faith" (faith for miracles), the latter which became extinct. Yet there is no such distinction in the New Testament. In it, faith is, first, direct revelation from God, and, second, our divinely empowered response of obedience to that revelation. Miraculous faith is not a defunct spiritual gift, because all faith involves a revelation from God. You can't have faith in Christ without a "propositional" revelation of doctrine (Matt 16:17)! Of course, one could argue that this revelation does not result in a new doctrine. True, but in each case the process of revelation is clear and ongoing. To throw out prophecy because it may involve the revelation of new doctrine, instead of clarifying and applying old doctrine is a pretty narrow requirement! In the case of the one being converted, the revelation of Christ is certainly new doctrine to the convert! Nonetheless, such miraculous spiritual gifts (prophecy, healing, tongues) posed problems for the Reformers because (to them) they would either reveal or prove new creedal doctrines. This they weren't allowing after the New Testament era—even though, according to Reformation theology, a doctrinal revelation about Jesus Christ happened every time someone got saved.

Miracles (including prophecy) then, turned into a political and polemical football in the Protestant conflict with Rome. The Protestants chose to punt. Miracles sailed all the way back into the first century. All this to give the Romanists terrible field position if they were to use the miracle football to score theological points (for the papists, miracles proved doctrine and prophecy created it). Instead of pointing to biblical evidence that neither was true, the Protestants bought into the premise and both over and under-reacted on this issue.

They over-reacted by the punt: denying post-apostolic miracles and spiritual gifts of revelation which the Bible itself simply does not teach. (Sola scriptura, where were you when we needed you?) The Reformers under-reacted by receiving the widespread doctrine that these miracles and gifts were intended by God to prove doctrines. They didn't understand that miracles don't prove the gospel—they *are* the gospel. Miracles and the charismata (gifts of grace and empowerment) actually are central to what God does in this world and the essence of his New Covenant. The Christian message is more than a system of paying people's way out of hell. So the Protestant denial that God expressed his power in present-day miracles caused subsequent theology to forfeit the game. *Sola scriptura* was unfairly penalized on this one! In any case, Jesus' answer to this "no-miracle" theology was, "You are mistaken, not understanding the Scriptures, or the power of God" (Matt 22:29).

Sola scriptura represented an under-reaction to the Protestant's opponents as the center of religious authority shifted for Northwestern Europe. In reaction to the office of pope as the last apostle, it was a simple matter for Reformation theology to include the spiritual gift of apostleship (1 Cor 12:28 and Eph 4:11) with all the other spiritual gifts that the Protestant team had punted back into the first century. The Protestant punt was so effective that even today few have the audacity to claim to have the gift of apostleship, since it is so contaminated with the image of a Pope and his total authority over the church. Almost everyone in the Protestant tradition, even Pentecostals, are a little bit cessationist when it comes to this gift! Those who do claim this gift, well. . .they better understand that a New Testament apostle was simply someone called by God to be "sent out" ("apostled," Luke 10) as a Spirit-filled missionary or church planter who has "seen the Lord" in at least a visionary or revelatory experience as Paul did. Bottom line, Protestants didn't need spiritual gifts of miracles and revelation because they had the Bible.

Traditional Protestant theology, then, offered a false choice: the authority of the Bible, or the authority of spiritual gifts which served to confirm Catholic doctrine. Protestantism developed its theology in an academic setting, with its emphasis on tradition, debate, the intellectual grasp of ideas, and a suspicion of such unscientific claims as prophecy and miracles. It used these tools somewhat uncritically to protest the power of the pope and his political control over people's eternal destiny and the economic benefits derived therefrom.

Hence, the great question of the time was, "How much does it cost to go to heaven?" The Reformers' answer was direct: "It's free, and here's why." The core of the Reformers' answer was the *ordo salutis* (here meaning the core sequence of salvation—with many variations): predestination/foreknowledge, calling, regeneration, justification, sanctification, glorification. The Holy Spirit's only modern role was to be active in these stages—nothing about spiritual gifts or miracles, since they passed away long ago. This limitation of the Holy Spirit's activity was the terrible omission of Protestant theology, since Scripture itself emphasizes (remember *sola scriptura*?) that the teaching and the goal of the Bible is the New Covenant, which is the gift of the prophetic Spirit of God. The ongoing activity of the Holy Spirit is the central spiritual dynamic between God and mankind that traditional Protestant theology has so marginalized. The next chapter develops this further.

---

1. The "punch line" or "action point" of Peter's keynote address—the earliest manifesto of the Church—in Acts 2 was the introduction of the New Covenant of the Spirit, citing Isaiah 59:21 in Acts 2:39. "'I, even I,' says the Lord, 'this is my covenant with them: the Spirit that I put upon you [Jesus in Luke 4:18] and the [prophetic] words I put in your mouth, I will put in the mouths of your children and your children's children forever.'" Acts 2 begins by noting that the day of Pentecost had come. This feast day celebrated God's giving of the Covenant (Law) to Israel. It was fitting that the *New* Covenant (the Spirit) would be also given on this day. See, Ruthven, "This Is My Covenant with Them: Isaiah 59.19–21 as the Programmatic Prophecy of the New Covenant in the Acts of the Apostles," *Journal of Pentecostal Theology* 17:1–2 (2008), (Part I) 32–47; (Part II) 219–37. This article also appears in Appendix IV as "'On Your Children's Children Forever': The Continuing Prophetic Spirit of the New Covenant" in Ruthven's *On the Cessation of the Charismata: The Protestant Polemic on Post-Biblical Miracles* (Tulsa, OK: Word & Spirit Press, 2011), 221–56.
2. If my treatment of Catholics (or Protestants, for that matter) seems a bit abrasive, it is my attempt to convey the spirit of the times, which were far removed from our more genteel, sensitive, ecumenical ethos. As with Protestantism, Roman Catholicism has evolved away from the worst excesses of polemics and violence that characterized an earlier era. My own experience with modern Roman Catholics has been uniformly pleasant: I gained my PhD from a Jesuit university (Marquette) where I was the only non-Catholic in a prayer group we started. In my classes, the theological split was not between the 50-50 Protestant-Catholic grad students, but between a couple of liberal Catholics and all the rest of us, most of whom had been influenced by the charismatic renewal with its high view of Scripture.
3. Luther repeats the "shrewd questionings of the laity" when he asks in Thesis 82 of his "Ninety-five Theses": "Why does not the pope empty purgatory, for the sake of holy love and of the dire need of the souls that are there, if he redeems an infinite number of souls for the sake of miserable money with which to build a Church? The former reasons would be most just; the latter is most trivial."

4. For a useful examination of the concept, see Mathison, *The Shape of* Sola Scriptura (Moscow, Idaho: Canon Press, 2001). See at <http://books.google.com/books>.
5. Even this limited connection with Scripture wasn't always the case among Protestants doing theology. For example, during the Cromwell era in England, the Puritans sought to impose Presbyterian orthodoxy on all the British Isles—by force, if necessary. When the Westminster Confession of Faith was first formulated (ca.1640s), the scholars sent a copy to the House of Commons for approval. Since charges had been flying around that the new Confession was written as a substitute for Scripture, this "secular" body bounced it back with the demand that every item in the new theology needed to be supported by Bible verses. The Westminster divines' scriptural support for cessationism (Heb 1:1–2) in paragraph 1 did little to inspire confidence in either their theology or their ability as exegetes! G. H. Milne, *The Westminster Confession of Faith and the Cessation of Special Revelation: The Majority Puritan Viewpoint on Whether Extra-biblical Prophecy Is Still Possible* (Bletchley, Milton Keynes, UK: Paternoster Press, 2007), 11. Milne's book documents the struggle over the continuation of charismatic experiences among some of the Puritan scholars who wrote the Confession and especially their founder, John Knox—a document that opens by denying these experiences existed after the New Testament was written! For a broader survey of this issue see, Leigh A. Kester, ***The Charismata in Crisis: The Gifts of the Holy Spirit in the Reformation Church of England,*** Ph.D. dissertation, Miami University, 1990.
6. It was *within the context of anti-charismatic polemics,* against both the papacy and the Radical Reformation, that Luther developed his concept of a "canon within the canon," i.e., that the doctrines and emphases of one group of books was subordinated to another group. In his "Preface to the New Testament" of 1522, Martin Luther distinguishes the "true and noblest books," i.e., Romans, Galatians, Ephesians, 1 Peter, and then the rest of Paul's letters and the first epistle and Gospel of John, from others in the New Testament.

   Luther's *sole criterion* for selecting "the heart and core of all the books" is that "these do *not* describe many works and miracles of Christ, but rather masterfully show how faith in Christ overcomes sin, death, and hell and gives life, righteousness, and blessedness." The discerning Christian prefers the Gospel of John over the Synoptics *simply because* it contains the fewest miracles! *The Works of Martin Luther* (St. Louis: Concordia, 1955–), v. 35, 361. See the discussion in P. Althaus, *The Theology of Martin Luther,* trans. R. Schultz (Philadelphia: Fortress Press, 1966), 83.
7. Thomas Boys, *The Suppressed Evidence, or Proofs of the Miraculous Faith and Experience of the Church of Christ in All Ages.* London: Hamilton, Adams & Co., 1832. Before reading, be brushed up on your German, French, Dutch, Latin, and New Testament Greek. Boys, a Cambridge scholar, assumes you can read his sometimes long quotations in all of these languages. He does a good job, however, in documenting appearances of spiritual gifts (prophecy, healings, etc.) before, during, and after the Reformation era.
8. Early on, Luther argued in his Ninety-Five Theses, against the papacy, that the ability to pardon sins for release from Purgatory was quite minor compared with the promised New Testament charismata. "We say, on the contrary, that even the present pope, and any pope at all, has greater graces at his disposal; to wit, the Gospel, powers, gifts of healing, etc., as it is written in I Corinthians xii" (Thesis 78).
9. Even Luther claimed he brought a friend back from the dead with his prayers. "In this instance our Lord God had to pay *me;* for I threw the bag of concerns before his door and I dinned his ears with all of his promises as to how he desired to favorably hear

our prayer—promises which I well knew how to document in Scripture. I put it to him that he had to grant my request if he expected me to continue to trust his promises." Cited in Theodore Jungkuntz, "Secularization Theology, Charismatic Renewal, and Luther's Theology of the Cross," *Concordia Theological Monthly* 42:1 (Jan 1971), 12–13. In the theme song of the Reformation, Luther could affirm: "The Spirit and the gifts are ours through Him Who with us sideth." For a balanced survey of the Reformers' views on miracles, see Pavel Hejzlar, "John Calvin and the Cessation of Miraculous Healing," *Communio Viatorum* 49:1 (2007), 31–77. For a more extended treatment, Daniel Gilbert, "The Pneumatic Charismata in the Theology of John Calvin: A Study of Calvin's Pneumatology Focusing on His Concepts and Interpretation of the Pneumatic Charismata in His Life and Works" (Unpublished PhD Thesis, University of Aberdeen, 2005).

10. Jon Ruthven, *On the Cessation of the Charismata.* rev. ed., 12–14. On the *pagan* source of cessationism and the New Testament response, see Gene L. Green, "'As for Prophecies, They Will Come to an End': 2 Peter, Paul and Plutarch on the 'Obsolescence of Oracles.'" *JSNT* 82 (2001), 107–122. Against the mainstream orthodox Christians, who held that "the gift of prophecy shall continue in all the Church until the end," heretic groups like the Montanists, Manicheans, Arians, Gnostics, and the Pseudo-Clementine tradition claimed that the charismata would cease with them! G. S. Shogren, "How Did They Suppose 'The Perfect" Would Come: 1 Corinthians 13:8–12 in Patristic Exegesis," *JPT* 15 (1999), 99–121.
11. **Petrus A. Pienaar, "Doctrinal Obstructions for the *Charismata* in the Reformed Doctrine of Supreme Providence: A Systematic Theological Research"** D.Th. dissertation, University of South Africa, 1999. Pienaar examines a key doctrine of Calvin that vitiated a desire for spiritual gifts in the Church: his doctrine of providence. Pienaar asserts that Calvin derived this doctrine from pagan Greek philosophy and the aberrant teaching of Montanism concerning suffering. He concludes: "A thorough investigation of the Scriptural proof texts usually cited for supreme providence revealed that in fact no such evidence exists. This research finds that an unbiblical doctrine is allowed to annihilate the miraculous gifts of the Holy Ghost and impede the growth of the Reformed churches."
12. The experience of miracles and "revival" phenomena never really died within the Protestant tradition. For example, "during the persecution of the Jansenists in 1782 a deacon, named Pâris, died and was canonised by the popular voice. Miracles were said to have been wrought at his sepulchre in the cemetery of St. Médard; fanatics flung themselves down on the tomb and writhed in horrible convulsions. So great was the excitement and disorder that the Archbishop [Fleury] of Paris denounced the miracles as the work of Satan, and the Government ordered the cemetery to be closed. The next morning a profane inscription was found over the entrance to the cemetery: *'De par le roi défense à Dieu / De faire miracle en ce lieu.'* ('By order of the king, God is forbidden to work miracles in this place')." Cited from Thomas Okey, *The Story of Paris.* 2nd ed. (New York: E.P. Dutton & Co., 1911), 245, n.152. See also Thomas Boys, n5, above.
13. Actually, they're at it again. As of this writing, Pope John Paul II is on his way to being canonized as a saint. A nun with Parkinson's disease was believed to be healed when her order prayed to John Paul II. I don't deny that the healing happened, but I wonder why the order couldn't have prayed to God through Jesus (the one mediator between God and man), who, in my opinion probably did the healing anyway. So the

use to which the miracle is being put, proof of sainthood, is problematic to most Protestants —and to me.

14. Under the heading, "The Principle of Temporary Gift [*sic*]," Zane Hodges appeals to the Protestant axiom that apostleship was limited to the first century. "Too often it is incorrectly assumed that the existence of a given spiritual phenomenon in the days of the primitive church must automatically presuppose that the same phenomenon should be apparent today. But no matter how often this assumption may be made, it is patently false. Strangely enough, its falseness can be demonstrated from the case of the supreme *charisma* [*sic*]—the spiritual gift par excellence—the gift of an apostle. That to be an apostle was itself a spiritual gift is clearly revealed in such passages as Ephesians 4:7–12 and 1 Corinthians 12:28–31, although through inattention to these Scriptures apostleship is often thought of as though it constituted a category entirely separate from the other spiritual gifts. But the inclusion of apostles along with prophets, teachers, miracles, and tongues in a list of *charismata* like that of 1 Corinthians 12:28 can leave no ground for question on this point. Accordingly, inasmuch as Protestant theology generally has clearly recognized the cessation of the apostolic gift in the first century, at the same time that it rightly denies any form of apostolic succession, all such Protestant theology becomes basically committed [*sic*] to the *principle* of temporary gift. For clearly the apostleship was itself temporary, and, if the principle be established, it is perfectly legitimate to inquire whether there may not be other first-century gifts which were likewise temporary." "Symposium on the Tongues Movement," *BibSac* 120:479 (July—Sept 1963), 226–27. Note that for Hodges, the starting point of showing the cessation of spiritual gifts is the unassailable Protestant doctrine denying apostolic succession of popes! Hodges' polemic was made much easier for the fact that the Pentecostals of this era, who were fundamentalists (like Hodges) first and charismatics second, agreed with the Protestant dogma that the gift of apostleship likely ceased. Since Hodges' authority rested on Protestant dogma, he was therefore freed from the *explicit command of Scripture* from the apostle Paul in 1 Cor 12:31 to desire the "greater gifts." Wouldn't this include "the spiritual gift *par excellence*—the gift of apostleship"? Hodges continues: "the inclusion of apostles along with prophets, teachers, miracles, and tongues in a list of *charismata* like that of 1 Corinthians 12:28 can leave no ground for question on this point." But the number one "apostle," Peter, "the first pope," seems to deny his special status as an apostle when he addresses his second epistle "To those who have *obtained a faith of equal standing with ours* in the righteousness of our God and Savior Jesus Christ" (2 Pet 1:1)!
15. Eldon J. Epp, *Junia: The First Woman Apostle* (Minneapolis: Fortress Press, 2005). Rena Pederson, *The Lost Apostle: Searching for the Truth about Junia.* (NY: Wiley Press, 2006). Conservative evangelicals are not too keen on a woman apostle: John Piper and Wayne Grudem, "An Overview of Central Concerns: Questions and Answers," in *Recovering Biblical Manhood and Womanhood: A Response to Evangelical Feminism,* eds. J. Piper and W. Grudem (Wheaton, IL: Crossway Books, 1991), 80.
16. For a thorough analysis of the complexity associated with apostleship, see Walther Schmithals, *The Office of Apostle in the Early Church* (London: SPCK, 1959).
17. See, e.g., John 14:26 || 1 John 2:27; Matt 10; Mark 3:14–15; 6:7; Luke 9 and 10. Prominent evangelical scholars today who follow this traditional Protestant line include, for example, Colin Brown, who claims that the programmatic charismatic ministry of Jesus in, say, Luke 4:18 cannot apply beyond Jesus himself: "no one else

may claim this anointing and this role." Similarly, Hebrews 2:4 "refers to the ministry of Jesus and the founding of the church. The passage is not talking about what happens when the gospel is proclaimed in each and every age." C. Brown, "The Other Half of the Gospel," *CT* 33 (April 21, 1989) 27. L. Smedes (ed.), *Ministry and the Miraculous: A Case Study at Fuller Theological Seminary* (Pasadena: Fuller Theological Seminary, 1987), *passim*. D. A. Carson applies the principle a step further: "The apostles and other writers of the New Testament must be viewed as something *other than* proto-Christians, models of what other Christians should enjoy and experience." D. A. Carson "The Purpose of Signs and Wonders in the New Testament," *Power Religion*, ed. M. S. Horton (Chicago: Moody, 1992), 102. More recently, a reworked PhD dissertation treats this issue in a similar way. Keith J. Hacking, *Signs and Wonders Then and Now: Miracle-working, Commissioning, and Discipleship* (Nottingham, UK: IVP, 2006). Hacking examines only the Gospels and Acts to suggest that, against the Pentecostal/charismatic view, espoused especially by the Vineyard movement, that miracle-working was done only by specially commissioned disciples in the New Testament era and was not to be expected to that extent today. In this Hacking follows a traditional Catholic/Protestant exaltation of apostles and "special saints" who "accredit" their status by miracles. Considering the level of scholarship to which Hacking was exposed, it is astonishing that he maintains this position that is largely passé. Certainly, he fails to examine the contemporary notion of a disciple as one who replicates his master's life and actions, as indicated in Paul's demand that his followers imitate him.

18. That is, John, Peter, and Paul. (Scripture itself does not claim Matthew as an author. This derives from later Church tradition. And so again we wonder, *Sola scriptura?*). Most of the apostolic writing came by a later addition to the original Twelve—Paul, who had "seen" Christ only in a vision and certainly didn't seem to meet the requirements of Acts 1:21–22. If Paul had physically seen Jesus during his earthly life, the experience didn't seem to "take" until the vision on the Damascus road—where he *truly* saw Jesus. Yet haven't other people since then had visions of Jesus?
19. On the question of the spiritual gift of apostle, see Jon Ruthven, *On the Cessation of the Charismata*, rev. ed., "Does the Gift of Apostleship also Continue?" Appendix II, 195–202. See also "Ephesians 2:20 and the 'Foundational Gifts'" *Journal of Pentecostal Theology* 10:2 (Apr 2002): 28–43. "Apostle" has been described in at least four ways in the New Testament: 1) the Twelve original followers of Jesus, 2) persons who had both seen and had been commissioned by the risen Lord (1 Cor 9:1; 15:1–11); 3) a missionary/church planter (Rom 15:19–20; 1 Cor 3:10–11); and 4) an emissary or missionary sent out by a particular church to perform specific tasks (2 Cor 8:23 and Phil 2.25). James Walters, "Phoebe and Junia(s)—Rom. 16:1–2, 7," in *Essays on Women in Earliest Christianity: Volume I*, ed. Carroll Osburn (Joplin, Missouri: College Press, 1995), 188.
20. For a more developed argument on this, see Appendix II of my book *On the Cessation of the Charismata: The Protestant Polemic on Post-biblical Miracles* (Tulsa, OK: Word and Spirit Press, 2011), 209–214.
21. Toward the end of his life, Aquinas had a vision of Jesus and came to regard the *Summa* as "like straw." Naturally, the Church kept the theology and ignored the vision, not displaying much curiosity as to why this "angelic doctor" would come to this distressing conclusion. Aquinas' confrontation reminds me of a line from the movie, "The Godfather": "Leave the gun, take the cannoli."

22. The *New International Version,* created by good traditional evangelical translators, can't bear Luke's word order that might imply emphasis: they change it to "word and deed."
23. The first paragraph of the WCF appears below with the supporting Scripture passages required by the dubious Parliament, though just how the appended Scriptures in the last three lines "support" these cessationist propositions is beyond my grasp.

    I. Although the light of nature, and the works of creation and providence do so far manifest the goodness, wisdom, and power of God, as to leave men unexcusable *[sic]* [Rom 2:14–15, 19, etc.]; yet are they not sufficient to give that knowledge of God, and of His will, which is necessary unto salvation [1 Cor 1:21; 2:13–14]. Therefore it pleased the Lord, at sundry times, and in divers manners, to reveal Himself, and to declare that His will unto His Church [Heb 1:1]; and afterwards for the better preserving and propagating of the truth, and for the more sure establishment and comfort of the Church against the corruption of the flesh, and the malice of Satan and of the world, to commit the same wholly unto writing [Prov 22:19–21; Luke 1:3–4; Rom 15:4], which makes the Holy Scripture to be most necessary [2 Tim 3:15; 2 Pet 1:19]; those former ways of God's revealing His will unto His people being now ceased [Heb 1:1–2].

    However, the WCF 5.3 seems to leave a back door unlocked, just in case: "God, in his ordinary providence, maketh use of means, yet is free to work without, above, and against them, at his pleasure." In other words, in their language, "without means" would mean, necessarily, an "immediate" or direct work or revelation of God, that is, a miracle! There are serious biblical and logical problems with this residual concept of "means" and miracle, but we'll blame that on St Thomas Aquinas, who (according to 16th century Protestants) was a dark ages Catholic after all!
24. It would seem that Church history (and history generally) consistently documents the predictable emergence of human leaders who jealously guard their power by claiming special knowledge or education. This is true not only of the famous Westminster Divines but also of the establishment of Lutheran clergy a few generations removed from their founder. Spontaneous expressions of piety and spiritual vitality tend to embarrass and threaten the power structure of a dead orthodoxy. Such was the case of the Quakers in England (against whom the Westminster Confession reacted) and the Pietists of Germany. The majority of Lutheran clergy issued a *fatwah* (so to speak) against the *Kinderbeten* (the children prayers) and others, called "Pietists," who were holding informal prayer meetings, unapproved by the clergy. "The major alleged charges against the Pietists contained in this decree were that they taught *direct inspiration (unmittelbare Eingebung)*, that one could become so perfect one did not need to go to Communion (*Stillestand*), that they had secret gatherings *(heimliche Winkelversammlungen)*, and that there was going to be a new kingdom of Christ on earth *(Chiliasmus)*. The *Landesobrigkeit* included the beliefs of Quakers, Schwenkfelders, and radical Pietists under a general umbrella of Pietism." E. J. Swensson, *Kinderbeten: The Origin, Unfolding, and Interpretations of the Silesian Children's Prayer Revival* (Wipf & Stock Pub., 2010), following Gerhard Meyer, *Gnadenfrei: Eine Herrnhuter Siedlung des schlesischen Pietismus im 18. Jahrhundert,* Nikolaus Ludwig Graf von Zinzendorf, Leben und Werk in Quellen und Darstellungen. Bd. 22 (New York: G. Olms, 1984), 21–23. A Schwenkfelder was a member of a Protestant group following the doctrines of the 16th-century German theologian and preacher Caspar Schwenckfeld, who challenged the Lutheran beliefs of justification by faith and consubstantiation (a theory defining

the relationship of Jesus to the Eucharist). Not getting this relationship "right" was a big deal, in fact, a hanging (or burning) offense in those days.

25. The Reformers were very much children of their time. For example, after Jews failed to embrace the Reformation, Luther wrote a 65,000 word rant, *On the Jews and Their Lies* in 1543. Robert Michael, in *Holy Hatred: Christianity, Antisemitism, and the Holocaust* (New York: Palgrave Macmillan, 2006), cites Luther: Jews are "a base, whoring people, that is no people of God, and their boast of lineage, circumcision, and law must be accounted as filth" (111). They are "full of the devil's feces . . . in which they wallow like swine" (113). Luther recommended the confiscation of all Jews' money and property and that they be "shown no mercy or kindness" (Michael, "Luther, Luther Scholars, and the Jews," *Encounter* 46:4 [Autumn 1985], 343). He even suggested their total extermination (343–344). Scholars point to these statements as precedent for Hitler's Jewish holocaust. Luther certainly knew of Romans 9:1–5, but his theology here certainly does not derive from Scripture! You don't want to know Luther's final solution for retarded children.

    Similarly, Calvin signed off on the execution of a religious opponent (Servetus, by all accounts a pious, good man) by burning him at the stake for insisting that one couldn't find the doctrine of the Trinity in the Bible. Many, if not most, New Testament scholars today also have similar trouble relating Scripture to the creedal statements on the Trinity. In any case, the Trinity is not mentioned in the New Testament, but it *is* the emphasis of traditional theology. *Sola scriptura?* (For the record, I personally affirm the essential point of the Trinity, but I can understand the difficulty of Servetus's finding in the New Testament the odd, discredited technical language the later Greek philosophers used to describe the Trinity.)

    I seriously doubt that either of these Reformation leaders consulted the New Testament for guidance on how to solve *these* problems! So why do people today feel so chained to everything else these guys wrote? Isn't it likely that the rest of their theology was also shaped as much (or more) by their culture and traditions as by Scripture?

26. E.g., "Is it lawful to pay taxes to Caesar or not?" Jesus immediately saw the underlying trap in their question: they used "lawful" in two senses, combining two legal systems, the Jewish Torah and Roman law. The Jewish law forbade idolatry and graven images, hence the reference to the image on the coin. Roman law demanded taxes (up to an incredible 20% on every sale of any kind). If Jesus answered with either option, he was in serious trouble with either the Jews or the Romans. On handling "theological" questions, we all could learn from Jesus's application of Prov 26:4–5 (e.g., Matt 12:10; 22:23–46; Mark 10:2–9; 12:19–34; 13:3; 14:60, etc.). Jesus answered honest questions in a straightforward manner (Mark 9:28–29), or if the questions were not right, he would go to a more important but related issue (Mark 13:3–37; John 9:2–3), and always he responded in a way that forced the questioner to face his own spiritual condition (Mark 10:17–23; 15:2–5; 14:61–65; Luke 23:8–9).

27. A powerful insight from Calvin, who argued that to understand Scripture properly, one needed the "testimony/witness" of the Spirit to make it relevant. Evangelicals were reminded of this by Bernard Ramm, *The Witness of the Spirit* (Grand Rapids: Eerdmans, 1959). Calvin was likely basing this on the teaching of Scripture itself in 2 Cor 3. It is tragic that Calvin did not follow this insight to its conclusion, because, as we shall show, this is the core experience of the Bible—the very goal of the New Covenant, around which the New Testament itself is built. Perhaps relevant to

Calvin's experience of the Spirit: rumor has it that Calvin may have actually spoken in tongues! <www.holyspiritmiracles.com/2010/04/did-john-calvin-speak-in-tongues.html> (Accessed 21 July 2011) As big a deal (to some) as a pope getting married!

28. For a re-examination of Protestant vocabulary as against the Scripture, see the proposed sequel to this work, tentatively titled *How Protestants Rewrote the Bible.*

PART TWO
SCRIPTURE EMPHASIS VS. A THEOLOGY OF PREPARATION

Moving beyond the traditional emphasis on the cost of salvation and a focus on intellectualized doctrines, Part II lays out what the Bible emphasizes is the characteristic way that God works in the lives of his people. This he does by revealing himself in direct prophetic communication into the heart and by signs and wonders (Jer. 32:20) resulting in the strenuous "testing" of that communication. The purpose of God's dealings with Israel in this characteristic emphasized process was to shape them into a "holy priesthood" and therefore a "light to the nations" who could transmit God's message and power to the world. This purpose extended the implicit mandate to Adam (mankind) to commune with God, acknowledge God's creation, and to "guard and serve" his living world against the power of evil—a mandate carried forward by the major role models in the Bible. This mandate is echoed to the "twelve"—the New Israel of God—in Mark 3:14–15 and implicitly repeated in the Great Commission of Matthew 28:19–20. Part III continues this investigation via an examination of major themes of the Old and New Testaments.

2

INTRODUCTION AND METHOD:

THE PROTESTANT "THEOLOGY OF PREPARATION"

All of the foregoing criticism of Protestant theology is implicitly based not on what the Bible says, but what it emphasizes. We have just shown some key themes in Protestant theology and what it emphasizes. This chapter shows the emphasis of Scripture and how it contrasts with this traditional theology, which, for a great many of us, was our "cradle faith."

The central point of this book is that Protestant theology's emphasis on salvation stressing repentance and baptism, suggests a theology of preparation. But preparation for what? By contrast, the Bible emphasizes the goal of the Christian life, the goal for which Protestant theology is, at best, only an initiation, a good start. We all agree that the ultimate goal is intimacy and relationship with God, but what is ignored—even denied—in traditional theology is the process (direct, immediate, prophetic communication with God) of getting there.

The message and goal the Bible emphasizes, then, is the process of the Spirit of God revealing God's will (instruction, wisdom) directly into believers' hearts. In other words, the goal of the Bible for the Christian life on this earth is believers' reception of, or immersion into, the Holy Spirit, whose main purpose is to reveal and empower. This relationship with the Holy Spirit enables believers to achieve the ultimate goal of intimacy with God himself and his glory.

Protestant theology primarily prepares us for this gift of the Spirit of prophecy and revelation—a theology that essentially stops at the first half of the message of John the Baptist (the preparation of repentance and baptism, based on the sacrifice of Christ, the "Lamb of God").[1] Beyond that, Protestant theology effectively denies John's explicit, central New Testament mission of Jesus: "he will baptize you in the Holy Spirit" (a concept tightly correlated with prophecy and spiritual gifts). The end result in Protestantism is that the only role for the Spirit now is to enhance the stages of the *ordo salutis*—preparation for heaven.

How does one go about proving this apparently outrageous claim that the central mission of Jesus is to bring us the New Covenant prophetic Spirit? After all, this is certainly not the direction the church has taken since the second century! Could it be that the church, like the Israelites in Exodus 20:19, insisted on avoiding God's voice by substituting human mediators and documents instead? Yes, the goal of the whole Bible was always direct communication, resulting in the New Covenant Spirit: the prophetic "words in the mouth" (Isa 59:21 > Acts 2:39 and God's "instruction" written internally, that is, in the heart—Jer 31:33 > 2 Cor 3; Heb 8—12).

OUR LOOSELY-APPLIED METHOD

So far I've given prominence to emphasis: what does traditional Protestant theology emphasize and what does the Bible emphasize? To answer the question, "What's wrong with Protestant Theology?" we must have some kind of standard by which to judge wrong and right.

My proposal is this: 1) I shall lay out how we know the Bible emphasizes something; obviously it can't simply be what I think is an emphasis; we must show objective standards. 2) I shall then employ these various standards to show a transparent and consistent result.

For each aspect evidence for my thesis, I will first indicate which method(s) of determining biblical emphasis I will use. The following is a list of commonsense methods for determining emphasis in all literature.

Contemporary content-analysis methods for establishing emphasis may be applied to Scripture via the following procedures, that is, by determining . . .

1. the percentage of a document's space devoted to a subject;[2]
2. the frequency with which a subject is discussed or mentioned;[3]
3. repetition;[4]
4. statements that appear to summarize larger amounts of material;[5]
5. statements of personal or group goals, e.g., what is prayed for, hoped for, or expression of objectives in terms of spiritual development (e.g., Phil 3:8–11), commands, etc.;
6. summaries of a person's ministry, e.g., Acts 10:38; 1 John 3:8; Rom 15:18–19; 2 Cor 12:12, etc.;
7. statements of the general Christian mission or commission (Mark 3:13–14; Matt 28:19–20; Luke 9 || Matt 10; Acts 1:8), etc., indicating the central raison d'être of the New Testament;
8. whether or not the text actually says a subject is important (e.g., Mark 12:28, the first commandment);
9. the climax (action point) of a speech or list (e.g., Acts 2:38–39).[6]

It is possible that these various devices could produce contradictory results, but at least the conflict would be fought out on biblical grounds rather than on external agendas.[7] These simple hermeneutical devices are not new, but in biblical studies they have not been used consistently enough by evangelicals.[8] If applied to the extent possible, they would allow the biblical text rather than traditions to dictate a hierarchy of emphases and values. Obviously, we cannot apply all of these criteria to every word or paragraph of the Bible if we don't want a book the size of a library! As we go along, I will occasionally point out the emphasis pattern to underscore a point being made. Although most of the time the emphasis pattern will be self-evident, I ask that you keep the issue of emphasis in the back of your mind when reading.

You will note that I often lay out large sections of Scripture for later comment. This is because while reading these passages I was struck by their power and beauty and found them so very effective if allowed to speak in their own voice. I know it is against the usual academic good form to cite long biblical passages, but I think this scholarly protocol is often a subtle attempt to minimize the force of the holy, written word of God. Please don't quickly jump over these biblical passages, but carefully and thoughtfully ponder as you read, allowing the Spirit to speak to you through his written word to discover its own emphasis.

MOVING BEYOND THE PROTESTANT THEOLOGY OF PREPARATION TO THE EMPHASIS OF SCRIPTURE

How do we prove this? The core experience in Scripture is the word/voice/message of God spoken directly into one's heart.[9] This experience is modeled and taught from every possible angle. We are trying to push the principle of *sola scriptura* to a new, more complete level to show that this core experience of the hearing and testing of the revelation of God's word in the heart is the central theme of the Bible from several lines of biblical evidence. It is against the "religious" tradition that tries to deny or diminish the process of direct, immediate revelation to the heart. Each of these five proofs expresses a biblical emphasis that leads to the same conclusion: God speaks directly to us today and empowers us with his Spirit. To create faith his word will necessarily be tested with all kinds of distractions and persecutions until the word is vindicated.

Proof 1: The word or wisdom of God is the creative power of all creation. (Genesis 1 and Proverbs 8 answer the old philosophical question, "Why is there something and not nothing?")

Proof 2: The first proof sets the pattern for the core plot line for almost all of the narratives in the Bible: God speaks directly to someone, who is then expected to respond appropriately even through great frustration and stress, before the word is fulfilled (Heb 11). Think of the pattern for the patriarchs Noah, Abraham, Isaac, Jacob, and Joseph, and then recall how direct revelation and response through severe trials is also the plot line for Moses, Joshua, the children of Israel, the judges, kings, and prophets. In the wisdom literature (Job, Psa, Prov, Eccl), it is clear that the wisdom comes "from above" as a word from the Lord: "The fear (attentive listening) of the Lord is the beginning/source of wisdom" (Prov 1:7). The plot line is advocated here: "Get wisdom"—that is, revealed guidance from the Lord.

In the New Testament, the identification of Jesus is through prophets —"The testimony of Jesus is the Spirit of prophecy" (Rev 19:10). Jesus himself is presented as a model for hearing the Father's voice and obeying (John 5:30). In Acts, in developing the New Covenant of Isaiah 59:21, the apostles and evangelists are constantly guided by the voice of God, thereby encountering persecution and suffering. The plot line of biblical narrative is unvarying: hearing (implicitly or not) the voice of God and obeying through frustration and resistance.

Proof 3: A second line of evidence derives from the central temptation of mankind. Speaking of emphasis, what does the Bible hold out as the issue facing humanity? To hear and obey the immediate word of God or not. Eve and Adam did not; Jesus did. Jesus' thesis response to the three temptations is, "Man does not live by bread alone, but by every word that proceeds from the mouth of God" (Matt 4:4).

Proof 4: The New Covenant is the answer to the temptation narratives. It is the solution and goal of the Bible: the essence of the New Covenant consists of the immediate message of God directly into the heart. The two "New Covenant" passages that identify the goal and purpose of the entire Bible are mainly Jeremiah 31:31–34 and Isaiah 59:21.

Proof 5: This revelatory essence of the Bible's message is shown from summary statements about it, the substance of the commissions to Jesus' disciples, and the focus of New Testament prayers.

Proof 6: Faith expresses the core value and central living-out pattern of the Christian life. The nature of faith involves a hearing of God's immediate word and responding appropriately. Faith is closely related to the kingdom of God, that is, the ruling activity of God that involves a "hearing" of faith for it to be actualized.

BIBLICAL NARRATIVES OVERWHELMINGLY TEACH THE NORMATIVE AND CENTRAL EXPERIENCE OF THE IMMEDIATE AND PERSONALLY REVEALED WORD AND ITS TESTING (THE LIFE OF FAITH)

This section will show (once we've removed the filter of traditional theology) that the plot line of the biblical narratives can be reduced to two basic elements: 1) God usually reveals instructions immediately into the protagonist's heart; and, 2) he or she then goes through great testing of that word—"Every word of God is tested/smelted/refined." (Prov 30:3).[10] This testing is required (and therefore recurs so constantly) to move people from the bad habit of depending upon their own mental decision-making to "inquiring of the Lord" or "walking in faith," that is, hearing and heeding God's voice.

CAN WE APPLY THESE "UNIQUE" EXPERIENCES IN THE BIBLE TO OURSELVES? DON'T THEY HAVE TO BE SANITIZED FIRST?

The Bible itself says these stories are "written for our instruction" (Rom. 15:4; 1 Cor. 10:11). Doesn't this strongly imply that we are not to change these stories to fit our theology? Doesn't it mean that the experiences with God described in these stories are intended to apply to us? When James generalizes to "the effective prayer of a righteous man can accomplish much" based on the case of Elijah praying for a miracle (5:16–18), doesn't this teach that we are to pray for miracles? Certainly, Jesus urges us to have faith (hear from God and act accordingly) in order to see miracles (e.g., Mark 5:34—and just about every other place faith is mentioned in the Gospels).

THE TRADITIONALIST FILTER ("VEIL"):A REGRESSION FROM THE NEW COVENANT TO THE OLD

Problem is, if we are shaped by traditional theology, we will read these stories with a traditional Protestant filter: every time we read about God's speaking to one of these Bible characters, we semi-consciously translate the event: since God can't speak directly to me today, how I apply this to myself is to remember that I hear from God only by reading Scripture.

In other words, traditionalist Protestants regress in exactly the opposite direction that Paul describes in 2 Corinthians 3: from the prophetic Spirit that writes God's law/teaching in the heart, to written words that must be interpreted and applied by men. Protestantism lives in the Old Covenant era of John the Baptist—the Gospel of Preparation: "repent and be baptized for your sins."

But the punch line of John's message is that one "mightier than I" will come and he will "baptize you in the Holy Spirit." Protestantism has no real place for this promise, except that the Holy Spirit will help out in convicting of sins in the preparation phase. Its cessationism demands that Jesus not bring the Spirit of prophecy that reveals his word directly into the hearts, as the normative expression of the New Covenant. Remember? The goal of Protestantism is to get you out of hell and into heaven, and be "good" in the meantime, while the true calling or goal of the New Covenant—to be a prophet of God—is off the Protestant table! In doing this, Protestants miss the core message of the whole Bible, the Bible they claim to protect and defend from further revelation. If you're a traditional Protestant getting enraged right now and saying, "This isn't what Protestantism is all about!" Then think back on the emphasis of all the sermons you've heard this past year. Look at the emphasis of your systematic theology textbooks. Isn't it all about how Jesus came to take away your sins rather than the New Testament emphasis on Jesus's mission for the Spirit—that he introduced (Isa 61:1–2), modeled (in his miracles and ministry), ratified (on the cross), vindicated (resurrection), commissioned and bestows this New Covenant Spirit? Think about it. This New Testament paradigm is the original biblical *sola scriptura* pattern of Jesus' mission!

The contrast between these two paradigms of Jesus's mission—Protestant and that of the New Testament—appears clearly in the way Protestantism typically interprets the work of the Spirit that Jesus introduced. For example when I use this Protestant interpretive veil/filter, if a New Testament miracle happens it translates into a metaphor of the Protestant gospel of salvation: that is, the blind "see" the light of the gospel; the deaf "hear" the word of truth; the lame "walk" the paths of righteousness; the "dead" are made "alive" by spiritual rebirth, and so forth.

And if the Bible story is about receiving the Spirit, it gets translated into the experience of regeneration unto salvation and being convicted of sins. Both of these experiences are divine revelation, incidentally—but, on traditionalist Protestant terms, they don't count as miraculous charismata! As the Bible uses the terms, the word that is implanted in our hearts by the Spirit and comes out of our mouths as words of "prophecy, wisdom, and revelation" is for Protestants memorized Scripture! While God can, and most often does, use memorized Scripture in prophetic revelation and application, using only human wisdom in applying Scripture is not the word of God in the biblical sense. This process of the word limited to scriptural exposition and application is the essence of human tradition of the scribes and Pharisees that Jesus condemns (John 5:37b–39).

Saying that there can be no more direct, immediate "words from the Lord" to someone today because that would add to Scripture is like saying that Congress can't pass any more laws today because that would add to the Constitution! Ideally, both Scripture and the Constitution guide and restrict their subsequent expressions (or they at least should). Prophecy and revelation are both like new laws in that they should appropriate application of the original documents into real life. Neither the Scriptures nor the Constitution are changed by these applications that they themselves authorize.

Just as the Constitution expects the enactment of new laws that apply constitutional principles, so Scripture urges preaching, prophecy, and miracles as applications of the intention and message of Scripture. Clear, biblical commands about prophecy and other spiritual gifts—for example: "let us use," "strive to excel [in spiritual gifts]," "desire earnestly," "do not quench," etc.—are simply ignored and flouted by cessationists.[11] Moreover, just because some laws are unconstitutional and because some prophecies are unscriptural doesn't mean that you throw the baby out with the bath water and give up your obligation to pass laws or seek God's revelation. Rather, the right approach is to correct the inappropriate actions and move on (1 Cor 14:29; 1 Thes 5:19–20).[12]

This cessationist view that spiritual gifts were given only to prove New Testament doctrines and therefore ceased after the New Testament was written is like an ambulance worker detecting your heartbeat to prove you're still alive. According to cessationist logic, as soon as your heart has proved you are alive by beating, it should stop beating because it has fulfilled its purpose. (A lifesaving hint: make sure your ambulance worker is not a cessationist before you pass out!) No. Like your heart, spiritual gifts were given for the ongoing organic life of the church.[13]

As for the Protestant demythologizing,[14] or metaphorizing, process, we can trace its use throughout church history. Allegory on miracles was developed to a high art by Reformation theologians since they had no other use for New Testament prophecy except as pre-written Scripture, or for miracles except as proof for the authoritative status of Jesus or the apostles. In application, miracle stories came to be used as metaphors of receiving salvation, that is, becoming heaven-bound.

SO JUST HOW DOES DIRECT REVELATION APPEAR IN THE BIBLE, AND HOW DOES IT APPLY?

But why are these New Testament stories told? If they are "given to us for our instruction" (1 Cor 10:11), then it seems clear that the characters are held up as "examples for us" (1 Cor 10:6). But examples of what? The short answer: faith. The Scriptures, again, are "written for our instruction, that through perseverance and the encouragement of the Scriptures we might have hope" (Rom 15:4). This hope is very close to the notion of faith, which is a revealed assurance that a communication from God is coming true (Heb 6:11–12).

The Epistle to the Hebrews spells out how this faith process works. After a long discussion of the New Covenant of the Spirit inaugurated by Jesus "the author and finisher of our faith" in chapters 8—10, the next chapter gives a series of examples of how this New Covenant faith is modeled in life. Chapter 11 is the so-called "gallery of the faithful," displaying role models for hearing and obeying God.

Chapter 11 at first describes the nature of faith: a divinely-revealed assurance, a kind of experience of God's revealed promise.[15] Faith is not assent to a creed or to a set of beliefs but the process of hearing God in our hearts and obeying (the essence of the New Covenant). The rest of the chapter gives examples of this faith: people hearing, obeying, and suffering as they obeyed. Are they held out to us as models or not? Aren't they exemplars of the pattern of "hearing God" (which produces divine assurance) and faithfully obeying that word through the resulting suffering?[16]

Hebrews 11:6 says this hearing-and-obeying pattern is the only way God has for redemption: "Without faith it is impossible to please Him, for he who comes to God must believe that He is, and that He is a rewarder of those who seek Him." The first part of faith is the New Covenant process of hearing God directly and receiving his word immediately into one's heart; the second part is obeying this word, no matter what. That is the only way we can please God—or even approach him! The devil has Scripture in his heart, but not faith! See the difference? Faith is a different way of knowing than memorizing Bible verses or theology or a creed. Human intellectual interpretation of Scripture is the Old Covenant way of knowing, which still must be understood and appropriated by faith if one is to approach God. This is why seminaries and Sunday schools fail: because they substitute a memory of the mighty acts of God (no longer occurring) for first-hand experience of God's power. Paul generalized "whatever is not of faith is sin" (Rom 14:23c), indicating the Bible's own criterion, or standard, by which we know things.[17]

OVERVIEW OF EXAMPLES OF FAITH IN SCRIPTURE

The Scriptures give us examples (narratives) of how we live out this generalization. The subsequent chapters of Part II summarize some of these examples, and continue to trace the narrative portions of the Bible to see the repeated pattern of God's word coming to an individual (or group) and the testing that comes as a result of receiving that word. Chapter 3 explores the Pentateuch (the first five books of the Bible); Chapter 4, Israel's later history; Chapter 5, the prophets and wisdom literature. Then Part III explores the biblical emphasis thematically: Chapter 6, The Central Issue of Humanity—Temptation Narratives; Chapter 7: The Goal of the Bible—The New Covenant; Chapter 8: The Essence of the Gospel of the Kingdom; and Chapter 9: The New Covenant Spirit in Word and Power.

NOTE ON O. PALMER ROBERTSON'S TWO-STAGE NEW COVENANT THEORY OF CESSATIONISM

In *The Final Word: A Biblical Response to the Case for Tongues and Prophecy Today* (Carlisle, NJ: Banner of Truth Trust, 1993), 78–81, author O. Palmer Robertson offers the ingenious (and circular) argument that the explicit New Testament commands may be appropriately denied today, such as, to "desire earnestly spiritual gifts, especially that you may prophesy" and "do not forbid to speak in tongues," or, "the eye [one spiritual gift] cannot say to the hand [another spiritual gift], 'I have no need of you'; or again the head to the feet, 'I have no need of you'" (1 Cor 12:21. Cessationism denies this New Testament principle!) These commands, according to Robertson, are somehow part of a scheme of progressive revelation—"stages of the new covenant"—within the New Testament. The fact that these commands are in the New Testament may express only an early stage of God's covenant plan: after God causes these gifts to cease, these commands are no longer relevant today.

Robertson offers some examples of the two-stage pattern. He cites Jesus at one point commissioning his disciples to take no provisions with them (Luke 10:4), whereas later (Luke 22:36–38) he commands them to take along a purse or bag (with money) and to buy a sword.

But is this in fact a contradiction, indicating two stages in the New Covenant? Not at all. In Luke 22:37 Jesus issues a sardonic command with the gist, If you're going to sin, do it now, because Scripture is to be fulfilled: "He was numbered among the transgressors." Proof of their already not trusting in God's provision was their bright response: "Lord look! Here are two swords!" Jesus' irony went right over their heads. He responded wearily (or sarcastically?), "It's enough!"

The context of the Luke passage is the problem of temptation—particularly the temptation to rely on oneself instead of God. The Jewish custom for the night of Passover also involved remaining awake all night to commemorate the "watch" for their deliverance of the Exodus. Jesus did this, but the disciples fell asleep and therefore into temptation. Jesus therefore asked, "Couldn't you 'watch' with me for even an hour?" (Matt 14:37–41). Robertson, like the disciples, misses the point of the passage in claiming that these two commands (not to take provisions, then to take them) contradict each other, thereby representing two stages of the New Covenant. Jesus' point is exactly the opposite of what Robertson intends: Jesus is not moving from one phase of the New Covenant to another, but rather confirming the same point: trust in God rather than the resources of a "transgressor."

He further misses the point when he contrasts the two other apparent contradictory commands of Jesus that he uses to prove two stages in the New Covenant Jesus' command for the first commission to go "only to the house of Israel" (Matt 10:6; cf.15:24) and then to "all nations" (Matt 28:19). This is superficially a two-stage movement of the covenant, expanding from its being offered to "the Jew first" and only then also to the Gentiles. This sequence fulfills Scripture: Isa 59:19–21 (its universalism predicated on the offer of the covenant to "Jacob") where the covenant of the Spirit is offered both to the "men of Israel" as well as to "all flesh" (Acts 2:22, 17 > Joel 2:28).

But this argument is also from an analogy to "those who are afar off—that is, as many as whom the Lord God shall call" (Acts 2:39). This analogy has no bearing on the universal and permanent command for the gift of the Spirit to Jew and Gentile (with the prophetic words in the mouths of their children's children). In the context of offering the covenant to the Jews and Gentiles, Paul also paraphrases Isa 59:21 > Rom 11:29: "For the charismata and calling of God are irrevocable—not called back." Is this universal principle of Isaiah and Paul abolished from Scripture by the higher revelation of cessationism?

So what does the term charismata mean? In all of the remaining eight cases of charismata in the New Testament, every one of them refers to spiritual gifts that necessarily imply prophecy and likely also miracles and other revelatory gifts (Rom 12:6; 1 Cor 1:7; 12:4, 9, 28, 30, 31 and 1 Tim 4:4).

The bottom line here—unlike the analogy with Robertson's two-stage covenant theory denying spiritual gifts: "desire spiritual gifts" then, effectively "don't desire spiritual gifts"—is that Robertson's precedent simply describes the geographical expansion of the Covenant of the Spirit. Yet this pattern was always implicit in God's plan for miracles to be shown for all mankind: "[Thou] who hast set signs and wonders in the land of Egypt, and even to this day both in Israel and among mankind; and Thou hast made a name for Thyself, as at this day" (Jeremiah 32:20). Acts 2:17 and 39 make this same point abundantly in the movement from "men of Israel" to "all flesh" and to "those who are afar off, even as many as the Lord your God shall call."

Simply because the Covenant of the Spirit moves from one stage to another geographically does not prove that the essence of the Covenant (prophetic revelation to mankind) changes in stages. The most unlikely of scenarios is that such revelation was offered to the earliest believers but then withdrawn later (again, Isa 59:21 > Acts 2:39 and Rom 11:29). Against Robertson is the overwhelming evidence of history that spiritual gifts appeared constantly in the church.

The other example of New Testament contradiction Robertson offers is the command to Gentile Christians to abstain from "things contaminated by idols, and from fornication and from what is strangled and from blood" (Acts 15:20), which Robertson identifies as at variance with 1 Cor 8:4, 9: "Paul declares that God has made all foods clean and that offering a piece of meat to an idol has no effect on its eatability [sic] so long as a weaker brother is not led into sin" p. 80–81.

This is no contradiction at all. In Acts 15:21 the reason for the restrictions on the new Gentile Christians is the same as Paul's in 1 Cor 8, that is, to avoid unnecessary offense to Jews because Jews who keep the law are in "every city." Besides, specific instructions in Acts 15:20 are for all Gentiles under the Noahic law, the Jewish tradition being spelled out almost word-for-word in Jubilees 7:20–28. Acts is not imposing Jewish law on the Gentiles but the generally-accepted laws of God to identify righteous Gentiles! The principles underlying both Acts 15 and 1 Cor 8 are identical: not giving offense to a weaker brother—in both cases those who were still under the Old Covenant of the written law.

Most crucially, the only possible example of some sort of dispensational rescinding of a command that Robertson offers—the shift from Jews alone to Jews and Gentiles—does not apply to the commands to prophesy and not to forbid speaking in tongues. Why? Because unlike the examples he gives, nowhere does the New Testament rescind the commands to seek or employ spiritual gifts in any way shape or form. In fact, many passages indicate they will continue until the end of this age. Against the clear commands and teaching of Scripture, Robertson can only speculate, without evidence, that somehow there might be a two-stage dispensation at work within the New Covenant.

Most fatal of all, Robertson's cessationism takes us backwards from the New Covenant of the Spirit—a term that was virtually synonymous with revelation and prophecy in New Testament times—to a covenant that is written. (Didn't Paul address this issue in detail in 2 Cor 3?) This cessationism is the doctrine of the scribes and Pharisees, the rabbinic doctrine of "it is not in heaven" (Deut 30:11–13) regarding the Law's being given to mankind.

It is interesting that in 2 Cor 3 Paul appeals to direct, immediate revelation, as Jesus did, when faced with the same temptation by the devil: Deut 30:14 and Jesus: Deut 8:3 > Matt 4:4 || Luke 4:4. The essence of the New Covenant is that God's revelation is moving from written revelation toward the internal revelation of the Holy Spirit. Robertson's cessationist scheme represents a regression into the mode of revelation of the Old Covenant! This does not mean that we do away with Scripture in favor of direct revelation. Not at all. Scripture is given as a deposit of the Christian tradition that provides the limits on what can and cannot be affirmed in a prophecy. Accordingly, we must resist Robertson's hermeneutic, which, like liberal higher critics, rejects the authority of scriptural commands simply because it does not fit his preconceived, post-biblical doctrine.

Against Robertson and cessationism generally, we affirm that prophecy and spiritual gifts do not create doctrine; they only apply doctrine to specific cases just as Old Testament prophets applied the Law of Moses. Cessationists wrongly insist, however, that for a prophecy to be truly revealed by God, it must be written as Scripture! Nowhere in the New Testament is this requirement ever applied for prophecy! In claiming this, cessationists themselves are creating a new, extrabiblical doctrine that denies the clear teaching and commands of Scripture! Maimonides (AD 1135–1204) approvingly anticipates this Protestant theology in summarizing Jewish tradition with respect to the cessation or limitation of prophecy: "It is said 'It is not in heaven'—you thus learn that henceforth no prophet is authorized to innovate anything."[18]

---

1. The "lamb of God," as every Jew in Jesus' time would pick up, is a way of talking about the Passover lamb—a covenant meal, strengthening and preparing the Israelites for their exodus from Egypt. Similarly, Jesus, as the Lamb of God was mediator of the New Covenant" whose body (and blood) was to be eaten as a signature-in-blood, removing all past violations of the covenant, thereby qualifying one to receive the Spirit (the New Covenant: Isa 59:21 > Acts 2:39; Jer 31:31–34 > 2 Cor 3; Heb 9:15; 12:24). It's no accident that 1 Cor 11 (the covenant/communion chapter) is placed just before the long discussion of the Holy Spirit charismata in chaps. 12—14, and the long section on Jesus as mediator of the New Covenant (Heb 8—10) is placed just before the chapter on faith (hearing and obeying the voice of the covenant Spirit) in Heb 11.
2. E.g., the percentage of the exodus story (or, Pentateuch) devoted to the events at Sinai. Does this imply that the issuing of the Covenant was unusually significant to the narrative?
3. To be quite banal, the fact that "God" (i.e., the various names) is mentioned many times certainly indicates an *emphasis*. But less obviously, what about "son" or the fourth most frequent noun in the Old Testament, "land"? See, e.g., K. Krippendorff, *Content Analysis: An Introduction to Its Methodology* (London: Sage Publications, 1980), 13–20.
4. Note how Ruth is repeatedly called "the Moabitess" or "Michal, daughter of Saul" long after they both are introduced. Or the famous "in our image and in our likeness" (Gen 1:26) and the chiastic: "created man in his own image, in the image of God he created him" (1:27). So P. J. Stone, *An Introduction to the General Inquirer: A Computer System for the Study of Spoken or Written Material* (New York: The Similmatics Corp., 1966), 11.
5. When the New Testament writers condense his ministry into a sentence or two they show Jesus in opposition to the reign of the devil which appeared as demonic

possession, sickness, the disruption of nature, or sin: it was "for this purpose that Jesus appeared, to destroy the works of the Devil" (1 John 3:8; Acts 10:38). Summary statements about Jesus' mission abound throughout the text of the Gospels, with references to healing and exorcisms: Mark 1:34||Matt 8:16||Luke 4:40–41; Mark 3:10||Matt 4:15||Luke 6:19; Luke 4:15; 7:21; 13:33; Luke 9:11||Matt 14:14; 15:30–31; 19:2; 21:14.

6. Rev 18:13 "the bodies and lives of humans" are the *last* (and cheapest?) on the list of commodities traded in Babylon the Great. Acts 2:38–39 represents the "action point" of arguably the most important sermon (certainly the first) in the history of Christianity. The action point is to prepare (by repentance and baptism) to receive the New Covenant Spirit of prophecy as must all who respond to the Christian message ("children's children forever" Acts 2:39 alluding to Isa 59:21).
7. See, e.g., K. Krippendorff, *Content Analysis: An Introduction to Its Methodology* (London: Sage Publications, 1980), 13–20.
8. Eta Linnemann, for example, has used a form of content analysis to undermine some of the basic tenets of higher criticism of the Gospels. *Is There a Synoptic Problem?* Trans., R. Yarborough (Grand Rapids: Baker, 1992), 182–83.
9. Just to be clear on my personal view of Scripture: I believe that it is the word of God written (at least from God's perspective), that it is, in its entirety, inspired by God, inerrant, authoritative for all people at all times, as interpreted and applied by the New Testament. When serving in seminary I taught approvingly the 1978 Chicago Statement on Biblical Inerrancy (text online at http://www.bible-researcher.com/chicago1.html). This is not to say that I agree with subsequent commentaries on this statement, especially those who assume that a high view of Scripture requires a denial of continuing "revelatory gifts" such as prophecy and words of wisdom and of knowledge. Spiritual gifts continue in the church *because* a high view of Scripture *demands* they continue as the central experience, authority, and mission of both Jesus Christ and his Church.
10. An important contribution to this theme is Marty Middelstadt, *The Spirit and Suffering in Luke-Acts: Implications for a Pentecostal Pneumatology.* Vol. 26 of *Journal of Pentecostal Theology:* Supplement series (NYC: Continuum Press, 2001).
11. See the note at the end of this chapter on O. Palmer Robertson's two-stage New Covenant theory of cessationism.
12. The Old Testament standard of killing a false prophet instantly is not applied in the New Testament. The New Testament policy of mercy breaks sharply from the Old Covenant's sanctions on aberrant prophecy. The New Testament policy calls for correction and grace for those inexperienced in hearing God's voice when prophesying and teaches that such knowing is "in part" or as "in a mirror dimly" (1 Cor 13:9–12). This leniency very well may also have been the case in the Old Testament "sons/school of the prophets" in 2 Kings chapters 2, 4, 5, 9. These were both correct and incorrect in their prophecies and certainly they weren't stoned for their errors! The standard cessationist argument that New Testament prophecy ceased often refers to this Old Testament death penalty as applicable to modern "false" prophecies. The New Testament teaching simply transcends this Old Covenant law in the community of Christian believers.
13. Against cessationism that must use the most opaque interpretive gymnastics to find biblical support, the Scripture is explicit and clear about the purpose of prophecy and the spiritual gifts: "The New Testament [the holy, divinely-inspired, eternally-sealed,

universally-applied, and unchanging, written word of God] describes the *function of prophecy* in a variety of cases. The earliest prophets of the New Testament, Zacharias, Elizabeth, Simeon, Anna, John the Baptist, and Mary, are all seen as proclaiming or identifying the Messiah, but sometimes in the form of a psalm of worship (Luke 1:67–79; 1:42–45; 2:25–26; 2:36; 1:76; 1:46–56, respectively). Peter receives a vision concerning the barriers between Jews and gentiles (Acts 10:11–17) and Paul, his apostolic call (Acts 9:3–8). These are not signs accrediting the gospel but the means by which aspects of the gospel are revealed, presented, and executed. But the function of prophetic revelation seems to lose its accrediting function altogether when Joseph is warned for the safety of his family in a revelatory dream (Matt 2:12, 13, 19, 22). Repeatedly those spreading the gospel are encouraged, warned, and directed by the Spirit through various revelations (Acts 5:3; 8:26, 29; 9:10; 10:3, 19; 11:27–30; 16:6–10; 18:9–10; 21:4,10–12; *cf.* 27:23). The obvious lesson we learn from these many experiences is that believers may expect similar revealed encouragement, guidance, and warning! The Book of Acts describes prophecy explicitly as having 'exhorted' and 'strengthened' the community (Acts 9:31; 15:32), just as Paul describes its function in 1 Cor 14:3; *cf.* 1 Thess 5:11–22; 1 Pet. 4:10. 'The one who prophesies, speaks to people for their upbuilding *(oikodomēn)*, encouragement *(paraklēsan)* and consolation *(paramythian)*.' The one who prophesies "edifies the church" (14:4). From prophecy an outsider or unbeliever will be 'convicted' *(elegchetai)*, 'called to account' *(anakrinetai)*, and 'the secrets of his heart will be revealed' (14:25). Conversion and worship will result from this prophetic revelation. This *explicit* function of prophecy is tied neither to an apostle nor necessarily to Scripture, but to specific, often unknown human needs. As long as the gospel is to be preached and applied, i.e., 'to the end of the age' (Matt 28:20), these functions of worship, prophetic guidance, encouragement, exhortation, edification, and conviction will continue to have relevance, and, if function determines duration, sufficient relevance to continue to the Parousia of Christ." *On the Cessation of the Charismata*, rev. ed. (Word & Spirit Press, 2011), 70. An utterance of prophecy can be *recorded* in Scripture (Matt 11:13; Mark 12:36; Acts 1:16; 4:35; Rev 22:18–19), but its being recorded does not exhaust its stated biblical purposes. Scripture is a product of revelation, as is prophecy, but New Testament prophecy is clearly not intended as simply Scripture awaiting its written form, as Paragraph 1 of the Westminster Confession of Faith has been interpreted.

14. Demythologizing is a process labeled as such by the extremely radical critic of the New Testament, Rudolf Bultmann (1884–1976). His interpretive procedure for miracles is to claim that they cannot realistically be taken literally, since we are in the age of modern science, so that no one today would ever believe such nonsense. Therefore, he claimed, one must remove the miracle "husk" of this primitive, backward worldview from the "kernel" of metaphorical truth that might lie beneath this miracle story. Bultmann was a great fan of Luther. But while Luther believed that miracles really happened in New Testament times, both he (leading the Protestant tradition) and Bultmann shared the practice of applying the meaning of the miracles today via the metaphors of salvation described above. B. B. Warfield insisted in *Counterfeit Miracles* (New York: Scribners, 1918), 177–178, that Jesus' healings were an "object lesson" of his "substitutionary work," which made "no promise that this relief [from sickness] is to be realized . . . in this earthly life." Disease is an expression of natural law and as such may not be "suspended in our case" (James 5:14–18, notwithstanding).

15. Hebrews 11:1 seems to be saying that "faith" is a kind of present *prophetic experience* of the reality ("substance/essence") of God's promise that is not yet confirmed by visible, physical confirmation, that is "knowing in the Spirit"—prophetically experiencing—a future event. Faith is therefore the revealed experience / taste of exactly the event that is not yet seen—the presence of the future.
16. Albert Bandura, who has been called the most prominent psychologist in the USA, insisted that imitating a role-model's behavior was the most effective process for learning complex (social) behavior. Is it accidental, then, that the Bible places a premium on this form of learning, as we model on the lives of the major figures of both the Old and New Testaments, particularly on the life of Jesus, whose ministry was offered principally as "an example" for his disciples of all ages? To deny the central process (hearing God and obeying that word) in the lives of the biblical role models, because of an alien and contrived doctrine (cessationism), is to deny the very heart of God's message and teaching method to the readers of Scripture. On the power of the modeling process, see these works by A. Bandura: *Principles of Behavior Modification* (New York: Holt, Rinehart and Winston, 1969); and *Psychological Modeling: Conflicting Theories* (Chicago: Aldine Atherton, 1971).
17. The technical term for the study of knowledge and criteria for distinguishing knowledge from opinion or hunch is epistemology. Interestingly, the Greek root underlying this English word is *epistēmē,* which means "knowledge"; however, its root is *pisteuō,* which translates as "I believe." I don't wish to make too much out of the connections among words, but at the least this connection illustrates a relationship between faith and knowledge that many have recognized from even non-religious perspectives.
18. Maimonides, *Mishneh Torah, Foundations of the Torah 9:1–4,* cited in Michael Walzer, *The Jewish Political Tradition. Volume 1: Authority* (Yale Univ. Pr., 2000), 269.

3

EMPHASIS ON THE WORD OF POWER

THE PENTATEUCH

Let's start at the very beginning. I used to believe that Genesis chapter 1 was a kind of prologue—a natural history introduction—to the good stuff: the stories about people. But since then I've decided that Genesis 1 sets up a very important pattern, integrated with the stories to follow, about God's central agenda.

What Genesis 1 seems to be saying is: "This is the way the universe is created and sustained—by the powerful word of God. It's far more than information. It is information and creative power. At the first two stages of creation we see the formula: "God said," then "God named." Then at each stage, or day, of the creation of life, "God said" and at the end of the period, he affirmed it as "good," or "very good," at the completion. So at the beginning and the end of each day, God's word goes forth—at the beginning as mighty, creative power and again at the end of the creative act as confirmation.[1]

The point is Genesis is setting a pattern showing that the whole world comes into being and is affirmed by the powerful word of God. Since mankind is the climax of this creative word, the text seems to be teaching this: if the whole universe is begun and supported by God's mighty word, and since you (mankind) are part of that created order, then your very life is begun and sustained by God's word of power. Hence, being "in" God's word is to exist—"In him we live and breathe and have our being," (Acts 17:28). I will suggest later that faith is being in God's word of life and power—"The righteous man shall live by his faith" [Hab 2:4 || Rom 1:17]—hearing, heeding God, and acting appropriate to that hearing.

Notice here that this pattern of the word (God speaking) is repeated at every stage. Remember our hermeneutic of emphasis? The repetition of "word" is a very big deal in Genesis 1. It's trying to get our attention. The "word" or God speaking is also repeated at the point of emphasis in the book—the lead chapter! One would think this "mighty word" repetition is the thesis statement—the central theme—for the whole book of Genesis. What else does this first section emphasize?

The plot line of the Patriarchal Narratives (and Israel's early leaders) is similar to that of Adam and Eve: God's word comes to them in a dream or in an unspecified way, and then their faithfulness grows and is strengthened as that word is tested. In fact, that pretty much sums up their stories!

ADAM

Adam is offered as a prototypical human. In the New Testament, he is contrasted with Christ, the "second Adam," who succeeded where the first Adam failed (Rom 5; 1 Cor 15). Adam was made in the "image and likeness" of God, proclaimed to be God's creation, given authority over creation and a mandate to guard life against evil; he was tempted and he disobeyed, resulting in nature becoming subject to turmoil and anarchy by his lost authority.

By contrast, Jesus was described as one with God and the image of God (1 Cor 15:45–49), one who came with authority to proclaim life (John 10:10); he was infused with the Spirit of God; he entered into temptation (Matt 4 || Luke 4); and he went forth "as one with authority" to proclaim the kingdom (ruling) of God in healing and delivering from Satan's ruin—to "destroy the works of the devil" (1 John 3:8).

Interestingly, the mandate for Jesus' twelve disciples, representing the chosen of God (Mark 3:14–15) carries the same core themes: "that they might be with Him [to be like Him], and that He might send them out to proclaim [prophesy], and to have authority to cast out demons."

Again, in setting the precedent for mankind, the text shows Adam frequently in conversation with God without any sense that this is unusual—unless one appeals to one's own religious experience (or lack of it) to override God's word.

CAIN AND ABEL

Cain and Abel (Gen 4) are offered as the first example of a contrast between one who hears and obeys and one who does not. God is speaking to Cain throughout the story, offering a promise of "lifting up the countenance" (joy?) if he would obey and "master" the sin "crouching at the door." Even after Cain told this to Abel (verbally acknowledging that he understood the choice), he still kills his brother (4:8). The rest of the story replicates the narrative of Adam and Eve after their sin: God's charge (v 8), Cain's denial (v 9), revolt against Cain by the ground; expulsion from the land; the threat of death (vv 10–14); God's provision for Cain's protection (v 15); and the removal from "the presence of the Lord" (v 16).

Up until this last point, there is constant communication recorded between God and Cain! Cain fails his test in offering an appropriate sacrifice and then, after telling his brother about it, kills his brother (one fourth of the world's population!). But nothing in the text indicates that it is unusual for this communication with God to take place! If Scripture is written for our instruction (Rom 15:4), should we deny that such communication with God can occur with us, simply because Scripture is written? Scripture itself here seems to be affirming that conversations with God can occur—normatively—even if the human interlocutor is evil, much less a righteous man like Noah.

NOAH

The story of Noah is the stuff of kids' Bible picture books, but if you read it in the original Hebrew it is awesome literature—beautifully and skillfully written. But again, the narrative is the standard "Genesis plot": God speaks/reveals/commands, then comes resistance and stress, then God vindicates his word, and life is preserved. It seems clear that Noah's story is offered as instruction, and, unless we put on that Protestant filter over our eyes, the story is about "hearing" God and obeying—that is, living in faith.

We know the story. The opening summary statement from God is, "My Spirit shall not always strive (probably "remain") with man forever" because he is "flesh" and will live only 120 years! (Gen 6:3). The Spirit is associated here with sustaining life (also 6:22), but the overwhelming association of "my Spirit" in the Old Testament is with prophecy and revelation. The remaining context indicates that like Cain, despite the presence of the Spirit, wickedness accelerates (vv. 4–7). There is more than a hint that demonic activity was rampant as well. "The sons of God came into the daughters of men" (v. 4), where at a bare minimum, the emphasis was on power and fame, and especially on a heart not hearing God's Spirit, but instead "that every intent of the thoughts of his heart was only evil continually." The term "heart" in the Bible means not simply the place of emotions (like a Valentine heart), but the center of spiritual perception and thought—who the person really is.

As before, all nature suffers the consequences of this evil, this time in a flood. Get the pattern? Our sin and unwillingness to take proper authority over nature and over the evil power against it results in catastrophe. This failure is a really big deal in the Book of Revelation in which the great plagues on creation are responses to great sin—that is, "greed, which is idolatry" (Rev 18) and giving allegiance to the demonic, rather than taking authority against it.

In contrast to his society which did not heed the voice of the Spirit comes "righteous, blameless" Noah who "walked with God." (6:9). "Can two walk together unless they be agreed?" In other words, Noah was used to talking, as well as walking, with God. So when God gives nine verses of communication about building an ark, Noah does not seem surprised.[2]

Noah's righteousness is evident and emphasized. Note the

repetition: "Thus Noah did; according to all that God had commanded him, so he did" (6:22). The lesson: when God tells you to do something, do it; you can both hear him and obey him. Noah is our example according to Romans 15:4 and 1 Corinthians 10:6, 11.

The same pattern in Genesis 7: God speaks to Noah (vv 1–4), "And Noah did according to all that the Lord had commanded him" (v 5). Note that Noah's mission was to preserve life, against the consequences of sin, much like the mandate to Adam and Cain. The sacrifice of animal life on an altar was a kind of substitute for the destruction of nature because mankind had ignored God's self-revealing (8:20—9:1). Noah, again, by his righteousness, reasserts his authority over nature and hears the command "to be fruitful and multiply" (9:1–7).

To sum up: against a background of great evil that would result in the destruction of nature, 1) God spoke to Noah about protecting life and nature; 2) Noah obeyed and life was preserved in spite of appalling circumstances; 3) Noah's authority over nature (as originally with Adam) was affirmed (9:1–3).

ABRAHAM

If ever the Bible presented a fully-human role model for us to follow, it's Abraham. The New Testament sums up Abraham's power of example: "Abraham believed (had faith in) God, and it was reckoned to him as righteousness" (Gen 15:6 > Rom 4; Gal 3:5–9). When I used to read this verse, quoted several times in the New Testament, I would "translate" it, "Abraham believed God, and even though it wasn't really 'righteousness' (doing really good things), God kinda cooked the books and made faith look like righteousness—even though we really know it wasn't." In other words, it was like the sacrificial system: we all have to die for our sins, but if we sacrifice an animal, God in his grace will make that count as if *we* died and forgive us. Abraham's faith was like a merit from God that he borrowed to deposit into his "righteousness account."

This interpretation fits well with traditional Protestant theology, but I doubt this is what it means. God is consistent here: he is talking about the power of hearing him and seeing the power that results from obedience. He is talking about "miraculous faith" (you know, the kind that some Protestants say is extinct?)—faith that produces miracles. Proof of this is how Paul relates hearing and faith in Galatians 3:5, "Does he then, who provides you with the Spirit and works miracles among you, do it by the works of the Law, or by hearing with faith?"

The very next verse is about the exact same kind of miraculous faith that Abraham had: "Exactly in the same way (*kathōs*) Abraham believed God and it was accounted to him as righteousness." The divinely-revealed assurance, that is faith, and obedience to that word, is what God's idea of righteousness is. Abraham, when he had faith, was in the New Covenant mode: the "teaching" of God internalized in his heart, rather than externalized on a document. How did Abraham's faith—in "exactly the same way"—produce the miracles in his life? By a hearing(!) of faith! What is a "hearing of faith"? By having the Bible read to you? Possibly, but Abraham didn't have any Bible! Necessarily then, he is modeling for us a direct, immediate perception of God's voice in his heart: "a hearing of faith" followed by action that precipitates conflict and opposition!

So God holds out Abraham's behavior here as the ideal to be imitated. God expects us to hear His voice directly and internally and obey against all opposition. So faith is not some kind of substitute for righteousness that God in his mercy somehow lets slide but is rather the very ideal and goal of how he wants to relate to us! "Righteousness" is not simply "being good" or ethical (the works of the Law) but is doing something the right way in God's eyes. Faith is hearing/heeding God's revealed message. It is God's right way—the only way—of living: you can't approach or please him without it!

So how does this play out in the Old Testament narrative of Abraham? Abraham, "the friend of God," is cited as a faithful role model for us today (Rom 4:16; Gal 3:6, 14; Heb 3:16; 11:8, 17; Jas 2:23). God spoke directly to Abram (12:1) at 75 years of age to leave all his extended family to go to another land that God would show him. This is a much bigger deal in that culture than, say, moving to Iowa nowadays! Very scary! As Abram arrived in the land, God then promised the land to Abram and his descendants (12:7). God promised the land again to

Abram (13:14–15) after miraculously protecting his wife and himself from the Pharaoh.

Genesis 15 records a long dialogue between Abram and the Lord, who promises a huge number of descendants and much of the land of the Fertile Crescent. Chapter 16 is the story of the slave girl, Hagar, whom Abraham used to produce a son, Ishmael. When she conceived, Abram's wife, Sarai, caused Hagar to flee into the wilderness. The angel of the Lord spoke to her there and encouraged her to return to Abram's house.

Chapter 17 records that the Lord again spoke with Abram, changed his name to Abraham and entered into a covenant with him, sealed with the ritual of circumcision. God promised an everlasting covenant giving the land of Canaan to Abraham and a son with Sarai (now Sarah). Ishmael would become the father of a great people, the Arabs, but would not be the chosen son of the covenant. Chapter 18 records God's promise again of a son to Abraham, who would be a blessing to all nations. The last half of this chapter is a long negotiation between Abraham and God for the protection of wicked Sodom, where not even 10 righteous men could be found.

In Genesis 20:7, Abraham is identified as a prophet (one who hears and obeys God and has power to heal, in this case, Abimelech of Gaza).

In Genesis 21:17, God hears the voice of Ishmael who, with his mother, was dying of thirst. Chapter 22 records the biggest test for Abraham: God asks that he sacrifice his long-awaited son, Isaac. Against every instinct and reason ("How could a good God ask this? This sounds more like the devil talking! I've waited so long for this only son. This is an evil act, I must have heard God wrong"), Abraham obeys God's word.

A summary of Abraham's life and his inheritance from God: He was greatly blessed in serving all mankind because "Abraham obeyed my voice and kept my charge, my commandments, my statutes, and my laws" (Gen 26:4–5)—none of these were in written form. The New Testament summarizes his chief virtue: "Abraham had faith [he was a prophet who heard and obeyed God] and this was his righteousness" (Rom 4:3, 9, 13). Abraham is the most important example or role model in the New Testament outside of Jesus. Abraham clearly demonstrates the pattern of faith: receiving a word from the Lord and having that word tested. Abraham, because he experienced the "hearing of faith," is called a prophet (1 Chr 16:16–22; Psa 105:9–15).

So to follow the example of Abraham (without the Protestant filter), we must become prophets! Abraham's story, after all, is "written for our instruction"! The Scripture itself again is teaching us to exercise spiritual gifts—"earnestly desire to prophesy" (1 Cor 14:39)! Like Abraham, his sons are also prophets: Christians, that is, those who have faith, are "sons of Abraham" (Gal 3:7).

ISAAC

Isaac's career is relatively brief (Gen 24—26). He believes and passes on the blessings God gave to Abraham and his descendants to Jacob (26:24). These blessings are seen as prophetic and, because they are, they cannot be withdrawn once given (Gen 27:37).

JACOB

Jacob, who negotiated the inheritance (birthright) away from his older brother, Esau (Gen 25:33–34), "sealed the deal" by deceitfully receiving his dying father Isaac's blessing from his deathbed (Gen 27). Shortly afterward, running for his life from his brother Esau's rage at being tricked, Jacob encounters God in a vivid dream. Here God reaffirms the covenant with Abraham and Isaac that Jacob's descendants would inherit the land of greater Israel and that his descendants would be numerous (Gen 28:12–15). Jacob endured trickery from Laban, having to work 14 years for his wife, Rachel, instead of the agreed-upon seven (Gen 29—30). So Jacob "managed" Laban out of a good deal of wealth, even though Laban tried to cheat Jacob repeatedly. God speaks again at five more important times:

1. to Jacob, to confirm that the amazing growth of his flocks was God's doing; and for him to leave Mesopotamia (Gen 31:11–13);

2. to Laban, not to do evil to Jacob (Gen 31:24);
3. and to Jacob, that his enraged brother Esau would not harm him (Gen 28:15; 32:9, 12);
4. to Jacob, to go back to Bethel and worship (Gen 35:1);
5. to Jacob at Bethel, where God changed Jacob's name to Israel and reaffirmed the covenant about many offspring and extensive land named for him (Gen 35:9–12).

Between all of these "words" from the Lord are extensive tests that would cast doubt on God and his words. Jacob's experiences carry the same emphasis as the other major figures in Genesis: the centrality of the word of God coming directly to them. These experiences are clearly intended as normative for the reader—otherwise, why is this communication with God so centrally stressed in these stories if they are not offered as inspiration for the normal way of relating to God? The same plot line continues in the stories of Joseph.

JOSEPH

Joseph is the last major figure in Genesis (chs. 37—50). The central theme of his life is the same as that of his ancestors: God reveals his word immediately to him, then this word is tested with great stress and suffering. As a teenager, Joseph had two dreams revealed to him, first, that his brothers would one day bow down to him; second, that even his mother and father would join the brothers and bow to him (Gen 37:6–11). The brothers were jealous and sought to kill him by selling him as a slave. After performing well as a slave in Egypt, Joseph was betrayed by the wife of Joseph's master.

Joseph was imprisoned, but the Lord helped him prosper even there. Shortly afterward, the Pharaoh's cupbearer and baker were imprisoned. They both had dreams that Joseph, by the Lord's revelation, interpreted: the cupbearer was restored to office, while the baker was killed. For two more years the cupbearer forgot his promise to remember Joseph, but when the Pharaoh had a puzzling dream, the cupbearer remembered Joseph, who interpreted Pharaoh's dreams correctly. Because Pharaoh discerned that "the Spirit of God" dwelt in Joseph (Gen 41:39), he chose Joseph to be the chief administrator during the seven predicted good and seven more poor agricultural years. By God's guidance, Joseph stored up huge amounts of grain and then accumulated much wealth for the Pharaoh when the famine struck, since the people paid high prices for grain.

Among these famine-stricken people was the family of Joseph from the land of Israel. The brothers come down to Egypt to buy food. Joseph tests to see if his brothers had learned about loyalty to each other and to their family since they sold Joseph into slavery. Ultimately, God's word is vindicated as Joseph's dreams are fulfilled—with the brothers doing some pretty serious bowing, just as the dreams describe!

Should we not assume that the "Spirit of God" dwelling in us, as in Joseph's story, is a good thing? And that if this is the case, doesn't that mean that, just as in the story, "the Spirit of God" means we are able to interpret revealed dreams (and have them ourselves) as he did? If not, then what is the point of these stories—that God later changes his mind and that we are only to "dream" of having such direct communication with God? That's what rabbinic Judaism and traditional Protestantism is trying to tell us! And yet the story of Joseph is a story for all of us: if God has truly given us a dream or another kind of revelation, we must pass the tests that will come against it and remain faithful before it will be fulfilled—in real life in this century!

The main point of Genesis is this: in these stories, God invites us to shift from the way we usually think and conduct our lives, and instead, to move from the Old Covenant mode of mediated revelation (the written word) to a life in the ideal—the original New Covenant of God's knowledge and instruction written directly in our hearts. He wants us to live in an intimate relationship with Him where we listen carefully and obey him—even under great stress and persecution. Why should we shift in this way? Because the Bible tells us so! Here we are not trying to add to Scripture by receiving personal revelation but rather to follow and obey Scripture! The stories of God's speaking to his servants of course do not end here. Moses is the next great example of the life of faith—hearing and heeding God—but the basic plot line is the same.

MOSES

The Book of Exodus emphasizes the process of God's word and power to deliver His people. Exodus picks up the story of Joseph's children who greatly multiply but become slaves in Egypt under a new Pharaoh "who did not know Joseph." God hears the cries of his covenant people, and after many years, Moses is born. Since at that time all male babies of the Hebrews (the descendants of Abraham, Isaac, Jacob, and Joseph) are to be killed, the baby Moses is set adrift on the Nile River in a little water-tight basket. God protects his life, when just a little way downstream he is discovered and adopted by a daughter of the Pharaoh. Moses is raised in the royal court, but knows the fate of his fellow Hebrews. When an Egyptian guard mistreats a Hebrew slave, Moses secretly (he thinks) kills the guard in defending his people. Moses soon discovers that this killing—and his sympathy with his people—is known to the pharaoh. Moses quickly flees far to the east, to Midian (now NW Saudi Arabia). For 40 years, until the age of 80, Moses herds sheep—a disgusting occupation to Egyptians and a real come-down for Moses, whose life seems to have hit rock bottom—for 40 years!

Then God's word comes to Moses in the form of a burning bush. In a fairly long dialogue, God commands Moses to deliver the children of Israel from Egypt (Exo 3—4). Again, aside from the burning bush and a serious self-confidence problem, Moses does not seem surprised that a conversation with God can occur.

Moses then hears a series of commands from the Lord resulting in 10 plagues on Egypt, each associated with one or more of the Egyptian gods:

1. Water to blood, killing all fish and other water life (god Khnum, guardian of the Nile; Hapi, god of Nile, birds, fishes, marshes; the Nile was the bloodstream of Osirus; Nu was god of life of Nile)
2. Frogs (Heqt, goddess of childbirth; highly revered; Egyptians could not kill a frog on penalty of death)

3. Lice ("diggers" that penetrated skin; Egyptian priests could not enter temple if infected; they took elaborate precautions)
4. Gnats and flies (actually "swarms" possibly of flesh-eating flies or scarab, the dung beetle that pushed sun disk [Ra] across sky)
5. Disease on livestock (anthrax? affected Bull = Apis, with sun-disk [Ra] between horns; Israelites worshiped "golden calf" in wilderness; Hathor = cow goddess, mother of Pharaoh; Khnum, ram god)
6. Boils (affront to Imhotep, scientist/healer/god; also Serapis god of healing and Thoth, ibis-headed god of science and healing)
7. Hail and thunder (affront to Nut, sky goddess, mother of Isis and Seth, protectors of crops, which were ruined from hail)
8. Locusts (Nepri, the god of grain; Ermutet, the goddess of childbirth and crops? Isis is silent once again. Thermuthis, the goddess of fertility and the harvest. Seth, god of crops)
9. Darkness (Main deity, Ra, sun-god; Horus, god of light)
10. Death of the first-born of all humans and animals who do not have marked doorposts. (Directed against "all the gods of Egypt" who could not protect the most valued of society: the firstborn. No response from Meskhenet, the goddess who presided at the birth of children; Hathor, one of the seven deities who attended the birth of children; Min, the god of procreation; Isis, the goddess of fertility; Selket, the guardian of life; Renenutet, the cobra-goddess and guardian of Pharaoh).

As with Adam and Noah and their authority over the forces of chaos, each of the plagues represents a counter-attack on one of the gods of Egypt. Because of the great sin of Egypt, nature is in equally great revolt against the nation and its gods, none of which has any authority over it compared to Yahweh, the Creator of it all. The God of Israel is demonstrating his authority as Moses prophetically announces each plague.

What is important to make clear: each of the commands for a new plague came as a revelation from God to Moses. Note that for each plague, the text specifies a contrast for the reader to note: Moses believed God, while the Pharaoh "hardened his heart" (refused to hear God's revelation). Are we getting this central theme?

The great deliverance finally came through a lot of disappointment — and then was tested again, and again, and again. The Israelites were massed at the Red Sea ahead, while the Pharaoh and his army were trapping them from behind. In this great, stressful time, God spoke to Moses: "Lift up your staff and divide the sea!" Let's read the story (Exo 13:18—14:31):

> 18 So God led the people around by the desert road toward the Red Sea. The Israelites went up out of Egypt armed for battle. 19 Moses took the bones of Joseph with him because Joseph had made the sons of Israel swear an oath. He had said, "God will surely come to your aid, and then you must carry my bones up with you from this place." 20 After leaving Succoth they camped at Etham on the edge of the desert. 21 By day the LORD went ahead of them in a pillar of cloud to guide them on their way and by night in a pillar of fire to give them light, so that they could travel by day or night. 22 Neither the pillar of cloud by day nor the pillar of fire by night left its place in front of the people.
>
> Then the LORD said to Moses, 2 "Tell the Israelites to turn back and encamp near Pi Hahiroth, between Migdol and the sea. They are to encamp by the sea, directly opposite Baal Zephon. 3 Pharaoh will think, 'The Israelites are wandering around the land in confusion, hemmed in by the desert.' 4 And I will harden Pharaoh's heart, and he will pursue them. But I will gain glory for myself through Pharaoh and all his army, and the Egyptians will know that I am the LORD." So the Israelites did this. 5 When the king of Egypt was told that the people had fled, Pharaoh and his officials changed their minds about them and said, "What have we done? We have let the Israelites go and have lost their services!" 6 So he had his chariot made ready and took his army with him. 7 He took six hundred of the best chariots, along with all the other chariots of Egypt, with officers over all of them. 8 The LORD hardened the heart of

Pharaoh king of Egypt, so that he pursued the Israelites, who were marching out boldly. 9 The Egyptians—all Pharaoh's horses and chariots, horsemen and troops—pursued the Israelites and overtook them as they camped by the sea near Pi Hahiroth, opposite Baal Zephon. 10 As Pharaoh approached, the Israelites looked up, and there were the Egyptians, marching after them. They were terrified and cried out to the LORD. 11 They said to Moses, "Was it because there were no graves in Egypt that you brought us to the desert to die? What have you done to us by bringing us out of Egypt? 12 Didn't we say to you in Egypt, 'Leave us alone; let us serve the Egyptians'? It would have been better for us to serve the Egyptians than to die in the desert!" 13 Moses answered the people, "Do not be afraid. Stand firm and you will see the deliverance the LORD will bring you today. The Egyptians you see today you will never see again. 14 The LORD will fight for you; you need only to be still." 15 Then the LORD said to Moses, "Why are you crying out to me? Tell the Israelites to move on. 16 Raise your staff and stretch out your hand over the sea to divide the water so that the Israelites can go through the sea on dry ground. 17 I will harden the hearts of the Egyptians so that they will go in after them. And I will gain glory through Pharaoh and all his army, through his chariots and his horsemen. 18 The Egyptians will know that I am the LORD when I gain glory through Pharaoh, his chariots and his horsemen." 19 Then the angel of God, who had been traveling in front of Israel's army, withdrew and went behind them. The pillar of cloud also moved from in front and stood behind them, 20 coming between the armies of Egypt and Israel. Throughout the night the cloud brought darkness to the one side and light to the other side; so neither went near the other all night long. 21 Then Moses stretched out his hand over the sea, and all that night the LORD drove the sea back with a strong east wind and turned it into dry land. The waters were divided, 22 and the Israelites went through the sea on dry ground, with a wall of water on their right and on their left. 23 The Egyptians pursued them, and all Pharaoh's horses and chariots and horsemen followed them into the sea. 24 During the last watch of the night the LORD looked down from the pillar of fire and cloud at the Egyptian army and threw it into

> confusion. [25] He made the wheels of their chariots come off so that they
> had difficulty driving. And the Egyptians said, "Let's get away from the
> Israelites! The LORD is fighting for them against Egypt." [26] Then the
> LORD said to Moses, "Stretch out your hand over the sea so that the
> waters may flow back over the Egyptians and their chariots and
> horsemen." [27] Moses stretched out his hand over the sea, and at
> daybreak the sea went back to its place. The Egyptians were fleeing
> toward it, and the LORD swept them into the sea. [28] The water flowed
> back and covered the chariots and horsemen—the entire army of Pharaoh
> that had followed the Israelites into the sea. Not one of them survived. [29]
> But the Israelites went through the sea on dry ground, with a wall of
> water on their right and on their left. [30] That day the LORD saved Israel
> from the hands of the Egyptians, and Israel saw the Egyptians lying dead
> on the shore. [31] And when the Israelites saw the great power the LORD
> displayed against the Egyptians, the people feared the LORD and put
> their trust in him and in Moses his servant (Exo. 13:18—14:31 NIV).

So the Israelites escaped by means of a spectacular miracle from God, but they were ready to start complaining immediately (no different from us, really)! Another test came when the Israelites lacked water (Exodus 15:25–26 NIV, emphasis mine):

> [25] Then Moses cried out to the LORD, and the LORD showed him a
> piece of wood. He threw it into the water [which was undrinkable], and
> the water became sweet. There the LORD made a decree and a law for
> them, and there he tested them. [26] He said, *"If you listen carefully to the
> voice of the LORD your God* and do what is right in his eyes, if you pay
> attention to his commands and keep all his decrees, I will not bring on
> you any of the diseases I brought on the Egyptians, for I am the LORD,
> who heals you."

This is an important principle: Hear, or heed, the voice of the Lord, for health and healing. This passage is presented as a key marker, a milestone in the Exodus experience.

Then the Israelites are tested again. Note God's reason for the testing (Exo 16:2–4 NIV, emphasis mine):

> 2 In the desert the whole community grumbled against Moses and Aaron. 3 The Israelites said to them, "If only we had died by the LORD's hand in Egypt! There we sat around pots of meat and ate all the food we wanted, but you have brought us out into this desert to starve this entire assembly to death." 4 Then the LORD said to Moses, "I will rain down bread from heaven for you. The people are to go out each day and gather enough for that day. *In this way I will test them and see whether they will follow my instructions."*

The point of this passage, then, comes in a summary statement—an expression of emphasis: "In that way I will test them, whether they will follow my instruction or not." Again, the key for this whole book of Exodus is hearing and obeying. The plot line never changes!

Here is still another test of whether or not the Israelites would listen (and learn) about the voice of God (Exo 17:2–7 NIV, emphasis mine):

> 2 So they quarreled with Moses and said, "Give us water to drink." Moses replied, "Why do you quarrel with me? Why do you put the LORD to the test?" 3 But the people were thirsty for water there, and they grumbled against Moses. They said, "Why did you bring us up out of Egypt to make us and our children and livestock die of thirst?" 4 Then Moses cried out to the LORD, "What am I to do with these people? They are almost ready to stone me." 5 The LORD answered Moses, "Walk on ahead of the people. Take with you some of the elders of Israel and take in your hand the staff with which you struck the Nile, and go. 6 I will stand there before you by the rock at Horeb. Strike the rock, and water will come out of it for the people to drink." So Moses did this in the sight of the elders of Israel. 7 *And he called the place Massah and Meribah because the Israelites quarreled and because they tested the LORD saying, "Is the LORD among us or not?"*

Note again the emphasis of the summary statement in verse 7! They actually renamed a location in memory of a failure to hear and heed God! This should tell us something about the emphasis and intention of this narrative: to exhort and warn us about the central theme: trusting God by hearing and obeying Him!

Another passage in the life of Moses shows the impulse of Scripture to spread the practice of "inquiring of the Lord" more broadly. The religious impulse is to limit the ability to hear God to the super-saints. But here and in Numbers 11, Moses empowers others to develop their ministry of hearing God and instructing others. In response to his father-in-law Jethro, Moses explains his action as judge: *"Because the people come to me to inquire of God.* When they have a dispute, it comes to me, and I judge between a man and his neighbor, and make known the statutes of God and His laws" (Exo 18:15–16, emphasis mine). It doesn't appear that at this point these laws have been written.

In Numbers 11, a similar scene develops. Moses gathers 70 elders around him to help him serve the people. This biblical kind of "service" or leadership required revelation from the Spirit. So to equip them for this service, the elders were then filled with the Spirit and prophesied. Immediately afterward, it was reported that two more elders, back at the camp, were also prophesying.

This was too much for Moses's number two man, Joshua. He was not used to anyone displaying the Spirit of God in anyone but Moses and himself. He seemed threatened by all this prophecy suddenly spreading all over the place, as Joshua saw it diluting the authority that he and Moses had monopolized up until now. (Sound familiar? Ah, yes! The traditional response to the charismata appearing in someone other than an accredited "saint"!) Joshua urged: "'Moses, my lord, restrain them.' But Moses said to him, 'Are you jealous for my sake? Would that *all* the Lord's people were prophets, that the Lord would put His Spirit upon them!'" (Num 11:28–29). Romans 11:29 and 1 Corinthians 14:1, 5 echo this godly impulse of Moses. Joshua saw prophecy as accrediting status (as do traditional Catholics and Protestants), but Moses saw the coming of the Spirit as empowering for service. Conflict over those two competing viewpoints have plagued the people of God ever after.

An even larger vision for God's anointing appears a few verses later (Exo 19:4–6 NIV, emphasis mine):

> 4 'You yourselves have seen what I did to Egypt, and how I carried you on eagles' wings and brought you to myself. 5 *Now if you obey me [my voice] and keep my covenant,* then out of all nations you will be my treasured possession. Although the whole earth is mine, 6 you will be for me a kingdom of priests and a holy nation.' These are the words you are to speak to the Israelites."

Bear in mind that a priest discerned the voice of God with the purpose of communicating it to others. "A holy nation" did not mean, as most Protestants would think, "a nation of really good, moral people" but rather a people set apart as priests or prophets for God's service: to communicate God's will to the surrounding nations. This vocation the church inherited: to be filled with the prophetic Spirit, or word, to evangelize and make disciples of the world. Protestantism, like the misguided Joshua, has tried to limit that prophetic gift exclusively to the apostles (= their Moses, the lawgiver) or to the writers of the New Testament! Once again, religion gets in the way of God's purposes! Traditional religion always wants to build a pyramid of power, with the power concentrated at the top, rather than embrace God's desire to see all empowered and commissioned by the Spirit to walk in faith and power.

THE KEY TEMPTATION IN THE FORMATION OF THE COVENANT

As one of the world's famous, yet unsung theologians, Bono has said: "Religion is what happens when the Spirit has left the building."[3] We shall discuss this at greater length below under "Covenant," but it is important to point out here that a key development that appears in the focal point of the Exodus—the offering of the covenant—is that God offers Israel the opportunity to speak directly with him. In this, God offers the essence of the New Covenant!

But the Israelites cannot bear being in the intense presence of God and demand mediated revelation, rather than immediate revelation as finally realized in the New Covenant (Exo 20:19–20, emphasis mine):

> 19"Then they said to Moses, 'You! You speak and we will listen; but *let not God speak to us, lest we die.*' 20And Moses said to the people, 'Do not be afraid; for God has come in order to test you, and in order that the fear of Him may remain with you, so that you may not sin.'"

To get the New Testament take on this, read Hebrews 12. The punch line? "See to it that you do not refuse him who speaks" (v 28). In this, the old human tendency to avoid direct communication with God is clear: in our sinfulness, we are always fearful in the presence of God.[4] The history of the church is the history of the conflicting tendencies to want to draw near to God and at the same time seek mediators (Popes, saints, Mary, priests, big pastors, evangelists, theologians) who will "do our magic" for us, rather than our personally entering boldly into the holy place! "There is one Mediator between God and man, the man, Christ Jesus" (1 Tim 2:5). Our calling is to emulate Jesus and his ministry in the power of the Spirit. Traditional theology is terrified at that. It says: "That's too big a job for us! We're unworthy! Besides, it's blasphemous to claim miracles or spiritual gifts like Jesus did, because if we claimed miracles, we'd be trying to prove we are God!" This is a faux-humble way of avoiding God's call to serve him in the way of power and suffering—that is, by his plan for us! But this avoidance is the traditional Protestant way—a way that so many of us take, mingling us right in with the crowd at Mt. Sinai!

In contrast with the human tendency to seek human mediators to help avoid the direct voice of God, the Lord can provide his own mediator when He emphasizes His process of communication for the conduct of the nation's life.

20 "See, I am sending an angel ahead of you to guard you along the way and to bring you to the place I have prepared. 21 Pay attention to him and listen to what he says [lit: obey his voice]. Do not rebel against him; he will not forgive your rebellion, since my Name is in him. 22 If you listen carefully to what he says [his voice] and do all that I say, I will

be an enemy to your enemies and will oppose those who oppose you. [23] My angel will go ahead of you and bring you into the land of the Amorites, Hittites, Perizzites, Canaanites, Hivites and Jebusites, and I will wipe them out. (Exo 23:20–23 NIV)

Just who this angel is, is unclear. But the principle of guidance remains the same: "truly obey his voice and do all that I say." Again, the voice of God could be delegated ("My name is in him"), as through one of the patriarchs or Moses, or directly to an individual. In any case, the theme of God speaking to his people is the central experience of the Exodus, if not the whole Old Testament.

Further on, when Moses delayed his return from the presence of the Lord and was receiving his instructions for Israel, the people revolted in idolatry. The dialog between Moses and God is instructive, as Moses assumes the role of an intercessor for his people (Exo 32). The communication between God and Moses is intense, but it demonstrates the tension between God's justice and his mercy. It would appear that God subtly assigns to Moses the task of protecting the people from God's wrath as a way of communicating the seriousness of the failure to hear and obey God's instructions (Exo 23 > 32:34 and 33:2).

A key story about Moses has to do with his constant communication with God "face to face" in Exodus 33. This passage describes a "tent of meeting" in which Moses converses with God regularly. "Thus the Lord used to speak to Moses face to face, just as a man speaks to his friend. When Moses returned to the camp, his servant Joshua, the son of Nun, a young man, would not depart from the tent" (33:11).

SUMMARY

This is the theme of the stories of Moses and the Exodus, the explicit reason for the Israelite's wilderness wanderings—to "test" them: "Remember how the Lord your God led you all the way in the desert these forty years, to humble you and to test you in order to know what was in your heart, whether or not you would keep his commands" (Deut 8:2).[5]

The summary statement (showing emphasis) of God's strategy for the Israelites appears early in Deuteronomy (4:32–40 NIV):

> 32 Ask now about the former days, long before your time, from the day God created man on the earth; ask from one end of the heavens to the other. Has anything so great as this ever happened, or has anything like it ever been heard of? 33 Has any other people heard the voice of God speaking out of fire, as you have, and lived? 34 Has any god ever tried to take for himself one nation out of another nation, by testings, by miraculous signs and wonders, by war, by a mighty hand and an outstretched arm, or by great and awesome deeds, like all the things the LORD your God did for you in Egypt before your very eyes? 35 You were shown these things so that you might know that the LORD is God; besides him there is no other. 36 From heaven he made you hear his voice to discipline you. On earth he showed you his great fire, and you heard his words from out of the fire. 37 Because he loved your forefathers and chose their descendants after them, he brought you out of Egypt by his Presence and his great strength, 38 to drive out before you nations greater and stronger than you and to bring you into their land to give it to you for your inheritance, as it is today. 39 Acknowledge and take to heart this day that the LORD is God in heaven above and on the earth below. There is no other. 40 Keep his decrees and commands, which I am giving you today, so that it may go well with you and your children after you and that you may live long in the land the LORD your God gives you for all time.

This communication was so vital that Moses' assistant and successor, Joshua, would maintain a constant presence with the Lord, replacing Moses in the Tent of Meeting when Moses conducted his business in the camp.[6]

If these narratives are "written for our instruction," then we must be clear as to what the nature of this instruction really is! It is not about deriving our own principles from reading Bible stories but about learning how to hear the voice of God! It seems clear that the dominant theme of the Exodus story is the process of hearing the voice of God and responding to it appropriately (what we now call faith).

---

1. A miracle in Mark 7:37 evokes a response from the bystanders: "He has done all things well." Does this response echo God's benediction over his own creative work in Gen 1? H. Hendrickx, *The Miracle Stories* (San Francisco: Harper & Row, 1987), 13.
2. As you're reading this, you probably aren't surprised as you think back over times when God spoke to your heart. I know I can remember lots of them, but a really unusual case came when I was in Korea. My interpreter for my theology classes at the huge Yoido Full Gospel Church in Seoul invited me to the English class she was teaching. A young Korean lady opened a class with the most perfect, complete prayer in English I had ever heard: flawless, fluent, and rich diction, spoken better than the most articulate, native-born American academic. There was no standard prayer jargon in this prayer either. I know *I* could not have put together a prayer like that! My Korean interpreter nudged me: "She's speaking in tongues." I didn't catch on at first, because as I heard this prayer, I kept fretting about what on earth I could teach these kids about English. I thought from the prayer that this had to be a super-advanced English class. But then I personally discovered that the speaker normally knew only a few English words she would speak in a strong Korean accent! There is no way she could have uttered that prayer on her own ability.

   Anyway, after I recovered enough from my astonishment to teach them to say with an American accent: "Larry O'Reilly really, really loves the Lord!" If you can get a Korean through that sentence with all those American-sounding Ls and Rs, you've accomplished another miracle! Significantly, the little gal who prayed so perfectly at the beginning of the class had a very tough time with my (to them) fiendishly difficult sentence! Um, so "tongues have ceased"? And this wasn't even preaching the gospel to foreigners as many cessationists insist must accompany tongues! I've kicked myself since then for not paying more attention to the content of the prayer which I considered at the time to be a kind of superficial ritual to start the class (I missed it because I made it all about me: worrying I would look bad by not having anything to teach these highly sophisticated students)! For many more such cases, see Ralph W. Harris, *Spoken by the Spirit: Documented Accounts of "Other Tongues" from Arabic to Zulu* (Springfield, MO: Gospel Publishing House, 1973), or, more recently, Jordan D. May, *Global Witnesses to Pentecost: The Testimony of 'Other Tongues'* (Cleveland, TN: Cherohala Press, 2013).

   My point here is that if God could speak so clearly through someone who had no real grasp of the language, then why not directly into our hearts, even if it's "in part" or "as in a glass darkly"?
3. Some of my older, unhip friends asked that I put in this footnote explaining that Bono is a song writer/rock star with the group U2, noted for his charity efforts for Africa and for his cool sunglasses.
4. This is spelled out in a summary by Moses: "These are the commandments the Lord *proclaimed in a loud voice* to your whole assembly there on the mountain from out of the fire, the cloud and the deep darkness; and he added nothing more. Then he wrote them on two stone tablets and gave them to me. 23When you heard the voice

out of the darkness, while the mountain was ablaze with fire, all the leading men of your tribes and your elders came to me. 24And you said, "The Lord our God has shown us his glory and his majesty, and we have heard his voice from the fire. Today we have seen that a man can live even if God speaks with him. 25But now, why should we die? This great fire will consume us, and *we will die if we hear the voice of the Lord our God any longer.* 26For what mortal man has ever heard the voice of the living God speaking out of fire, as we have, and survived? 27*Go near and listen to all that the Lord our God says. Then tell us whatever the Lord our God tells you. We will listen and obey."* 28The Lord heard you when you spoke to me and the Lord said to me, "I have heard what this people said to you. Everything they said was good. 29Oh, that their hearts would be inclined to fear me and keep all my commands always, so that it might go well with them and their children forever!" (Deut 5:22–29, emphasis mine).

This sinful human reaction to the experience of God (or to the so-called "supernatural") receives a modern assessment from Peter Berger.

Sociologists who deal with religion often like to refer to the etymology of the Latin word *religio*. Supposedly it derives from the verb *religare*—to re-bind. If so, this points to a very valid insight, most fully formulated by the classical sociologist Emile Durkheim—namely, that religion provides the symbolic ligature that keeps a society together. I understand that Latinists reject this etymology for a different, and actually more interesting one: *Religio* derives from *relegere*—to be careful. In other words, the supernatural is a very dangerous reality—one has to approach it with great caution. This understanding was brilliantly formulated by Rudolf Otto, arguably one of the greatest twentieth-century historians of religion, in his book, *The Idea of the Holy*. Religion is always based on an experience, on whatever level of intensity or sophistication, with a reality that is intensely dangerous. (If I were writing a paper for an AAR conference, I would of course say "a *believed* reality"—as a sociologist, I might refer to the famous statement by W.I. Thomas, "If people define a situation as real, it is real in its consequences.")

. . . .

One can build a whole theory of religious institutions from Otto's key insight. At the origin of all religious traditions there is an experience of the numinous. Religious institutions have two functions: to preserve the memory of the experience, so that it can be handed on to future generations who did not have it themselves; and to prevent the numinous experience from invading everyday reality in such a way as to make impossible the ordinary business of living. In this sense, every religious institution is an exorcism. It cannot be my purpose here to go on theorizing in this way. Let me just get back to the two events with which I started this post. It is difficult to think of two institutions as different from each other than the Roman Catholic church and the American Academy of Religion. Yet both are similar in one not unimportant way: They provide procedures to keep the supernatural at bay. The church does this by legal and bureaucratic procedures. The discipline of religious studies does it by—well, *by studying it*. Both mechanisms avoid encountering the supernatural directly in its terrifying reality. (The American Interest: blogs.the-american-interest.com/berger/2010/11/26/defanging-the-supernatural/).

5. See the summary statements, indicating *emphasis*, about the reason God called out his people: Deut 6:16; 8:16; Exo 15:26; 16:4, 7; 17:2, 7; 20:20; Jdg 2:20, 21; Psa 78:41, etc.

6. On a personal note, I try a similar pattern of meeting with the Lord in our church six days a week, offering intercession for our people. I have a wonderful prayer partner, whose ministry of intercession is beginning to expand to others. We are learning through various trials that God is leading us into increasing intimacy and constant communication with him, and from that, greater power in his miraculous gifts to his church. These Old Testament stories resonate so much more clearly with us, simply because we have similar, confirmed communication with God. These are really exciting times for us. Dreams and visions, "words" from the Lord, and "faith," are all ways of hearing God confirm his intention before the event happens, and are all part of our ministry experience these days.

4

EMPHASIS ON THE WORD OF POWER

ISRAEL'S HISTORY

Chapter 4 moves beyond the leadership of Moses (some time between 1445 and 1290 BC) to Israel's subsequent history, beginning with the conquest of the Promised Land under Joshua. This chapter covers the historical stories of Israel until the story ends in the Post-exilic era when Judah (the Jews) returned from exile in the mid-400s BC. Again, the emphasis of this whole period remains the same: God speaks and performs wonders as his normal pattern of revelation to his people—a pattern he expects the reader to emulate.

JOSHUA

The lead section of Joshua (1:1–9, 16–17, emphasis mine) features God speaking—again:

> After the death of Moses the servant of the LORD, the LORD said to Joshua son of Nun, Moses' aide: 2 "Moses my servant is dead. Now then, you and all these people, get ready to cross the Jordan River into the land I am about to give to them—to the Israelites. 3 I will give you every place where you set your foot, as I promised Moses. 4 Your territory will extend from the desert to Lebanon, and from the great river, the Euphrates—all the Hittite country—to the Great Sea on the west. 5 No

> one will be able to stand up against you all the days of your life. As I was with Moses, so I will be with you; I will never leave you nor forsake you. 6 Be strong and courageous, because you will lead these people to inherit the land I swore to their forefathers to give them. 7 Be strong and very courageous. Be careful to obey all the law my servant Moses gave you; do not turn from it to the right or to the left, that you may be successful wherever you go. 8 Do not let this Book of the Law depart from your mouth; meditate on it day and night, so that you may be careful to do everything written in it. Then you will be prosperous and successful. 9 *Have I not commanded you?* Be strong and courageous. Do not be terrified; do not be discouraged, for the LORD your God will be with you wherever you go."
>
> 16 Then they answered Joshua, "Whatever *you have commanded us* we will do, and wherever you send us we will go. 17 Just as we fully obeyed Moses, so we will obey you. Only may the LORD your God be with you as he was with Moses." (Josh 1:1–9, 16–17 NIV, emphasis mine)

It's all about hearing God and obeying in a "strong and courageous" manner! Faith!

Notice here the relationship of the immediate word that comes directly to Moses and Joshua and through them to the Israelites on the one hand; and on the other, the instructions that are in the written covenant "that shall not depart out of your mouth." It seems that until recent times the custom was to read out loud (e.g., Acts 8:30). So the exhortation here is most likely to read aloud the book of the Law regularly (Deut 17:19), and in this way, the covenant "shall not depart out of your mouth."

My point is that even though the Law is written, it coexists constantly with immediate revelation from God—long after it was written (2 King 17:13; Neh 9:26–30; Isa 29:10–13). Jeremiah, Ezekiel, Zephaniah, and Zechariah all foresee times when the law and prophecy cease together under conditions of godlessness (Lam 2:9; Ezek 7:26; Zeph 3:4; Zech 7:12)! Contrary to cessationism (and Paragraph 1 of the Westminster Confession), prophecy and the written word do not compete with each other, nor is the written word to replace the immediate, revealed word, but the written word is to be understood and applied by the word of prophecy.[1] Prophecy has the advantage over the written word in that it can be much more clear and specific in applying God's message.

The next chapter of Joshua tells about faith, derived from hearing about God's mighty works and acting appropriately. Joshua 2:9–13 recounts the story of Rahab who had faith in God and who elicited a promise from the two Israelite spies to save her family. Rahab (the prostitute) later became an ancestor of Jesus Christ (Matt 1:5; Heb 11:31; Jas 2:25).

In chapter 3, the Lord again speaks to Joshua about crossing the Jordan River:

> [7] And the LORD said to Joshua, "Today I will begin to exalt you in the eyes of all Israel, so they may know that I am with you as I was with Moses. [8] Tell the priests who carry the ark of the covenant: 'When you reach the edge of the Jordan's waters, go and stand in the river.'" [13] And as soon as the priests who carry the ark of the LORD—the LORD of all the earth—set foot in the Jordan, its waters flowing downstream will be cut off and stand up in a heap." (Josh 3:7–8, 13 NIV)

Actually, the Jordan River is known to do this, when clay banks upstream are undermined by the current, collapse, and stop the flow of the river.[2] After the successful, miraculous crossing, Joshua set up a memorial for the word of the Lord and its fulfillment (Josh 4:1–7):

> [6] "In the future, when your children ask you, 'What do these stones mean?' [7] tell them that the flow of the Jordan was cut off before the ark of the covenant of the LORD. When it crossed the Jordan, the waters of the Jordan were cut off. These stones are to be a memorial to the people of Israel forever." (Josh 4:6–7 NIV).

So this fulfilled word from the Lord to Joshua about the miraculous crossing of the Jordan is presented as very important. This event was to be taught to successive generations.

Now the big question is, "Why bother?"

If we read this account through the Protestant filter (or veil), the reader cannot receive this account as teaching about hearing and obeying God's voice as Joshua experienced it. The children in this story are clearly instructed that their identity is shaped by the miracle-power of God at one point in history.

But this was more than a history lesson. Was it not to establish the nature of God and his intervention in history on their behalf? Clearly the lesson here is: if you hear and obey God, the same kinds of miracles can continue in your history! This was an object lesson, not only about what God did in the past, but about our present reading of the present nature of God and our relationship to him.

If God did not intend to teach this, then what is the purpose of this story? Is it that, "I am the Lord thy God: I change . . . I am not the same yesterday, today and forever?" Or, "I am the God of Abraham, Isaac, and Jacob, but I change gears at Moses and Joshua?" Or, "Once the Law of God was written, you don't need to expect any more miracles like the Jordan; that's why you should erect these stones—to remind you that the time of miracles is over; God doesn't work that way any more!"

But this cessationism is not what God was telling the Israelites (Deut 4:3–7 NIV):

> [3] You saw with your own eyes what the LORD did at Baal Peor. The LORD your God destroyed from among you everyone who followed the Baal of Peor, [4] but all of you who held fast to the LORD your God are still alive today. [5] See, I [Moses] have taught you decrees and laws as the LORD my God commanded me, so that you may follow them in the land you are entering to take possession of it. [6] Observe them carefully, for this will show your wisdom and understanding to the nations, who will hear about all these decrees and say, "Surely this great nation is a wise and understanding people." [7] What other nation is so great as to have their gods near them the way the LORD our God is near us whenever we pray to him?

This passage, and especially verse 7, implies strongly that the distinctiveness of the Lord, the God of Israel, was the fact of communication: God both spoke and listened; He then fulfilled his promises—and continues to do so!

> "Now I am about to go the way of all the earth. You know with all your heart and soul that not one of all the good promises the LORD your God gave you has failed. Every promise has been fulfilled; not one has failed." (Josh 23:14 NIV)

The final movement into the land of Israel concludes with a warning from the Lord not to follow other gods. The aged Joshua sets up a stone as a sign commemorating the covenant all Israel made to follow the words, or Law, of God. Joshua speaks (Josh 24:23–27 ESV, emphasis mine):

> 23 He said, "Then put away the foreign gods that are among you, and incline your heart to the LORD, the God of Israel." 24 And the people said to Joshua, *"The LORD our God we will serve, and his voice we will obey."* 25 So Joshua made a covenant with the people that day, and put in place statutes and rules for them at Shechem. 26 And Joshua wrote these words in the Book of the Law of God. And he took a large stone and set it up there under the terebinth that was by the sanctuary of the LORD. 27 And Joshua said to all the people, "Behold, this stone shall be a witness against us, for it has heard all the words of the LORD that *he spoke to us*. Therefore it shall be a witness against you, lest you deal falsely with your God."

Like Adam, Noah, the Patriarchs, Moses, and Joshua, the Israelites shared a three-part expectation: 1) to listen to God, 2) to affirm his word, and, 3) to take authority over the areas God had assigned them. The patriarchs are all called prophets, since their central lifestyle was hearing and obeying God's voice (1 Chr 16:16–22; Psa 105:15). This role plays out also in the book of Judges.

JUDGES

The judges whose stories we read are not guys in long black robes who sit behind a big desk deciding legal matters. These judges were unlikely, flawed people, who had one big thing in common: against a background of local or national sin and failure, the judges all heard the voice of God, eventually obeyed it, and as a result, saw God's miraculous deliverance. It would seem that this central theme has a fairly clear application to the reader: when one finds oneself (and one's constituents) in a situation of sin and failure, this is time to cry out to the Lord, hear/heed his voice, do what he says, and see his rescue.[3]

But right from the first verse, the pattern is set (Jdg 1:1–2 NIV):

> After the death of Joshua, the Israelites asked the LORD, "Who will be the first to go up and fight for us against the Canaanites?" 2 The LORD answered, "Judah is to go; I have given the land into their hands."

But the process of heeding the word of the Lord, taking authority over the land, and conquering it was incomplete. Eventually, Joshua and the generation that followed him, passed on. The new generation did not know (experience) the Lord as their fathers had done. The following portion of Judges 2 summarizes (giving emphasis) the pattern of the Book of Judges (Jdg 2:10–22 NIV, emphasis mine):

> 10 After that whole generation had been gathered to their fathers, another generation grew up, who knew neither the LORD nor what he had done for Israel. 11 Then the Israelites did evil in the eyes of the LORD and served the Baals. 12 They forsook the LORD, the God of their fathers, who had brought them out of Egypt. They followed and worshiped various gods of the peoples around them. They provoked the LORD to anger 13 because they forsook him and served Baal and the Ashtoreths.
>
> 14 In his anger against Israel the LORD handed them over to raiders who plundered them. He sold them to their enemies all around, whom they were no longer able to resist. 15 Whenever Israel went out to fight,

> the hand of the LORD was against them to defeat them, just as he had sworn to them. They were in great distress. [16] Then the LORD raised up judges, who saved them out of the hands of these raiders. [17] *Yet they would not listen to their judges but prostituted* themselves to other gods and worshiped them. Unlike their fathers, they quickly turned from the way in which their fathers had walked, the way of obedience to the LORD's commands. [18] Whenever the LORD raised up a judge for them, he was with the judge and saved them out of the hands of their enemies as long as the judge lived; for the LORD had compassion on them as they groaned under those who oppressed and afflicted them. [19] But when the judge died, the people returned to ways even more corrupt than those of their fathers, following other gods and serving and worshiping them. They refused to give up their evil practices and stubborn ways. [20] Therefore the LORD was very angry with Israel and said, "Because this nation has violated the covenant that I laid down for their forefathers and *has not listened to me,* [21] I will no longer drive out before them any of the nations Joshua left when he died. [22] I will use them to test Israel and see whether they will keep the way of the LORD and walk in it as their forefathers did."

The result is that the settlement of each tribe of Israel is corrupted by the local demonic deities (idolatry in those days was fairly similar to Satanic cults today). So the Israelites lose their God-given power and authority, and in short order find themselves in trouble and bondage.

When they finally cry out to the Lord, God calls a "judge" to rise up, organize his or her people, and, at least partially, strike out against those who were oppressing them. It was not simply a matter of "obeying God's laws" but first and foremost, hearing God's voice as to how to deal with the crisis. The following shows how this pattern unfolds:

Othniel was the first judge. The Spirit of the Lord comes upon him (this means he became a kind of prophet—receiving revelation and power from God). He delivered Israel from bondage for 40 years[4] (3:1–11).

Ehud was a "left-handed" man (not an advantage in that superstitious culture), but the Lord "raised him up" for a mission against the oppressor, Moab. It's a gruesome story of an assassination like you'd read in a Godfather episode, but it got the job done. (3:12–30).

Shamgar "struck down 600 Philistines with an ox goad; and he also saved Israel" (3:31). Not much of a story, until you realize that an ox goad is usually a fairly flimsy stick, sharpened at the end, used to poke an ox in his behind to get him moving. Not much of a weapon to take on 600 Philistines, but it showed, obviously, that God's power was "made complete in weakness" and that even the Philistines got the point.

Deborah's story is more developed (Jdg 4–5). Here God speaks in a prophecy, when Deborah's army general, who seemed to be a bit of a wimp, refused to go to war without her. Deborah prophesied that the enemy leader would be taken out by a woman (actually, a woman nailed his head with a tent peg). For a woman to score like that was a real humiliation in those days, both for the enemy leader and for the Israelite general who wimped out on his divine authority. Yet this came about from a word from the Lord.

Chapter 5 is the proclamation and affirmation of God's word. This is really gripping and powerful poetry—great literature—and a form of prophecy, extolling the mighty works of God.

The account of **Gideon** (Jdgs 6–10) lays out a fascinating study of how a totally defeated agnostic about the practice of hearing from God is gradually convinced that hearing and empowering can actually happen. The Bible is unique in the major religions in that its account of human nature (and weakness) is so brutally realistic. Some readers can relate to the level of defeat and hopelessness described in Judges 6, a hopelessness that makes it very difficult to believe that God cares to speak with them. Perhaps our anger at God makes us not want to communicate with Him. But Judges 6 shows the amazing patience of God with someone who is even a tiny bit interested in hearing his voice. In the next chapter, Gideon is tested even further with the impossible demand to whittle down his forces to a scant 300. (Actually, as I write this, I'm in a similar situation with a venture that I believe God called me to. The problem with faith is that you're never absolutely sure because God leaves freedom of choice! The only difference in my case, the loss of my life isn't threatened by it!)

The crucial point from this passage is that Gideon's victory started with direct, personal communication—even though this communication was for him very hard to start. The story goes on (chapters 8—10) to show that leadership of God's people comes from a calling and communication with God; it does not continue automatically (8:27), and leadership certainly does not come by "inheritance" or from human power struggles (chapters 9—10).

The rest of the Book of Judges continues to show, especially in the case of Samson, that God uses very flawed people, but the process of direct, immediate, revealed communication with God is central to these teaching stories—indicating the emphasis of Scripture in this section. This is also true in the books of Samuel and Kings.

THE EMPHASIS ON GOD'S WORD OF POWER: THE CENTRAL THEME OF THE PERIOD OF THE KINGS

Placed as prominently as possible in the single scriptural unit (Books of Kingdoms) known as the two books of Samuel and two books of Kings is the call of Samuel the prophet. Samuel is a transitional figure between the era of the Judges and the beginning of the unified kingdom of Israel —a period in the early 1000s BC. The worship of the Lord had become corrupted because people who should have been aware of God's voice weren't: "In those days the word of the Lord was rare; there were not many visions" (1 Sam 3:1). While this rare condition might be common for traditional Protestant cessationists, the Scripture considers it a bad thing.

Scripture takes up a whole chapter (1 Sam 3) showing how difficult it is sometimes to get someone to communicate directly with God, as it was for Moses and Gideon.[5] Traditional Protestants will worship and pray, but the prayer (if they're playing by their cessationist rules) is definitely one-way. If God talks back, they're surprised—or in denial.

In Samuel's case, the text says something highly significant, "Now Samuel did not yet know the Lord: The word of the Lord had not yet been revealed to him" (1 Sam 3:7). Here it seems that knowing the Lord necessarily involves receiving revelation! This is where the traditional Protestant theology that denies personal propositional revelation gets a little shaky: Can one really know God without receiving the Spirit of revelation (Matt 16:17; John 14:17; Eph 1:17; 1 John 3:24; 4:13)?

At any rate, from the point of view of emphasis, the calling and communication with Samuel is the starting point for this history covering the 500 year period of Israel's kings. It confirms the central theme of the Books of Kingdoms: the prophetic communication to God's people (1 Sam 3:19–4:1 NIV):

> 19 The LORD was with Samuel as he grew up, and he let none of his words fall to the ground. 20 And all Israel from Dan to Beersheba recognized that Samuel was attested as a prophet of the LORD. 21 The LORD continued to appear at Shiloh, and there he revealed himself to Samuel through his word. 4:1 And Samuel's word came to all Israel.

Both of the two volumes of Samuel contrast the actions of Samuel and Saul, then those of David and Saul, the central difference being that Saul, who was chosen to be king and who had the Spirit of prophecy come upon him (necessary for leadership, 1 Sam 10:10 and 13), failed at key points to obey the word of the Lord (ch 15) or refused to inquire of the Lord (14:19; 28:16) when the Lord tested him. In so doing, he opened himself to demonic influence (16:14–15; 18:10; 28:8).

As a point of emphasis, the story of Saul centers on chapter 15 which explains the failure of his rule, in contrast to David who would replace him (vv 10–11, 19–22 NIV):

> 10 Then the word of the LORD came to Samuel: 11 "I am grieved that I have made Saul king, because he has turned away from me and has not carried out my instructions." Samuel was troubled, and he cried out to the LORD all that night.
>
> 19 "Why did you not obey the LORD? Why did you pounce on the plunder and do evil in the eyes of the LORD?" 20 "But I did obey the LORD," Saul said. "I went on the mission the LORD assigned me. I

> completely destroyed the Amalekites and brought back Agag their king. [21] The soldiers took sheep and cattle from the plunder, the best of what was devoted to God, in order to sacrifice them to the LORD your God at Gilgal." [22] But Samuel replied: "Does the LORD delight in burnt offerings and sacrifices as much as in *obeying the voice of the LORD?* To obey is better than sacrifice, and to heed is better than the fat of rams."

How many times is it emphasized here about hearing and heeding the word of the Lord? This is the key concept in the narratives of Israel. Saul was "rejected . . . as king over Israel." This reputation for rejecting God's voice may have contributed to the sardonic expression, "Is Saul also among the prophets?" (1 Sam 10:11–12; 19:24) By contrast, the Scripture portrays an important life summary of David at the end of his life (2 Sam 23:1–2 NIV, emphasis mine):

These are the last words of David: The oracle of David son of Jesse, the oracle of the man exalted by the Most High, the man anointed by the God of Jacob, Israel's singer of songs: [2] *"The Spirit of the LORD spoke through me; his word was on my tongue."*

In the interim, David, unlike Saul, is constantly and consistently portrayed as "inquiring of the Lord" about decisions (1 Sam 22:10; 23:2, 4, 9–12; 30:8; 2 Sam 2:1; 5:19, 23; ch 7). So David's career followed the archetypal mandate God assigned to mankind: 1) to hear, or heed, him; 2) to acknowledge God's mandate verbally and prophetically; and 3) to guard against and take authority over the forces that seek to oppose God and his rule.

God's speaking immediately to people's hearts in 1—2 Samuel is clearly emphasized: the phrase "the word of the Lord" or "the Lord spoke" or "said" as a prophecy occurs 26 times! This total does not include the numerous times the text mentions the fulfillment of these prophetic words. This pattern of emphasis increases in the next books.

1 AND 2 KINGS

The history of the kings who followed David's reign shows a spotty, but general trend away from hearing the voice of the Lord. Direct, prophetic revelation was the central mode of communication from God to Israel. But this mode only intermittently functions properly. Even when God communicated prophetically, such communication was often ignored or challenged.

One prominent case is that of Solomon. In establishing his rule against several challenges after his father died, God commended Solomon for his humility and his first choice of "wisdom" from God in order to rule effectively (1 Kng 3:7–12). The text makes it clear that it is wisdom revealed from God (1 Kng 3:28; 4:29; 5:12; 10:24)—wisdom "which God had put into his heart." In this, the "Books of Kingdoms" (1—2 Samuel, 1—2 Kings) expresses the ideal of governing not only a kingdom, but one's life by the wisdom revealed from God. This is simply another way of describing "walking by faith," or heeding "the word of the Lord."

From the mass of material emphasizing the centrality of "the word of the Lord" in the experience of Israel in 1 and 2 Kings, and all of the prophetic revelation described there, let us choose three major stories that illustrate the importance, the complexity, and the ambiguity of the great lesson of the Bible: hearing and heeding God's direct revelation. These stories are fairly extensive, a very good indication of their importance. Their themes overlap to some extent, but they all are about this question: "How do you know it's God's voice?" (the great question of the serpent). All of them deal with pressure from politicians and religious figures. But the following themes diverge by slightly different aspects of the difficulties of certainty in receiving the crucial experience of mankind: hearing the word of the Lord.

1. The case of the young prophet from Bethel who obeys the "word of the Lord" with great results, only to waver in his faith by acceding to the religious authority and reputation of an old prophet who claims a contradictory word from the Lord (1 Kng 13).
2. Following the spectacular miracle of Mt Carmel, Elijah's loss of faith in God's plan for his covenant people, specifically in

how that plan is communicated via the voice of God (1 Kng 18—19).

3. The case of Micaiah, a prophet who was outnumbered 400 to one and faced extreme political, religious (really, demonic) pressure to doubt his word from the Lord (1 Kng 22).

CASE #1 ON THE DIFFICULTY IN HEARING THE VOICE OF GOD AGAINST IDENTIFYING WITH A FAILED RELIGIOUS TRADITION (1 KINGS 13)

Rodney Dangerfield used to complain: "I don't get no respect! I came home the other day, and my kid said, 'Go to your room!'" Unlike our youth culture, ancient Israel tended to respect their elders. (All right, not the sons of Noah, Isaac, Moses and the Israelites, Eli, Samuel, David, and some others, but generally.)

The story in 1 Kings 13 has a lot more to it (to me) than when I first read it. What started out as a story about a minor issue (cultural influences) in hearing the word of God suddenly took on huge significance for the central theme of this book: "What's wrong with Protestant theology?" It's about the enormous conflict between voice of God and human religion comprised of human traditions and human authority. Remember Bono's observation? "Religion is what happens when the Spirit has left the building!"

Atheists love to attack religion—especially fundamentalist religion. They refuse to distinguish Islamic Fundamentalism from Christian Fundamentalism—deliberately. On the road to attacking Jesus, they try to equate him with the many evil people who hijacked his movement (such as popes and crusaders) and who did a lot of evil things.[6] The same approach is used to discredit anyone who claims to hear the voice of God: "Yeah, like Jim Jones and the Ayatollah Khomeni"—even as 38% of Americans affirm that they have sensed God speaking to them.[7]

So I don't want to make an opposite mistake here and claim that Protestant theology has nothing in common with Jesus and his mission. In fact, the core ideas of Protestantism I would redefine as my own:

- *Sola scriptura* (when taken to its logical end of letting Scripture speak for itself and its own emphasis, not just Scripture's being mined to support already-established doctrines);
- *Sola gratia* (when grace is defined biblically) as primarily "generous charismatic empowerment"; and
- *Sola fide,* especially when we mean by "faith" the "hearing/heeding of God's immediate, revealed voice."

So this story from 1 Kings 13 is right down this alley—it is a case study of church history's central problem: the direct, immediate revelation and power of the Spirit in the heart (the essence of the New Covenant) replaced by human status and tradition.[8]

It's a good idea to read 1 Kings 13 first before continuing with this commentary.

Now, notice how the prophet from Judah is told "by the word of the Lord" (a phrase occurring three times in five verses) to go outside his own country, north, to Bethel to "cry against" an illicit altar—while an "old prophet" from the same village is passed over. The young prophet from Judah shouts out against the altar and the sacrifice being offered by a king, no less! When the king reaches out to do him harm, the king's hand freeze-dries. The king then begs the man of God to "intercede with the Lord your God" to heal him—with no indication of "Gee, I'm sorry I sinned or disobeyed God."

The man of God intercedes and the king is healed. The king offers a big reward and a covenant meal. Perhaps he thought, "This kid's got game—he could help me politically!" But the offer is abruptly refused: "Even if you were to give me half your possessions, I would not go with you, nor would I eat bread or drink water here. For I was commanded by the word of the Lord: 'You must not eat bread or drink water or return by the way you came'" (13:8–9). So he courageously snubbed the king; he would not be tempted with government money, protection, or prestige.

What brought him down, however, was the power of traditional, discredited religion. Look at the details of the text. Why is it that the active "man of God" had to travel from Judah, when the "old prophet" from Bethel was on location? Why would the old prophet be so eager to eat with the younger man, even after the old prophet knew of God's command to the younger to go straight back to Judah? What did the old prophet have to gain by lying about his "word of the Lord" from an angel? Here we see the younger man of God from Judah so sure about his instructions that he would insult a king (a very dangerous move), and yet he lets another's prophetic claim overrule his own! Keep in mind that eating with someone in that culture was a kind of covenant relationship with them—joining them, so to speak.

The younger prophet didn't stop to ask discerning questions, such as, "If there were an old, experienced prophet in this town, why did God have to bring me all the way up from Judah to do this job?" Or even more basically, "Why is God so emphatic about my not eating with (covenanting with) anyone up here?" The young guy didn't need the approval of the king, but maybe it didn't seem so bad if he hung out with another prophet—especially one who is older and more experienced. "After all," he might have puzzled, "The old prophet did get a word from the Lord, one that contradicts mine. So whose word should I follow: mine (a rookie) or a word from an older, more respected prophet?"

How is this different from anointed servants of God seeking training from prestigious, accredited seminaries that instead of confirming faith, often mislead and "stretch" their students faith beyond the breaking point? (More of this in the chapter, "How Protestants Messed up Discipleship.")

The seriousness of diverting from the word of the Lord comes home to both prophets when the younger prophet finally gets back on the road and is killed by a lion. This seems so very "Old Testament" in its severity, but it drives home the point that God's commands are, in fact, a matter of life and death—one simply cannot disobey the voice of God and not expect consequences! That is exactly what both prophets discovered! The sad thing is that when the old prophet gets an actual word from the Lord, it's to confirm the original word the younger prophet received and the consequence for disobeying it.

So what can we learn from this "word of the Lord" story? The seductive power of dead church tradition and its great history! If identifying with all of this (glorious religious institutions, beautiful buildings and libraries, big ministries on TV, grand theologies) for its prestige and because it is so "cool" and "relevant" conflicts with the word of the Lord in our heart, then we should remember the fate of the prophet from Judah. It may not be a lion that kills us, but we will be just as dead.

Jesus covers this issue in Matthew 7:13–29. He is talking about the narrow gate and way, as opposed to the superhighway with all the traffic; he then specifies this with following false prophets. Yet like the old prophet from Bethel, if they are not obedient to the authority of Jesus' words, their disobedience leads to destruction.

Jesus' words represent the true biblical tradition revealed to the church (1 Cor 15:1–8; 1 John 1:1–5), but this biblical tradition (as shown in this book) will lead you to the covenant of the Spirit—away from religious tradition to the immediate witness of the Spirit. The Bible itself teaches that the normative way we are to relate to God is communication directly through His prophetic Spirit in our hearts.

So the lesson of the story of the two prophets: it is not good to trade God's orders to you in exchange for directions from those who have had a big reputation for experiences in the past or prestigious religious traditions that no longer have life. Rather we are to hear and obey the word of the Lord that we know God has given us and to walk by faith (hearing and heeding God's word in our heart).

The next case is about a great prophet who becomes so discouraged that he actually acknowledges that he is like his faithless ancestors, who, after seeing great miracles of deliverance, lost faith in God's great plan and refused to hear the voice of God. Thank God, he was wrong.

CASE #2 ON THE DIFFICULTY IN HEARING THE VOICE OF GOD AGAINST DEPRESSION AND THE COLLAPSE OF FAITH: ELIJAH (1 KINGS 17—19)

Elijah is the model prophet. In the New Testament, he is the example of Old Testament prophecy in that he appears with Moses, symbolizing the witness of the Law and the prophets to Jesus on the Mount of Transfiguration. The Epistle of James describes Elijah as a "man with emotions similar" to all of us while offering him as an example to us of powerful prayer (Jas 5:17–18). Paul contrasts the spiritual seeing and hearing of Elijah with Israel (ancient and contemporary) who, while a remnant was graced, the rest of Israel were given a "spirit of stupor, eyes so that they could not see and ears so that they could not hear, to this very day" (Rom 11:8). This New Testament passage clarifies that whether one has the perception of revelation or not is based on being a receiver of grace or not.

Here, then, is the problem of this case study (1 Kng 17—19): How can we trust the "word of the Lord" when we've seen great miracles and then immediately afterward see God's plan totally collapse—and us with it! This surprise is a huge test of faith to trust the word of the Lord. It certainly has happened to me, and probably to you as well!

The pattern is set in chapter 17 where, after Elijah is miraculously fed by ravens at the Brook Kerith, the water dries up. The word of the Lord had directed Elijah to go to a ravine (Kerith) and hide from Ahab. God sends ravens with food. The creek dries up, and the word of the Lord came again directing Elijah to a foreign town (Zerephath) well north of Samaria (Ahab's country) to have a widow (of all people) supply food. Again, God's word comes to Elijah that they would not run out of food until rain came. It proved to be true—"in keeping with the word of the Lord that came to Elijah" (17:16).

Then calamity strikes: after the amazing miracle of unceasing food, the widow's son gets sick and dies. Her reaction is bitter: "What do you have against me, man of God? Did you come to remind me of my sin and kill my son?" (17:18). The son is brought back to life and given to his mother. "Now I know that you are a man of God and that *the word of the Lord from your mouth* is the truth" (17:24, emphasis mine). Yes . . . but! The lesson Elijah is shortly to learn about how one hears from God is going to be repeated with stunning intensity.

Elijah, the ideal prophet, showed amazing faith (hearing and obeying God) in coming right up to King Ahab who had "hit contracts" out on Elijah in every surrounding nation (1 Kng 18:10)! With incredible chutzpah, Elijah challenges Ahab's idolatrous Baal prophets to a contest on Mt. Carmel just west of the then capital Jezreel and next to the Mediterranean Sea (now on the southern edge of modern Haifa, Israel).

We know the story in chapter 18 of how the prophets of Baal and Elijah each set up altars offering a bull. Whichever deity provided fire for the sacrifice was to be regarded as the true God. The prophets of Baal cried and screamed and bloodied themselves (typical of Satanic cults): "Come on baby, light my fire!" (which is where that song comes from). There was no sound; Baal did not answer. He was supposed also to be the thunder god, but not a peep.

Then Elijah, to prove there was no trickery involved in his divine fire, poured a lot of water (most likely seawater) on the altar until it even filled a trench around it. The Lord then sent fire that behaved in a particularly odd way: it not only burnt up the sacrifice, but also the wood, the stones, the wet soil and "licked up the water" in the trench. The only fire to act like that would be lightning, which is appropriate, since Baal was portrayed as standing on the back of a bull (fertility symbol) throwing a lightning bolt.[9] Baal was also believed to be the rain god. Most importantly, this miracle was done—against Baal—because of the word of the Lord (1 Kng 18:36).[10]

But just when God had scored an amazing victory, dispatched the 400 Baal prophets, and turned the spiritual life of the whole nation around on a dime, Jezebel counterattacks: "May the gods deal with me, be it ever so severely, if by this time tomorrow I do not make your life like that of one of them" (1 Kng 19:2).

Elijah is surely stunned. He runs for his life some 120 miles south, ditching his servant in Beersheba, the southernmost town of Judah, and continuing alone 15–20 miles into the desert where he slumps under an umbrella-shaped broom tree, hungry, thirsty, exhausted—and apparently furious at God: "Take my life; I'm no better than my ancestors."

"Take my life" I get, but what does he mean by "no better than my ancestors"? If you look at a map, you will see that Elijah is in the very wilderness that claimed those who escaped from Egypt in the Exodus. Elijah is essentially saying as they did, "Yes, we saw huge miracles of the plagues on Egypt, the parting of the Red Sea, all the big noise, earthquakes and fire of Mt. Sinai, but so what? The government is trying to kill us. We're all alone in the desert and we're going to die here! You call this a deliverance!"

God doesn't say a thing at this point. He just lovingly provides food and water (as he had for the Israelite ancestors). Elijah snarfs it down, rolls over, and goes to sleep again. After a while the angel nudges him awake and gives him more food and water: "Get up and eat or the journey is too much for you."

Elijah then takes off on the 40-day journey to Mt. Horeb (Sinai), the place where God offered the covenant to Israel. What Elijah was about to experience parallels the experience of his fathers.

When the people saw the thunder and lightning and heard the trumpet and saw the mountain in smoke, they trembled with fear. They stayed at a distance and said to Moses, You! You speak to us and we will listen. *But do not have God speak to us or we will die"* (Exo 20:18–19 emphasis mine).

Elijah finally reaches Mt. Horeb and hides in a cave. Note the literary pattern A-B-A (1 Kng 19:9–14 NIV, emphasis mine):

> A) [9] And the word of the LORD came to him: "What are you doing here, Elijah?" [10] He replied, "I have been very zealous for the LORD God *Almighty* [a little sarcasm here?]. The Israelites have rejected your covenant, broken down your altars, and put your prophets to death with the sword. I am the only one left, and now they are trying to kill me too."
>
> B) [11] The LORD said, "Go out and stand on the mountain in the presence of the LORD, for the LORD is about to pass by." Then a great and powerful wind tore the mountains apart and shattered the rocks before the LORD, but the LORD was not in the wind. After the wind there was an earthquake, but the LORD was not in the earthquake. [12] After the earthquake came a fire, but the LORD was not in the fire. And after the fire came a gentle whisper. [13] When Elijah heard it, he pulled his cloak over his face and went out and stood at the mouth of the cave.
>
> A) Then a voice said to him, "What are you doing here, Elijah?" [14] He replied, "I have been very zealous for the LORD God Almighty. The

> Israelites have rejected your covenant, broken down your altars, and put your prophets to death with the sword. I am the only one left, and now they are trying to kill me too." (1 Kng 19:9–14)

What is the point of all this? Notice that 49 times (!) 1 and 2 Kings uses the phrase "the word of the Lord came" and another 8 times "God spoke" to someone as a revelation. Talk about emphasis! But specifically, this paragraph takes it a step farther by zeroing in on the normative process by which we hear God's voice.

Elijah's fathers in the wilderness after the Exodus couldn't seem to recognize God's voice unless it literally exploded at them—and then it terrified them so much they didn't want to communicate, except through a mediator. Moses explains that this is the only way God could get their attention: he had to scare them that they might not sin (Exo 20:20).

By contrast, God was telling Elijah that it doesn't have to be that way: he is not "like his fathers," and God in fact speaks almost imperceptibly to his listening heart. But why this odd literary pattern (A-B-A) where Elijah has the exact same (A) speech two times?

Elijah says that the big experiment with Israel and its Covenant is kaput. He is the last survivor of God's covenant people. God has failed, and Elijah needs to explain all this to God—twice.

Oddly, God answers Elijah by contrasting the way he had to speak to Elijah's ancestors in the wilderness (thunder, fire, earthquakes) against the way he speaks to a person who "gets" the covenant. The normative way one hears from God is the "still, small voice"—a kind of intuited whisper, more felt than heard. This then is the important answer to Elijah's loss of faith: just listen to Me! In other words, our first step in God's plan for us is the hearing of God's voice. Elijah doesn't seem to get this. He "patiently" (through gritted teeth) explains the problem to God—twice.

But finally God moves to answer Elijah's question point-for-point: "You've been zealous for my plan that you see as a failure? Here then is my tiny little whisper to you, dude: You're afraid of kings? Go anoint two of them into my covenant of kingship! You think all the prophets are dead? Go anoint a leader of dozens of prophets! You're afraid of your enemies' swords? They will be killed by the swords of those you anoint! You think you're the only one left? Right! You along with seven thousand others! I'm not going to let you quit the team, Elijah. In fact you are "the chariots and horses of Israel"—the real fighting force! If you'd just listen. Now get out of here and do what you're told!"

The truth is, Elijah must not take responsibility for God's success or failure. Elijah has only one job: to hear God's whisper and obey it. Period. The central point of this book.

It seems, then, that Elijah stopped being depressed.

Are you depressed?

Think about it.

CASE #3: ON THE DIFFICULTY IN HEARING THE VOICE OF GOD AGAINST HOSTILE POLITICAL AND RELIGIOUS PRESSURE, DRIVEN BY A LYING SPIRIT: MICAIAH (1 KINGS 22)

"I just got a 'word' that I should marry Lori" (somebody says), "but is that 'word' from God or from the devil?" Some of us hear this a lot from young, inexperienced believers. Older believers have the same problem but have learned they won't be regarded as mature if they admit they're not sure, either.

Actually, the lesson of this chapter seems to be saying something like Jesus once said: "Wisdom is vindicated by all her children" (Luke 7:35). Said another way: "if you intuitively sense revelation, you'll know it when you hear it." St. Paul says you can settle problems with prophecy by two or three witnesses and let the others discern (1 Cor 14:29). On the other hand, he says, "The man without the Spirit does not accept the things that come from the Spirit of God, for they are foolishness to him, and he cannot understand them, *because they are spiritually discerned*" (1 Cor 2:14, emphasis mine). Hearing revelation with human reasoning without the Spirit is like trying to receive a TV picture on an egg beater.

The previous two cases (three if you count the story of Gideon) are all about discernment—how to hear the voice of the Spirit. But this case focuses on the issue of raw discernment: to whom are you really listening, and how do you know?

First Kings 22 addresses exactly this problem in hearing the word of the LORD. The setting is at the end of the reign of Ahab, and the king of Judah is identified as Jehoshaphat ("Yahweh judged"). This chapter follows the central theme of the Old Testament so far: hearing and obeying the word of the LORD. The king of Israel asks Jehoshaphat and his army to join him in recovering Israelite territory by attacking Aram (an enemy on the northeast border of Israel, probably Aram-Damascus, roughly the area of modern Syria today).[11] Jehoshaphat agrees on the attack but first wants to "inquire of the LORD." Ahab obliges and assembles 400 prophets, all of whom agree "the Lord will give [victory] into the king's hand" (1 Kng 22:6). Jehoshaphat seems a little dubious about their qualifications: "Can't we inquire from a prophet of the LORD?" (Were these 400 rent-a-prophets replacing the 450 prophets of Baal that Elijah had killed?) Some translations use the lower case "Lord," correctly translating *adonai*, which the king of Israel is likely using to refer to Baal, as opposed to "LORD" or the God of Israel, Yahweh. For clarity, we will follow this Lord/LORD distinction only in this story. In any case, these prophets who at first prophesied in the name of the "Lord [*adonai-Baal*]," later deceptively adapt their "revelation" source to Yahweh (LORD) after they are challenged by Jehoshaphat:

> 11 Now Zedekiah son of Kenaanah had made iron horns and he declared, "This is what the LORD says: 'With these you will gore the Arameans until they are destroyed.' 12 All the other prophets were prophesying the same thing. "Attack Ramoth Gilead and be victorious," they said, "for the LORD will give [victory] into the king's hand." (1 Kng 22:11–12 NIV)

Jehoshaphat and the king of Israel both seem to have the sense that all these prophets aren't getting it right: Ahab knows of Micaiah, who never says anything good about him, but the king (remembering his quasi-repentance and his experience with Elijah on Mt Carmel) probably doesn't want to kill Micaiah either. Ahab probably senses that Micaiah will not agree with his plans. To keep Jehoshaphat on board, he orders Micaiah before him. Like the 400, Micaiah is briefed on what is the "right" prophecy to make (22:13). Micaiah insists that he will only say what the LORD has told him. Finally Micaiah stands before the impressive kings and their impressive thrones and all the impressive prophets prophesying madly about the big victory—like a big pep rally.

So the king of Israel asks the big question and Micaiah gives the "right" answer: "Attack and be victorious, for the LORD will give it into the king's hand" (22:15). Something about Micaiah's voice (sarcasm?) or about his answer (it didn't ring true?) smoked out the king's real discernment of the truth and his angry response: "How many times must I make you swear to tell me nothing but the truth in the name of the LORD?" In either case, it was not just Micaiah the prophet, but Ahab (as well as Jehoshaphat) who knew the word of the LORD when they heard it! Here we see that all the prophets in the whole country—who quite possibly thought they had a word from the LORD (they were deceived after all)—couldn't fully convince either of the kings, both of whom knew deep down in their hearts the true word of the LORD.

Micaiah was arrested and jailed, but not before he explains in some detail how there could be such chaos in discerning the word of the LORD. He describes a heavenly court, with the LORD as king. Everybody's giving the LORD "advice" until he decides to put a lying spirit into the mouths of the prophets "of yours" because "the LORD has decreed disaster for you!" This doesn't sit well with the head of the prophets' union: "Then Zedekiah son of Kenaanah went up and slapped Micaiah in the face. 'Which way did the spirit from the LORD go when he went from me to speak to you?'" You can read the rest to see how the "word of the LORD" was vindicated.[12]

The point of this story: the leaders knew that they knew what God's word was! They were able to discern the true and false prophets! If you honestly take the time to "inquire of the Lord" and honestly listen, you will eventually "get it." This story, like the others, wants you to believe that these subjective "words of the Lord" can be trusted and will be fulfilled.

Well, they "got it," but to "hear" is one thing; to obey is another (they didn't). It takes both hearing and obeying to have "faith" or "righteousness" (Jas 1:22; Rom 2:13).

SUMMARY OF SAMUEL AND KINGS

The process of revelation of the "word of the Lord" and its testing is the central theme of the books of Samuel and Kings. The process for the "word of the Lord" is its revelation either directly into hearts, or via a prophet who immediately experienced this word to be communicated to others. The purpose of these books stresses the central emphasis and importance of hearing the "word of the Lord" and the certainty of its fulfillment.

If these books are "written for our instruction," then what do they instruct? Simply this: the reader is to make it a practice to "inquire of the Lord" for decision-making; then the reader is to expect, even under difficult circumstances, to hear subjectively the "word of the Lord" personally (the "still, small voice"—the internal "whisper" of God) and expect to see it fulfilled either in our behavior or in that which was predicted. This biblical instruction that is the central emphasis of these books is denied for us today, implicitly or explicitly, in traditional Protestant theology!

THE HISTORIES OF CHRONICLES AND EZRA-NEHEMIAH

A note on how "history" is done: All history is written from a point of view. Biblical history is dismissed by some secular academics because it is religious history, while they themselves also write from a profoundly religious point of view, which they view as superior: that is, atheism or agnosticism (Rom 1:18–22). As an article of religious faith, the biblical historians interpret events as being shaped by God. Equally, secular historians, as an article of their religious faith, *deny* that historical events are shaped by God—an equivalent and opposite faith position! One point of view is no less religious than the other! One side says, "God did it." The other side claims, "No, he didn't!" Both are religious or theological positions!

In fact, modern historians often impose a Marxist, atheistic religious motivation on historical figures by describing all their actions in terms of "class struggle" or "economic forces," instead of accurately reporting the explicit, stated religious motives of the historical figures they describe. For example, instead of accepting the miraculous events of the Exodus[13] as precipitating the founding story of Israel as a nation (I mean, who would make up a "founding story" of a nation as a bunch of whining, infighting, fleeing slaves?), such historians turn this event, on the scantiest of evidence, into an unconfirmable Canaanite slave revolt that fled into the hills to form the nation of Israel. There is, they say, no evidence of any Egyptian bondage and deliverance!

In today's news for instance, this same secular, Marxist, "class struggle" view is applied by journalists to Islamic terrorism. This view does not seem to comprehend that these murderous acts are religiously —actually spiritually—driven. The Marxist assumption is that this must be an economically-based movement of poor, underclass middle-easterners, struggling against American imperialist, capitalist oil companies. Those reporting are utterly confounded by the fact that most Islamic terrorists in the West are well-educated, even affluent! Wherever possible, the press erases or avoids references to any Islamic motivation to this terrorism—as in the case of US Army Major Hassan who was shouting "Allahu akbar" ("Allah is greater/greatest") as he was killing 13 and wounding dozens of others at Ft. Hood, Texas.[14] So despite the fact Major Nidal Hassan clearly felt motivated by his Muslim religious sensibilities, the agnostic "religious commitment" of the media would not allow Hassan's Muslim motivation to be known as a factor in the murders. Thus for journalists and historians to insist that biblical history is "religious" and therefore biased shows their own historiography is blindly hypocritical.

So history—whether your own or others'—is best validated by your own experience rather than being based on the agnostic speculations of detached academics. If you have experienced healings, miracles, and the voice of God, then the stories of the Bible come as no surprise to you: you understand them at essentially the same level they happened and were recorded. Whereas for a desiccated old academic, who bitterly lost his Sunday School faith years ago, it is important to push as many students as possible into his "cool" world of angry unbelief and denial. Misery loves company. Such sour disillusioned professors evangelize for their cause every bit as much as the most radical Christians do for theirs —though at the expense of others, taxpayers or, in the case of many seminary professors, at the church's expense!

These agnostics believe in the separation of Christian church and state, but not the separation of their agnostic religion from tax-supported schools and universities. In fact, they (and the ACLU) insist on agnosticism as being established as the state religion over the objections of the vast majority. To the intellectual elite, it is not simply that all of creation moved from simple forms of life to more complex, but they claim that God cannot have any input into this process.[15] Materialistic evolution is a religious idea that is part of the new, court-legislated state religion of the US and the West—not much different from that of the old Soviet Union, when atheism was also the state religion![16]

Having said all this, we can affirm that the ones who wrote Chronicles from a religious point of view did so unapologetically, tacitly knowing that it is impossible to write history from a point of view that is not religious. More specifically, the authors of Chronicles and Ezra-Nehemiah focused on the religious issues of the return from Exile, the rebuilding of the temple, the hereditary jobs of the priests and Levites (Chronicles opens with nine chapters of genealogies to get these jobs straight), and a particular focus on the importance of following the Covenant Law of God.

HISTORY SHAPED BY PROPHECY

Despite an emphasis on the written law, the books of Chronicles, Ezra, and Nehemiah continue to be saturated with the underlying theme that the people of God were to be guided by the prophetic word. For example, as in all the preceding Old Testament narratives, the prophets consulted with the Lord on key decisions: "the word of the Lord" (13 times), "inquired of the Lord" (10 times), the practice of "seeking the

Lord" (15 times), or simply praying for help or guidance (36 times). The prophets appear at the very center of important activities some 46 times. So these so-called "priestly" Scriptures emphasize the process of hearing from God. Key summary statements emphasize God's revelation in initiating and shaping the actions of God's people. For example:

> [14] Furthermore, all the leaders of the priests and the people became more and more unfaithful, following all the detestable practices of the nations and defiling the temple of the LORD, which he had consecrated in Jerusalem. [15] The LORD, the God of their fathers, *sent word to them* through his messengers again and again, because he had pity on his people and on his dwelling place. [16] But they mocked God's *messengers, despised his words and scoffed at his prophets* until the wrath of the LORD was aroused against his people and there was no remedy. (2 Chr 36:14–16 NIV)

> [20] *You gave your good Spirit to instruct them.* You did not withhold your manna from their mouths, and you gave them water for their thirst. . . . [30] For many years you were patient with them. *By your Spirit you admonished them through your prophets.* Yet they paid no attention, so you handed them over to the neighboring peoples. (Neh 9:20, 30 NIV, emphasis mine)[17]

The Books of Chronicles emphasize that it was the prophets (the ones who heard directly from God) who recorded much, if not all, of Israel's history from God's point of view (emphasis mine):

> [29] As for the events of King David's reign, from beginning to end, they are written in the records of *Samuel the seer, the records of Nathan the prophet and the records of Gad the seer,* (1Chr 29:29 NIV)

> [29] As for the other events of Solomon's reign, from beginning to end, are they not written in the records of Nathan *the prophet*, in the *prophecy* of Ahijah the Shilonite and in the *visions* of Iddo *the seer* concerning Jeroboam son of Nebat? (2 Chr 9:29 NIV)

As for the events of Rehoboam's reign, from beginning to end, are they not written in the records of Shemaiah the prophet and of Iddo the seer that deal with genealogies? There was continual warfare between Rehoboam and Jeroboam. (2 Chr 12:15 NIV)

The other events of Abijah's reign, what he did and what he said, are written in the annotations of the *prophet* Iddo. (2 Chr 13:22 NIV)

> The account of his sons, the many *prophecies* about him, and the record of the restoration of the temple of God are written in the annotations on the book of the kings. And Amaziah his son succeeded him as king. (2 Chr 24:27 NIV)

> The other events of Hezekiah's reign and his acts of devotion are written in the *vision of the prophet* Isaiah son of Amoz in the book of the kings of Judah and Israel. (2Chr 32:32 NIV)

After the Exile, the prophets play a central role in reconstituting the political and religious life of God's people.

> Now Haggai the *prophet* and Zechariah the *prophet,* a descendant of Iddo, *prophesied* to the Jews in Judah and Jerusalem in the name of the God of Israel, who was over them. 2 Then Zerubbabel son of Shealtiel and Jeshua son of Jozadak set to work to rebuild the house of God in Jerusalem. And the *prophets of God were with them, helping them.* (Ezra 5:1–2 NIV)

> So the elders of the Jews continued to build and prosper under the preaching [*binvu'at* lit. *"prophesying"*—Protestant bias here?] of Haggai the prophet and Zechariah, a descendant of Iddo. They finished building the temple according to the command of the God of Israel and the decrees of Cyrus, Darius and Artaxerxes, kings of Persia. (Ezra 6:14 NIV)

The Old Testament "church" received constant input from the prophets, just as God intends in the New Testament church in the form of the New Covenant Spirit of revelation. Even in the books of Chronicles and Ezra-Nehemiah which emphasize adherence to the written law of God, emphasize prophecy revealed directly as the means of being guided as a nation.

SUMMARY OF CHRONICLES, EZRA AND NEHEMIAH

Despite their emphasis on the temple worship and obedience to the written law, these so-called "priestly" documents in the Scripture still continue the Old Testament emphasis on the centrality of the immediate revelation of God to guide his people.

At this point, we will review how Scripture leads us more into the interior life of the prophets, focusing not simply on the content of their revelations, as is usual in Protestant commentaries, but on the neglected *process* of hearing God's voice.

---

1. Predictably, at least one Jewish scholar suggested that this early reference to the "book of the law [that] shall not depart from your mouth" is also the point Isaiah (59:21) is making about *continuing* the *Old* Covenant. Alexander Rofé suggests how the content of the Isaiah 59:21 covenant would fit the period: While he recognizes that the terms "'Spirit' and 'word' belong to prophetic stock, . . . there is little doubt that they have been reinterpreted here to designate the Torah." Alexander Rofé, "The Piety of the Torah Disciples at the Winding-Up of the Hebrew Bible" in *Bibel in jüdischer und christlicher Tradition: Festschrift für Johann Maier zum 60. Geburtstag* (Frankfurt am Main: Hain, 1993), 83. Certainly, this is *not* how Luke interprets this passage in Acts 2:39 (or Paul in Rom 11:29), who both see the fulfillment of the covenant promise as, broadly, the gift of prophecy, or *charismata* (Paul). Of course, the later traditional Protestant impulse to regress into the Old Covenant written Law instead of prophetic revelation into the heart (2 Cor 3) again reflects the Jewish rabbinic, scribal mentality of choosing the wrong "tree" or the wrong approach toward Scripture—as Jesus was tempted to do in the wilderness (Matt 4 | | Luke 4).
2. The stopping up of the Jordan occurred several other times in recorded history: on July 11, 1927, it stopped flow for 22 hours; in 1906 it stopped flow for 24 hours; in 1834 and in 1546, on Jan. 14, it stopped for two days; again in 1534 and 1267, on Dec. 8, it stopped up for 10 hours; and in 1160 during the time of the Crusaders. The miracle, of course, was that God predicted exactly when the river would cease its flow, allowing the Israelites to cross over.
3. On our theme in Judges, see Lee Roy Martin, *The Unheard Voice of God: A Pentecostal Hearing of the Book of Judges.* (Blandford Forum, Dorset, UK: Deo Pub., 2008). Martin examines the words, or speeches, of Yahweh.

4. In Scripture, 40 years represents a generation; also, multiples of 4 imply a period of probation or testing.
5. Something like God's calling to Samuel happened to a friend of mine back in his "hippie days". He told me that he was a little buzzed on marijuana late one night, got the munchies, stopped in at a 7–11 convenience store for some junk food, got back in his car and came up to a stoplight. He was about to start through the intersection when the light changed, but at that moment he heard his name being clearly called from the back seat: "Roger!" He was startled; he turned to look back before moving forward. The car beside him started into the intersection and, he said, literally exploded from the impact of a huge 18-wheeler blasting through the red light. The people in the car were annihilated. To this day, my Jewish friend, who is not particularly walking with the Lord, feels that God called his name and literally saved his life. He wonders, "why me, and not the people in the other car?" I wonder too. He is absolutely certain that the calling of his name was not drug induced. If you ask around, though, you will find that the stories like Samuel's calling may not be so unusual—and that God in his mercy can and will talk to anybody.
6. Of course there are some religions that begin badly and stay that way. But that charge does not apply to Jesus! The evil that happens in his name is very different from what he did and taught. This is *not* fundamentally true with Mohammed. "Muslim radicals" are those who go back to "the root" (= radical); that is, modeling themselves exactly on the words and deeds of their founder. One of the points of this book is that if we did the same with Christianity, we would have a somewhat different religion than Protestantism displays.
7. "In a 1994 Gallup poll that surveyed more than 1,000 adult Americans, 36 percent said God spoke to them directly. Fifty percent believed God spoke through the Bible, while 38 percent believed God spoke through an internal feeling or impression." (http://bit.ly/q85H9X)
8. J.N.D. Kelly, *Early Christian Doctrines* (New York: Harper and Row, 1960), 58–59. A. Ehrhardt, "Christianity before the Apostles Creed," *HTR* 55 (1962), 107. H. Chadwick, *The Early Church* (Baltimore, Penguin Books, 1967), 53. H. von Campenhausen, *The Formation of the Christian Bible* (trans. J. A. Baker, Philadelphia: Fortress Press, 1972), 234; and his *Ecclesiastical Authority and Spiritual Power in the Church of the First Three Centuries* (London: A. and C. Black, 1969), 297, where the "unbalanced ascendancy of office" displaced charismatic expression. J. Pelikan, *The Christian Tradition 1: The Emergence of the Catholic Tradition* (Chicago: University of Chicago Press, 1969), 106.
9. Just after seminary, when I had delusions of becoming a scholar, I wrote an article, "A Note on Elijah's 'Fire from Yahweh,'" *The Journal of the Evangelical Theological Society* 12 (1968), 111–115. In it I argued that it was possible that the Lord actually set up this miracle when he instructed Elijah to drench the altar with highly-conductive seawater at a time of the evening sacrifice (sundown), when the highest probability for a lightning strike would occur, in advance of lightning-causing turbulence from an oncoming storm off the sea "the sound of the rushing of rain" (18:41). This combination provided the "jumping off point" for lightning. The miracle of course, was the timing, in response to Elijah's prayer, certainly not because Elijah *planned* and tried to *manipulate* a lightning strike—in this case, a "bolt from the blue." These modern observations make it no less a miracle, but it does show us in later times that the "fire" was indeed lightning, highlighting the contrast with Baal's reputation as a

lightning thrower and his inability to perform—and providing increased historical plausibility to the story for the modern scientific mind. The same is true for the description of one of Goliath's relatives (2 Sam 21:20), who probably suffered from an endocrine disorder, gigantism (too much growth hormone), which is indicated by the detail "a huge man with *six fingers* on each hand and *six toes* on each foot—24 in all" (emphasis mine). Like the Elijah story, the original writer would not have known about any possible scientific confirmation for his accurate description of a growth disorder: he just wrote what he actually saw or heard.

10. Does God really predict stuff like rain in our time? Sometime in March 1977, a local news lady from our newspaper was calling up local pastors (since there had been a bad drought in Nebraska for three years) asking for their thoughts on whether or not God answers prayer for rain. When she asked me what I thought, I was ready with the standard theology that God does answer prayer, blah, blah, blah. Suddenly, however, I felt this electric rush come over me (I really felt it was the Spirit of God) and I began to blurt out: "Yes, I do believe God answers prayer for rain, and what's more, since God's people are praying, the next month will come within an eyelash of a record for rain." But I caught myself when I could just see her pounce on this with a headline: "Pastor Says, 'Build Ark: Floods Coming!'" Besides, what if I was wrong? So I chickened out.

    Well, in sharp contrast to the previous three years, that month it began to rain, and rain all through March, which registered the eighth most amount of rain for that month since records were kept since 1887! It was too late to call the news gal and say, "Um, well, I shoulda said . . . ." But at least I have a tiny appreciation for how tough it was for Elijah, with his life on the line, to go public with a prediction that lightning would strike—that very afternoon on his altar—with 400 other prophets disagreeing! Anita Fussell, "Doubts Dampen Prayers for Rain," *Sunday Journal-Star Religion*, March 6th 1977, 10B.

11. Remember that Ahab and his family probably lost a lot of political clout after the Mt. Carmel fiasco. The fiasco made it clear that Jezebel, his queen, was the real power behind the throne forcing the wrong gods onto Israel—or to put it into more modern terms her political statement was: "We are no longer a Jehovah [*Christian*] country." Perhaps to get the king of Judah on board, Ahab's prophets were instructed to attribute their revelation to the Lord (kind of); they waffle between *adonai* (Baal?) and Yahweh. This unpopularity set him up later for a military coup by Ahab's general, Jehu. Sound familiar? What do most politicians do when they're down in the polls? Start a war!

12. Sneakily, Ahab tries to divert attention from himself as the main target in battle by not dressing in royal robes, but throws his friend, Jehoshaphat, under the bus by insisting that *he* wear royal robes. It doesn't work: God's plan is vindicated by some random enemy soldier who shoots an arrow into nowhere and it "happens" to hit Ahab, who is wounded, then dies on the spot where "the word of the Lord" said he would (1 Kings 21:19–21; fulfilled in 22:38). The rest of the "word of the Lord" to be fulfilled applied to the remainder of Ahab's household (2 Kings 9:6–9; 2:10).

13. Greta Hort, "The Plagues of Egypt," *Zeitschrift für die alttestamentliche Wissenschaft* 69:1–4 (1957), 84–103; [Part 2] 70:1–2 (1958), 48–59. Hort argues convincingly that the Exodus account of the plagues of Egypt was historically credible in that they followed an ecological chain of events that followed quite logically and naturally from the previous one. Each plague also represented a specific Egyptian god's loss of control

over its "turf," showing in each case that it was Israel's God, Yahweh, who controlled all of nature right up to the firstborn of the Pharaoh of Egypt who was also considered to be a god to the Egyptians. On the broader historiographical issues, see the somewhat acerbic K. A. Kitchen, *On the Reliability of the Old Testament* (Grand Rapids/Cambridge: Eerdmans. 2003), or his much earlier work, *Ancient Orient and Old Testament* (Chicago: Inter-Varsity Press, 1966).

14. See Ruthven, *The Prophecy That Is Shaping History: New Research on Ezekiel's Vision of the End* (Fairfax, Virginia: Xulon Press, 2003).
15. Rarely are contemporary scientists as candid about their considered opposition to anything divine as the Harvard population biologist Richard Lewontin: "Our willingness to accept scientific claims that are against common sense is the key to an understanding of the real struggle between science and the supernatural. We take the side of science *in spite of* the patent absurdity of some of its constructs, *in spite of* its failure to fulfill many of its extravagant promises of health and life, *in spite of* the tolerance of the scientific community for unsubstantiated just-so stories, because we have a prior commitment, a commitment to materialism. It is not that the methods and institutions of science somehow compel us to accept a material explanation of the phenomenal world but, on the contrary, that we are forced by our a priori adherence to material causes to create an apparatus of investigation and a set of concepts that produce material explanations, no matter how counterintuitive, no matter how mystifying to the uninitiated. Moreover, that materialism is absolute, for we cannot allow a divine foot in the door." "Billions and Billions of Demons," a review of Carl Sagan's *The Demon-Haunted World: Science as a Candle in the Dark* in *New York Review of Books* 44:1 (9 Jan. 1997), 28–32 (www.nybooks.com/articles/archives/1997/jan/09/billions-and-billions-of-demons/; requires fee).
16. Against *theistic* evolution, *materialistic* evolution claims that all movement from lower to more advanced forms of life did so strictly by random, mechanical, natural means, without any divine input. Many Bible-believers observe that Genesis 1 describes a process moving from the preparation of the oceans and land to simple life forms, to more complex forms, to, finally, mankind. Some disagree as to whether or not God used existing life forms to modify them "after their kind" or whether He created each species completely afresh. There might be a sense in which both could be true. Materialistic evolutionists, however, deny that He had *anything* to do with it! In other words, an incredibly complex and sophisticated something came out of nothing—a daunting scenario that takes more faith than I have to believe! The most recent scientific claim, based on a study of complex proteins, is that all life emerged from one single cell. On the one hand, that seems to confirm the linear evolution scenario (whether shaped and continually modified by God or not) and, on the other, undercuts the claim that the origin of life was spontaneous—from random collisions of elements—because one would expect that the first cells would be popping up all over the place, independently. This single-cell origin theory would also undercut the frantic search for life on other planets that depend on the spontaneous, multiple-origins, something-from-nothing scenario. (www.sciencedaily.com/releases/2010/05/100519205503.htm).

    An organization that manages to reconcile good science with sound biblical interpretation is Reasons to Believe, founded by astrophysicist Dr. Hugh Ross (www.reasons.org).
17. Note how the term, "Spirit" is used here synonymously with prophecy.

5
EMPHASIS ON THE WORD OF POWER
PROPHECY AND WISDOM

It may seem a little odd having a separate section for the prophets in our survey of biblical literature, since all of the preceding is about the centrality of the prophetic experience. However, the prophets are key players in offering God's guidance to the politicians, yet are typically ignored as generalized in the following text about the repeated behavior of the children of Israel:

> "Woe to the obstinate children," declares the LORD, "to those who carry out plans that are not mine, forming an alliance, *but not by my Spirit,* heaping sin upon sin; [2]who go down to Egypt *without consulting me"* (Isa 30:1–2, emphasis mine).

The New Testament insists that we emulate the prophets in their mission: "Brothers, *as an example* of patience in the face of suffering, take the *prophets who spoke in the name* of the Lord" (Jas 5:10, emphasis mine; Heb 11). This section, then, examines the central experience of the prophets found within the writings named after them. This will be a highly selective survey, seeking the markers of emphasis within these books. We are working on the premise that Scripture presents these men as role models (see Heb 11) to be emulated, since even such an authority as Moses expressed the desire that "all of God's people be prophets" (Num 11:29).

Isaiah has regularly occurring experiences with the word of the Lord: "The Sovereign Lord has given me an instructed tongue, to know the word that sustains the weary. He wakens me morning by morning, *wakens my ear to listen* like one being taught" (Isa 50:4, emphasis mine). This is the "hearing of faith" that should by now be familiar to us from Scripture. This "morning by morning" emphasizes the repetition in Isaiah's life. His prophecies come upon him as a kind of load, or "burden" (*massa'*), which Isaiah not only can feel, like a pressure,[1] but also "see" as a prophetic vision (13:1, cf. Hab 1:1). The prophetic Spirit, therefore, comes "upon" someone (Isa 11:2; 32:15; 42:1; 44:3; 59:21; 61:1) in a palpable way. As from Genesis 1 onwards, the presence or Spirit of the Lord typically results in speech coming forth.

Jeremiah describes the prophetic drive within him as "a fire in my bones." This feeling arises when he is discouraged at the strong opposition he encounters: "the word of the Lord has brought me insult and reproach all day long. But if I say, 'I will not mention him or speak any more in his name,' his *word is in my heart* like a fire, a fire shut up in my bones. I am weary of holding it in; indeed, I cannot" (20:8–9). Over 70 times Jeremiah uses the familiar phrase "the word of the Lord" that comes to him as a prophetic revelation.

In Jeremiah's circles it seems that the phrase "burden of the Lord" for a prophecy was hijacked by false prophets (Jer 23:33–40), so he is forbidden to apply the term even to a genuine prophecy. In reference to this problem, Jeremiah has a long discussion on "How do we know a prophecy is from the Lord?" (Jer 23:9–40). Jeremiah lists ways to tell if prophets are false: they are immoral (23:10, 14–15) and they "lead the people astray" (23:13, 32). If these prophets had really stood in God's presence, the result would have been that they "would have turned them [Israel] from their evil ways" (23:22). So a test of a prophet is a resulting moral lifestyle in himself or in those he addresses.

But the greatest emphasis of this section is the simple assertion that these false prophets "speak visions from their own minds, not from the mouth of the Lord" (23:16), with the result that their hearers forget the Lord (cf. Deut 13 and 18):

> 25 "I have heard what the prophets say who prophesy lies in my name.
> They say, 'I had a dream! I had a dream!' 26 How long will this continue
> in the hearts of these lying prophets, who prophesy the delusions of
> their own minds? 27 They think the dreams they tell one another will
> make my people forget my name, just as their fathers forgot my name
> through Baal worship. 28 Let the prophet who has a dream tell his
> dream, but let the one who has my word speak it faithfully. For what has straw to do with grain?" declares the LORD. (Jer 23:25–28 NIV)

The test for false prophecy then is not a claim to revelation but that the result of their prophecy is it causes "my people to forget my name" and to follow other gods. This appears to be the same test as found in Deuteronomy 13:1–5 and 18:18–22. Similarly today it is possible to follow the idolatry of the scribes who refused "to hear the one who speaks" (Heb 12:25; John 5:37–39).

A little historical note here on the problem of discerning revelation and throwing the prophetic baby out with the bath water: from its very beginnings (early 1500s) in its university setting, Protestant theology has been shaped by an academic, intellectualized mindset of "human wisdom." The Enlightenment (1640s through 1700s) came into being by reacting primarily to constant infighting over whose "revelation" or theology was correct. The cherry on the sundae came with the controversies over witch trials (early 1600s), wherein nobody knew what to believe: who is a witch and who isn't. One test was to put a suspected witch on a dunking stool and force her under water. If she died, she wasn't a witch, but if she lived (supernaturally), then she was a witch, so they'd burn her at the stake—a win-win way of getting rid of surplus unmarriageable women. Thoughtful people decided this was crazy, so they searched for a way of knowledge on which everyone could agree.[2] In this move, philosophy adapted the religion of the scribes—away from the biblical experience of personal New Covenant revelation toward human intellect. They had the arrogance to call this move into spiritual darkness "Enlightenment" (Rom 1:21; 1 Cor 1:19–24; 2:5, 12–14; 8:2–3).

Unfortunately, costly casualties of this Enlightenment quest for certainty were the rejected ideas of experience, enthusiasm, or personal revelation that every sect and aspiring prophet appealed to for his or her authority. The Reformation had already decided (against Catholic claims) that such miracles and prophecies existed only to accredit apostles or New Testament doctrine. So the Enlightenment formalized human wisdom into a "scientific method" that could discover all reliable knowledge. Today among conservative Protestants, you hear this Enlightenment solution applied to charismatic or prophetic confusion by saying, "I don't rely on *experience* but on the *facts* of Scripture." Trouble is, this statement has a huge problem: Experience (directly hearing the voice of God) is probably the biggest fact that Scripture emphasizes. The human tendency to take refuge from this fact in seeking to substitute a knowledge of God with a knowledge of Scripture ends up being completely circular—since the emphasis of Scripture itself ironically leads back to the centrality of God's voice!

So, since hearing from God seems to be an emphasized habit in a prophet's life, and since the prophets and their miracle-faith are held out to be role models for the readers of Scripture (Heb 11; Jas 5:17), then what we learn from the prophets' experiences should be applied to us. After all, "the gifts (charismata—always a reference to prophetic activity in the New Testament) and the calling (probably a reference to being called, as were the prophets) of God are not withdrawn" (Rom 11:29, paraphrasing Isa 59:21). This notion of "calling" begs investigation.

THE "CALLING" EXPERIENCE OF THE MAJOR PROPHETS—IS THIS OFFERED TO THE READER?

Isaiah, Jeremiah, and Ezekiel all record very moving encounters with God when they are called to be prophets. Many Christians today can relate a similar sense of calling into service for God. What is significant with these prophets, however, is the nature of their mission: What exactly were they called to do? More importantly for us, why must we follow a traditional theology that insists that these "calling" accounts are not "for our instruction" and that we must reject these stories as something that can't apply to us?

Traditional Protestantism places the calling as a kind of experience of the Spirit, the first step in the *ordo salutis* that draws one toward salvation. When we think about it, isn't this a revelation experience? In one of the most crucial, defining stories of the New Testament, didn't Jesus respond to Peter's confession by saying, "Blessed are you, Simon son of Jonah, for this was not revealed to you by man [lit: flesh and blood], but by my Father in heaven." This role of revelation in recognizing Jesus is summarized in Revelation 19:10, "The testimony of Jesus is the spirit of prophecy."

The three calling passages of the major prophets, Isaiah, Jeremiah, and Ezekiel come in Isaiah 6, Jeremiah 1, and Ezekiel 1—3. What are the characteristics that all three callings share?

- First is the contrast of the glory of God and the human weakness of the prospective prophet (Isa 6:1–7; Jer 1:4–8; and Ezek 1:3–28).
- Second is the cleansing of the lips, expressing that the message is holy, that is, separated from human contamination (Isa 6:5–7; Jer 1:6–19; Ezek 1:28—3:4).
- Third, the prophet is told not to be afraid of those to whom he is sent (Isa 6:5, 9–12; Jer 1:6–10, 17–19; Ezek 2:3—3:15, 22–26).
- Fourth, God indicates that the prophet will not necessarily experience success—at least in the short term (Isa 6:9–12; Jer 1:10–17; Ezek 2:3–7; 3:4–21, 24–27).
- Fifth, the central point is: "the word of the Lord" comes to these prophets (Isa 6:8; Jer 1:2, 4, 9–13; Ezek 2:8—3:4, 10, 11, 14c, 24–26, esp. 27). There is no confusion that it is God who is speaking to them.

It is important to note, however, that the revelatory experiences of these prophets are quite different, even though they share these themes. Accordingly, people today will experience a variety of revelation experiences that accompany God's calling: dreams, visions, impressions, audible voices, words from others sent from God, circumstances, healings, miracles, special provisions, financial blessings, etc. Some may experience something like this only once in a lifetime or periodically; others, like Isaiah (50:4), daily.

We should not assume, however, that the prophets of the Old Testament received a word from the Lord at will. Even the best of prophets had to wait on the Lord, seeking him diligently before the word came. Jeremiah, for example, had to wait on God for 10 days for an answer that was rejected by the very ones who asked for the word (Jer 42:7). Daniel prayed for 21 days for the interpretation to a vision experienced (Dan 10)—the revelation from the angel was delayed by "the prince, or king, of Persia" (Dan 10:12–14). So just because someone was called a prophet does not mean he receives instant revelation on demand!

GOD'S IDEAL PERSON: A PROPHET

A prophet is expected to obey God's mandate as given to Adam for mankind: 1) to express our identity with God ("image and likeness," Gen 1:26–27); 2) to respond to God's revelation with verbal expression (Gen 2:20, 23); 3) to rule over and guard God's creation (Gen 1:28; Gen 2:15; including the serpent, Gen 3:1).

Similarly, prophets 1) encounter God's presence; and 2) utter God's word in response; 3) and their commission is to guard and protect God's creation, specifically, his chosen people.

The bottom line for our purposes is that the prophets of the Bible represent the ideal expression of godly humanity. Proof of this is that a prophet, after all, is sometimes simply described as "a man of God." Paraphrasing Moses' wish that *"all the Lord's people* were prophets" (Num 11:29), the apostle Paul addresses the entire church through the ages: "I would like *all of you* to speak in tongues, but I would *rather have you prophesy.* He who prophesies is greater than one who speaks in tongues, unless he interprets, so that the church may be edified" (1 Cor 14:5). Notice that the reason Paul wants everyone to prophesy is not to produce a body of prophecy that will turn into the New Testament canon but rather "that the church may be edified." How are they to be edified? "For *you can all* prophesy in turn so that everyone may be instructed and encouraged" (1 Cor 14:31, emphasis mine). Note here that the New Testament canon of Scripture is offering the reader a promise: that all can prophesy—at least in the sense of receiving revelation ("All who are led by the Spirit of God are the sons of God" Rom 8:14. "In Christ Jesus, you are all sons of God through faith [a gift of revelation]" Gal 3:26). This promise is consistent with the prophetic essence of the New Covenant—the goal of the Bible—that we shall examine further. The reason that all can prophesy is that "everyone may be instructed and encouraged/edified/built up" (1 Cor 14:31). It does not say that prophecy is for the building up of the texts of Scripture!

Further, "If an unbeliever or someone who does not understand comes in while everybody is prophesying, he will be convinced by all that he is a sinner and will be judged by all, and the secrets of his heart will be laid bare. So he will fall down and worship God, exclaiming, 'God is really among you!'" (1 Cor 14:24–25). So another purpose for prophecy is, by revelation, to "read the mail" of the unbeliever to bring him into the presence of God (fall under the power) and into repentance.

Again, the central theme of the Bible, hearing the voice of God and obeying it through the resulting tests, comes to its highest human expression in the normative experience of the prophets. We now turn to a different genre of literature that also emphasizes this theme: the so-called "Wisdom" literature.

THE CENTRALITY OF THE WORD OF POWER: PSALMS AND PROVERBS

The Books of Psalms and Proverbs, of course, appear in a different literary form (poetry and proverb) from that of the narratives we have just reviewed. But the content, yes, even the emphasis, remains the same: God continues characteristically to reveal his word and show his mighty power. Psalms covers a range of subjects, focusing mostly on the "word" of God in the form of his law and commandments, which appear as direct revelation or Scripture. Almost all the time, however, the distinction is not spelled out and must be discerned from the context. We cannot assume, however, as traditional Protestantism might, that all references to God's law, commandments, judgments, precepts, decrees, statutes, word, etc., are to the written law of Moses. Contrary to the conventional wisdom, as often as not, these terms appear to describe God's direct revelation to the individual—a foretaste of the direct revelation of the New Covenant (Isa 59:21 > Acts 2:39 and Jer 31:31–34). The Book of Psalms also shows an interest in the history of God's mighty working for Israel as well as serving as a painfully honest collection of quite personal spiritual experiences and struggles with God.

The Book of Proverbs appears to be a collection of precepts, or rules, for us to follow. But the underlying theme of this book is that the first thing one should seek is wisdom (Prov 4:7), that is, the communication of God's will directly into one's heart (inner being and thoughts). As elsewhere in the Old Testament, the central process is assumed: namely, that God communicates by mighty deed and revealed word directly and immediately into the heart of the individual and the nation. Because of space limitations, we can only sample a few passages to make our point.[3]

In the Psalms, the themes of the previous Scriptures continue: God's voice, or word, is often described, as are his mighty works. The Psalms serve as a kind of spiritual diary, both of individual writers and of the nation as a whole. They provide us with a candid and honest glimpse into the common religious experience of God's people—the experience of his revealed words and deeds are emphasized.

For example, in the famous repentance passage of David, the solution to his sin—indeed, to the human condition—is interesting: it is the internal revelation of the (prophetic) Holy Spirit in the "inner parts/heart":

> 6 Surely you desire truth in the inner parts; you teach me wisdom in the inmost place. 7 Cleanse me with hyssop, and I will be clean; wash me, and I will be whiter than snow. . . . 10 Create in me a pure heart, O God, and renew a steadfast spirit within me. 11 Do not cast me from your presence or *take your Holy Spirit from me*. (Psa 51:6, 10–11 NIV, emphasis mine)

Note the parallel construction of verse 6, through which "truth" and "wisdom" appear as synonymous, both located in the "inner/innermost" places of the person. What this double expression emphasizes is the same emphasis as the New Covenant (Jer 31:33–34)—that is, the goal of the Bible! Accordingly, as in Proverbs, also in Psalms: "the fear of the LORD is the beginning of wisdom" (111:10). In other words, revelation begins with listening, as Paul said: "Faith comes by hearing, and hearing through the word of Christ" (Rom 10:17).

In Psalms the phrase "word of the LORD" is an immediate utterance, or revelation, from God—not Scripture—since it seems to be immediate ("the word from your lips" 17:4); the "word of the Lord" made the heavens (33:6); it was a prophecy uttered by Joseph that proved true (105:8, 19); it was the word at Sinai that was more than the tablets of stone (68:11); it is obeyed by angels (103:20); it was a word of physical healing and rescue from the dead (107:20); God's word is expressed in parallel with "laws and decrees" (147:19), which could end up as Scripture, but in the same context, his word "runs swiftly" to cause hail, snow, frost, and wind—not an action of Scripture (147:15–18)! None of these examples could be caused by a document of Scripture but only by an action of God.

Psalm 119 focuses on the word of God in human experience some 25 times. Protestant tradition has shaped generations to mentally convert the term "word" in this Psalm to "Scripture." Hence, the verse "Thy word have I hid in my heart that I might not sin against thee" (119:11) means to a Protestant: "I have memorized a lot of Scripture that when I am tempted to sin I prevent it by recalling the relevant Scripture." Certainly, this is an admirable practice, but the "word" throughout this Psalm does not seem to be Scripture, but the revealed, prophetic word in one's heart. How do we know this? The language of the following section seem to suggest that the "decrees/laws/statutes/precepts/ways/word/commands" could well be written, but, more likely, they are directly revealed to the writer of this Psalm—and by extension to its readers. This verse conceptually is very close to "walk by the Spirit and you will not fulfill the desires of the flesh" (Gal 5:16; also Rom 8:4).

> 12 Praise be to you, O LORD; teach me your decrees. 13 With my lips I recount all the laws that come from your mouth. 14 I rejoice in following your statutes as one rejoices in great riches. *15 I meditate on your precepts and consider your ways. 16 I delight in your decrees; I will not neglect your word. 17 Do good to your servant, and I will live; I will obey your word.* 18 Open my eyes that I may see wonderful things in your law. 19 I am a stranger on earth; do not hide your commands from me. 20 My soul is consumed with longing for your laws at all times. 21 You rebuke the arrogant, who are cursed and who stray from your commands. 22 Remove from me scorn and contempt, for I keep your statutes. 23 Though rulers sit together and slander me, your servant will meditate on your decrees. 24 Your statutes are my delight; they are my counselors. 25 I am laid low in the dust; preserve my life according to your word. 26 I recounted my ways and you answered me; *teach me your decrees.* 27 Let me understand the teaching of your precepts; then I will meditate on your wonders. (Psa 119:12–27 NIV, emphasis mine)

In v 12, if the Psalmist were reading the decrees, why would he ask the Lord to teach them? Indeed, in the next verse and others, these are "laws that come from your mouth" not from a written document (13,

72, 88). In verses 16–17, the promise that he "will not neglect your word" implies direct communication, as the term "word" most frequently does in the Old Testament. "Do good to your servant, and I will live" seems to imply an action on God's part (speaking?) that results in a corresponding divine action: "I will live." This is paralleled in a second, human action: "I will obey your word." (It's easier to do if one is alive). Similarly, God is requested to "open my eyes" (revelation?) "that I might see wonderful things in your law"—apparently direct revelation or illumination of Scripture in this case. Another act from God is that he will preserve the life of the Psalmist "according to [His] word" (vv 25, 37). This physical healing cannot be an act of written Scripture but of the power of God. Moreover, God answered the Psalmist as he reviewed his own ways; he then asks God to teach his decrees so that he might "understand the teaching" [paralleled with] "wonders"—again, both are apparently revelatory (v 27). Elsewhere, the writer expects that specific promises will be fulfilled based on God's word (vv 28, 37, 41–43, 49, 57–58, 65, 74, 81, 88–90, 107, 114, 117, 140, 147–49, 161–62, 170).

Several times, then, the Psalmist receives teaching directly as revealed. This echoes the standard operating procedure from all the preceding Scripture we have surveyed. More importantly, this revealed teaching in Psalms anticipates the ideal state of the New Covenant: "no longer will you need anyone to teach you" (John 14:26; Heb 8:11; 1 John 2:27, cf. Col 3:16 > Jer 31:33–34), in which the New Covenant word is put directly into one's heart (Ps 119:11) or (prophetically) into the mouth (Ps 119:43), "of your children and children's children forever" (Isa 59:21 > Acts 2:39). Because word and mighty act (miracle) are different aspects of God's revelation, Psalms emphasizes their remembrance and recounting.

REMEMBERING MIRACLES IN PSALMS

Just as the "word" represented the revelation of God, so did his mighty works, since God continually "bears witness" through "signs, wonders and mighty works" (Heb 2:4).[4] God's people were expected not simply to experience God's miracles, or merely to remember them, but to teach and proclaim them to others, particularly their children.

The Old Testament seems to recognize ongoing signs and wonders throughout its history. For example, Jeremiah says, "You performed miraculous signs and wonders in Egypt and *have continued them to this day, both in Israel and among all mankind,* and have gained the renown that is still yours" (Jer 32:20, emphasis mine). Jeremiah's inspired prayer does not seem to indicate that signs and wonders correlate only with the revelation of new doctrine, as traditional Protestants insist. In response to an apparent cessation of miracles, Habakkuk, who was writing Scripture, petitions God: "I stand in awe of your deeds, O LORD. Renew them in our day, in our time make them known" (Hab 3:2 NIV). Daniel also expresses a summary statement, or a generalization, to emphasize God's characteristic activity: "He rescues and he saves; he performs signs and wonders in the heavens and on the earth" (Dan 6:27). Daniel in 4:2 proclaims God's mighty works: "The signs and wonders that the Most High God has worked for me I am pleased to recount." This generalization of how God reveals himself via miracles is repeated in Hebrews: "God also testifying to it [the great salvation] by signs, wonders and various miracles, and gifts of the Holy Spirit distributed according to his will" (Heb 2:4).[5]

Similarly, there are summary statements in the Psalms emphasizing how God characteristically works throughout the ages:

> Praise the Lord, O my soul, and forget not all his benefits—who forgives all your sins and heals all your diseases, who redeems your life from the pit and crowns you with love and compassion, who satisfies your desires with good things so that your youth is renewed like the eagle's. (Psa 103:2–5 NIV).

Traditional Protestant theology will emphasize God's present, contemporary benefit of forgiving sins but will downplay anything that looks like the present, contemporary miracle of healing "all your diseases." In heaven, maybe, but not now! We are told, essentially, to disobey Scripture and "forget the benefit" of healing! We are forgiven now, but the summary statement of God's guaranteed benefit of healing applies only to heaven! This hermeneutic seems to apply in the same way to Matthew 8:17 and 1 Peter 2:24.

By contrast, the following passages teach that each generation is to declare these mighty works (miracles) to the next generation. They imply that the generations are to declare not only the mighty works of the Exodus and of the recorded history of Israel but also all of God's mighty acts in all generations, including one's own, just as Jeremiah declares God's signs and wonders in his own generation—even among "all mankind." Psalm 104:22 affirms "*all* his works *everywhere* in his dominion" (my emphasis). These are some of the commands in the Psalms (emphasis mine throughout) to teach and recount God's mighty works, including those experienced personally:

> 4 One generation will commend your works to another; they will tell of your mighty acts. . . . 10 All you have made will praise you, O LORD; your saints will extol you. 11 They will tell of the glory of your kingdom and *speak of your might, 12 so that all men may know of your mighty acts and the glorious splendor of your kingdom.* (Psa 145:4, 10–12 NIV)

> 16 With the mighty deeds of the LORD God I will come; I will remind them of your righteousness, yours alone. 17 O God, from my youth you have taught me, and *I still proclaim your wondrous deeds.* 18 So even to old age and gray hairs, O God, do not forsake me, *until I proclaim your might to another generation, your power to all those to come.* 19 Your righteousness, O God, reaches the high heavens. You who have done great things, O God, who is like you? (Psa 71:16–19 ESV).

> 4 We will not hide them from their children, but *tell to the coming generation the glorious deeds of the LORD, and his might, and the wonders that he has done.* 5 He established a testimony in Jacob and appointed a law in Israel, which he commanded our fathers *to teach to their children, 6 that the next generation might know them, the children yet unborn, and arise and tell them to their children, 7 so that they should set their hope in God and not forget the works of God,* but keep his commandments; 8 *and that they should not be like*

> *their fathers,* a stubborn and rebellious generation, a generation whose heart was not steadfast, whose spirit was not faithful to God. [9] The Ephraimites, armed with the bow, turned back on the day of battle. [10] They did not keep God's covenant, but refused to walk according to his law. [11] *They forgot his works and the wonders that he had shown them.* (Psa 78:4–11 ESV)

> [12] *I will meditate on all your works and consider all your mighty deeds.* [13] Your ways, O God, are holy. What god is so great as our God? [14] *You are the God who performs miracles; you display your power among the peoples.* [note plural!] (Psa 77:12–14 NIV)

> Give thanks to the LORD, call on his name; *make known among the nations* [plural!] *what he has done.* [2] Sing to him, sing praise to him; tell of all his wonderful acts. [3] Glory in his holy name; let the hearts of those who seek the LORD rejoice. [4] *Look to the LORD and his strength; seek his face always.* [5] *Remember the wonders he has done, his miracles,* and the judgments he pronounced. . . . (Psa 105:1–5 NIV)

> Then they cried to the LORD in their trouble, and he saved them from their distress. [20] *He sent forth his word and healed them; he rescued them from the grave.* [21] *Let them give thanks to the LORD for his unfailing [continuing] love and his wonderful deeds [miracles] for men.* [22] *Let them sacrifice thank offerings and tell of his works* with songs of joy. (Psa 107:19–22 NIV)

> *Remember the wonders he has done, his miracles,* and the judgments he pronounced, (1Chr 16:12 NIV)

So what do these commands have to do with expecting miracles today? These repeated commands show emphasis, certainly. However, the purpose of insisting on recounting the mighty works (miracles) of God is to raise the level of appreciation and expectation that God will work similarly in the lives of the hearers. It is pointless to "tell of your power, to make known to all people your mighty deeds" if God's power is no longer operating. It's like saying, "Jesus Christ is the same yesterday, and maybe tomorrow, but um . . . not today."

Perhaps partly as a result of the exploding Pentecostal-charismatic movement worldwide, belief in miracles is spread broadly into the popular culture.[6] A 2003 Harris poll revealed that 84% of the public believed that miracles occur today.[7] A later, differently phrased poll indicated that 73% of adults believed in miracles,[8] a figure that agrees with results of 1,100 physicians' responses, 74% of whom believed that miracles occurred in the past. Interestingly for this study, 73% agreed that miracles occur today. A surprising result showed that 55% of the physicians claimed to witness medical miracles in their practice.[9] The recent trends over the past decades show a persistent, even growing belief in the miraculous today. It is compelling that an Israeli survey published at the end of 2008 claimed that 82% of Jews believe in miracles and that 41% claimed to experience miracles of their own.[10] (Can someone quote Jer 32:20 again?)

It would appear, then, the so-called "post-Christian" era has not taken deep root in the everyday experience of human life. Instead, the doctrine of cessationism seems to be losing ground even in our "secular" culture.[11] Miracles, then, are God's way of revealing himself—every bit as much as he does in words. Note that Jesus, Paul, and the obedient Christian community are described as being active or empowered in "deed and word" (Luke 24:19; Rom 15:18; Col 3:17; 2 Thes 2:17)—a phrase that has the overtone of miracle and inspired utterance.[12]

The main point of this section is to show that the "wisdom" that is emphasized in Proverbs, Ecclesiastes, Job, Psalms, and Song of Songs (or Song of Solomon) simply continues to emphasize the most valued process in the Bible: the immediate, prophetic revelation of God to his people—that is, hearing and heeding God.[13]

HEARING GOD IN PROVERBS

The Book of Proverbs has the most to say about wisdom and its related ideas. Wisdom is close to the concepts of "knowledge," "righteousness," and "faith." In the Bible, these are the product of revelation. A key verse of Proverbs (1:23) is likely mistranslated in the NIV. A more appropriate translation from the KJV follows. Note the synonymous parallel, where the first stanza repeats the second in different words:

> Behold, I will pour out my Spirit upon you
> I will make known my words to you

This verse shows a familiar pattern of the "pouring out" of the Holy Spirit resulting in revelation.[14] This revelation by the Spirit is the essence of the New Covenant, as we shall see below in Chapter 7. This revealed wisdom, or "words," expresses the central theme of Psalms and Proverbs: wisdom.

Proverbs emphasizes the importance of acquiring wisdom. Since we are emphasizing emphasis in this book, we must reiterate that Proverbs actually claims "Wisdom is the first priority [Heb: *reshiyt*, 'beginning']; therefore, whatever else you acquire, acquire understanding" (4:7). As in the previous Old Testament books we have examined, we see that the goal of hearing God's voice (wisdom) is the most important—the principal—goal of all.

One gains wisdom by listening to one's father and mother (1:8; 23:22–25; 30:17) or from other wise people. A mocker resents correction; he will not consult the wise (15:12). Ultimately, however, wisdom derives from God: "The Lord gives wisdom, and from his mouth come knowledge and understanding" (2:6). Note the sense of direct immediacy "from his mouth" of this wisdom. Jesus said exactly the same thing about how one "lives," that is, "on every word that proceeds from the mouth of God" (Matt 4:4). Isn't Jesus talking about wisdom or revelation here?

Note also that Proverbs emphasizes that the "fear of the Lord," which involves attentive, serious listening, is the beginning (starting point—a statement of emphasis) of wisdom (1:7; 9:10; 15:33). Accordingly, Wisdom herself is personified in two long passages in Proverbs, chapters 1 and 8. In each case, Wisdom promises to reveal herself directly to the seeker: "if you had responded to my rebuke, *I would have poured out my Spirit to you and made my thoughts known to you"* (1:23; 8:1, my emphasis). In 14:33 we have a parallel of the revelation of the Law into the heart in the New Covenant in Jeremiah 31:33: "Wisdom reposes in the heart of the discerning and even among fools she lets herself be known."

Not listening to Wisdom is the same as "hating knowledge" and choosing not to "fear the Lord" (1:29; 8:13–14; 15:33). So it is crucial to listen! Note the triple emphasis at the conclusion of the famous Proverbs 8 passage about how to get Wisdom: you listen to her, diligently!

> *Now then, my sons, listen to me; blessed are those who keep my ways.* [33]*Listen to my instruction and be wise; do not ignore it.* [34]*Blessed is the man who listens to me,* watching daily at my doors, waiting at my doorway. [35]For whoever finds me finds life and receives favor from the Lord (Prov 8:32–35 NIV, my emphasis).

So the punch line of this Wisdom chapter, which lays out the method for conducting a godly life, emphasizes the process of listening to Wisdom, that is, "fearing" or "hearing" God. Wisdom, then, appears to be a synonym for faith (hearing and heeding God)—the biblical way of "knowing" or "knowledge." Going this way is the same as choosing the Tree of Life rather than the Tree of the Knowledge of Good and Evil (knowing by human ability only).

In this connection, one is commanded to meditate (focus on, consider, think about) the words or commands of the Lord. Again, those words or commands appear to be in large part experienced, not as reading, but as direct and immediate revelation. This same theme appears frequently in the Psalms.

SUMMARY OF PSALMS AND PROVERBS

Psalms continues the theme of hearing God's voice (or sometimes not), obeying Him, and seeing His mighty works. Psalms expresses a kind of poetic, but very real and honest record of personal religious experiences in ancient Israel. The central experience is the perception of God's word or law in the heart. We may not dogmatically assume the traditional Protestant understanding that these terms refer to written documents or Scripture. At very least, the process of hearing God's word or law (or other terms like precepts, commandments, judgments, etc.) involves revelation, whether direct revelation to the heart (as is the goal of the Bible in the New Covenant) or illumination (by revelation) of the written law. The important point is that God communicates with his people directly and personally as normative.

Proverbs is not simply a collection of pithy sayings to guide our behavior in some legalistic way. Rather, Proverbs emphasizes gaining wisdom, which is the direct revelation of God into the heart—no different in principle than the charismatic or prophetic "word of wisdom" in the New Testament. Again, this is the goal of the Bible, the essence of the New Covenant.

SUMMARY OF THE OLD TESTAMENT EMPHASES

The enormous emphasis on faith (hearing God and obeying through suffering) in Scripture is clear, since it is placed as prominently as possible in the key narratives, e.g., the temptation of Eve and Adam (Gen 3), the call of Noah, of Abraham, (Gen 12), Jacob (Gen 37:5); the dreams of Joseph, the call and guidance of Moses (Exo 3), the Covenant at Sinai (Exo 19), the call of the prophets (1 Sam 1; Isa 6; Jer 1; Ezek 1—3), and the dominant themes in the Psalms and Proverbs. The explicit purpose of the defining wilderness experience for 40 years was to learn to live by hearing and obeying "every word that comes from the mouth of the LORD" (Deut 8:3). The Epistle to the Hebrews notes the flow of the dominant theme in the Old Testament to its climax in the New Testament:

> In the past God spoke to our forefathers through the prophets [role models] at many times and in various ways, but in these last days he has spoken to us by his Son, whom he appointed heir of all things, and through whom he made the universe. The Son is the radiance of God's

> glory and the exact representation of his being, sustaining all things by his powerful word (Heb 1:1–3 NIV).

As we shall see subsequently, Hebrews emphasizes the role of Jesus who mediates the New Covenant, which prominently promises the voice of God as "living and active" as its central element "today" (Heb 3:7–9; 3:15; 4:7–12)—a voice that today must not be refused (12:25). Indeed, the revelatory miracles and word of God come to all of mankind (Jer 32:20; Rom 1:18–21; 2:15; 10:18–20; 11:29).

To summarize, then, the three-fold mandate for mankind follows:

1. Ultimately, the purpose of our creation is intimacy with God, inasmuch as we are made "in his image and likeness," and the central process in man's relationship with God is to hear and obey God's voice. (The issue of humanity's temptation in Gen 3).
2. The Old Testament commands to speak forth prophetically his mighty works, his wisdom and praise, and,
3. To take authority over His creation (life and his people) to guard it and protect it against evil.

When we reflect on the mission of all the role models in the Old Testament, we see they all operated under this three-fold mandate. This mandate necessarily involves testing and suffering, as it confronts the forces of evil that attempt to destroy God's creation. Hence, the one who hears God's voice and obeys its mandate will encounter resistance, suffering, and even death, before ultimately being vindicated. This later becomes the defining issue for Jesus in his wilderness (40-day) experience: "Are you going to be a man of the Spirit, a true 'son' of God (a prophet who hears God's voice) or a rabbi who teaches from his own traditions—as the devil was tempting him to do?" (See the discussion, "What's Cookin' in Akhnai's Oven?" below.)

This prominence occurs also in the didactic teaching of the New Testament (e.g., 1 Cor 1—3; Rom 1; Gal 3; Heb 11 and Jas 1:2, 5–8; 2:14–26). The prominent location of this teaching in these books shows the centrality of revelation and action in the life of faith: the choice between the revelatory knowledge and experience of God (the life of faith) or alienation from God based on one's own desires and mental resources.

To avoid repetition by examining each New Testament book individually, this study will trace the theme of the New Covenant throughout. Here we show that traditional Protestantism, because of its cessationist bias, got its understanding of the New Covenant quite wrong. It is not simply the substitute of Christ's death for Old Testament animal sacrifices that constitutes the New Covenant (that death ratifies the New Covenant), but rather—the New Covenant is the coming of the Spirit to the individual.

Before we try to show the Bible's answer to the incorrect view of the New Covenant, we must first review an important emphasis of Scripture to determine its central issue for mankind, that is, the choice between hearing and heeding God's voice or following human "wisdom."[15] Accordingly, the next major section deals with this very issue.

---

1. This "weight of glory" (2 Cor 4:17) is a very common experience today among charismatics, many of whom will tell you that when they feel the "presence of the Lord" strongly, it's like a "weight" pressing us down, sometimes to the point we can no longer stand. The Hebrew word "glory" *(chabod)* has, after all, its primary meaning, "weight" and appears to be a synomym for the "presence" or "Spirit" of God. This seems to be described in 2 Chr 5:14: "the priests *could not stand* to minister because of the cloud, for the glory of the Lord filled the house of God" (nas), also Ezek 1:28; 3:23; 44:4; 1 Pet 4:14. Some experienced the "hand" of the Lord upon them apparently as a physical pressure 2 Kng 3:15; or simply in proximity to his "glory": sometimes to fulfill His purposes in a way normally not desired: 1 Sam 5:6; 6:5; Acts 13:11. The similar and more common biblical description of the "weight of glory" experience is "the Spirit of the Lord *upon*" someone, sometimes "mightily," e.g., Jdg 13:25; 14:6; 14:19; 1Sam 10:6; 16:13, even drawing comparisons to drunkenness (Acts 2:15–18; *cf.* Luke 1:15; Eph 5:18).
2. For a good survey of these developments see James C. Livingston and Francis Schüssler Fiorenza, *Modern Christian Thought, Vol. 1: The Enlightenment and the Nineteenth Century,* (Minneapolis: Fortress Press, 2nd ed., 2006), 5–82.
3. God teaches through creation itself and through the knowledge/wisdom of wise ones in the community, e.g., Isa 28.23–26 with Psa 19. God's voice through man's interaction with creation and acknowledging such learning from God's design in creation as also part of God's revelation, which the truly wise receive with gratitude. Creation is a mighty deed of God. It is only when deistic views of God smother

biblical theism that people no longer see "what nature teaches" (not a major biblical theme, to be sure) as intentional communication from God.

4. On this continuous process of revelation through miracles and the charismata expressed in Heb 2:4, see Ruthven, *On the Cessation of the Charismata,* revised and expanded version (Tulsa, OK: Word & Spirit Press, 2011), 87–88, esp. note 197.
5. *Synepimarturountos*—present participle of continuing action, modifying a past act, but which nonetheless is written to show normative "attesting" as in other cases where the gospel is presented (Acts 15:8, 12; Rom 15:19; 2 Cor 12:12; 1 Thes 1:5).
6. David C. Lewis. *Healing—Fiction, Fantasy or Fact?* (London: Hodder & Stoughton), 1989. Lewis, holding a PhD in Social Anthropology, analyzed 1,890 questionnaires from the Harrogate Conference (UK), led by John Wimber in 1986. Lewis chose 100 responses at random and followed up on reported healing experiences over a period of six months to a year, using established social science protocols (see pp. 15–16 and Appendix A).
7. The Harris Poll #11, February 26, 2003.
8. The Harris Poll #90, December 14, 2005.
9. The survey was conducted by HCD Research and the Louis Finkelstein Institute for Religious and Social Studies of the Jewish Theological Seminary in New York, December 23, 2004. (http://bit.ly/nD0ySE)
10. The Ynet-Gesher poll was conducted by the Panels Research Institute and included 500 respondents that constitute a representative sample of the adult Jewish population in Israel. Published December 23, 2008 in YNet News (http://bit.ly/pTQ6g3)
11. "Much of the strong belief in the supernatural is being driven by the growth in Pentecostalism and charismatic churches, said John Green, a Pew senior fellow in religion and American politics." Jacqueline L. Salmon, "Most Americans Believe in Higher Power, Poll Finds." *Washington Post,* Tuesday, June 24, 2008; A.2. (http://bit.ly/ohGSA7; for fee). See also James Arlandson, "Do Miracles Happen Today?" *American Thinker* (Jan 13, 2007) (http://bit.ly/ovgH86). As a representative of a widespread healing movement in Christianity, see the interview of Todd White on Sid Roth's "It's Supernatural" TV program (http://bit.ly/r4FU1m). With programs such as Roth's on TV constantly documenting miracles, it is difficult for traditional cessationism to hold the field.
12. The miraculous nature of the term "deed" in the above expression is confirmed in contemporary rabbinic materials according to G. Vermes, *Jesus the Jew: A Historian's Reading of the Gospels* (Philadelphia: Fortress Press, 1973), 78–82. Echoes of these summaries of how Paul "preached" the gospel appear also in other writers, e.g., in Acts 26:17–18 and Heb. 2:4, though in this latter case, as in Gal. 3:5 and 1 Cor. 1:5–8, the confirmation of the gospel was God working via a distribution of spiritual gifts in members of the various congregations. F. F. Bruce, "The Spirit in the Letter to the Galatians," *Essays on Apostolic Themes* (Peabody, MA: Hendrickson, 1985), 37–38. The niv and others miss the charismatic and miraculous flavor in its translation of Rom 15:18, where it translates "word and deed" as "in what I have said and done."
13. The Protestant tradition treats Ecclesiasticus (Sirach) and Wisdom (of Solomon) as secondary, apocryphal books, though they fit in the wisdom tradition.
14. The conservative Protestant niv misses the significance of the "pouring out" metaphor, which is connected with the *Spirit* in the Old Testament, not simply with expressing one's "heart." The word in the Hebrew text is *ruach,* not *lev* ("heart"). See:

Isa 32:15; 44:3; Ezek 39:29; Joel 2:28–29; Zech 12:10; so also, Acts 2:17, 18, 33; 10:45; Rom 5:5.

15. For a survey of theories on the nature of the New Covenant see Femi Adeyemi, *The New Covenant Torah in Jeremiah and the Law of Christ in Paul* (New York: Peter Lang, 2006), 1–80. Adeyemi acknowledges the role of the Spirit in the New Covenant, but only to interpret and apply the commands of the New Testament, which become the new Torah. In this view he fails to appreciate the radical nature of the promised prophetic Spirit in which direct, immediate communication with God becomes normative "Torah" in the heart. Adeyemi has simply replaced one set of written rules for another, contra 2 Cor 3.

PART THREE
THEMES OF SCRIPTURE VS. PROTESTANT TRADITIONS

Part III moves from a survey of the Old Testament materials to significant themes emphasized in both Testaments, Old and New. These themes are major emphases in the Bible, so it is important to examine what it is that these themes, in fact, emphasize. We discover that choosing not to hear God's voice of power is the central temptation to all of mankind (ch. 6). Moreover, the goal of the Bible is the New Covenant, the content of which is, unsurprisingly, the experience of the prophetic Spirit—hearing God's voice (ch. 7). Part III, then, includes a survey of the central theme (emphasis, again) in Jesus' ministry: the kingdom of God and its relation to our thesis (ch. 8). Finally, we can test our thesis by showing how the theme of the experience of the prophetic Spirit is emphasized in some key books of the New Testament, three of which play prominently as sources of traditional theology (ch. 9).

6

THE CENTRAL ISSUE OF HUMANITY

TEMPTATION NARRATIVES

In creation (Genesis 1), God set the pattern: all the universe, all life, survives by the central rule—God's word creates and sustains everything.[1] God commands Adam's involvement in ruling, "guarding and serving" the world. Adam begins this process by learning his authority over creation. Like God, he names, or calls, the different living beings, acknowledging God's creative acts. This occurs as an important instructional prerequisite before the greatest creative action with Adam: the creation of Eve, Adam's "suitable helper." At her creation, Adam's "word" comes forth, acknowledging their relationship and naming her.

God also commanded Adam that while every tree of the garden was available to him, including the tree of life, the fruit of only one tree, the tree of the knowledge of good and evil, was off limits.

Why? And what does this have to do with this book?

Simply this: the Genesis story up to this point establishes the central reality—that the power of God's word is everything. It creates, it sustains, it now warns and guides. Direct communication with God is assumed. Obviously, Adam is not reading all this from the Bible. What Adam hears, he obeys.

This process is laid down for the reader as a pattern to be followed—otherwise, why write it? Both Jesus and Paul emphasize this pattern. "Jesus said, 'Exactly as the Father has sent ['apostled'] me, in exactly the same way

I send you.' And when He had said this, He breathed on them, and said to them, 'Receive the Holy Spirit'" (John 20:21b–22). In so doing, like Adam, Jesus created a new race of men (breathing on them) and commissioned them to be empowered by the Spirit of revelation and prophecy.[2] Jesus also personifies the power of the word that creates and sustains the universe: "in Him all the universe coheres, holds together" (Col 1:16–17).

THE CENTRAL TEMPTATION TO MANKIND: INDICATOR OF THE CORE MESSAGE OF THE BIBLE

What comes next shows how important this "hearing and obeying" really is. How is this importance indicated by the emphasis of Scripture? The temptation narratives (Gen 3 and Matt 4:1–10 || Luke 4:1–13) in their literary structure are placed prominently and strategically in the mature lives of the first and second Adam. In both cases, the very lifeline from God to man is threatened: How does one define and live out one's relationship with God? By hearing and obeying (faith) or by following another way?

What is important here, is that the Bible emphasizes—by placing these stories in the narratives of the first Adam and second Adam (Christ) and by the fact that the temptations are essentially the same issue—whether one hears and obeys God's voice or seeks a substitute. So in terms of importance, no issue is more vital than the central temptation to us: to hear God or not.

The big test was for the whole world and Adam's authority over it. Proverbs generalizes into an emphasis: "Every word of God is tested" (in the sense of smelting or refining metal in intense heat—Prov 30:5).

"DID GOD REALLY SAY?"—THE ISSUE FACING ADAM, "MANKIND," "EVERYONE" (GENESIS 3)

The first words out of the serpent's mouth represent the central issue of the temptation of Eve and Adam. Theology generally recognizes that the content of this temptation story represents the primal issue for all mankind: that is, to hear and heed God's voice, or not. Again, the issue here is that when the snake asked this question, Eve and Adam did not go scurrying off to read their Bible to determine what God said or didn't say; rather, it's clear they already had memorable conversations with God.

Nevertheless, the issue was (and is), to whom do we listen? The two trees (Life and Knowledge) represent the primal human choice: do we listen to God or to the "wise" snake disguised as our own intellect? That old "intellectual stimulation," "academic excitement," and "joy of learning" is not a recent invention ("the woman saw that the fruit of the tree was good for food and pleasing to the eye, and also desirable for gaining wisdom"). In fact, after 188 semester hours of graduate work and 25 years of teaching theology, it's only recently occurred to me that Eve's primal excitement about learning was essentially spiritual adultery!

I can hear the reaction now: "he's really anti-intellectual!" Now that's a bad thing in our culture, like being a racist or a communist (well, at least, a communist back in the 1950s). We spend billions trying to stimulate the "love of knowledge." At least that's what was inculcated into me at the universities I attended, beginning with the University of Nebraska, where even the middle of the football field displayed a huge "N," which, we all knew, stood for "Nolledge."

Yet we can distinguish between "our heart burning within us" (Luke 24:32) and "the lust of the flesh, the lust of the eye and the pride of life" that "is not of the Father, but is of the world" (1 John 2:16 > Gen 3:6). Does every theologian and Christian teacher have a clear idea of this distinction when preparing lesson plans? I'm not always sure I do. Haven't we all fantasized at one time or another about how our stirring preaching or teaching will have a great "wow factor" to our audience? Knowledge is always used in our culture for status and prestige. Remember "grades," "degrees," "excellence"?

Surely, though, we can argue that knowledge is not bad; it's good to learn everything you can; after all, "knowledge is power." Exactly! But whose power? And for what purpose? Paul says that "knowledge puffs up" (causes pride), and with pride comes conflict (1 Cor 8:1; Prov 13:10).[3]

If we are looking for emphasis, we find it in the first three chapters of 1 Corinthians that deal with the issue of the two trees of Genesis 3. At this point I recommend stopping to read these first three chapters. The point here is not simply that there are two different ways of knowing, but far more importantly, that we should conduct our lives based on hearing from God—his wisdom revealed to us. "He will keep you strong [confirmed by spiritual gifts] to the end, so that you will be blameless on the day of our Lord Jesus Christ. God, who has called you into fellowship with his Son Jesus Christ our Lord, is faithful" (1 Cor 1:8–9). As we shall see, this goal statement (remember emphasis?) is a paraphrase of the New Covenant from Jeremiah 31:33—"'This is the covenant I will make with the house of Israel after that time,' declares the LORD. 'I will put my law in their minds and write it on their hearts. I will be their God, and they will be my people.'" See the parallel? Revelation leading to fellowship with God.

We see a good example of puffed up knowledge and the conflict pride brings in 1 Corinthians 1—3. Just as Adam and Eve were alienated from God and from each other because of their decision to become "wise" in their own ability, so the Corinthians began fighting over whose doctrine was superior (1 Cor 1:11–21). As we shall see in Part V when we talk about the New Testament method of training Christian workers, Paul is at pains to contrast God's way of knowing against the competitive pride of the Greek academy that the Corinthians were so used to.[4] These new Greek-influenced Christians immediately began treating the gospel as an interesting set of ideas that should be explored by human debate and intellectual jousting—almost exactly like the scribes and Pharisees of Jesus' time. Somebody once said that the Greeks (as the Jews) had to turn everything into a contest. The Corinthians caught onto the "theology game" really fast. So they crammed the ideas of their newly-adopted Christianity into their long-established, pagan academic systems. Today much Christian education emulates this pattern.

Here is an example of the power of this pagan, intellectualized, "wrong tree," Greek "group-think": I used to have a cartoon on my seminary office door of a preacher and his wife driving home after church.

> She: "That was a powerful sermon you gave this morning, dear! That new man in the last row was sobbing all the way through it. Who was he?"
>
> [Long silence]
>
> He: "That was my old hermeneutics professor."[5]

Of course, the point of the joke was that the pastor's wife didn't catch that the professor's tears were not in response to Holy Ghost conviction but to her husband's poor performance in the "theology game." A sermon that she thought elicited tears of repentance instead brought tears of wounded pride because a former student had learned so little about the "proper" rules of interpreting Scripture. The pastor's failure here was only that he failed in displaying human wisdom, not that he failed at God's requirement of communicating godly wisdom! So the joke was all about the competing "wisdom" systems in 1 Corinthians 1—3 and in Genesis 3.

This brings us back to the central theme of the Bible and of this book: that seeking God and hearing his voice is central to everything; it's the starting point of all we do. And like the issue of Genesis 3, the temptation of Eve and Adam, hearing the voice of God first is the precise point of the temptation of Jesus, the second Adam.

Just as Adam was tempted and just as Moses fasted in God's presence for forty days in the wilderness (Exo 34:28) to receive the Covenant, so Jesus was tempted in the wilderness for forty days to introduce a New Covenant—the covenant of the Spirit (2 Cor 3). The temptation of Jesus was a temptation to remain in the Old Covenant of the written law vs. the New Covenant of the Spirit written in the heart (Jer 34:33). The devil wanted Jesus to conduct his life by following the traditional religious-scribal process for interpreting Scripture by trying to force God to act according to human desires (fleshly or demonically inspired), rather than by a "hearing of faith" in which God takes the initiative and reveals his will directly to the heart.

This was the central conflict between early Christianity and Judaism: New Testament Christianity relied first on the witness of the Spirit as a guide to Scripture, while the Jewish tradition explicitly and consciously denied the voice of God, or of the Spirit, in applying Scripture. Traditional interpretation was delegated to the professional scribes and rabbis.[6]

Some might say, "This temptation narrative isn't simply about Scripture, because both the devil and Jesus quote it." True. Yet we can't miss that the issue is about how Scripture is applied. Jesus does not do away with the Scripture or the Law (Matt 5:18–20) but fulfills the dominant theme of Scripture by inaugurating the New Covenant of faith (hearing and heeding God's revelation, Gal 3:24–26). So that it is by faith (or being led by the Spirit, Rom 8:16) that we become sons of God.

Let's look at the temptation text of Matthew 4:1–11:

> Then Jesus was led by the Spirit into the desert to be tempted by the
> devil. 2After fasting forty days and forty nights, he was hungry. 3The
> tempter came to him and said, "If you are the Son of God, tell these
> stones to become bread." 4Jesus answered, "It is written: 'Man does not
> live on bread alone, but on every word that comes from the mouth of
> God.'" 5Then the devil took him to the holy city and had him stand on
> the highest point of the temple. 6"If you are the Son of God," he said,
> "throw yourself down. For it is written: 'He will command his angels
> concerning you, and they will lift you up in their hands, so that you will
> not strike your foot against a stone.' 7Jesus answered him, "It is also
> written: 'Do not put the Lord your God to the test.'" 8Again, the devil
> took him to a very high mountain and showed him all the kingdoms of
> the world and their splendor. 9"All this I will give you," he said, "if you
> will bow down and worship me." 10Jesus said to him, "Away from me,
> Satan! For it is written: 'Worship the Lord your God, and serve him
> only.'" 11Then the devil left him, and angels came and attended
> him. (NIV)

In the Matthew temptation, the thesis (or emphasis) statement of Jesus about this new/old way of understanding God's will is to live by "every word that comes from the mouth of God" (Deut 8:3).[7] The other two temptations are simply variations of the first: what or whom do you consult before acting on a principle of Scripture? Tradition? Satan? Or the voice of God himself? For Matthew, the key answer is the quotation from Deuteronomy 8:3 and "every word that comes from the mouth of God."

In citing this crucial answer to Satan, Jesus is meticulously following the Old Testament spiritual role models (patriarchs and prophets), who heard from the Lord and obeyed—and who sought revealed wisdom as the first priority. After this temptation Jesus demonstrates precisely how he "lives by every word" from God: he inaugurates the kingdom of God (Matt 4:17) in power; "preaching the good news of the kingdom, and healing every disease and sickness among the people" (Matt 4:23). Conceptually, this Matthean account is the same as Luke's account, in which Jesus returned from his temptation "in the power of the Spirit" (Luke 4:14).

Luke emphasizes Jesus' response to the temptation with the same answer as Matthew (the citation of Deut 8:3: "man does not live on bread alone"), implying the Spirit of revelation and prophecy.

> Jesus, full of the Holy Spirit, returned from the Jordan and was led by the Spirit in the desert, [2]where for forty days he was tempted by the devil. He ate nothing during those days, and at the end of them he was hungry. [3]The devil said to him, "If you are the Son of God, tell this stone to become bread." [4]Jesus answered, "It is written: 'Man does not live on bread alone.'" [5]The devil led him up to a high place and showed him in an instant all the kingdoms of the world. [6]And he said to him, "I will give you all their authority and splendor, for it has been given to me, and I can give it to anyone I want to. [7]So if you worship me, it will all be yours." [8]Jesus answered, "It is written: 'Worship the Lord your God and serve him only.'" [9]The devil led him to Jerusalem and had him stand on the highest point of the temple. "If you are the Son of God," he said, "throw yourself down from here. [10]For it is written: 'He will command his angels concerning you to guard you carefully; [11]they will lift you up in their hands, so that you will not strike your foot against a stone.'"

> [12]Jesus answered, "It says: 'Do not put the Lord your God to the test.'" [13]When the devil had finished all this tempting, he left him until an opportune time. [14]Jesus returned to Galilee in the power of the Spirit, and news about him spread through the whole countryside. (Luke 4:1–14 NIV)

Luke does not mention Matthew's "thesis statement" of Deuteronomy 8:3b ("but by every word that proceeds from the mouth of God"). Why? In the first place, the typical Jewish reader would automatically finish the quote; so it is quite possible that Luke is using a teaching device to plant the quotation more firmly in the readers' minds.[8] Furthermore, it's possible he does not want to detract from his emphasis on the Holy Spirit (the Spirit of prophetic revelation) as Jesus' answer. The opening verse shows that, in addition to being "led" into the wilderness by the Spirit (as in Matthew), Jesus leaves his baptism in the Jordan River "full of the Holy Spirit"! The temptation narrative is bracketed by an emphasis on the prophetic, revelatory Holy Spirit ("Jesus returned to Galilee in the power of the Spirit").

In fact, unlike Matthew, Luke emphasizes the outworking of the Spirit in the next story immediately following: the crucial announcement of his mission as being the Holy Spirit-anointed prophet sent to those who would reject him (Luke 4:16–32 > Isa 61:1–2) as the Israelites had historically rejected God's prophets. The religious people in Jesus' home town didn't like to be seen for what they were: rejecters of God's prophetic word. They wouldn't have done well in the temptation Jesus just experienced! They saw him as "Joseph's son" but not the Son of God. A true "son of God" hears God's voice—that's more than memorizing Scripture and being pleased with ourselves for doing so. It is, at a minimum, allowing God's Spirit to shape our understanding of Scripture.

This programmatic prophecy of Luke from Isaiah 61:1–2 ("The Spirit of the Lord is upon me . . .") corresponds to the programmatic prophecy of Acts, Luke's sequel, Isaiah 59:21. Acts 2:39 quotes from it:

> "As for me, this is my covenant with them," says the LORD. "My Spirit, who is on you, and my words that I have put in your mouth will not depart from your mouth, or from the mouths of your children, or from the mouths of their descendants from this time on and forever," says the LORD. (Isa 59:21 NIV)

So, in view of his emphasis upon the prophetic Spirit, did Luke have this idea "every word that comes from the mouth of the Lord" in mind when he omitted what Matthew had emphasized? Luke's answer makes clear the role of the covenant Spirit in hearing God's voice against the temptation to apply Scripture to his life improperly. As Matthew, Luke emphasizes the role of God's voice at the center of Jesus' existence as the Son of God (our role model for our existence as children of God).

Indeed, the relative roles of the Spirit and Scripture in 2 Peter 1:19–21 makes this very point:

> And we have the word of the prophets made more certain, and you will do well to pay attention to it, as to a light shining in a dark place, until the day dawns and the morning star rises in your hearts. [20] Above all, you must understand that no prophecy of Scripture came about by the prophet's own interpretation. (NIV)

Peter is encouraging the use of prophecy in his church community "as a lamp in a dark place" until the heavenly state arrives, at least in one's heart in this present age. Peter seems to be dealing with the same issue facing Jesus in his temptation: what takes priority? Prophecy or Scripture? Peter seems to come to the same conclusion as Jesus, that the Spirit has priority in guiding us—even to interpret Scripture; because, contrary to the practice of the scribes, the revelation of God both wrote and interprets Scripture—since Scripture itself was generated by "men moved by the Holy Spirit [who] spoke from God." The argument then is this: if Scripture was inspired by the Spirit, it should also then be interpreted by the Spirit, as an activity of the "prophetic word made more sure" that guides us like a "lamp in a dark place." As Paul says, "no one comprehends the thoughts of God [even those written in

Scripture] except the Spirit of God" (1 Cor 2:14) on whom we must depend to interpret Scripture. Likewise, we must resist the notion that the gift of prophecy adds new Scripture or that personal revelation from our Holy Spirit teacher ever contradicts it. While Scripture itself strongly encourages personal revelation, it also provides the unchanging, inerrant framework for judging the validity of that personal revelation.

Again, we must emphasize that the temptation narratives of both the first and second Adam relate to the same issue: does one heed the immediate, revealed voice of God or not?[9] It's as simple as that—and just as central to the plan of God for mankind. As we have seen, the temptation narratives are a way of identifying the core value—the central theme of the Bible—in how God deals with all humans. How does one prove this? By the fact, according to Scripture, that everyone has a conscience—a body of information that is revealed to them by God.

CONSCIENCE: A TASTE OF THE NEW COVENANT REVELATION?

Conscience provides us with a glimpse of the New Covenant of God's Law "written in the heart," that is, by divine revelation. A hint of this is from the apostle Paul's parallel expression that even the Gentiles "show that the requirements of the law are written on their hearts, their *consciences also bearing witness*" (Rom 2:15, my emphasis). Note that the idea that one's conscience can bear witness seems to suggest a kind of independent witness—independent of one's own witness or consciousness. Is this what is described in the very form of the word itself, conscience, translated literally from the Greek: *syneidisis,* that is, "with-knowledge"? So you have personal, human knowledge, but also another knowledge "with" that knowledge. So how does this "with-knowledge" that is not our own arrive within us?

It is clear from the New Testament that one's conscience is knowledge revealed from God himself! How do we prove this? Thirty times the Greek term for "conscience" appears in the New Testament. Of those 30 passages, 15 show from the context that one's conscience is revealed from God (e.g., Rom 9:1; 2 Cor 1:12; 5:11; 1 Tim 1:19; Heb 10:22). This is another case of exegetical emphasis, showing the universal experience of God's direct and immediate, propositional revelation.

Traditional Protestants, especially those who wrote the Westminster Confession of Faith, would say, well, of course, this is what we call "general revelation," which is a knowledge of Christ insufficient for salvation. Such knowledge does not reveal new doctrine but at best "the requirements of the Law written on [the Gentiles'] hearts."

Yet aren't these requirements the dreaded "propositional revelation"? Aren't they doctrines? Certainly new doctrines—at least new to the recipients? Don't Gentiles today, all around the world, who have never heard the gospel, receive this kind of "propositional revelation" today? We read in Romans 1 that just as a believer of the revealed gospel moves from "faith into faith," so the unbeliever also receives revelation "revealed from heaven" that "God has made plain/clear to them" and is therefore "clearly seen" (Rom 1:17–21). Romans 1 goes on to show that God's wrath is revealed when this "plain, clear" revelation is suppressed and "their foolish (God-denying) hearts are darkened" (1:21). So the law is written in their hearts just as it is in the New Covenant mediated by Jesus Christ (Jer 31:33 > 2 Cor 3).

The parallel between knowledge through conscience and that through the New Covenant is shown in the following example. Hebrews 6:4–6 actually claims that when one would "fall away" from Christianity, s/he is actually falling away, not from some doctrine or creed, but is "falling away" from a *process* of ongoing revelation to the human heart—that is the central process of the New Covenant that is stated in five different ways in Hebrews 6:4–6.[10] Talk about emphasis! So just as the New Covenant can be denied, so the revelation received in one's conscience can be suppressed, made weak (1 Cor 8:7, 10) or seared (1 Tim 4:2).[11]

So our argument here is that the process of revelation is a universal and permanent activity of God's to all mankind, as shown by the biblical phenomenon of conscience as a taste of the New Covenant.[12]

CONCLUSION

The general point of Chapter 6 is that the Bible points to the central temptation of mankind, which is whether or not we hear God or heed our own human wisdom. This central choice, offered to both the first and second Adam—the archetypes of all of humanity, shows that God emphasizes hearing his voice as central and normative in human experience. This emphasis is shown by the role of God's revelation to all of mankind, that is, in our conscience, which is a prototype experience of God's New Covenant of the Spirit, in that conscience is specific revelation to all.

The next section makes the same point with slightly different framing: just as the temptation narratives encapsulate the central issue confronting mankind (to hear God or not) and as our conscience reveals this fact, the Bible also shows that the goal of the Bible is the New Covenant, which also shows us how God's central desire is realized as we hear, heed, and have loving fellowship with Him through the revelation of His Holy Spirit.

---

1. Heb 1:3. This notion of an intelligent, outside power tweaking and sustaining the universe is gaining ground, even to the point of consensus, in modern astrophysics. Scientists, confronted with the overwhelming odds of even atoms holding together by "random chance," are forced to conclude that some intelligent force is constantly overcoming the odds and maintaining this "impossible balance" within nature. See Granville Sewell, *In the Beginning: And Other Essays on Intelligent Design* (Seattle, WA: Discovery Institute Press, 2010.) and Hugh Ross, "Big Bang—The Bible Taught It First," *The Creator and the Cosmos*, 3rd ed. (Colorado Springs: NavPress, 2001), 23–29.
2. Remember that, in biblical theology, the term "Holy Spirit," when involving a person, has a strong flavor of that person's being empowered as a prophet—to do things prophets do, e.g., receive revelation, prophesy, and perform miracles.
3. The arrogant claim to the ultimacy of human knowledge ("science," "facts," "reality") against the foolishness and superstition of Christian believers is the central theme of atheists. For examples, check the responses to articles on creationism or intelligent design in any major news journal online. This theme also is prominent in the popular writings of the resurgent atheist movement today, e.g., Dawkins, Hitchens, Gould. In this they fit the familiar pattern of Romans 1:18–32, which goes on to describe the remarkably modern consequences of their denial of God. They are quite up front about their choice: to follow their own wisdom rather than the revelation of God. The

most prominent atheist in our time, philosopher Anthony Flew, recently changed his mind, however.

4. Although the Corinth of Paul's day was Roman and not Greek Corinth, elements of Hellenic culture such as love of oratory and the existence of various schools of philosophy continued to thrive and justify our reference to things Hellenic.
5. Hermeneutics is the science of biblical interpretation.
6. See discussion about their doctrine of "It is not in Heaven," p. 138, n. 7
7. Remember, it was *always* God's immediate voice coming to the role models for Israel (the Patriarchs, Moses, Joshua, the Judges, the prophets, etc.) that was the central way God communicated—the ideal, preferred way. Jesus' way of the New Covenant was simply the continuation of God's plan for communicating and communion.
8. This "complete-the-sentence" technique may not work as well in our culture: see Ben Stein's struggle in "Ferris Buehler's Day Off": "Anyone? Anyone?" (http://www.youtube.com/watch?v=dxPVyieptwA)
9. Recall that in normative Judaism, the decision was "no": the will of God was decided by the application of human wisdom (proper exegesis and logic) to the Law that was once-and-for-all delivered to the teachers/scribes to teach others.
10. For it is impossible to restore again to repentance those who have once (1) been enlightened, who have (2) tasted the heavenly gift, and have become (3) partakers of the Holy Spirit, and have (4) tasted the goodness of the word of God and (5) the powers of the age to come, if they then commit apostasy, since they crucify the Son of God on their own account and hold him up to contempt. (Heb 6:4–6 rsv).
11. An excellent treatment of conscience from the natural law tradition, wholly compatible with Scripture, is J. Budziszewski, *The Revenge of Conscience: Politics and the Fall of Man* (Dallas: Spence Publishing, 2000; Eugene, OR: Wipf & Stock, 2010).
12. In fact, this is often the case in the Muslim world today, where many report vivid revelatory dreams of "Issa" (Jesus) as the way to God. In the same way God reveals himself in signs and wonders to all mankind "even to this day" (Jer 32:20).

7
THE GOAL OF THE BIBLE
THE NEW COVENANT

One of the ways literature emphasizes specific features is by expressing a goal or objective: that is, saying where this document is taking me, identifying its main point. Often this purpose for the document will appear in its title. In that case, consider the title defining document of Christianity. The New Testament, right? Testament is another word for covenant: New Testament expresses a New Covenant.

A couple of definitions:

The Old Covenant is expressed in the written laws of God given at Mt. Sinai through Moses (found in Exodus through Deuteronomy). It was a kind of written treaty between God and his people, with stipulations, which if kept or broken would result in consequences (see Deut 28).

The New Covenant represents a radically different approach. Someone in the New Covenant experiences the Holy Spirit of prophecy revealing God's message into the heart. In this way, one really knows God (Isa 59:21; Jer 31:31–34) because He speaks directly to the individual instead of leaving an ancient, written set of directives left to be interpreted and applied by professionals (Deut 17:11; 30:12).

Before we can talk about the New Covenant, we need to make sense out of the Old Covenant and how it fits the big picture of God's revelation in the Bible.

THE OLD COVENANT AS PLAN B: "PUT IT ALL IN A MEMO, AND WE'LL GET BACK TO YOU."

The Old Covenant (the words of God written) was given as a concession to Israel's fearful rejection of God's communicating with them directly (Exo 20:19). They had watched the many times that Pharaoh's "heart was hardened" after encounters with God.[1] In other words, Pharaoh just could not get or hear God's message as faith (hearing and obeying). He may have heard in some sense, but the Pharaoh refused to obey.

Similarly, it seems that this Pharaoh disease was contagious even to the Israelites. They heard God's voice at Sinai, but it scared them so much they demanded a go-between: Moses and the Law. But God still did not write them off; he saw a future for them. Instead he gave a written word to Israel as a concession to their hardness of heart just as he allowed, say, divorce (Matt 19:8).

But Ezekiel noted that in the future, God would "remove from them their heart of stone" (Ezek 11:19; 36:26) and would "put a new Spirit in them" (Isa 44:3; Jer 31:33; Ezek 37:14; 37:14; 39:29). This is exactly what Paul sees as fulfilled in the New Covenant of the Spirit (2 Cor 3:3 > Jer 31).

Paul puts this another way: "Those who are led by the Spirit," Paul says, "are not under Law/Torah" (Gal 5:18). When "walking in step with the Spirit . . . there is no law" (Gal 5:23). The "new deal," or the New Covenant, brought a whole new way to relate to God: instead of all the stipulations of an elaborate and impossible covenant or contract that no one could fulfill, the faithful would enter into God's loving, revealing presence as his adopted children—those who internalized his power and divine nature (2 Pet 1:4). In this way, as mature sons and daughters who hear God's voice, he can then "sign off" on the old Law and thereby "fulfill in us who walk by the Spirit the righteous commandment of Torah" (Rom 8:4).[2]

The New Covenant, then, is the promise of the Spirit fulfilled by his words in our mouth (Acts 2:39 > Isa 59:21) or is the voice of God (Heb 3:7, 15; 4:7; 12:25) to which we respond in loving obedience. The point is that the normal Old Covenant mentality did not allow the word of the Lord to penetrate the heart, whereas under the covenant of the prophetic Spirit, God can reveal himself and have it get through. In the New Covenant era, God's word or revelation does not need to languish, unread or unfulfilled in a written form, subject to misuse and misapplication by a cadre of professional religionists.

So as Plan B (the Old Covenant), God's communication functioned as a kind of "guardian/instructor" (Gk: *paidagōgos*, lit., "child-leader") to take us to Christ and faith (Gal 3:24–25), that is, the New Covenant of the Spirit. The written Scripture could act only as a mirror—to show our dirty faces (our sin), but it didn't actually wash our faces! By contrast, the New Covenant Spirit, which now indwells us, not only guides us as to the content of God's will but also motivates us to do it. In fact, under the New Covenant, the answer to sin is not simply to stop sinning but to "walk in the Spirit" (the revelation and guidance of God) and, in this way, we "will not carry out the desires of our weaknesses" (Gal 5:16).

Beyond that (and this is central), the New Covenant Spirit empowers us with his gifts to fulfill God's calling for us. The New Covenant isn't simply a list of new laws we have to obey, even with help of the Spirit, but rather, is a whole new way of living in maturity and in constant communion with God who has moved us from a "have to" religion to a "want to" relationship.

Under the Old Covenant we were like an immature kid: the Law served as the "pedagogue/babysitter," who supervised us and tried to keep us out of trouble. Under the New Covenant, we have become mature, adult participants in the family business of guarding and serving God's created order: restoring people to health, faith, and obedience to God, as well as driving out demons—in other words, fulfilling our calling as prophets of God and living out the New Covenant. This is the commission to Adam, that is, to mankind, reaffirmed to Jesus' disciples. In the New Covenant we have become not just servants but friends in intimate relationship with God, who, like a father relating to his adult child, will remember our (childhood) "sins no more."

As the people of God mature, they move from very specific laws to a whole new way of living, as we see here in these progressive directions—

> *To a five-year-old: "Never go into the street!"*
> *To a 10-year old: "Look both ways before you cross the street!"*
> *To an 18-year-old: "Please drive to the market and get the groceries on this list. Drive safely!"*
> *To a married 25-year-old: nothing.*

Why? It's all automatic and internalized now. Well, it should be, anyway! (If not, this is usually where the wife takes over as the external law). Mature life has moved beyond being constantly reminded of rules for survival to actually living and achieving. To be sure, the rules are internalized, but they are now made flexible and appropriate to the situation. They are no longer the focus of life: we don't exist to keep rules; rather the old rules supplement and serve God's mission for which we are prepared in so many other ways than rule-keeping. The mature life is the life in the Spirit: a life of communion with God, of faith and of charismatic empowerment to heal, redeem, and disciple others to do the same.

A LITTLE MORE DETAIL ON THE COVENANTS

Since our argument here is that the New Covenant is the goal of the Bible and therefore its central emphasis, it might be useful to investigate how the Bible portrays this centrally important goal.[3]

The New Testament writers emphasize the desirability and superiority of the New Covenant over the Old (Matt 4 || Luke 4; Acts 2:39 > Isa 59:21; Matt 26:28 || Mark 14:24 || Luke 22:20, cf. John 6:54–56, 63; 1 Cor 11; 2 Cor 3; Heb 8—10 [esp. 8:5–13; 9:14–15; and 12]).

Given the nature of the Law as described in the New Testament, it would appear that the Israelites failed the test on two points: 1) they refused the offer of God speaking directly to them—thereby inaugurating Plan B, the Old Covenant, and postponing the offer of God's direct voice until it reappears in the New Covenant. 2) Moses expresses a paradox for the Israelites: on the one hand he urges them, "Do not be afraid," yet he says that God has presented himself in a frightening way (Exo 20:20).

How does one untangle this?

Maybe what's going on here is that God is presenting the classic dilemma of all mankind when we encounter God in all his power, glory, and holiness: our sinfulness wants to flee, but the Spirit and plan of God draws us to him. The word of God—communication with him—demands suffering, beginning with the suffering of confronting our own fear, failure, and selfishness.

For example, when we see or hear of great healings and miracles around us, we can respond in three ways. Two are inappropriate: 1) we can react in revulsion because the presence of God evokes fear or shame, as Peter reacted in response to a miracle (Luke 5:8). 2) Or, we may have a desire to be part of a miracle movement, but not necessarily for God's glory. In these first two examples, we may want to jump into the ministry of spiritual gifts, but all the while fearing failure for ourselves and God ("ashamed of the gospel"?). We might then exert our own efforts or "believe real hard" because we don't yet see "the power of God unto salvation." Still fearful and disappointed, we rationalize: "I just don't have the gift" or "it's not me failing, there's probably some sin or resentment in this guy's life," or we justify some other back-door through which we flee.

But there is an appropriate way of approaching God's presence and power. Those who are experienced will tell you they feel the same fear issues, but that they see results when they are in that "glory zone" or "feel the anointing" or have "aggressive assurance" that comes from being in the presence of God. Those experienced in the power of God often spend many hours in prayer before moving out to minister in healing. A student of mine apprenticed himself to the great healing evangelist, Reinhard Bonnke, who would drag him out of bed every morning at 4:30 to pray intensively until about 9:00 when it was time to go to work. To hear God clearly (the first part of faith) takes a lot of intensive listening! The New Testament shows Jesus modeling prayer some 26 times—even "with loud crying and tears" (Heb 5:7). If he needed to do it, what about us? And, just like Jesus, spending a lot of time in prayer does not excuse us from constantly being in the presence of God or "walking in the Spirit."

So let's look closer at Moses' paradox: "God has come in order to test you and in order that the fear of him may remain with you so that you may not sin" (Exo 20:20). This verse may mean two things: God is presenting himself in a fearful way to scare you into obedience; or the Israelites were presented with the choice of fearing, that is, hearing and heeding his internal voice (God's speaking to them) so that they may not sin. This idea is precisely the point of the New Testament covenant of the Spirit: "walk in rank with the Spirit and you will not fulfill the desires of your weakness (flesh)" (Rom 8:4; Gal 5:17–19). It seems clear that they chose the former interpretation; they coped with this terror of God by begging Moses to mediate between them and God. It is instructive how Hebrews 12:18–28 explains the difference between the two covenants to early Jewish believers who were persecuted for their life in the Spirit of Christ:

> You [the Messianic Jewish readers] have not come to a mountain that can be touched and that is burning with fire; to darkness, gloom and storm; 19to a trumpet blast or to such *a voice speaking words that those who heard it begged that no further word be spoken to them,* 20because they could not bear what was commanded: "If even an animal touches the mountain, it must be stoned." 21The sight was so terrifying that Moses said, "I am trembling with fear."
>
> 22But you have come to Mount Zion, to the heavenly Jerusalem, the city of the living God. You have come to thousands upon thousands of angels in joyful assembly, 23to the church of the firstborn, whose names are written in heaven. You have come to God, the judge of all men, to the spirits of righteous men made perfect, 24to Jesus the mediator of a New Covenant, and to the sprinkled blood that speaks a better word than the blood of Abel.
>
> 25*See to it that you do not refuse him who speaks.* If they did not escape

> when they refused him who warned them on earth, how much less will we, if we turn away from him who warns us from heaven? [26]At that time his voice shook the earth, but now he has promised, "Once more I will shake not only the earth but also the heavens." [27]The words "once more" indicate the removing of what can be shaken—that is, created things—so that what cannot be shaken may remain. [28]Therefore, since we are receiving a kingdom that cannot be shaken, let us be thankful, and so worship God acceptably with reverence and awe. (my emphasis, NIV)

Despite the response of the Israelites, God was then, and is now, offering the ideal of direct communication (Heb 12:25. Note the three present tense verbs: "speaks," "warns," "are receiving"). This ideal is the central characteristic of "receiving a kingdom that cannot be shaken" (v 28). Certainly Moses and Joshua had it, but the Israelites as a whole chose what we (and the church before us) mostly choose—something or someone to buffer between us and a holy God. The Israelites chose Moses and the Law. Later generations chose canon law, priests, apostles, popes, etc., to be mediators. It's no accident that among Catholics, Mary is called "Mediatrix." The pope is called a "substitute" Christ—*vicarius Christi* (as are the bishops).[4] The spirit of religion always wants to keep a distance from God by interposing substitutes—all to avoid direct communication and communion with God. Jesus, of course, is our Mediator, but a "mediator of the New Covenant"—not a mediator like the saints, not a written document, or a pope, but rather a Mediator who facilitates and introduces us into direct, personal communication with God (Luke 22:20; 1 Cor 11:25; Heb 8:6; 9:15; 12:24).

Several passages show us that the bestowal of the (prophetic, revelatory) Spirit is the central element of the New Covenant. The one most often cited in the New Testament is Jeremiah 31:31–34.

> "The time is coming," declares the LORD, "when I will make a *new covenant* with the house of Israel and with the house of Judah. [32]It will not be like the covenant I made with their forefathers when I took them by the hand to lead them out of Egypt, because they broke my covenant, though I was a husband to them," declares the LORD. [33]*"This is the*

> *covenant I will make with the house of Israel after that time,"* declares the LORD. *"I will put my law in their minds and write it on their hearts.* I will be their God, and they will be my people. [34] No longer will a man teach his neighbor, or a man his brother, saying, 'Know the LORD,' because *they will all know me, from the least of them to the greatest,"* declares the LORD. "For I will forgive their wickedness and will remember their sins no more." (emphasis mine, NIV)

What is new here is the process of communicating between God and the New Covenant person: the Law will no longer be written on stone or some such but will be internalized through the new reality by which they now "know the Lord." But how does one "know the Lord" in the biblical tradition? How about that key phrase from 1 Samuel 3:7 (NIV)?

> Now Samuel did not yet know the LORD: The word of the LORD had not yet been revealed to him.

Note the parallel sentence construction explaining how one knows the Lord: by revelation of the Lord's word. There are at least 134 passages of Scripture showing how one knows the Lord. In the Old Testament it is in every case because God reveals himself either by his miracle power or by his word given directly to an individual.[5] In the New Testament, God reveals himself in a similar way—that is, the gospel is announced in "deed and word" (Luke 24:19; Rom 15:18; Heb 2:4). In fact, the Gospel of John seems to have been written to refute the prevailing Jewish notion that a knowledge of God was a matter of studying Torah and the teachings of the rabbis, instead of being revealed directly to the human heart.[6]

It is clear from Scripture that the essence of the New Covenant is the presence of the communicating, prophetic Spirit in our heart (Isa 59:21 > Acts 2:39; Jer 31:33 > 2 Cor 3; Heb 8—12). This is a gift of faith—the Spirit of God's Son within us crying "abba," "Daddy!" (Gal 4:6).

Beyond this, when we are challenged to explain our relationship with God, we are promised a New Covenant phenomenon of "teaching" in the heart: that the "Holy Spirit will teach *(didaksei)* you at that time what you should say" (Luke 12:12—the same word also in John 14:26, citing Jeremiah 31:34 [38:34 LXX]).

But what about all this in traditional Protestant theology? In their denial of this sort of direct, prophetic revelation in the heart, traditional Protestants are soul mates with the "theologians" (the scribes) of Jesus' time. A strong denial that God spoke directly to people was a cornerstone of the Jewish approach to interpreting Scripture.[7] Torah study was the core of rabbinic Judaism based on the doctrine "It is not in heaven" (Deut 30:12).[8] The rabbis took this passage to justify the rabbinic authority to interpret the Scriptures for the rest of us—to the exclusion of even God himself—who had apparently recused himself from giving any more revelation, since he entrusted it entirely into the hands of the rabbis (scribes and Pharisees)! You can guess who made up that rule; rather like the Westminster Confession's creators or the pope (who declared himself infallible)!

With this mindset, then, the Torah itself is said to explain the phrase "not in heaven" as justifying rabbinic authority to interpret the Torah. The Talmud explains that "(The Torah) is not in heaven" means that even God's prophets, miracles, or his own direct words would not determine the meaning and application of the Law, but rather only by the interpretive decisions and teachings of the rabbis! Scripture and its interpretation by the professionals had become the only vehicle for God to communicate to mankind![9] As Jesus said, "Thus you nullify the word of God for the sake of your tradition" (Matt 15:6).

This is why Jesus' teaching in John 5:37–47 is so relevant to the Judaism of his time—and to ours. It also underscores the crucial importance of the New Covenant which reversed (in Jer 31:31–34) this rabbinic and Westminster Confession idolatry of human teaching and authority! Jesus himself said: "But the Helper, the Holy Spirit, whom the Father will send in My name, He will teach you all things, and bring to your remembrance all that I said to you" (John 14:26; also 1 Cor 3). Cessationism is essentially rabbinic Judaism's doctrine of "it is not in heaven"!

But Jesus attacks this position vigorously:

> And the Father who sent me has himself testified concerning me. You have never heard his voice nor seen his form, [38] nor does his word dwell in you, for you do not believe the one he sent. [39] You diligently study the Scriptures because you think that by them you possess eternal life. These are the Scriptures that testify about me, [40] yet you refuse to come to me to have life. (John 5:37–40 NIV)

What is Jesus saying here? He is saying that the scribal-rabbinic doctrine of "it is not in heaven," which is also the doctrine of cessationism, is invalid. Jesus is saying that it is the intention of the Father to send a "prophet like Moses" (Deut 34:10–12) but he qualifies by adding "you do not believe (receive revelation) in Him whom He sent." This is crucial: belief in Jesus involved a process of divine testimony which the scribes denied, specifically, these traditionalist religionists denied the testimony of God in his voice, his form, and the possibility of his prophetic word abiding in you. This intent of the Father is not merely the process of human interpretation of Scripture which was the core of rabbinic theology and much of traditional, scholastic Protestantism! Instead Jesus insists that the Father has not excluded himself from the human process of interpreting Scripture, nor has he caused revelation directly to the human heart to cease as Jewish "cessationism" insisted.

Jesus was showing that it is exactly the opposite of Jewish cessationism— it is in order to fulfill the New Covenant that all of these revelation functions must be active! Indeed, the central characteristic of the Messiah, and presumably his followers, is that . . .

> "The Spirit of the LORD will rest on him—the Spirit of wisdom and of understanding, the Spirit of counsel and of might, the Spirit of knowledge and of the fear of the LORD—and he will delight in the fear of the LORD. He will not judge by what he sees with his eyes, or decide by what he hears with his ears" (Isaiah 11:2–3 NIV).

The rabbinic doctrine of "it is not in heaven," excluding divine communication from the interpretation of Scripture, finds its critique in

John 5:41–47 quoted below. In this passage, Jesus outlines the "it is not in heaven" doctrine of rabbinic Judaism: accepting praise from men for their piety and knowledge of the Scriptures. As Paul says, "Where is the wise man? Where is the scholar? Where is the philosopher of this age? Has not God made foolish the wisdom of the world?" (1 Cor 1:20).

> [41]"I do not accept praise from men, [42]but I know you. I know that you do not have the love of God in your hearts. [43]I have come in my Father's name, and you do not accept me; but if someone else comes in his own name, you will accept him. [44]How can you believe if you accept praise from one another, yet make no effort to obtain the praise that comes from the only God? [45]But do not think I will accuse you before the Father. Your accuser is Moses, on whom your hopes are set. [46]If you believed Moses, you would believe me, for he wrote about me. [47]But since you do not believe what he wrote, how are you going to believe what I say?" (John 5:41–47 NIV)

In John 5:1–45, Jesus attacks the prideful academic system of the scribes (rabbis) who are not motivated to build their careers by communicating the love of God, but by accumulating a reputation for intellectual debate ("besting" was the term they used) and memorization of both Scripture and the past debates over the interpretation and application of the Torah. Accepting "praise from men" as a religious practice, that is, approval or accreditation as a scholar, is a universal human failing. Even St. Paul complained that members of the very church he founded now were requiring (as was the Greco-Roman custom) "letters of recommendation"—something like a diploma or accreditation from him!

His response was, essentially, "Why do I need 'praise from another' to prove my status, when you saw for yourselves the power and salvation of the Spirit of Christ working in me?" (1 Cor 3:1–6). As a "minister of the New Covenant" (Spirit), he didn't need a human system of approval. In fact, Jesus demands a forced choice between the "honor of men" on the one hand, and "faith" with the honor of God on the other (John 5:44).[10] On some level, seeking the "praise of men" (accreditation, academic degrees) for work that God has commissioned and approved is something like asking my dog to bark its approval of my library.[11]

Despite their vast knowledge of Scripture, Jesus essentially makes the argument emphatically reflected in this book about the voice of God as a major theme in the Bible (John 5:45–47). He points out: You claim to know and place your faith in Moses (that is, in his writings—the Torah: Genesis through Deuteronomy), but Moses, not I [Jesus], will accuse you before the Father at the last judgment. Why? Because you don't follow his emphasis in his narratives about the key human examples who hear the voice of God (as we did in Part II, above). Ultimately Moses' writings witness to Me and what I am modeling for you: hearing the Father's voice and coming "in His name" (in His authority, character, and His way of revealing Himself directly). Since you don't perceive the message of Moses' writings by faith (hearing God —a completely different approach compared to your prideful, competitive human 'wisdom'), how can you grasp what I am telling you without your having faith? Because both Moses and I use God's way of knowing, that is, by revelation."

See how closely the scribal interpretive approach fits with the famous "protector" of Scripture, Benjamin Warfield, who said, "the objective [human, scientific] method is . . . indispensable to the accurate attainment of the mind of the Spirit."[12] Really? Why not simply consult the "mind of the Spirit" directly as the Bible requires?

Why not? The spirit of the scribes!

An earlier version of Warfield's "objective" method that seeks religious control was already in force in the Cromwell era. The academics, when they wrote the Westminster Confession of Faith were reacting against the Quakers and even against their founder, John Knox, who had experienced gifts of the spirit at that time, and were not protecting Scripture. Rather, they were protecting their status and perks as scribes who refused to advance from the Old Covenant into the New Covenant of the Spirit.[13] Let's call it what it is: religious support for Cromwell's coup. These Westminster academics inserted themselves as the mediators of gospel truth against anyone claiming religious (and political) authority. This essentially was an attempt to create a new Protestant college of Cardinals in support of Cromwell. Sensing this, the English Parliament demanded at least a partial return to the priesthood of all believers by requiring transparent scriptural (and more broad-based) authority for this new theological edict, the Westminster Confession of Faith.

By contrast, within the context of discussing the core value of the Christian experience—the revealing New Covenant Holy Spirit—Hebrews 6:1–6 encourages the reader to "imitate those who through faith and patience inherit *what has been promised*" (my emphasis). What is this promise if it isn't what has immediately been so emphatically described in vv 4–5: ". . . those who have been once enlightened, who have tasted the heavenly gift and have become partakers of the Holy Spirit, and have tasted the goodness of the word of God and the powers of the age to come." True to the biblical tradition, this promise/covenant is accompanied by persecution and suffering—the very thing that was tempting the first readers of Hebrews to deny their experience of the prophetic Spirit and Jesus who made it possible.

> 6But the ministry Jesus has received is as superior to theirs as the covenant of which he is mediator is superior to the old one, and it is founded on better promises. 7For if there had been nothing wrong with that first covenant, no place would have been sought for another. 8But God found fault with the people and said: "The time is coming, declares the Lord, when I will make a new covenant with the house of Israel and with the house of Judah. 9It will not be like the covenant I made with their forefathers when I took them by the hand to lead them out of Egypt, because they did not remain faithful to my covenant, and I turned away from them, declares the Lord. 10This is the covenant I will make with the house of Israel after that time, declares the Lord. I will put my laws in their minds and write them on their hearts. I will be their God, and they will be my people. 11No longer will a man teach his neighbor, or a man his brother, saying, 'Know the LORD,' because they will all know me, from the least of them to the greatest. For I will forgive their wickedness and will remember their sins no more" (Heb 8:6–11 NIV).

Several observations are worth noting here:

First, the New Testament term, "promise" (Heb 8:6) is synonymous with "covenant,"[14] that is, not only the traditional "going to heaven," but more specifically, the covenant of the promised Spirit (Isa 59:21; Jer 31:33–34; also Matt 3:11 with parallels and John 1:33). This is the "promised eternal inheritance" of Hebrews 9:15; 12:26 (so also Acts 2:33; Gal 3:14; Eph 1:13; 1 Pet 1:3–4). The Gospel of John constantly refers to "life" or "eternal life" which is understood by traditional Protestants as "born again" now, but mainly as "going to heaven." By life or eternal life John is more likely referring to the promised New Covenant Spirit described in the passages above.

Second, several Old Testament promises foretell the New Covenant Spirit: beginning with Moses' prophetic desire that "all Israel would be prophets" (Num 11:29). Other Old Testament promises also foresee the outpouring of the Spirit: Ezekiel 11:19; 36:26–28; 37:14; 39:29. The Spirit that is placed upon the Servant (Jesus) in Isaiah 11:2; 42:1; 61:1 would one day be "poured out on your offspring" (Isa 44:3; 59:21). The central characteristic of the Messiah and his followers is the action of the Spirit on them, that is, the New Covenant "word" that is continually revealed

Third, the results of the New Covenant are two-fold: a) "I will be their God and they will be my people," and, b) no need for external teaching in order to know God. In a chiastic (X-shaped) structure, the content of the covenant concludes with "for I will forgive their wickedness and remember their sins no more."

> "This is the covenant I will make with the house of Israel after that time," declares the LORD.
>
> A) "I will put my laws in their minds and write them on their hearts.
> B) I will be their God, and they will be my people.
> B') No longer will a man teach his neighbor, or a man his brother, saying, 'Know the Lord,' because they will all know me, from the least of them to the greatest.
> A') For I will forgive their wickedness and will remember their sins no more" (Jeremiah 31:33–34).

"Wickedness" and "sins" appear to be the opposite of the process of hearing and heeding the internalized will of God (written on inner parts and heart). In other words, we are back to the two trees of the temptation in the garden: the tree of life offers a knowledge of God by hearing his voice. The wrong tree offers death by our refusing "the One who speaks."

Fourth, the term for sin in this passage is *adikia* (unrighteousness: not doing something God's way, but Eve's way) and *hamartia* ("missing the target"). The target that needs to be hit would seem to be the process of hearing and heeding the voice of God. Seen from the point of view of God's ideal behavior, both of these descriptions of sin represent not hearing God's voice. This is why Paul can say, "Walk in step with the Spirit, and you will not fulfill the desires of the flesh [your human weakness]" (Gal 5:16).

GOD'S VOICE VS. HIS LAW?

Does the New Covenant really say that when we are hearing God's voice and that God remembers "our sins no more" that somehow the Law has no relevance to us? "Knowing" in the New Covenant seems to involve communication and a "reset" toward the ideal relationship with God. Jeremiah 31:31–34 suggests that by giving us the New Covenant Spirit in our hearts God has dealt with our sin issue. God's teaching being written directly on the heart involves something like "I will forgive their wickedness and remember their sins no more."

Compared to the Old Covenant, which includes a hopeless list of sins one must remember to avoid, the New Covenant is a radical new way of relating to God. It is not a list of new rules from the New Testament replacing rules from the Old Testament, nor is it simply Old Testament rules one must memorize, expand upon, apply, and perform as the scribes and Pharisees did. On the other hand, Jesus came, not to do away with the Law, but to fulfill it (Matt 5:17)—to get at its true intent. Consequently all of the Old Testament laws for temple worship and sacrifice have been superseded by the work of Christ. Hence Paul can say, "if you are led by the Spirit you are not under the law" (Gal 5:18).

The function of the Law was to point out the attitudes and actions that alienated us from God. So, when we start with a communicating relationship with God based on the atonement of Christ, past sins are no longer an issue for Him, because the goal of the Law (fellowship with God) has been achieved. How, then, do we understand the specific demands of the Law today, both in the Old and New Testaments?

The answer seems to be that when we begin to mature by receiving the Spirit of adoption as sons (those who replicate the Father's attitudes and behavior), our actions vis-à-vis the Law move in two paradoxical directions at the same time: toward more stringent attitudes and toward more flexibility. Jesus' teaching leads us to look behind the specific laws of God to see his heart. For example, the Old Testament commands not to murder or commit adultery. In New Testament teaching, however, we grow up when we realize that who we really are is found in our attitudes: even secret hatred toward someone is like murder and so is unacceptable (Matt 5:21–24). Adultery is not simply the act of sex outside of marriage but an attitude of the heart, or imagination (5:26–27)—what you would do if nobody could find out. New Covenant righteousness is not simply something people can see but who you really are inside.

On the other hand, some laws in the Old Testament are very rigid and specific which in a mature understanding apply in a different way. For example, we do not need, as some Orthodox Jews, to apply the extremely rigid application of the law by not eating cheeseburgers because the Law says not to boil a baby goat in its mother's milk (Deut 14:21), but rather to avoid idolatrous religious practice.[15] If you have no temptation to join a pagan cult that boils baby goats in their mother's milk, then this law makes little sense in our situation. What makes even less sense is to separate all pots, pans, and dishes based on whether they even touched milk or meat in the incredibly faint chance that a few molecules of goat milk may be cooked with the meat of a baby goat—as is kosher law among Orthodox Jews. This precaution seems to go far beyond God's intent of this law to avoid idolatry. In any case, wisdom, or God's direct guidance, will likely clarify this *halakah* for you (Rom 12:14–23; 1 Cor 7:40).

If, on the other hand, you mutilate your body by tattooing yourself with symbols or words that do not glorify God (as was the case among the pagan idolaters in the Old Testament), then probably Leviticus 19:28 applies to us. If you have (or are) a teenage kid, you know this is a live issue today! Or it will be when you turn 35, need a good job, and you expect to be taken seriously at a job interview. (Can you tell I went through all this with my 18-year-old son?) Again, the New Covenant Spirit provides guidance if we seek it (Jas 1:5; 3:13–17).

This kind of interpretation is essentially what Jesus was following when accused of breaking the Sabbath by shucking kernels of grain or healing on that day (Mark 2:23–28; 3:2–5). Later, Paul basically says that Old Testament dietary or Sabbath rules are optional under the New Covenant (Rom 14:1–18; Col 2:16–17)—only "let everyone be convinced in his own mind." "For the kingdom of God is not a matter of eating and drinking, but of righteousness, peace and joy in the [New Covenant] *Holy Spirit,* because anyone who serves Christ in this way is pleasing to God and approved by men" (Rom 14:17–18, my emphasis). The relationship of the Law (including the commands of the New Testament) to the New Covenant of the Spirit is complex. But the simplest explanation may be that we should know the commands of the Bible very well and keep them as background in our mind. Then, when we seek God about a course of action, the Spirit of God can apply these commands appropriately to our situation, just as Jesus did during his temptation.

For example, as children, we are taught rather rigidly to obey traffic laws. When we are adults, we are mature enough to know that if we come to a stuck red light against us at four in the morning with no traffic and we are rushing to the emergency room a person who is hemorrhaging blood, we understand that saving a life trumps obeying a mindless, dysfunctional traffic light. As the Book of Proverbs reminds us, we are to interpret the rules—and all of life—using wisdom, that is, revelation from God (Prov 26:7; Ecc 1:13).

So, at this point in our study, what is wrong with traditional

Protestant theology? This is it! Well, at least this is the main thing: religious tradition downplays the essence of the New Testament, that is, the New Covenant and its emphasis on the internal revelation of the Spirit. In so many ways, the human religious tendency is to revert to a system of laws rather than to walk in intimate communication with God.

The next section shows how Scripture emphasizes the "voice of God" by noting its major role in four substantial concepts relating to the essential nature of the gospel as described in the New Testament.

---

1. Exo 4:21; 7:3, 14, 22–23; 8:15, 19, 32; 9:7, 12, 35; 10:1, 20, 27; 11:10; 14:4, 8.
2. I am following here Gordon Fee, *Paul, the Spirit, and the People of God,* (Peabody, Mass.: Hendrickson Pub., 1996), 102–103.
3. It is ironic that we are arguing for the experience of God's prophetic Spirit to be central to the New Covenant, when traditional Calvinistic covenant theology explicitly denies the possibility of that experience!
4. Tertullian (ca. ad 160–ca. 220), in a rare opinion among the Church Fathers, suggested (correctly) that the *Holy Spirit* was the *vicarius Christi.* This suggestion is probably based on John 14:16, 26, that is, on the Holy Spirit's substituting for Christ in preventing error and performing miracles in the Church (*On the Veiling of Virgins* 1). The current Catholic catechism teaches that both the pope and the bishops are vicars of Christ. Second Vatican Council, *Dogmatic Constitution Lumen Gentium* 27.
5. Some 134 cases: Exo 6:7; 7:5,17; 8:10, 22; 9:29; 10:2; 14:4, 18; 16:6, 8, 12, 15; 18:11; 29:46; 33:11–12; Lev 23:43; Num 16:28, 30; Deut 4:34–36; 7:8–9; 8:2–5; 18:22; 29:6; 31:13–15; Josh 3:7,10; 4:24; 23:14; 24:1–14; 1 Sam 3:7; 6:8–9; 17:46–47; 1 Kng 8:60; 17:23–24; 18:37–39; 20:13, 28; 2 Kng 5:15; 19:19 Job 12:7–10; Ps 9:10, 20; 20:6; 46:8–10; 83:13–18; 100:3; 109:27; 135:5–6; Isa 37:20; 40:28; 41:20; 43:10–13; 44:7–8; 45:3–7; 49:23–26; 55:5, 13; 60:16; 63:13; Jer 5:22; 16:21; 22:16 (in the poor); 24:6–7; 31:34; Ezek 5:13; 6:7, 10, 13, 14; 7:4, 9, 27; 11:10, 12; 12:15, 16, 20; 13:14, 21, 23; 14:8; 15:7; 16:62; 17:21, 24; 20:20, 26, 38, 42, 44; 21:5; 22:16, 22; 23:49; 24:24, 27; 25:5, 7, 11, 17; 26:6; 28:22, 23, 26; 29:6, 9, 16, 21; 30:8, 19, 25, 26; 32:15; 33:29; 34:27; 34:30; 34:27,30; 35:4, 9, 15; 36:11, 23, 38; 37:6, 13, 14, 28; 38:23; 39:6, 7, 22, 28; 39:21–22, 28–29; Joel 2:26–28; 3:16–20; Mic 6:5; Zech 2:11; 6:15. In the New Testament, this consistent pattern may be what Paul has in mind when he describes the gospel as "the power of God toward/into salvation" (Rom 1:16), or "the kingdom of God does not consist of talk, but of power" (1 Cor 4:20, so also 1 Cor 2:4; 1 Thes 1:5).
6. John 8:47; 10:1–8, 27–28; 12:38–46; 16:13–15; see also: Matt 11:25–27 || Luke 10:21–22; 16:17; Luke 2:26; Rom 1:17–22; 10:8–9, 20; 1 Cor 2:10.
7. It was believed by Jews, during the time of Jesus, that even though an exceptionally righteous rabbi might merit the Holy Spirit (i.e., the gift of prophecy), his generation did not merit it, therefore, the gift of the Spirit had ceased. See the discussion on the genesis of the doctrine of cessationism in early normative Judaism in *On the Cessation*

of the Charismata, revised and expanded edition, pp. 12–15. The normative Jewish position on the restricted availability of the Spirit stood in stark contrast to the message of the Pentecost sermon, which concluded with the affirmation that the Spirit was promised to "all people" forever (Acts 2:39 citing Isa 59:21). Indeed, like Acts 2, the Gospel of John and Hebrews both affirmed as their central message the mission of Jesus to ensure that God would continue to speak to all people at all times (see especially the "thesis statement" of John and Hebrews as their respective first verses).

8. Deut 30:12–14 is quoted by the apostle Paul in Rom 10:6–8: "It is not in heaven, that you should say, 'Who will go up to heaven for us to get it for us and make us hear it, that we may observe it?' Nor is it beyond the sea, that you should say, 'Who will cross the sea for us to get it for us and make us hear it, that we may observe it?' But the word is very near you, in your mouth and in your heart, that you may observe it." Paul picks up on the implications of the last qualifier (Deut 30:14) *and turns it away from* the cessationist rabbinic view *toward the New Covenant.* "The word is near you, in your mouth and in your heart—*that is, the word of faith* which we are proclaiming, that if you confess with your mouth Jesus as Lord, and believe in your heart that God raised Him from the dead, you shall be saved; for with the heart man believes, resulting in righteousness, and with the mouth he confesses, resulting in salvation. For the Scripture says, 'Whoever believes in Him will not be disappointed'" (Rom 10:8–11, my emphasis). The requirement of belief in the heart "that God raised [Jesus] from the dead" probably moves beyond a mere creedal confession about the resurrection, but more a specific way of requiring that one believe in the present power of God in miracle as a variant expression of discerning God's revelation (faith). Again, the New Testament makes no distinction between "saving faith" and "miraculous faith."

   In this passage, Paul appeals to the *revelation* inherent in the *New* Covenant that emphasizes the revelation of *faith* and [revealed, prophetic] *confession:* the pattern from Adam onward: "for with the heart man *believes,*" resulting in righteousness (not works of the Law or memorizing Scripture, but hearing from God!), and, like Adam, acknowledges God's mighty acts: "with the mouth he *confesses,* resulting in salvation"! As in Acts and elsewhere, *revelation* is associated with *utterance:* the Holy Spirit and prophecy.

9. The "it is not in heaven" doctrine is expounded in a story from the Talmud, "The Oven of Akhnai" (*Bava Metzia* 59b), in which a dispute about interpreting the Law breaks out among some prominent early rabbis. A rabbi Eliezer believes, against the majority, that his contrary interpretation is correct. To prove it, he causes a tree to be uprooted and thrown 100 cubits (some said, 400); he also made a stream to flow backwards. To top it all off, the heavenly voice (*bat qol*) went forth to the debaters saying, "Why are you disputing with R. Eliezer, for the Halakhah is as he claims everywhere." So what do you want for a nickel? Shouldn't that end the discussion if *God himself* came down on the side of R. Eliezer?

   Well, the majority opinion, even today, stands firm, *even against the voice of God* on the principle that once God revealed the written Law (Torah) to mankind, it remained for only the scribes (rabbis, experts in the *Torah*/Law) to interpret it. Miracles and even the voice of God were not enough to interfere with the mandate of the scribes to interpret and apply the Law to mankind. They based this interference ostensibly on Deut 30:12, but more firmly on Deut 17:11. If rabbis divide over an interpretation (*halakah*), they are "to incline toward the majority [the many]" (Exo 23:2) and not to seek God for the understanding. This position, as we have seen in the biblical material outlined above clearly violates the overwhelming teaching and modeling of the Hebrew Scriptures themselves! Nevertheless, a modern Jewish scholar summarizes the consensus of his community on excluding any divine input (prophecy, miracles, illumination) in interpreting the Law, once it was given by God:

If the law is the product of the agreement of people and sovereign, and itself creates the sovereign, the sovereign must be bound by it. The Holy One is the God of Israel because of the covenant at Sinai and that covenant, though dictated by Him, doesn't create Him as its interpreter. The Law, rather, is not in Heaven and doesn't require Heavenly intervention to be understood. So, God's sovereignty itself requires His withdrawal from the system; the covenant, and its internal logic, must be allowed to work itself out without further divine intervention. We, not the human or divine Authors of the covenant, must take control of it. (Cited from online lecture by Daniel Greenwood at Hofstra University: http://bit.ly/oF5tSl)

Most Christians would be aghast at people's rejecting the voice of God as authoritative, especially when they *acknowledge* it is the voice of God. Isn't this similar to Jesus' saying about blasphemy of the Holy Spirit (Matt 12:31–32, also Heb 6:4–6)? This certainly clarifies Jesus' complaint in John 5:37b–39 against the scribes. If we think about it, however, this Jewish position is not far removed from that of scholastic Protestantism (paragraph 1 of WCF), or of many conservative evangelicals today. A sage of the early Hellenistic period summarizes the position of rabbinic Judaism: "Up to now prophets have prophesied by the holy spirit [*sic*], from now on, incline your ear and listen to the words of the sages" (*S 'Olam Rab.*, 30). For a literature review on the cessation of prophecy in Judaism see Benjamin D. Sommer, "Did Prophecy Cease? Evaluating a Reevaluation," *JBL* 115.1 (1996), 31–47.

10. "*How can you believe,* when you receive glory [accreditation, ratings] from one another, and you do not seek the glory that is from the *one and* only God?" Jesus here actually forces a choice on the academics of his day: "believe" or "receive glory from one another" instead of God.
11. This analogy is borrowed from C.S. Lewis.
12. Warfield, "The True Method of Procedure in the Interpretation of the New Testament," p. 35, contained in a folio, *MSS Material on the New Testament,* located at the Alumni Alcove of Speer Library, Princeton Theological Seminary.
13. On this, see Milne, *The Westminster Confession of Faith and the Cessation of Special Revelation,* 165–76, see especially his chapters 4–6. This is an excellent book on the problems of cessationism challenging the production of the infamous "Paragraph 1."
14. Instead of using the word, "covenant" (lxx, *diathēkē*), Luke substitutes the term "promise" *(epangelia)* of the Spirit (Luk 24:49; Acts 1:4; 2:33; 3:39). Elsewhere in Acts, this substitution is retained: Acts 7:17; 13:21, 32; 26:6-7. In this Luke seems to follow biblical usage generally, where *epangelia* refers to covenant: Rom. 4:13–14, 20; 9:4, 8; 15:8; 2 Cor 6:16—7:1; Gal 3:14–17, 29; 4:23–28; Eph 1:13; 2:12; 3:6; Heb 4:1; 6:12, 13, 15, 17; 7:6; 11:9, 13, 17; 8:6; 9:15; 10:36; 11:39; 2 Pet 3:9. Indeed, the terms "covenant" and "promise" are placed in synonymous parallel in Gal 2:12; Eph 3:17; Heb 8:6; 9:15, cf. lxx 1 Ch 16:16; Neh 9:8. So in Peter's direct quotation of the Isaiah prophecy, the substitution for covenant is clear: "This *promise (epangelia)*—covenant—is to you and to your children and to all that are afar off" (Acts 2:39). If, then, we substitute "covenant" for Luke's "promise" with respect to the outpouring of the Spirit, then his theme of the Isaiah 59 fulfillment stands out more sharply (Luke 24:49; Acts 1:4; 2:33). Certainly, St Paul follows Luke's pattern regarding the covenant

mediators, i.e., "our competence is from God who has made us competent to be ministers of a new covenant, not in a written code but in the Spirit; for the written code kills, but the Spirit gives life" (1 Cor 3:6). Similarly, Heb 8:15. These New Testament passages appear to repeat the message of the new covenant prophecy of Jer 31:31.

15. Apparently this was an idolatrous (voodoo-like) Canaanite ritual to ensure fertility, as described in Ugaritic texts found at Ras Shamra. Besides being, on its face, a particularly cruel act, it was likely that its association with pagan idolatry (witchcraft) led to its being forbidden three times in the Law (Exo 23:19; 34:26; Deut 14:21). It is likely that many of the dietary laws of the Old Testament appeared mainly for this reason, rather than because, for example, eating shellfish or pork is unhealthy. But for an opposite opinion, see the revised classic by S. I. McMillan and David E. Stern, *None of These Diseases* (Grand Rapids, Mich.: F.H. Revell, 2000).

8

THE ESSENCE OF THE GOSPEL OF THE KINGDOM

This chapter shows by means of emphasis and summaries the core nature of the biblical message: the powerful, creative voice of God and its testing. After a brief note introducing the nature of the gospel ("God's Spell"), this emphasis is shown by examining. . .

- the New Testament message from Jesus: the kingdom of God;
- the mission of Christian disciples in the commissioning accounts; the content and objective of New Testament prayers; and
- the central theme of five key New Testament books, showing that the essence of the New Testament message follows the Old Testament in its emphasis upon the revealed "word" of God into the human heart.

GOD'S SPELL: "THE POWER OF GOD UNTO SALVATION"

Before addressing the theme of the kingdom of God—the central term to describe Jesus' mission that was mostly ignored by traditional Protestantism—we first note the interesting history of our familiar term, "gospel." Even at the end of the sixth century AD, this English term clearly reflected an experience of the gospel that was, by necessity, forced back into the New Testament emphasis of the power of God.

The word *gospel* was invented cleverly by some of the first missionaries to Britain, who needed a clear alternative to the powerful curses (spells) of the dark arts produced by the native shamans and their capricious, evil gods. These early apostle-evangelists, accordingly, translated the *theos/deus* (deity) of the New Testament into something more comprehensible and in extreme contrast to the evil, fearful gods of the natives. So they called the deity of the Bible "Good." As a further, brilliant act of contextualization to counter the curses ("spells") of these satanic religions, the missionaries then came up with the Christian alternative: "Good's spell," or "God's spell," today known as "gospel." This powerful, victorious spell of Good was certainly more than a list of doctrines or even ideas about Jesus. If it were to compete with the impressive occult power of the Druids, the gospel indeed had to be identified as "the [miracle] power of God unto salvation."[1] If only evangelical missionaries to unreached areas of India or Africa today could show the same spiritual sophistication as these sixth-century monks!

THE KINGDOM OF GOD: THE GOSPEL THAT JESUS BROUGHT

Indeed, even today, when true biblical Christianity confronts such manifest demonic power, Christian workers must resort to a gospel from Jesus, not merely derived about Jesus: it takes more than affirming religious information. The New Testament describes the gospel from Jesus as the kingdom of God: "I must preach the good news of the kingdom of God . . . *because that is why I was sent*" (Matt 4:17; Luke 4:43, my emphasis). Jesus' central mission represents far more than the vague "kingdom" of traditional theology meaning the "visible Church" (Roman Catholics) or the "invisible Church" (referring to "true believers" by Protestantism).

By contrast, the kingdom of God in the New Testament is described directly or indirectly as God's ruling power in action. We can see proof of this primary meaning in some New Testament descriptors: "If I by the

Spirit/finger of God cast out demons, then the kingdom of God has come upon/to you" (Matt 12:28 || Luke 11:30). Paul backs this up: "The kingdom of God does not consist in talk but in [miracle] power" (1 Cor 4:20). Mark 9:1 and possibly Revelation 12:10 refer to the outpouring of the Spirit of power and prophecy on the church in the New Covenant era beginning at the day of Pentecost. My favorite verse describes the promise of the Spirit: "God did not give us a spirit of timidity, but a Spirit of—characterized by—[miracle] power, of love, and of self-discipline" (2 Tim 1:7), a verse that is similar in content to Romans 1:16.

The kingdom elsewhere is associated closely with acts of healing and exorcism (Matt 4:23; 9:35; 10:7–8; Luke 4:40–43; 8:1–2; 9:2, 11; 10:9, 11; John 3:5–6; Acts 8:12–13; Rom 14:17). Overwhelmingly, however, the New Testament is not as interested in a theological description of the kingdom as much as it emphasizes the diligent, even desperate importance of entering it, especially Matthew 13; or 11:12 "From the days of John the Baptist until now, the kingdom of heaven has been forcefully advancing, and forceful people lay hold of it" (NIV), or "the kingdom of heaven has experienced violence [because] violent people grab it or snatch it away aggressively *(arpadzousin)*" (Matt 11:12 || Luke 16:16).

This violence expresses the connection between the kingdom and those who would enter it. They do so by aggressive, persistent faith. This involves receiving a revelation about the kingdom and responding singlemindedly with all our heart, mind, and strength. The kingdom of God is the New Covenant relationship of being led by the Spirit into a ministry of life and power in intimacy with God in Christ Jesus (Matt 13).[2]

The New Testament was written for our involvement in the kingdom of God. The nature of the kingdom is expressed in the typical way God reveals himself: in divine power (1 Cor 2:4–5; 4:19–20). Accordingly, true Christian "preaching" (presenting the kingdom) is necessarily expressed in *dunamis* (miracle power: Rom 15:19; 2 Cor 12:12; 1 Thes 1:5; 1 Pet 4:6). Nowhere in the New Testament is the miracle nature of the kingdom of God more evident than in Jesus' commissioning of his disciples to carry on his mission. They were commanded: "to preach as you go, saying, 'the kingdom of heaven is at hand.' Heal the sick, raise the dead, cleanse lepers, cast out demons" (Matt 10:8).

THE "IMITATION OF CHRIST": FOLLOWING THE NEW TESTAMENT COMMISSIONINGS REAFFIRMS THE CHARISMATIC ESSENCE OF THE GOSPEL, THE EMPHASIS OF THE NEW TESTAMENT MESSAGE

The commissioning accounts describe Jesus sending out his disciples on their first outreach without him (Matt 10; Mark 6; Luke 9 and 10). The explicit reason (emphasis) the twelve (the new Israel, the people of God) were selected is recorded in the earliest Gospel (Mark) in a somewhat cryptic, but highly significant formula: "He appointed twelve," designating them apostles ("ones sent out") . . .

- that they might be with him; and
- that he might send them out to proclaim; and
- that they would have authority to drive out demons (Mark 3:14–15).

This commissioning, then, expresses the core mission of the disciples, including the readers of these words. Compared with the curriculum of modern churches and seminaries today, this is indeed an odd agenda. We could argue further that this is the core mission for all mankind, since God commanded Adam similarly in the Garden of Eden. Adam was made in God's own image for the purpose of . . .

- life-giving communication and obedience (Gen 2:16–17; 3:1);
- proclaiming with words a response to the miraculous creation of God (Gen 2:19), as God himself did in the stages of creation in Genesis 1 (and prophetic speech was the first response to God's mighty presence at Pentecost);

- "serving and guarding" (Gen 2:15) the garden; against whom becomes clear only in the next chapter: the serpent—the representative of everything demonic (Rev 12:9).

So with Mark 3 it seems that the universal divine calling or mandate (biblical emphasis) is to . . .

- experience closeness with God/Christ;
- proclaim (prophetically?); and
- protect God's creation from the evil one(s).

This seems to explain the mandate of Jesus (and Paul, his apostle), who were "mighty in word and deed" (prophecy and miracle) as an expression of their intimacy with, and mandate from, God (Luke 24:19; Rom 15:18–19). If this universal mandate is good enough for Jesus and for Paul, then it should come as no surprise that Jesus commissioned his disciples to do the same thing. We will discuss this fully in Part V.

THE PRAYERS OF THE NEW TESTAMENT OVERWHELMINGLY CONFIRM THE NEW COVENANT EMPHASES ON REVELATION, POWER, AND RELATIONSHIP

This section demonstrates that biblical prayer has a clear purpose: to realize God's goals. Not surprisingly, then, the objectives or goals of prayers in the New Testament align very closely with the New Covenant Spirit themes of Isaiah 59:21 and Jeremiah 31:33. Against traditional Protestant cessationism, what is prayed for in the New Testament is primarily revelation, i.e., signs and wonders, prophecy. If we are to follow traditional religious cessationism, then we must eliminate almost all of the New Testament teaching on prayer, because the New Testament teaches overwhelmingly to pray for God's revelation and power! Prayer is one more case of cessationist theology ripping out huge sections of the Bible while claiming to protect it. Cessationism denies what the Bible is trying centrally to affirm! As Jesus said to the scribes: "you know neither the Scriptures nor the power of God" (Mark 12:24).

The goals for New Testament prayer, then, emphasize the three main themes in the New Covenant:

1. **Revelation: the mighty Word** (Isa 59:21 > Acts 2:39) and Torah-in-the-heart (Jer 31:33 > 2 Cor 3; Heb 8:8–10). "Knowing" the Lord (hearing or experiencing his power) is the goal of the New Covenant. This personal knowledge of God is closely related to prayer.[3]
2. **Power**: which prayer releases to change physical conditions. This theme is inferred from the nature of the prophetic Spirit poured out in fulfillment of Isaiah 59:21 in a clarifying reference to Isaiah 61:1–2: that is, the Spirit's coming upon Jesus and his programmatic experience. The prophetic Spirit is omnipotent: many New Testament references connect the asking in prayer with unlimited possibilities.
3. **Healing human attitudes**: toward reconciliation and relationship (with God and man). The knowledge/experience of God's will and power is equivalent to the final expression of the New Covenant goal: "I will be their God, and they will be my people" (Jer 31:33).

PRAYER AND RECEIVING REVELATION

Prayer and prophecy or revelation appear in causal relationship even before Jesus' birth. There was a climate of prayer around the angelic revelation to Zechariah, John's father (Luke 1:10–11), and in the story of the prophetess Anna who worshiped "with fasting and prayer night and day" (Luke 2:37) for around 60 years. Three decades later, as a model for all to follow, Jesus was baptized in water "to fulfill all righteousness" —doing everything the right (God's) way (Matt 3:15). When Jesus receives the Spirit and revelation, Luke records that Jesus "was praying" (Luke 3:21–22) "and as he was praying, heaven was opened and the Holy Spirit descended on him in bodily form like a dove. And a voice came from heaven: 'You are my Son, whom I love; with you I am well pleased.'"

Accordingly, Jesus instructs his followers to trust God and pray that he will give "the Spirit" (Matt 7:11), that is, "good gifts" (Luke 11:13) "to those who ask him." Revelation came to a pagan Gentile, Cornelius, who "distinctly saw an angel of God" who commended him for his prayers (Acts 10:1–6, recounted in vv 30–31). Similarly, Peter received a vision from the Lord when he was praying (10:9, recounted in 11:5). Finally, Paul was "praying in the temple" when he was warned by revelation to flee Jerusalem (22:17).

As a general principle, James emphasizes the connection of prayer and revelation: "If any of you lacks wisdom, he should ask God, who gives generously to all without finding fault, and it will be given to him" (1:5). This wisdom is "from heaven" (3:17) and must be received in "faith" (an obedient hearing from God, 1:6). In John's Gospel, the Spirit of revelation is also described as "the gift of God" or "living water" received in Jesus, which is given if one asks (John 4:10). Similarly, Paul's urging believers to "pray constantly" seems related to the exhortation to prophesy (1 Thes 5:17–20). If confusion occurs over an expression of tongues, one is to pray or ask God for clarification (1 Cor 14:13) or be content that one's spirit is praying with an "unfruitful" mind (14:14). Perhaps related to this is the discussion on the role of the Spirit in prayer in Romans 8:26–27.

> In the same way, the Spirit helps us in our weakness. We do not know what we ought to pray for, but the Spirit himself intercedes for us with groans that words cannot express. 27 And he who searches our hearts knows the mind of the Spirit, because the Spirit intercedes for the saints in accordance with God's will. (NIV)

In any case, when we are praying, the Spirit reveals and empowers in our weakness, unless our limited theology prompts us to resist such benefits. What is very important here is that when Paul prays for his churches, what does he pray for? He prays for the fulfillment of their New Covenant charismatic experience that is normative for all Christians.

> And this is my prayer: that your love may abound more and more in knowledge and depth of insight, [10] so that you may be able to discern what is best and may be pure and blameless until the day of Christ, [11] filled with the fruit of righteousness that comes through Jesus Christ—to the glory and praise of God. (Phil 1:9–11 NIV)

This prayer requests the themes of the New Covenant Spirit be realized in the readers—particularly the charismata of revealed knowledge and discernment. Something very like this appears in this greatly abbreviated but sufficient expression: "we pray most earnestly night and day that we may see you face to face and supply what is lacking in your faith" (1 Thes 3:10).

Again, for emphasis, this prayer for Paul's church is repeated in essentially the same way in Ephesians 1:15–23.

> [15] For this reason, because I have heard of your faith in the Lord Jesus and your love toward all the saints, [16] I do not cease to give thanks for you, remembering you in my prayers, [17] that the God of our Lord Jesus Christ, the Father of glory, may give you the Spirit of wisdom and of revelation in the knowledge of him, [18] having the eyes of your hearts enlightened, that you may know what is the hope to which he has called you, what are the riches of his glorious inheritance in the saints, [19] and what is the immeasurable greatness of his power toward us who believe, according to the working of his great might [20] that he worked in Christ when he raised him from the dead and seated him at his right hand in the heavenly places, [21] far above all rule and authority and power and dominion, and above every name that is named, not only in this age but also in the one to come. [22] And he put all things under his feet and gave him as head over all things to the church, [23] which is his body, the fullness of him who fills all in all. (Eph 1:15–23 ESV)

Note here that Paul's ceaseless prayer appears to be for his agenda, or goal, for the Ephesian church. Again, this goal follows the goal of the New Covenant (Isa 59:21; Jer 31:31–34), that is, revelation of him ("the God of our Lord Jesus Christ, the Father of glory"). Then following the word-power emphasis of the New Covenant in Acts 2:39 (< Isa 59:21), Paul emphasizes what is "the hope of his calling." Is it to be a prophet and experience these gifts? Not quite! Rather he wants to attain "the riches of the glory of his inheritance in the saints." Paul goes on to spell out what that "inheritance in the saints" is: "the exceeding greatness of his power" (*dunamis*—miracle power). Is it only to apostles in the first century? No: "to us who believe—have faith." Faith is the condition for receiving this power! According to what? The writing of the New Testament that caused all miracles to cease? No! Not only is faith the condition, but "according to the working of his mighty power" which the Holy Spirit is now bestowing on his church all over the world—and not only in this present "world," or era, but also in the "world to come."[4]

Hebrews says that in this age the believer has "tasted of the heavenly gift [Holy Spirit] . . . the good word of God [not just Scripture, but revelation] and the powers of the age to come" (6:5). Accordingly, the Christian has received the first fruits of the Spirit (Rom 8:23), that is, the down payment of the "inheritance until the redemption of those who are God's possession" (Eph 1:13–14; cf. 2 Cor 1:22; 5:5). This is a picture of this present age in which we have the same revelation and power as in heaven (as in the Lord's Prayer, Matt 6:10 || Luke 11:2). Though "now we know in part and prophesy in part" (1 Cor 13:9, 12), the kind of revelation and power we have in this present age up to its end is the same kind of revelation and power we will have in heaven, because we are getting part or a taste of this inheritance now, in this present age.

So, this is the agenda or goal of Paul's prayer: a church that experiences the revelation and miracle power of the age to come already, as a way of knowing the God of glory as expressed in the New Covenant prophecies (Isa 59:21 and Jer 31:33–34, see also Isa 44:3; Ezek 11:19; 36:26; 37:14; 39:29).

A similar emphasis appears in Colossians 1:9–12:

> For this reason, since the day we heard about you, we have not stopped praying for you and asking God to fill you with the knowledge of his will

> [New Covenant in heart] through all spiritual wisdom and understanding. [10] And we pray this in order that you may live a life worthy of the LORD and may please him in every way: bearing fruit in every good work [normally, charismatic ministry], growing in the knowledge [personal experience] of God, [11] being strengthened with all [miracle] power according to his glorious might so that you may have great endurance and patience, and joyfully [12] giving thanks to the Father, who has qualified you to share in the inheritance [promise/covenant] of the saints in the kingdom of light. (NIV)

This statement summarizes the Christian experience, elements of which are emphasized throughout the Bible and modeled in Jesus' life:

1. revelation/power
2. that is tested
3. thereby gaining a knowledge/experience/inheritance in God.

Assuming that Paul is not wasting his time in prayer, then this outline is central to his (and our) mission to what Christianity is all about.

Another category of prayer relating to revelation in the New Testament is prayer before choosing and commissioning disciples. To begin at the beginning: The choosing, or identification, of Jesus came as the "redemption of Jerusalem" by the prophetess Anna (Luke 2:38, cf. Isa 59:20), who fasted and prayed for over 60 years. Jesus himself was fasting (and presumably praying) in the wilderness for 40 days (as did Moses), before emerging "in the power of the Spirit" into his mission (Luke 4:14). It is therefore notable that Jesus prayed "all night" before he chose his disciples (Luke 6:12; see also Acts 1:24). In Acts 6:6, prayer preceded the choosing of the Seven who later became powerful evangelists (e.g., Stephen and Philip). Later, others were commissioned into Christian (and presumably also charismatic) ministry after prayer (Acts 13:3; 14:23; and 20:36).

The next section moves from prayer and revelation to prayer and its effect in the physical world.

PRAYER THAT RELEASES POWER TO CHANGE PHYSICAL CONDITIONS

A second category of prayer outcomes involves the power of God applied primarily to physical conditions as in healings, miracles, and changing the course of future events. Here are a few examples.

Early in the story of John, Jesus' forerunner, John's father Zechariah is told about the outcome of his prayer: "your prayer has been heard, and your wife Elizabeth will bear you a son, and you shall call his name John." (Luke 1:13). The familiar Lord's Prayer (Matt 6:9 || Luke 11:2) asks that God not only provide "daily bread," which involves a request for God to shape physical properties, but also asks for his kingdom to come. This kingdom is related to healing and the expulsion of demons.[5] Jesus is explicit that demons come out only by prayer (Mark 9:29). Scripture identifies the kingdom with *dunamis* (miracle power, or "mighty work"; Mark 9:1; 1 Cor 4:20; Rev 12:10). In Acts 1:6, 8, Jesus' answer to the disciples' question about the coming of the kingdom emphasizes divine power to witness to him effectively and globally. It follows, then, that the New Testament would instruct us to pray for the spread of the gospel (Matt 9:38 || Luke 10:12; Col 4:3; 1 Thes 5:25; 2 Thes 3:1). The first readers of the New Testament saw that prayer enabled key people to travel for ministry to the church (Rom 1:10–11; 1 Thes 3:10; Heb 13:19). The ensuing narrative of Acts shows how often such effective witness is accompanied by Holy Spirit power, along with suffering. A more specific connection of prayer to power is the story of Jesus' walking on the water, an event that occurred after extended prayer (Matt 14:22–33 || Mark 6:46–52).[6]

Prayer sometimes petitions God to strengthen faith and resolve. For instance Jesus prayed repeatedly and intensively before his arrest and crucifixion (Matt 26:36, 39, 42, 44 || Mark 14:32, 35, 39 || Luke 22:41, 44). In the midst of his praying for the "cup" of suffering to pass, he warned his disciples to "pray that you not fall into temptation" (Matt 26:41 || Mark 14:38 || Luke 22:40, 46); presumably, Jesus foresaw the disciples' temptation to deny him. Against the tradition that the Passover night was to be spent in a watch commemorating the Exodus, the disciples could not even watch with Jesus for a single hour. (Matt 26:40, 42, 45 || Mark 14:37–41 || Luke 22:45). Despite Peter's later denial, Jesus had already prayed against Satan who would "sift [Peter] like wheat" (Luke 22:31–32). Jesus continues however "but I have prayed for you that your faith may not fail; and when you have turned again, strengthen your brethren" (Luke 22:31–32 RSV). In these cases Jesus was perfectly reasonable to expect that prayer could induce God to change future events.

The same expectation pertains to Jesus' warnings that, during the time of a great persecution, his followers should pray "that [their] escape not take place in winter or on the Sabbath" (Jews weren't allowed to travel very far on the Sabbath—Matt 24:20 || Mark 13:18) and to "stay awake at all times, praying that you may have strength to escape all these things that are going to take place, and to stand before the Son of Man." (Luke 21:36).

The New Testament thus shows the emphasized themes of the New Covenant of the Spirit—revelation, power, and relationship with God—expressed in its own prayers.

The final New Testament theme about why we pray is that God offers unlimited possibilities in prayer. After Jesus caused a fig tree to wither as a sign to his disciples, Jesus emphasized the unlimited possibilities of praying in faith:

> [22] "Have faith in God," Jesus answered. [23] "I tell you the truth, if anyone says to this mountain, 'Go, throw yourself into the sea,' and does not doubt in his heart but believes that what he says will happen, it will be done for him. [24] Therefore I tell you, whatever you ask for in prayer, believe that you have received it, and it will be yours." (Mark 11:12–24 NIV)

It is crucial to remember here, that faith is not will power, nor wishing real hard, nor repeating a Scripture verse until either you or God "gets it." Rather, faith is hearing God's opinion on the matter. If God (not some principle or wish) reveals and assures that something is to be, then, and only then, does anyone have the right kind of faith to move a mountain. Jesus' example is expressed through these passages:

> So Jesus said, "When you have lifted up the Son of Man, then you will know that I am *the one I claim to be* and that I do nothing on my own but speak just what the Father has taught me [echo of New Covenant, Jer 31]. [29] The one who sent me is with me; he has not left me alone, for I always do what pleases him." (John 8:28–29 NIV, emphasis mine)

> I have testimony weightier than that of John. For the very work that the Father has given me to finish, and which I am doing, testifies that the Father has sent me. (John 5:36 NIV)

> Don't you believe that I am in the Father, and that the Father is in me? The words I say to you are not just my own. Rather, it is the Father, living in me, who is doing his work. [11] Believe me when I say that I am in the Father and the Father is in me; or at least believe on the evidence of the miracles themselves. (John 14:10–11 NIV)

So to do mighty works "in Jesus' name" is to do them in the authority of the hearing obedience that characterized Jesus' hearing obedience to the Father; that is, we are to imitate exactly Jesus in the way he heard and obeyed the Father. This truth is why Jesus can say to his disciples:

> [12] I tell you the truth, anyone who has faith in me will do what I have been doing. He will do even greater things than these, because I am going to the Father. [13] And I will do whatever you ask in my name, so that the Son may bring glory to the Father. [14] You may ask me for anything in my name, and I will do it. (John 14:12–14 NIV)

Discerning the Father's will and sensing assurance from him is how we are to ask "in Jesus name," that is, in the same authority that Jesus had from the Father.

It is not enough to yell out, "In the naym-uh Jee-zus" as if this is some magic incantation, as in a Harry Potter episode. We must understand that, according to the New Testament, we pray and expect miracles when we have heard and obeyed the Father in that specific case. If we appeal to some other principle (citing the right Scripture, or wishing hard enough, or some magic Christian words), we will fail, just as Jesus was tempted to do in the wilderness (Matt 4 | | Luke 4). We live by faith (hearing God's revelation and obeying), that is, "by every word that [immediately] comes from the mouth of God" (Matt 4:4). We hear better the more time we spend in God's presence. That's why people with successful healing ministries usually spend many hours in prayer before their meetings begin—not because a lot of prayer racks up points with God, but rather, because the more we enter into his presence, the more aligned we become with his will and resulting power.

To continue with the many promises for the virtually unlimited possibilities of prayer, we need to survey only the following:

> But seek first his kingdom and his righteousness, and all these things will be given to you as well. (Matt 6:33 NIV)

> Ask and it will be given to you; seek and you will find; knock and the door will be opened to you. [8] For everyone who asks receives; he who seeks finds; and to him who knocks, the door will be opened. (Matt 7:7–8 NIV)

> Now if I drive out demons by Beelzebub, by whom do your followers drive them out? So then, they will be your judges. (Luke 11:19 NIV)

> Again, I tell you that if two of you on earth agree about anything you ask for, it will be done for you by my Father in heaven. [20] For where two or three come together in my name, there am I with them. (Matt 18:19–20 NIV)

> But I know that even now God will give you whatever you ask. (John 11:22 NIV)

> You did not choose me, but I chose you and appointed you to go and bear fruit—fruit that will last. Then the Father will give you whatever you ask in my name. (John 15:16 NIV)

> In that day you will no longer ask me anything. I tell you the truth, my Father will give you whatever you ask in my name. [24] Until now you have not asked for anything in my name. Ask and you will receive, and your joy will be complete. (John 16:23–24 NIV)

> Now to him who is able to do immeasurably more than all we ask or imagine, according to his power that is at work within us, (Eph 3:20 NIV)

> You want something but don't get it. You kill and covet, but you cannot have what you want. You quarrel and fight. You do not have, because you do not ask God. [3] When you ask, you do not receive, because you ask with wrong motives, that you may spend what you get on your pleasures. (Jam 4:2–3 NIV)

> Dear friends, if our hearts do not condemn us, we have confidence before God [22] and receive from him anything we ask, because we obey his commands and do what pleases him. (1 John 3:21–22 NIV)

> This is the confidence we have in approaching God: that if we ask anything according to his will, he hears us. [15] And if we know that he hears us—whatever we ask—we know that we have what we asked of him. (1 John 5:14–15 NIV)

Cornelius, an officer in the Roman occupation army, described in Acts 10:2, was commended because he "prayed to God about everything."

This list is amazing when we consider the issue of emphasis. These many commands to pray for a virtually limitless range of requests make our case as to the effects of the promised Spirit modeled by Jesus in Luke 4:18–19 (< Isa 61:1–2) as his agenda, which is fulfilled for us and succeeding generations in Acts 2:39 (< Isa 59:21). This latter pair of passages is fulfilled by the Spirit's producing the mighty "words" in Jesus' mouth, which are then transferred into the mouths of his children (the 120 on Pentecost) and in the mouths of "their children's children, forever." Could it be that the mighty "words in the mouth" represent Spirit-inspired prophetic prayer of unlimited possibilities? Certainly, this seems to be Matthew's commitment in citing the crowds after a miracle by Jesus: "When the crowds saw it, they were afraid, and they glorified God, who had *given such authority to men*" (Matt 9:8; my emphasis).

The next chapter shows how the theme of the mighty, prophetic word of God appears to be summarized as normative in the church.

---

1. For some background to the invention of the term "gospel," see the report to Pope Gregory I: "I determined, through the aid of your prayers for me, to send . . . a monk of my monastery for the purpose of preaching [to the heathen in Anglia]. And he, having with my leave been made bishop by the bishops of Germany, proceeded with their aid also to the end of the world to the aforesaid nation, and already letters have reached us telling us of his safety and his work, to the effect that he and those that have been sent with him are resplendent with such great miracles in the said nation that they seem to imitate the powers of the apostles in the signs they display. Moreover, at the solemnity of the Lord's nativity [Christmas] which occurred in this first indication, more than ten thousand Angli are reported to have been baptized [really cold, if immersed!] by the same, our brother and fellow bishop" (Gregory I, *Letters* 30 [ad 597], *PNF* 12.2, 1163).
2. More on this under "Kingdom of God" in a sequel to this book: *How Protestants Rewrote the Bible*.
3. Note the connection between "word" and "power" in the notion of "testifying" in Acts 4:33: "And with great power the apostles were giving their testimony to the resurrection of the Lord Jesus, and great grace was upon them all." Acts 19:10–12 summarizes Paul's ministry as does the phrase "word and deed" (Rom 15:18, imitating Jesus, Luke 24:19). So also, the characteristic way God reveals himself: "God also bore witness by signs and wonders and various miracles and by gifts of the Holy Spirit distributed according to his will." (Heb 2:4). This is the normal, even exclusive, way that God reveals himself.
4. In this distinction between "this world" and the "world to come," Paul is following the traditional Jewish designation of *olam hazeh* and *olam habah*. Obviously, this same kind of mighty power that raised Christ from the dead and exalted him in power to the right hand of God has put all "principalities and powers" (demonic forces) "under his feet"—into a position of defeat and submission. So the New Covenant revelation and miracle power in the church is expressed "in this age" *(olam hazeh)*, up to and including "the age to come" *(olam habah)*.

5. Matt 4:23; 9:36; 12:28; Luke 9:2, 11; 10:9; 11:18, esp. 11:20; 1 Cor 15:24; Col 1:13, cf. Rev 11:17—"reign" here is the verb form of "kingdom"—see the context at v 15.
6. Is walking on the water a miracle that has ceased? I listened in on a phone conversation, December 2010, between Bill Johnson and an eyewitness to a 13-year-old boy walking out on the ocean water at Dana Point, CA, during a baptismal service. Nearby surfers noticed it first and were "freaking out." A teachable moment?

9
NEW TESTAMENT GREETINGS EXPRESS THE ESSENCE OF CHRISTIAN EXPERIENCE

In more formal churches we often hear a benediction on our way out the door, "Grace and peace to you from God our Father and our Lord Jesus Christ." When we take a closer look at this greeting or benediction, it seems that this "throwaway" line of greeting (like "Dear Sir" in a business letter) in the New Testament has a hugely more important meaning than a kind of generic blessing at the end of a church service. This greeting/benediction formula, occurring in various forms (emphasis, again), is actually stunning in what it does: this greeting encapsulates and reiterates the essence of the original Christian message some 17 times—all but one case.

How so? Could it be that "grace" ("generous, charismatic empowering") and "peace" ("wholeness, health, balance, harmony") are ways of focusing on the Holy Spirit, which in our present era is the essential operating principle of the church and the Christian life? Indeed, in most of the contexts for this greeting, the writer moves on immediately to speak of the works of the Spirit, summarized as grace and peace sent from "God our Father and the Lord Jesus Christ."[1] This proto-Trinitarian "grace and peace" formula seems to focus on the actions of the Spirit in all but one of these passages. Thus the central theme of the Bible—the New Covenant Spirit expressing itself in revelation and power, experienced in love and suffering—is again emphasized in still another form. The following offers a brief sketch of how each "greeting passage" introduces the normative life in the Spirit in their respective Christian communities:

ROMANS 1:7–11:

> To all in Rome who are loved by God and called to be saints: Grace and peace to you from God our Father and from the Lord Jesus Christ. [8] First, I thank my God through Jesus Christ for all of you, because your faith [hearing and obeying God] is being reported all over the world. [9] God, whom I serve with my whole heart in preaching the gospel of his Son, is my witness how constantly I remember you [10] in my prayers at all times; and I pray that now at last by God's will the way may be opened for me to come to you. [11] I long to see you so that I may impart to you some spiritual gift to make you strong (NIV).

Thirteen times in the New Testament the word translated "established" is used, often in the sense of "set in its proper place"; or as "strengthening" or "shoring up" one's position in the Christian life. In our Romans passage it seems to mean that the charism ("grace thing," spiritual gift) is intended not only to "strengthen," but to "put [the believer] in the proper place" in the charismatic body (Rom 6; 1 Cor 12). Note that charismatic empowerment is the object of Paul's prayer for the Roman church, as it is in his other epistles.[2]

ROMANS 16:20:

> The God of peace will soon crush Satan under your feet [the mission of Jesus in 1 Jn 3:8b]. The grace of our Lord Jesus be with you (NIV).

To paraphrase: the very mission of the believer is to experience the eschatological "peace" by crushing "Satan under your feet" [because] God's "grace [generous empowerment] is with you." So the summary statement in 1 John 3:8b echoes Luke 10:19—"authority to tread on serpents and scorpions"—the disciples' mission (Mark 6:7).

1 CORINTHIANS 1:3–7:

> [3] Grace and peace to you from God our Father and the Lord Jesus Christ. [4] I always thank God for you because of his grace given you in Christ Jesus. [5] For in him you have been enriched in every way [charismatic empowerment]—in all your speaking and in all your knowledge [spiritual gifts]— [6] because our testimony about Christ was confirmed [a word associated with signs, wonders and spiritual gifts, Heb 2:4] in you. [7] Therefore you do not lack any spiritual gift as you eagerly wait for our Lord Jesus Christ to be revealed (NIV).

Again, note the tight implication that "grace" and "peace" are or at least include the charismata. This is an excellent example of the greeting formula introducing the normative life in the spirit.

2 CORINTHIANS 1: 2–5:

> [2] Grace and peace to you from God our Father and the Lord Jesus Christ. [3] Praise be to the God and Father of our Lord Jesus Christ, the Father of compassion and the God of all comfort, [4] who comforts us in all our troubles, so that we can comfort those in any trouble with the comfort we ourselves have received from God. [5] For just as the sufferings of Christ flow over into our lives, so also through Christ our comfort overflows (NIV).

Note the word "comfort" is the same word (*paracletos*—Paraclete) as is used of the Holy Spirit in John 14—16. Here in five verses, the root *paraclete* is repeated (emphasis) nine times! "Grace and peace" represent "comfort" and appear to be actions of the Paraclete, the Holy Spirit. Here again is still another example of the connection between the standard New Testament greeting and the ideal community life in the Spirit.

2 CORINTHIANS 13:14:

> May the grace of the Lord Jesus Christ, and the love of God, and the fellowship of the Holy Spirit be with you all (NIV).

Note the goal of this climatic verse is that grace, love and fellowship of the Holy Spirit "be with you all." In other words, Paul is summarizing (which indicates emphasis) the essential experience of the Christian life that all should enjoy. Let us define the key terms of this "Trinitarian" experience (Lord Jesus, Father, Spirit):

- Grace of the Lord Jesus ("generous empowering of charismata" equals "grace things"),
- Love of the Father (love is the "more excellent way" in which we minister the "grace-things/charismata" 1 Cor 12:31), and the
- Fellowship of the Spirit (sharing, having-in-common;"body ministry" of charismata).

GALATIANS 1:3–4:

> Grace and peace to you from God our Father and the Lord Jesus Christ, 4 who gave himself for our sins to rescue us from the present evil age, according to the will of our God and Father (NIV).

Are we to assume that "grace and peace" represent the opposite characteristics of "the present evil age"? The context seems to indicate that this "evil age" represents the bondage to the Law, which merely accused us of our sin. The Galatians were tempted to return to this bondage and hopelessness of trying to keep the Old Covenant rules of the Law, rather than receiving the New Covenant of the Spirit for which

Jesus died, that is, to pay off the obligations of the Old Covenant. They already had received this miracle-producing New Covenant Spirit by a "hearing of faith" (3:5)—a revelation that characterizes the "Law written in the heart" (Jer 31:34), that is, the prophetic "words in the mouth" characterizing the New Covenant Spirit (Isa 59:21 > Acts 2:39).[3]

EPHESIANS 1:2–17:

> [2] Grace to you and peace from God our Father and the Lord Jesus Christ [note causal connection of "grace" and gifts]. [3] Blessed be the God and Father of our Lord Jesus Christ, who has blessed us in Christ with every spiritual blessing . . . . according to the riches of his grace, [8] which he lavished upon us, in all wisdom and insight . . . . when you heard the word of truth [a prophetic process, not just doctrines] the gospel of your salvation, and believed in him, were sealed [legally protected] with the promised Holy Spirit [characterized by charismata] . . . . [16] I do not cease to give thanks for you, remembering you in my prayers, [17] that the God of our Lord Jesus Christ, the Father of glory, may give you the Spirit of wisdom and of revelation in the knowledge of him. . . . (ESV)

This charismatic emphasis spelling out "grace and peace" is repeated: "that the God of our Lord Jesus Christ, the Father of glory, may give you a Spirit of wisdom and of revelation in the knowledge of him . . . ."

PHILIPPIANS 1:2–11:

> [2] Grace and peace to you from God our Father and the Lord Jesus Christ . . . . [5] because of your partnership in the gospel from the first day until now [recall how the "gospel" was presented in power Rom 15:19; 2 Cor 12:12; 1 Thes 1:5; Heb 2:4]. , [6] being confident of this, that he who began a good work in you [including the New Covenant gift of the Spirit] will carry it on to completion until the day of Christ Jesus. [7] . . . for. . . all of you share in God's grace [generous empowerment] with me. [8] God can testify how I long for all of you with the affection of Christ Jesus. [9]

And this is my prayer: that your love may abound more and more in knowledge and depth of insight [spiritual gifts], [10] so that you may be able to discern what is best and may be pure and blameless until the day of Christ, [11] filled with the fruit of righteousness [revelatory faith and spiritual gifts, Rom 1:17] that comes through Jesus Christ—to the glory and praise of God (NIV).

COLOSSIANS 1:2–14:

Grace to you and peace from God our Father. . . . we heard of your faith in Christ Jesus and of the love that you have for all the saints, [5] because of the hope laid up for you in heaven. Of this you have heard before in the word of the truth, the gospel, [6] which has come to you, as indeed in the whole world it is bearing fruit and increasing— as it also does among you, since the day you heard it and understood the grace [that word, again] of God in truth, [7]. . . Epaphras . . . has made known to us your love in the Spirit [the ideal existence of the believer on earth]. [9] And so, from the day we heard, we have not ceased to pray for you, asking that you may be filled with the knowledge of his will in all spiritual wisdom and understanding, [10] so as to walk in a manner worthy of the LORD, fully pleasing to him, bearing fruit in every good work [including the charismata] and increasing in the knowledge of God. [11] May you be strengthened with all [miracle] power, according to his glorious might, for all endurance and patience with joy, [12] giving thanks to the Father, who has qualified you to share in the inheritance of the saints in light. [13] He has delivered us from the domain of darkness [no revelation] and transferred us to the kingdom [the reign of the Spirit] of his beloved Son, [14] in whom we have redemption [the buying back of a slave], the forgiveness of sins [which frees us to enter the New Covenant of the Spirit] (ESV).

1 THESSALONIANS 1:1–7:

> 1 Paul, Silvanus, and Timothy, To the church of the Thessalonians in God
> the Father and the Lord Jesus Christ: Grace to you and peace. 2 We give
> thanks to God always for you all, constantly mentioning you in our
> prayers, 3 remembering before our God and Father your work of faith
> and labor of love and steadfastness of hope in our Lord Jesus Christ. 4
> For we know, brethren beloved by God, that he has chosen you; 5 for our
> gospel came to you not only in word, but also in power and in the Holy
> Spirit and with full conviction. You know what kind of men we proved to
> be among you for your sake. 6 And you became imitators of us and of the
> Lord, for you received the word in much affliction, with joy inspired by
> the Holy Spirit 7 so that you became an example to all the believers in
> Macedonia and in Achaia.

This passage provides the clearest indication that the grace and peace is identified or related with the Spirit. Note the progression of the gospel coming to the Thessalonians in power, then they imitate the apostles and the Lord in that process of bringing the gospel to others, thereby setting an example to be imitated in turn.

2 THESSALONIANS 1:2–9:

A second letter to the Thessalonians illustrates the significance of grace and peace as an action of the Spirit, again. This church is suffering persecution for their "abundantly growing" faith through which they will enter the kingdom of God—a synonym for the presence of the Spirit. The Thessalonians' faith will be vindicated by "mighty angels in flaming fire," while their adversaries will experience the "punishment of eternal destruction and exclusion from the presence of the Lord and from the glory of his might." For a cessationist, the punishment of eternal destruction and exclusion from the presence of the Lord would be very bad indeed, and yet "exclusion from the glory of his might" seems to be the cessationist's theological norm for this present age—

we're not supposed to see miracles today! St Paul, however, sees this exclusion as a bad thing on a par with damnation, since the very gospel is "the [miracle] power of God unto salvation."

2 TIMOTHY 1:2:

While 1 Timothy 1:2 does not spell out the themes of the Spirit as an expression of the "grace and peace" formula, its counterpart in 2 Timothy does so explicitly. Paul describes himself as gifted with apostleship "according to the promise" (a synonym for "covenant" which recalls his paraphrase of Isa 59:21 in Rom 11:29—"The charismata and calling of God are not withdrawn"). The "promise" is "of the life which is in Christ Jesus." Statistically, "life" correlates with and results from the Spirit's operation "which is in Christ Jesus." As we have seen, Jesus has essentially identified himself with the Spirit (John 14; 2 Cor 3:17); so to be "in Christ Jesus" is to be "in the Spirit."

This, then, is the setting for our formula, "grace . . . and peace . . ." which is followed by a reference to serving God "with a clear conscience."[4] Recall that a conscience is a result of revelation (keeping the New Covenant stipulations). Paul then traces the progression of faith (a revelatory hearing) through Timothy's grandmother, mother, and to him. Since Timothy has experienced revelation in faith, Paul can draw a conclusion ("Hence"—*di' hēn aitian*) he can "remind" him to rekindle the gift (charisma—"grace thing") of God imparted to Timothy by the laying on of hands (cf. Rom 1:11). "For God did not give us a Spirit of timidity but a Spirit of power and love and self-control" (v 7). Accordingly, Paul continues logically to spell out the works of the Spirit by encouraging Timothy not to be "ashamed . . . of testifying . . . but to share in suffering for the gospel in the power of God" (similar to Rom 1:16. Note also 1 Thes 1:5; Heb 2:4). Paul contrasts Timothy's being saved and called with a "holy"—sanctifying—calling not by "virtue of our works but in virtue of his own purpose and grace" (generous empowerment—charisma). Ultimately, Timothy is to guard this truth (the "grace, mercy and peace" of the Spirit "in Christ Jesus"—the essence of the gospel) "that has been entrusted to [him] by the Holy

Spirit who dwells within us." This passage again shows that the "grace and peace" formula usually introduces and reiterates a description of the gospel of the New Covenant Spirit and His activity expressed in His graces (charismata).

TITUS 1:4:

This verse also connects the "grace and peace" formula with a summary of the Spirit's work in normative Christian experience and which affirms a triune pattern of divine mission. Paul describes himself as a "servant of God and an apostle [a "sent-out one"] of Jesus Christ." The mission itself emphasizes the work of the Spirit of revelation: "to further the faith" [hearing and obeying] and their "knowledge of the truth which accords with godliness." Traditional theology would suggest that the term, "knowledge of the truth" means at least an intellectual grasp of "doctrine," or a primitive creed. But this is part of a tradition laid out in John's Gospel referring to "the Spirit of truth" . . . "which dwells in you" (14:17; 1 John 4:6), who will "teach you all things" (14:26)—a reference to the New Covenant Spirit (Jer 31:34). This "knowledge of the truth which accords with godliness" is a way of saying "this experience with the Spirit of revelation" (faith, knowledge of the truth) is God's way, that is, the normative pattern of Christianity." Moreover, we have mention of "eternal life" which God "promised ages ago . . . manifested in his word." Would the promise here, expressed in his "word" be an allusion to the covenant/promise (the words are synonymous in the New Testament) of Isaiah 59:21? "Eternal life" is more than simply going to heaven; it begins in the present as an expression of the Spirit revealing to us our "knowledge [experience] of God."[5]

These first three verses of Titus provide a background of the Christian experience of the Spirit leading to the declaration that Titus is Paul's "true child in a common faith"—again an experience of revelation. "A common faith" would traditionally be understood as a "common doctrine or creed," but this reading does not do justice to the context nor to the possible allusion to "child" in this common experience of the Spirit. Recall in Isaiah 59:21 that the prophetic word of the Spirit would not depart from "the mouths of your children, or from the mouths of your children's children, forever." It is apparent that Paul sees Titus as one of these prophetically gifted children. Titus 3:5–7 offers a similar summary of the normative Christian, charismatic experience: "renewal in the Holy Spirit, which he poured out upon us richly through Jesus Christ our Savior, so that we might be justified by his grace [generous empowering] and become heirs in hope of eternal life."

PHILEMON 1:3–6:

These verses carry forward the theme of "grace and peace" being described in the context as the normative experience in the Spirit:

> 3 Grace to you and peace from God our Father and the Lord Jesus Christ.
> 4 I thank my God always when I remember you in my prayers, 5 because I hear of your love and of the faith which you have toward the Lord Jesus and all the saints, 6 and I pray that the sharing of your faith may promote the knowledge of all the good that is ours in Christ.

"Love" and "faith" here are echoes of Paul's discussion of the charismata in 1 Corinthians 13:2 where he exhorts the readers to minister the gifts from the motive of love, rather than pride. Again, here in Philemon the situation is similar: the object of their faith (the revelatory gift of the New Covenant Spirit) has a double focus on "the Lord Jesus and all the saints," where the "sharing of your faith" promotes "the knowledge of all the good that is ours in Christ." Hence, the process of "faith" (hearing and obeying) toward ("into") the Lord Jesus results in a "knowledge" (experience) "of all the good that is ours in Christ." "All the good" clearly describes more than Protestant "salvation." More likely, it is, at minimum, following the vocabulary of the New Testament rather than the Reformation, a description of the promised life in the Spirit ("all that is ours"). Once again, there is a connection of the "grace and peace" formula with a description of the charismatic community in action.

1 PETER 1:2–13:

Here we see Paul is not the only New Testament writer to use the "grace and peace" formula to introduce the work of the Spirit as the normal experience of his readers. First Peter is a clear example of our pattern, though the formula is somewhat different: "May grace and peace be multiplied to you. Blessed be the God and Father of our Lord Jesus Christ!" The "grace and peace" again seems expressed in the normative experience of the Spirit in the community Peter addresses. This community is described as being "sanctified by the Spirit" (set apart as a priest/prophet); having been "born anew" based on the resurrection of Jesus (God's vindication in power); for "an inheritance . . . kept in heaven." During the time we journey toward heaven in this present age we are "guarded by God's power (*dunamis*—miracle power, a gift of the Spirit) "through faith" (the charismatic process of hearing and obeying). This same "guarding" is elsewhere described as the "seal of the Spirit" (1 Cor 1:22; Eph 1:13; 4:30), which protects us with the Spirit's gifts until we are delivered into the heavenly court. In the New Testament culture, no one could break a seal on a Roman imperial document on pain of death until it was delivered to its destination. Similarly, no human or demonic authority can break the guarding of us or the seal of the Spirit except the Father or Jesus (Rev 5:5).

The prophetic flavor of the experience of Peter's community is compared with the Old Testament prophets who also suffered, but only predicted the "grace" (generous empowerment) that was to be theirs—"the things which have been announced to you by those who proclaimed the good news to you through the Holy Spirit sent from heaven." While the emphasis is upon the grace and inheritance coming in the future, it nonetheless also describes the grace and power occurring in the present Christian life.

2 PETER 1:2–19:

This passage describes the nature of "grace and peace" formula clearly in terms of its implicit emphasis on the power and revelation normative to the believer. Note that before the formula, Peter makes the claim that the readers "have obtained a faith of equal standing" with the apostles. From the context, it is clear that "a faith" is not a correct creedal statement, but an ability to "hear and obey" at the apostolic level! He then modifies the formula by emphasizing that "grace and peace [can be] multiplied to you in the knowledge [experience] of God and of Jesus our Lord." He then repeats and spells out what he means by this "grace and peace" experience/knowledge by affirming that "His divine power *[dunameōs]*" has granted everything that relate to "life and godliness."

How? Via the knowledge—a revelatory experience, a charism, which "he has granted to us his precious and very great promises." Which promises? In the context of receiving revelation and power, it would seem that Peter is repeating the "punch line" of his crucial Pentecost sermon: "this promise/covenant is for you . . ." which is the fulfillment of Isaiah 59:21. He then notes how this gifting helps us escape the corruption of the world to "become partakers of the divine nature" which is characterized by faith ("hearing and obeying"), virtue, knowledge (a charism of revelation), love, etc. These characteristics promote effectiveness and fruitfulness "in the knowledge [revealed, charismatic experience] of our Lord Jesus Christ." As in Hebrews, Peter reminds the readers not to be shortsighted by forgetting that Jesus provided release from the Old Covenant and its laws, which now allows the reader to focus on their "call and election" as recipients of the New Covenant Spirit of power and revelation.

He notes that the core of the gospel is not "myths" because "we made known to you [caused you to experience firsthand] the power and coming" of Jesus. This experience with Jesus showed that Peter's testimony was not a fictional myth. He reminds them of the experience of God's immediate word on "the holy mountain" of the transfiguration. On this basis, then, he urges the use of "the prophetic word" which they would "do well to pay attention to this as a lamp shining in a dark place." This practice of heeding prophecy is to continue until the end of this age—"until the day dawns and the morning star [Jesus?] rises in your hearts." Then Peter argues, as the temptation narratives of Jesus do (Matt 4 || Luke 4), that the starting point for understanding Scripture (the process of *halakah*) is not by a human impulse but as "the Holy Spirit spoke from God." Again, this formula is immersed in a context saturated with descriptions of the normative church life in love and in the charismatic New Covenant Spirit. This is also true in 2 John, as well.

2 JOHN 1:1–9:

John the apostle, who wrote this brief letter, does not see "truth" as traditional theology might by identifying it with doctrine. Instead, John seems to be using the word as a synonym for the New Covenant Spirit. It is difficult imagining someone loving someone else "in the doctrine" or simply because they "know" doctrine! Rather, the language seems to indicate "Spirit," "which abides in us and will be with us forever." This last phrase could echo again, Isaiah 59:21, which describes the prophetic "words" of God not departing his children "forever."

By contrast, the "deceivers"—the untruthful—who, like the scribes of John 5:38 do not have his word [truth] abiding in [them], for [they] do not believe him whom he has sent." But to his readers, John refers to the one "who abides in the doctrine has both the Father and the Son." At first glance this RSV translation "doctrine" confirms the traditional view of "truth" as a creed, but the word translated "doctrine" *(didachē)* here is probably more an echo of John 14:26, which is referring to the New Covenant Spirit "who will teach *(didaksei)* you all things" (Jer 31:34). Once again, in different language, it would appear that John is confirming the role of the "grace and peace" formula as an introduction to the normative Christian life in the New Covenant Spirit and His love and giftings. Finally, we go to the last appearance of this formula, appropriately, in the last book of the Bible.

REVELATION 1:1–10:

This passage again demonstrates the huge role of the Spirit in the experience of the church. If we read this text from within the experience of the Spirit associated with the "grace and peace" formula, the traditional theological vocabulary must be recast into its original meanings. The opening words assume the readers' familiarity with the process of prophecy. Indeed, this was an immediate prophecy of John which was to be circulated among seven churches in western Anatolia. There is no explicit statement in this prophecy that it is to be regarded as canonical Scripture, even though he attempts, toward its end, to protect it from additions or deletions by false prophets (Rev 22:18–19).

The process of prophecy involves the claim that it is a "revelation" "made . . . known" by God via an angel to John. This writing seems to be the result of John's "witness to the word [prophecy] of God and to Jesus Christ's own testimony, that is, "to all [John] saw." John addresses the seven churches in Asia with the familiar formula, probably representing the works of the Spirit ("grace and peace") from the timeless God "and from the seven spirits who are before His throne, and from Jesus Christ, the faithful witness." Who are the "seven spirits"? Could they be the specific "revealers" assigned to the seven churches, rather like spirits of prophecy?

In any case, the role of Jesus, "who loves us and has freed us from our sins by his blood" is portrayed as the one who has broken the power of the Old Covenant in order to introduce us to the New Covenant of the Spirit: "He made us a kingdom [recall the tight association of Kingdom and Spirit in New Testament theology] of priests to His God and Father." An important role of a priest was to "inquire of the Lord" on behalf of God's people and in this sense he served as a prophet conveying God's immediate word. Indeed, John himself, is modeling this role for his readers: after all, "the testimony of Jesus is [expressed as] the Spirit of prophecy" (Rev 19:10). Indeed, following the biblical pattern, John is suffering "on account of the [prophetic] word of God, that is, the testimony of Jesus." Accordingly, he continues on into his prophecy by emphasizing his source: "I was in the Spirit—on the Lord's day."

CONCLUSION

All of these 17 "grace and peace" formulae are more than mere ritualized greetings. These greetings include, along with the Father and the Son, the Holy Spirit who is indirectly described as "grace and peace." In almost all of these contexts the greeting formula introduces a description of gifts of revelation and power to be ministered in love, all as normative in the Christian community. Here again, these greetings provide another emphasis pattern confirming our thesis, that the New Covenant Spirit of revelation and power with love and suffering is absolutely central to the Biblical message.

By contrast this greeting formula prominently shows that Jesus' mission was more than what traditional Protestantism emphasizes. Traditional doctrine affirms that Jesus came to "save sinners" by dying on the cross to pay for those sins in a substitutionary atonement. No priests should therefore receive payment to pray one out of Purgatory when Jesus grants us "unmerited favor" for our salvation.

Certainly all this is true, but the New Testament does not stop here: Jesus' death on the cross was one important link in a chain of actions he did to reach his goal: to baptize us with the Holy Spirit to empower us for our mission in the same way he was empowered. Jesus-as-Spirit actually indwells us when we have received him by faith in the experience of the Spirit. We cannot talk, at least in biblical terms, about being "Spirit-filled" if there is no corresponding outworking of Jesus' charismatic ministry in our lives. This experience in the Spirit ranges from gifts of apostleship to prophecy, miracles or revelation, to gifts of administration or hospitality. But the central characteristic of the Holy Spirit is revelation and prophecy. Prophecy includes all the things that prophets do: reveal secrets of the hearts, proclaim God's revelation, heal, perform miracles, prophesy about the future—all to evangelize as well as to build up and equip the church. These gifts are God's grace in action, the "grace-things" (charismata) that are never withdrawn (Rom 11:29).

What is most important, however, for this section, is that the New Testament has demonstrated that biblically, the presence of these genuine gifts in our life is also the presence of the living Christ—the Spirit living within us. Our baptism in the Spirit is not some theological add-on, but the central goal of the Bible, the central mission of Jesus, and is, in fact, the essential expression of Jesus Christ in the believer's life now.

The next chapter lays out how this theme permeates representative New Testament books.

---

1. The only scholarly reference I was able to discover that connected the standard apostolic greeting with spiritual gifts was in Judith Lieu's article, "'Grace to You and Peace' The Apostolic Greeting," *Bulletin of the John Ryland's Library at the University of Manchester* 68:1 (Aut 1985), 178. We seem to have independently arrived at the following conclusion, which she makes without elaboration on the "divine gifts": "[W]e see that the greeting, only to be expected in a letter, expresses far more than the conventional formalities. The distinctive Christian grace speaks both of the 'apostolic' authority of the sender and of the divine gifts given to the recipients."
2. 2 Cor 1:11–12; 9:14; Eph 1:16–17; 6:18–19; Phil 1:4,7; 4:6-7 (peace = Spirit?); Col 1:3–4 (faith); 1:9; 4:3–4; 1 Thes 1:2–5; esp. 1 Thes 3:10; 5:17–20; esp. 2 Thes 1:11; 3:1; 1 Tim 4:5–6; Phlm 5–6; cf. Rom 15:29.
3. Edmund K. Neufeld, "Christ and the Spirit in Galatians and 2 Corinthians 1—5: An Eschatological Comparison," PhD dissertation, Milwaukee: Marquette University, 1987.
4. Note that conscience is, like faith, a function of revelation. See pp. 127–128, "Conscience: A 'Taste' of the New Covenant Revelation?"
5. On this see D. A. Carson, on John 17:3, which defines "eternal life" as "not so much everlasting life as personal knowledge of the Everlasting One." *The Gospel According to John* (Leicester, UK: Apollos, 1991), 556.

10

THE NEW COVENANT SPIRIT IN WORD AND POWER

Our new paradigm of the Bible's being written around the immediate word of God and its power, the New Covenant Spirit, finds confirmation in the very Scriptures that are mined for support of traditional theology: the Gospel of John, Romans, and Hebrews. I also include Acts, having only recently understood it in a whole new way—a way that comports with the idea that the New Covenant is really the central experience of the Spirit, the prophetic word and power of God. Following is a thematic survey of these four key books.

JESUS AS THE (PROPHETIC) WORD OF GOD IN THE GOSPEL OF JOHN

The thesis statement (emphasis again) of the Gospel of John appears in its first line: "In the beginning was the Word, and the Word was with God, and the Word was God." Here are the twin emphasized themes of John: the fact of powerful revelation ("word"—a synonym for the Holy Spirit) identified with Jesus. John goes on to emphasize the point that God sent Jesus to model, teach about, and prepare for the process of hearing and obeying the Father.[1]

John also follows the biblical emphasis in connecting the revealed and uttered Word with the rejection and suffering of its proclaimers.[2]

The central issue in John, however, is "believing"[3] versus unbelief. This issue manifests itself in the way that people respond to Jesus and his mission from the Father. The chief issue and conflict in the Gospel of John concerns how we hear and obey God. I never understood the conflict in its proper historical setting until a Messianic Jewish colleague pointed out a story in the Talmud set around the time John's Gospel was being written. This conflict revolutionized the way I read John and its constant cycling of the issue of belief and how we hear God's voice.

WHAT WAS COOKIN' IN AKHNAI'S OVEN? TRADITIONAL RELIGION AND THE MESSAGE OF JOHN'S GOSPEL

Rabbinic Judaism seems to represent the traditional human religious impulse to avoid the immediate word of God and construct a less disturbing set of religious ideas and practices. The Gospel of John is almost obsessed with confronting this intellectualized, detached mentality with the word of God—the immediate revelation into the heart, which is the essence of the New Covenant Spirit.

After finally absorbing the central import of the Jewish scribal position on Scripture and its rejection of further revelation (the direct voice of God and miracles), one may read the Gospel of John with new eyes. The very center of Rabbinic Judaism is the written Torah ("teaching"/Law) and how it is understood and applied through the rabbis (experts in Torah). The Gospel of John, after all, was probably recorded within the time of the historical setting of the "Oven of Akhnai" story in the Talmud (Baba Mez'ia 59).[4]

Since I noticed the connection between John 5:37–45 and the "Oven" doctrine, I began to see that, indeed, the whole Gospel of John was written against the rabbinic way of knowing God, that is, by remaining firmly in the Old Covenant. This, of course, was the issue of Jesus' temptations—and for that matter, Eve's—and that also of traditional Protestant religion.

The first verses of John quote from the first chapter of the Bible and likewise emphasize the mighty word of God going forth to create the world. Jesus' mission follows the theme of the wisdom of God (the process of revelation) that was integral to the creation miracle (Prov 8:22–31; Psa 104:24).

Accordingly, John emphasizes some 85 times this process of revelation and its reception that occurs each time the issue of believing comes up, or "having faith"—hearing God's voice or "word." The Gospel of John spends chapter after chapter pounding home the same theme: in Jesus, God reveals himself in signs (revelatory miracles) and in word to those who "get it" by believing. This process is to be continued and even amplified (John 14:12) after Jesus ascends to the Father and returns in the Spirit (John 14:16–18).

John's teaching generalizes about hearing the voice of God—the central process of the New Covenant—some 38 times.[5] For example, the characteristic of one of Christ's sheep is to hear his voice (10:3, 4, 16, 27): "My sheep listen to my voice; I know them, and they follow me" (so, 3:29; 5:24, 30; 6:45; 8:43; 8:47) "He who belongs to God hears what God says. The reason you do not hear is that you do not belong to God." Remember the story of Achnai's oven?[6] The present-day voice of God was forbidden—as in traditional Protestant theology—although, thank God, many traditional Protestants defy their theology in practice!

Jesus, therefore, models hearing from God for his readers (John 5:30; 8:26, 38, 40; 14:24; 15:15 "everything that I learned from my Father I have made known to you," similar to the Spirit in 16:13 and 18:37). This pattern should come as no surprise, since this Gospel explicitly lays out Jesus' purpose and mission at the beginning in the prophecy of John the Baptist: "I myself did not know him, but he who sent me to baptize with water said to me, 'He on whom you see the Spirit descend and remain, this is he who baptizes with the Holy Spirit.'" (John 1:33). John 18:37 expresses the thesis statement of the New Testament—the central point of the whole Bible: "for this reason I was born, and for this I came into the world, to testify to the truth. Everyone on the side of truth listens to me." We will find this theme central to the Book of Acts.

THE BOOK OF ACTS: THE OPERATIONS MANUAL FOR THE CHURCH

Jesus' mission, then, is summarized at the beginning of John as being the "word." After Jesus has received the word/Spirit in Luke (and the other Synoptic Gospels), in Acts the Spirit remains on Him during his exaltation in heaven in order to baptize others in the word/Spirit (John 1:33). This New Covenant pattern is presented precisely in Isaiah 59:19–21. It is cited in typical rabbinic shortened form as the conclusion of the charter message of Christianity, the Pentecost sermon (Acts 2:39):

> So they shall fear the name of the LORD from the west,
> and his glory from the rising of the sun;
> for he will come like a rushing stream,
> which the wind of the LORD drives.
> "And a Redeemer will come to Zion,
> to those in Jacob who turn from transgression," declares the LORD.
> "And as for me, this is my covenant with them," says the LORD: "My Spirit that is upon you, and my words that I have put in your mouth, shall not depart out of your mouth, or out of the mouth of your offspring, or out of the mouth of your children's offspring," says the LORD, "from this time forth and forevermore" (ESV).

The fulfillment of these last two verses appears in Acts 2:38–39:

> Repent and be baptized every one of you in the name of Jesus Christ for the forgiveness of your sins, and you will receive the gift of the Holy Spirit. For the promise is for you and for your children and for all who are far off, everyone whom the Lord our God calls to himself (ESV).

Peter's "action point" of his sermon is nothing more than John the Baptist's agenda: the preparation for the Spirit in repentance and baptism, but then also the fulfillment of the New Covenant Spirit by way of Jesus. The importance of Jesus in all of this is fleshed out in Acts chapter 3 and 4 where the central issue of the trial Peter and John revolves around the name of Jesus and its power.

So Isaiah 59:19–21 shapes the early part of Acts in both content and structure.[7] The following is the abstract of my article developing this thesis, which set me on the path toward this book.

> Perhaps due to traditional discomfort with the continuing gift of prophecy in the Christian community, the New Covenant/promise of Isaiah 59:19–21 has received no significant attention in both theology and biblical studies. By contrast, Luke records the events of Pentecost in Acts 2 as not only the fulfillment of this Isaianic promised New Covenant, but as the template of the very structure of his chapter (and entire book) as well. Intertextual "dependence" [the connection of one Bible passage with another] via the use of identical words and phrases is less convincing if the underlying argument and narrative plot are not also demonstrated. Employing synonymous rather than identical expressions, Luke weaves Isaiah 59:19–21 into a coherent narrative flow in Acts 2, describing: 1) The powerful rushing sound 2) of the wind/Spirit and the "words in the mouth"/speaking (Joel 2) 3) which cause 4) the universal 5) fear of 6) the Lord's name and his glory. 7) In this way, the redeemer (Psa 16) 8) comes to Zion/Jerusalem 9) to Jacob/Jews, who, upon their repentance, 10) will receive the covenant/promise of the Spirit 11) that shall not depart from him nor from his children nor from their children forever. The conceptual and structural use of Isaiah 59:19–21 in the early chapters of Acts, then, solves a number of puzzles. This Isaianic prophecy serves as the programmatic statement for the Book of Acts, building upon its mirrored programmatic passage (Isa 61:1–2) of the first volume, the Gospel of Luke. In Luke, Jesus is the bearer of the Spirit; in Acts he is the bestower of the Spirit "for you, for your children, and for all who are far off."

Beyond this, as another indicator of emphasis, the Book of Acts seems even to be structured around the phrase "the word grew and multiplied," expressed variously.[8] Some 26 times, this prophetic "word" of God is uttered throughout the book. The "word" of power manifests itself in Acts in the fact that (conservatively) 27.2 percent of the text takes the form of miracle narrative. Recall that miracle and word are variant forms of God's revelation in "deed and word" ("God also testified to it by signs, wonders and various miracles, and gifts of the Holy Spirit distributed according to his will" Heb 2:4). The mighty word theme is complemented (as it is in most other biblical books) by the corresponding theme of suffering which we see in this case as mostly unjust imprisonments (based on Isa 24:14–23).[9]

Again, an important summary statement indicating emphasis comes to us from what some have called Paul's "theological tractate," the Epistle of Romans.

ROMANS: A SUMMARY STATEMENT OF THE BIBLICAL MESSAGE

The central biblical message, here again, is the ideal of hearing the voice of God with the consequences of heeding or rejecting it. Paul's Epistle to the Romans (perhaps along with Galatians) is the foundational source for classical Protestant theology—with its theme of the sinfulness of man resulting in God's justification and salvation by faith. Recently, however, biblical scholars are seeing the message of Romans as more about the Spirit of God.[10] Indeed, the themes of faith (hearing and heeding God), sin, justification, the Spirit, and reconciliation with God are all elements of the New Covenant as described in Isaiah 59:21 and Jeremiah 31:31–34, yet the emphasis of these two covenant passages focuses much more on the process of experiencing the prophetic spirit.

DESCRIBING THE GOSPEL

For the moment, let's suspend what we think we know about the term "gospel" *(evangelion)*. Now consider that in contrast to traditional religion, modern linguistics seeks a word's meaning from cues and associations within its context. Let's do this with the term "gospel" using four passages from Romans: Romans 1:1–6; 15:15–19; 1:16–17; and 8:13–16. As we do so, notice that these passages describe the gospel in terms of experiencing the Spirit. There is much more we could develop, but these are clear samples of how Paul understood the essential characteristics of the Gospel in the ultimate Protestant biblical resource, the Epistle to the Romans.

Romans 1:1–6 shows the nature of the gospel in part through the calling and experience of Paul and his readers.

> Paul, a servant of Christ Jesus, called to be an apostle and set apart for the gospel of God— [2] the gospel he promised beforehand through his prophets in the Holy Scriptures [3] regarding his Son, who as to his human nature was a descendant of David, [4] and who through the Spirit of holiness was declared with power to be the Son of God by his resurrection from the dead: Jesus Christ our Lord. [5] Through him and for his name's sake, we received grace and apostleship to call people from among all the Gentiles to the obedience that comes from faith. [6] And you also are among those who are called to belong to Jesus Christ (Rom 1:1–6 NIV).

As a glance at any modern commentary will tell you, this passage condenses a huge amount of material. But for our purposes, note that Paul identifies himself as . . .

- "a servant of Christ Jesus," who is further defined as one
- "called" (as prophets, as we saw above in Chapter 5)
- "to be an apostle" (at least 89 apostles in the New Testament), and
- "set apart" (as a priest or a prophet—a synonym for "sanctified"?)
- "for the gospel of God" (the "good message" from God).

Now he describes this gospel and how "we" (he and all of us) fit into this calling/mission/being set apart. This gospel, which is expressed and modeled in Jesus . . .

- was "promised [covenanted] through his prophets in the Holy Scriptures" (wouldn't this include Isa 61:1 with Isa 59:21 > Acts 2:39; Jer 31:31–34?)
- "regarding [focused on] His Son," a human descendant of David, but who
- "through the Spirit of holiness [set apart for ministry] was declared"
- "with [miracle] power *[dunamis]* to be the Son of God by his resurrection."

What does all this have to do with us? Well, like Jesus, through him and for his name's sake, we (all of us!) . . .

- received grace (charismatic empowering)
- and apostleship (charismatically endowed missionaries, "sent out ones"—"apostled"—an ordinary word for "sending" 132 times in New Testament)
- to call people from among all the Gentiles to the obedience that comes from faith (or "hearing of revelation")—the essence of the New Covenant (Jer 31:33)
- and you also are among those who are called to belong to Jesus Christ.

So the mission of Jesus ("through him and for his name's sake") according to this passage was to give "grace" or charismatic empowering. Note in verse 11 Paul replicates Jesus' mission—and ours —to "impart some spiritual gift (charisma or "grace thing") to make you strong." Remember, the exaltation of Jesus is for the purpose of "pouring out [as Spirit] that which you see and hear" (signs, wonders, and prophecy, charismatic gifts and ministries, Acts 2:33; Eph 4:7, 11–13).

The other gift Jesus gives is the gift of "sending out" (apostleship). Don't be horrified at becoming an apostle: remember that it's only the odd traditional Protestant idea that "apostles are popes limited to the first century." In the New Testament, everybody gets to play. Remember the command of 1 Corinthians 12:31? "Desire earnestly the best gifts [apostleship was first in the list in 1 Cor 12:28], especially that you may prophesy."[11] It is clear that not all in the Corinthian community were apostles, prophets, or miracle workers (1Cor 12:29), but what is clear is that these gifts were on the table for all Christians to "desire earnestly" (1 Cor 12:31; 14:1) and even to emulate, just as evangelicals today strive to fulfill the "Great Commission" (Matt 28:19–20) which, after all, was directed to the eleven apostles.

The purpose of these gifts is to not only edify the Christian community but to "call people from among all the Gentiles to the obedience that comes from faith." Again, the "call" is used (an echo of a call into prophetic ministry?) toward the nations (Gentiles), to what? "The obedience that comes from faith." Isn't this last statement simply a paraphrase of the New Covenant: "the Torah/Law written/revealed in the heart"?

Just to be sure his readers get it, Paul emphasizes again in this last point that his readers are "also among those who are called to belong to Jesus Christ." This last phrase is teaching that the "calling to belong to Jesus Christ" is like one called as a prophet to join the band of disciples to replicate the life of a "sent one" as did Jesus (who was an apostle from God—Heb 3:1) and Paul, who was sent by Jesus (Rom 1:1; Gal 1:1). Paul tells us to "Follow my example, as I follow the example of Christ" (1 Cor 11:1; 1 Tim 1:13–16; 1 Pet 2:21). This example-following of Jesus (and other apostles) is not optional: if one "belongs to Christ," one is necessarily a disciple who should be commissioned to do the works (and even "greater works" [John 14:12] "because I go to the Father"; it's now Jesus' job to bestow gifts and ministries). Example-following was not optional for the original 84 disciples (Matt 10; Mark 6:7–13; Luke 9—10), nor is this charismatic ministry and discipleship optional for us today. The universally recognized binding force of Jesus' last command to us, his church, is important in this connection.

The so-called "Great Commission" (Matt 28:19–20) involves our tapping into "all authority" (a term associated with exorcism of demons, Mark 3:15; 24:9–14; Mark 3:14–15; 6; 7; Luke 4:36; 9:1; 10:19). We tap into this authority of Jesus to disciple the nations so that they will "obey everything I [Jesus] have commanded you." This certainly involves the earlier commissions (Matt 10; Mark 3, 6; Luke 9, 10) to receive the "grace" (charismata) to assert "all authority" given to Jesus, who likewise bestows it on us.

To summarize the sequence:

1. Paul lays out his own commission for the gospel in verse 1 (to be a servant of Jesus Christ, an apostle, sent out and "set apart").
2. This process of being 'set apart' into the New Covenant Spirit is predicted in the Old Testament and fulfilled in the life of Jesus, who was also "set apart" by the Spirit of holiness and vindicated by the Spirit of [miracle] power (vv 2–4). In this process Jesus is the prototype for all believers.
3. Therefore, "we" (all "who belong to Jesus Christ"), because of Jesus' pattern, are to receive empowering ("grace") and apostleship (Rom 1:5, 11) and are called to have faith (revelation prompting obedience, Rom 1:5, 6, 8, 12), to be "saints" ("those set apart for ministry," Rom 1:7); and to mutually encourage others through faith (again, revelation prompting obedience, Rom 1:12), as well as to make "faith" known "all over the world" (Rom 1:8).

So Paul's mission tells us about the nature of the gospel. In the gospel we are called by the Spirit to emulate Jesus, that is, to be a servant and to obey the mandate to be "set apart" (as a priest or prophet). This being "set apart" into a ministry is characterized by the miracle power of the Spirit in order to make "faith" (hearing and obeying, as in the New Covenant) known among all people. Essentially the same point about the nature of the gospel found here at the beginning of the Epistle to the Romans is found at the end in Romans 15.

Romans 15:15–19, the latter of the epistolary bookends, summarizes Romans 1:1–6 as it expresses how the gospel is "fully proclaimed" by Paul's being "graced," a "servant," set apart in a "priestly duty," and by the "power of signs and miracles, through the power of the Spirit"—all so that the Gentiles might be similarly "sanctified" (set apart as priestly/prophetic servants) to present the gospel "fully" to others:[12]

> I have written you quite boldly on some points, as if to remind you of them again, because of the grace God gave me [16] to be a minister of Christ Jesus to the Gentiles with the priestly duty of proclaiming the gospel of God, so that the Gentiles might become an offering acceptable to God, sanctified by the Holy Spirit. [17] Therefore I glory in Christ Jesus in my service to God. [18] I will not venture to speak of anything except what Christ has accomplished through me in leading the Gentiles to obey God by what I have said and done— [19] by the power of signs and miracles, through the power of the Spirit. So from Jerusalem all the way around to Illyricum, I have fully proclaimed the gospel of Christ (Romans 15:15–19 NIV).

The gospel, or mission, of God, then, seems to involve calling (as a prophet), grace (charismatic empowering), and faith (immediate revelation and obedience)—all for the purpose of spreading (apostleship —"sending out") this experience to others.

What is absolutely crucial here when Paul describes his mission is an accurate translation of verse 19 that ends "by word and deed, by the power of signs and wonders, by the power of the Spirit of God—so that from Jerusalem and all the way around to Illyricum I have fulfilled the gospel of Christ."

Now we will examine how most Protestant translations almost unconsciously "clarify" this presentation of the Gospel by an addition that is totally unsupported by the text because it makes no sense to them in any other way. These translations are a presentation of the "gospel" as an entirely verbal process, hence: "I have fully preached the gospel of Christ" (KJV, Geneva, NAS, RSV, NET, NJB) or "proclaimed the gospel" (NIV, TNIV). Other translations come closer: "I have fulfilled the ministry of the gospel" (ESV), "I have caused to abound the Gospel" (Geneva), "presented the Good News" (NLT).

In the original Greek text there is no "preaching," "proclaiming," or "ministry"—these are added to reinforce the Protestant idea of how the gospel is delivered, that is, only verbally—using words. In traditional Protestantism, the gospel can be presented only as a spoken message.

So how else could it be demonstrated?

By contrast, Paul in our Romans' passage is simply practicing the normative way the gospel is presented. We see him in 1 Corinthians 4:19–20 confronting opposing preachers by testing how they presented the gospel. The test? Paul says, "I will find out not the talk of these arrogant people but their power." Then Paul appeals to the essence of his Christian program: "For the kingdom of God does not consist in talk but in power." Isn't this exactly what we see in the "programmatic statement" of Jesus in Luke 4:18 as he introduced his mission?

Accordingly, "by word and deed" (prophecy and miracle) is the way Jesus actually manifests his mission through the Spirit and in so doing this is what "fulfills" the gospel (kingdom) of Christ. Hence, the literal translation of Paul's statement: "I will not venture to speak of anything except what Christ has accomplished through me to bring the Gentiles to obedience—by word and deed, by the power of signs and wonders, by the power of the Spirit of God—so that from Jerusalem and all the way around to Illyricum I have fulfilled *[peplērōkenai]* the gospel of Christ." Here it is clear that the gospel of Christ is revealed in the characteristic way that God "bears witness" (Heb 2:4)—with empowered word (inspired utterance), with an emphasis on God's power. That is how Paul sees the gospel "fulfilled" or "completed"—and describes it as such. No traditional "three points and a poem" for his gospel presentations—at least to these Gentiles!

Romans 1:16–17 says the same thing, essentially, about the nature and mission of the gospel, except that it focuses more narrowly on the problem of receiving or rejecting faith: the "righteous one who lives by faith" or the wicked one who rejects God's revelation and descends into chaos and death.

I am not ashamed of the gospel, because it is the power of God for the salvation of everyone who believes: first for the Jew, then for the Gentile. [17] For in the gospel a righteousness from God is revealed, a righteousness that is by faith from first to last, just as it is written: "The righteous will live by faith" (Rom 1:16–17 NIV).

Several points are worth noting here:

1. Paul takes a stand against any who would suggest he should be ashamed of God's message and power. We see this crowd unveiled for who they really are in 1:28–32—those claiming to be wise.
2. The nature of the gospel is power (*dunamis,* "miracle/ mighty work") of God. Elsewhere Paul describes the kingdom of God as consisting "not in talk, but in power" (same word, 1 Cor 4:20).
3. This power gospel results in salvation (not simply going to heaven, but used mostly when talking of healing and deliverance miracles).
4. The point of this, however, is that this salvation comes to "everyone who believes" ("to all who are afar off—whomever God calls" Acts 2:39). The New Covenant of revelation into the heart or "faith" represents righteousness being revealed from God (God's way of doing things). And what is God's way? "Faith into faith" or "revelation into/toward more revelation"—the essence of the New Covenant (Isa 59:12; Jer 31:33). In other words, revelation begins with listening, as Paul said: "Faith comes by hearing, and hearing through the word of Christ" (Rom 10:17). In Romans 1:16–32 we also find a pivotal choice that parallels Adam's choice to "hear God and obey" (the tree of life) or eat from "the tree of the knowledge of good and evil." Adam's wrong choice rejected God's way of faith and life for the misery and death resulting from human prideful knowledge. This crucial choice is exactly what Romans 1:16–32 is all about: Do you live via faith (God's right way) or die by rejecting this knowledge of God seen so clearly in creation (just as Adam saw in creation in Genesis 2:19–20)?

Romans 8:13–16 includes a very important descriptor of a normative "child/son of God" as one who "is led by the Spirit of God" (Rom 8:14). More importantly, this larger passage paraphrases the New Covenant expressed in Jeremiah 31:33–34:

> "This is the covenant I will make with the house of Israel after that time," declares the LORD. "I will put my law in their minds and write it on their hearts. I will be their God, and they will be my people. 34 No longer will a man teach his neighbor, or a man his brother, saying, 'Know the LORD,' because they will all know me, from the least of them to the greatest," declares the LORD. "For I will forgive their wickedness and will remember their sins no more." (Jer 31:33–34 NIV)

Note how the Jeremiah passage is paralleled in the Romans passage below through these themes:

1. the prophetic Spirit leading/teaching the Law in the mind and heart,
2. which results in God's forgiving and remembering our sins no more,
3. which leads into the goal of a relationship with God as his people:

> Do not offer the parts of your body to sin, as instruments of wickedness, but rather offer yourselves to God, as those who have been brought from death to life; and offer the parts of your body to him as instruments of righteousness. 14 For sin shall not be your master, because you are not under law, but under grace. 15 What then? Shall we sin because we are not under law but under grace? By no means! 16 Don't you know that when you offer yourselves to someone to obey him as slaves, you are slaves to the one whom you obey—whether you are slaves to sin, which leads to death, or to obedience, which leads to righteousness? (Rom 6:13–16 NIV)

These three New Covenant themes (stated in Isa 59:21 and Jer 31:33–34) are clear in this Romans passage, as they are in many other passages throughout Paul's writings: the Spirit, forgiveness, intimacy with God.

In Paul's Epistle to the Galatians, we find them explicit.

GALATIANS: THE CONFLICT OF THE COVENANTS—AGAIN

Different New Testament text for this section, yet same issue. Just as John, Acts, Romans, and certainly Hebrews (following) are contending for the New Covenant expression of the Spirit against a regression into the Old Covenant of the written word and human wisdom, so the core of Galatians deals with the same issue.

By contrast, for the Reformers, especially Luther, the issue in Galatians dealt with a contemporary theological fight: are you saved (going to heaven) by "works of the Law" (legalism) or by "faith" (believing the creedal point that Jesus died for your sins so that you don't need to do acts of penance or "works")?

But this really isn't what Galatians is about.

Galatians is continuing the New Testament debate described in so many places (especially in 2 Corinthians 3): As a Spirit-filled Christian, does one regress back to the Old Covenant of the Jewish scribes to keep the rules they create by human pride, or does one enter the New Covenant by receiving the miracle-producing New Covenant Spirit, that is, living by faith—hearing directly into the heart and obeying God.[13]

Let's look at Galatians 3:1–9 to confirm this:

> You foolish Galatians! Who has bewitched you? Before your very eyes Jesus Christ was clearly portrayed as crucified. 2 I would like to learn just one thing from you: Did you receive the Spirit by observing the law, or by believing what you heard? 3Are you so foolish? After beginning with the Spirit, are you now trying to attain your goal by human effort? 4 Have you suffered so much for nothing—if it really was for nothing? 5 Does God give you his Spirit and work miracles among you because you observe the law, or because you believed what you heard? 6Consider Abraham: "He believed God, and it was credited to him as righteousness." 7 Understand, then, that those who have faith are

> children of Abraham. [8] The Scripture foresaw that God would justify the Gentiles by faith, and announced the gospel in advance to Abraham: "All nations will be blessed through you." [9] So those who have faith are blessed along with Abraham, the man of faith. (NIV)

This is exactly the temptation that Jesus faced in the wilderness (Matt 4 || Luke 4).

First, what are we talking about here? The punch line of this section is the foreseeing that God "would justify the Gentiles by faith." This is the gospel given in advance to Abraham! And what is that gospel? "Those who have faith (hear from God directly—remember, Abraham didn't have a Bible, Gen 26:5) are blessed along with Abraham, the man of faith."

Now, back to the beginning of the Galatians passage. What is the connection between Jesus being crucified, the "hearing of faith," and the miracles? As in Matthew 26:28 (par Mark 14:24 || Luke 22:20, 1 Cor 11:25) and five places in Hebrews, the blood of Jesus ratified/signed the New Covenant of the Spirit. Like the readers of Hebrews, the believers of Galatia don't get this. So Paul reminds them in v 1. He then proves this by asking if they received the Spirit of prophecy and miracles by following the written rules of the Old Covenant or by a "hearing of faith." The conservative Protestant translators of the NIV miss the point and unwittingly regress into Old Covenant, traditional religious thinking when they translate "hearing of faith" (a prophetic experience) as "believing what you heard" (that is, "accepting the creedal doctrine taught to you"). Obviously, receiving the prophetic Spirit and doing miracles is not a result of holding proper doctrine (the devil holds proper doctrine)! That's exactly the problem Paul is trying to correct!

No. Receiving the prophetic Spirit and doing miracles are the result of the revelation of faith—the "hearing of faith" which is a charismatic act! It is what happens when you enter the New Covenant of the prophetic Spirit—like Abraham did—the father of all "who have faith"!

The same pattern holds in the Epistle to the Hebrews: God reveals himself (his "word") through Jesus who receives, bears, and bestows the

Spirit to others. In Hebrews Jesus is presented primarily as the crucial mediator of the Spirit covenant.

THE MESSAGE OF THE EPISTLE TO THE HEBREWS: JESUS AS THE INDISPENSABLE MEDIATOR OF THE NEW COVENANT SPIRIT

The thesis statement of Hebrews, corresponding to John, is in the first verses of the epistle.

> Long ago, at many times and in many ways, God spoke to our fathers by the prophets, [2] but in these last days he has spoken to us by his Son, whom he appointed the heir of all things, through whom also he created the world. [3] He is the radiance of the glory of God and the exact imprint of his nature, and he upholds the universe by the word of his power. After making purification for sins, he sat down at the right hand of the Majesty on high (Heb 1:1–3 ESV).

Here again are the central themes of Jesus' mission and the plan of the whole Bible: God's "speaking" is emphasized as coming through the role models of Scripture ("prophets"—including the patriarchs and key leaders); but now, at the climax of history (the time of the New Covenant), through God's Son.

Jesus perfectly fits the pattern of all creation:

1. As the Wisdom, "through whom He made the universe" and sustains it (continuous present tense) "by his powerful word."
2. Doing this makes Jesus God's "Son," "the heir of all things," "the radiance of his glory and the exact representation of his being." In other words, doing exactly and perfectly what God wants to be done.
3. Jesus introduces the ideal relationship through his death; that is, he renders the Old Covenant "obsolete" by paying the death penalty of the Old Covenant. In his death he ratifies and mediates the New Covenant of the Spirit (Heb 8:6–12; 9:15; 12:24–25). We enter a new creation as we are "raised to

newness of life" with Christ in the Spirit. (Rom 6).Okay, this is important!

4. What is the first thing noted (emphasized) about Jesus in this thesis statement? He has spoken "in these last days" which means he continues to speak from heaven, as Hebrews 3:7; 4:7; and 12:25 emphasize! The core idea of the New Covenant is that God now writes his guidance/instruction directly and immediately into our heart (8:10–11). In fact, in v 3, Jesus is "sustaining all things [including us] by his powerful word." In other words, the Genesis 1 normative pattern of the mighty creative and sustaining "word" is applied here to all of us in the present as a continuous action! Remember here that "word" is not simply Scripture, but much more: the mighty word that creates and generates signs, wonders, and the charismata.

This speaking "in these last days" is done after Jesus ratified the New Covenant by providing "purification for sins." He now sits at the Father's right hand and now manages angels (messengers/communicators/ministering spirits) "sent to serve those who inherit salvation" (1:7, 14).

God testified to the "word" of Jesus "by signs, wonders and various miracles, and gifts of the Holy Spirit distributed according to his will" (2:4; 1 Cor 1:7–8), and continues to do so: "So, as the Holy Spirit says [present tense]: "Today, if you hear his voice, do not harden your hearts" (Heb 3:7, 15; 4:7, cf. 12:25; Mark 16:17–20; Jer 32:20).[14] Against traditional Protestantism (WCF, para 1), if the Epistle to the Hebrews is part of the New Testament canon that applies to all people in all ages, then the "Today" in this verse means "now" to the reader of these words.

Below is another passage (6:3–4) that is crucial to our understanding of the New Covenant as discussed above, where five times the prophetic word of God is the essence of what is rejected when one "falls away"—a notion to be identified with the "blasphemy of the Holy Spirit" (Mark 3:29 || Luke 12:10).

> It is impossible for those who have once been enlightened, who have tasted the heavenly gift, who have shared in the Holy Spirit, [5] who have tasted the goodness of the word of God and the powers of the coming age, [6] if they fall away, to be brought back to repentance, because to their loss they are crucifying the Son of God all over again and subjecting him to public disgrace (Heb 6:4–6 NIV).

The effects of this blasphemy (total rejection) of the Holy Spirit are eternal, if only because if one cannot "hear" and obey God's (prophetic) voice, one necessarily cannot "know" him. Again, the two essential parts of the New Covenant involve the prophetic word leading to the ultimate intimacy with God. The biblical emphasis is clear that one cannot "know" God without hearing and obeying his voice. Even being used in charismatic gifts of prophecy and miracles is no guarantee of one's ultimately "knowing" God if obedience is not part of the package (Matt 7:21–29). In traditional religion, miracles might "accredit" saints or apostles, but then again, they might not. The goal of God's revelation is intimacy and obedience, not simply expressions of power. Nevertheless, one cannot "know" God without receiving his revelation.

We examined the crucial "punch line" of Hebrews 12 previously in our discussion "A Little More Detail on the Covenants" and the verse that is the imperative of Hebrews: "See to it that you do not refuse him who speaks" (12:25). This theme is continued in chapter 13:7–8 which urges the readers to receive the "word" from leaders, then follow the process of receiving that word: "imitate their faith" (hearing God's voice and obeying). This "imitation" is implied in 1:1 (forefathers and prophets). Chapter 11 is offered as a long list of forefathers and prophets who are held out as examples (Jas 5:10). Certainly they looked for a heavenly city, but the constant that was repeated in each of their lives was that they lived by faith—that is, hearing and obeying God's voice.

This hearing and obeying should be done because of the divine, universal principle that "Jesus Christ is the same yesterday and today and forever." We are told to "imitate" Jesus to the same degree and extent that Paul did—in all the empowering and revealing charismata (1

Cor 4:16; 11:1; 1 Thes 1:5–7). Accordingly, it is Jesus who is the "author and finisher of our faith," which means that Jesus is our founder, leader, or initiator *(archēgon)* of our ability to hear and obey God, and moreover the one who completes our ability *(teleiōtēn)*. Against traditional religion, Jesus is not simply the one who formulated and fulfilled our doctrine ("the faith"), but the one who models and empowers the act of hearing and obeying God.

Why would God "also" testify so specifically "by signs, wonders and various miracles, and gifts of the Holy Spirit distributed according to his will" (2:4)? Could it be that this is the very charismatic, essential nature of the salvation that Paul, in "leading the Gentiles to obey God by word and deed . . . fully proclaimed/preached by the power of signs and miracles, through the power of the Spirit" (Rom 15:19; 2 Cor 12:12)? In other words, isn't the preaching of the gospel in the New Testament the combination of signs and wonders with a verbal explanation? That clearly seems to be the pattern in Acts and throughout the New Testament.

Bottom line: Jesus came to mediate the New Covenant by sacrificing his earthly life to remove sins. His death paid in full the Old Covenant, and prepared us for the New Covenant of the Spirit. This did not introduce a new set of "laws" but rather reaffirmed the original and ideal process of relating to God: hearing his "Torah"/instruction/guidance in our hearts and thereby knowing him, even as little Samuel knew God only when he heard his voice (1 Sam 3:7).

The nature of living out the New Covenant is seen in the Gallery of the Faithful in Hebrews 11: those who lived (and died) by faith (hearing God's voice and obeying)—God's new/old way of communicating in the New Covenant, that is, via the prophetic word/assurance/faith.

HEBREWS SPELLS OUT THE CORE VALUE–THE ESSENCE–OF ITS GOSPEL

It has always been the case that traditional religion has imposed its theology of "salvation" on the text of Hebrews. For the most part, the traditional Protestant notion of the New Covenant has emphasized that the animal sacrificial system of the Old Covenant has been replaced by the once-and-for-all sacrifice of Christ. In this way our sins can be forgiven, we are "saved," we can escape hell, and can now go to heaven. All of that is true, but it is derivative from the important point Hebrews actually makes, which is that the New Covenant is essentially "hearing" God's voice directly "today"—which is not the same as simply reading it in the Bible.

Proof of this is clear in Hebrews. The readers (including us) are warned about "falling away" after going through the "elementary teachings about Christ" (6:1). What are these teachings and how do they play out in the central experience of the believer? Note how these teachings—experiences, really—follow the sequence of John the Baptist's agenda for Jesus, and also that of John and Acts:

- repentance from acts that lead to death (Matt 3:2–12, 17 and parallels)
- faith in God (the revelation that is the basis of all these elements)
- instruction about baptisms (note the plural: in water and Spirit?)[15]
- the laying on of hands (reception of Spirit and His gifts for ministry (Acts 6:6–8; 8:17; 9:17; 19:6; 28:8; 1 Tim 4:14; 2 Tim 1:6)
- the resurrection of the dead
- eternal judgment (Matt 3:12 and parallels)

The central experience of the New Covenant, however, is the essence from which they "fall." This is crucially important to understand:

> It is impossible for those who have once been enlightened, who have tasted the heavenly gift, who have shared in the Holy Spirit, [5] who have tasted the goodness of the word of God and the powers of the coming age, [6] if they fall away, to be brought back to repentance, because to their loss they are crucifying the Son of God all over again and subjecting him to public disgrace (Heb 6:4–6 NIV).

Note that it is the prophetic revelation of the Holy Spirit expressed in five different ways from which the believer "falls away." Talk about emphasis! This experience of the revealing Holy Spirit is the central point of Hebrews—the New Covenant that the indispensable Jesus sacrificed so much to bring to us!

To deny or reject this experience and then attempt to return to it requires another "ratification" of the New Covenant by Jesus' blood and death—and that is not going to happen again. You are either in the New Covenant Spirit or you're not.

This denial of the Holy Spirit's ongoing revelation is the famous blasphemy of the Holy Spirit (Mark 3:29 and par). This is what makes Paragraph 1 of the Westminster Confession of Faith (". . . to commit the same wholly unto writing; which maketh the holy Scripture to be most necessary; those former ways of God's revealing his will unto his people being now ceased.") and similar traditional Protestant statements so terrifying: they explicitly deny the very core of what the New Testament affirms as central to the message of Scripture.

It is supremely ironic that this central and crucial denial of the prophetic revelation of the Spirit is in the service of "protecting" the canon of Scripture, when Scripture itself commands us "to desire earnestly the best gifts—especially that you may prophesy" (1 Cor 14:1)!

This description of what an apostate abandons is repeated in Hebrews 10:26–29.

> If we deliberately keep on sinning after we have received the knowledge of the truth, no sacrifice for sins is left, 27 but only a fearful expectation of judgment and of raging fire that will consume the enemies of God. 28 Anyone who rejected the law of Moses died without mercy on the testimony of two or three witnesses. 29 How much more severely do you think a man deserves to be punished who has trampled the Son of God under foot, who has treated as an unholy thing the blood of the covenant that sanctified him, and who has insulted the Spirit of grace? (NIV)

Continuing to "sin" results in no further remedy—Christ will not die again to ratify an even newer covenant. But when is this sin particularly egregious? "After we have received the knowledge of the truth." In popular Protestant theology "receiving the knowledge of the truth" means "we understand at least the basics of Christian doctrine." Yet among first century Jewish Christians it would mean the New Covenant experience of "the truth" as revealed knowledge from the Spirit.

But the act of apostasy involves three parallel elements:

1. Trampling the Son of God underfoot is not merely talking about Jesus, but is talking specifically about the nature of "son." A "son" is, in the Hebrew culture, one who characterizes a father. In this case, putting someone under one's foot is to show utter contempt, as is the case even today in the Middle East. When Saddam Hussein's statue was pulled down many whacked it with their shoes as the worst insult one could imagine—as was the case when the Iraqi news reporter threw his shoes at visiting United States president George W. Bush.
2. This passage, then, is saying that apostasy represents contempt for the son-pattern of God's plan—God's way of reaching out to us in love, in Jesus. In other words, it is denying the very mission and purpose of Jesus—to bring us the New Covenant Spirit of revelation, prophecy, and power. It is trampling under foot both that mission and the One who brought it. We see this exemplified further in the next parallel element where:
3. Treating "as an unholy thing the blood of the covenant that sanctified him" is a way of denying any significance to Jesus ratifying the New Covenant of the Spirit in his blood. And yet this is the truly divine act that makes Jesus supremely significant. "Sanctified him" means "commissioned for priestly or prophetic functions" much as indicated in Isaiah 59:21 and Jeremiah 31:33.
4. So treating the sanctifying blood of the covenant as "unholy" would be a so much greater evil than when a prominent

American actress betrayed beaten and suffering American POWs held in North Vietnam when she allegedly called them "hypocrites and liars" for their testimony of torture.[16] John McCain, the future senator and presidential candidate, was one of those prisoners whose blood was shed and body broken in covenant with his country, and who suffered all over again with emotional severity because of this peace activist. Her action was a bitter betrayal not only because it caused the suffering and death of her fellow citizens who tried to protect her and her people, but because she treated with utter contempt all this sacrifice and their code of honor to serve their country. This is what some of the readers of the Epistle to the Hebrews were doing to Jesus and his sacrifice that defends us from the powers of darkness and brings about the New Covenant of the Spirit for us.

5. The last act is even more clearly related to denying the voice of the Spirit: one who "has insulted the Spirit of grace."
6. "Insulting" we have discussed, but "Spirit of grace" needs amplifying. "Spirit," of course, refers to God's New Covenant Spirit of prophecy. This is emphasized by the use of the term, "Spirit of grace" (that is, *charis*, from which we get *charismata*– "grace things" or"gifts of the Holy Spirit." "Grace," then, as we saw above, does not primarily mean "unmerited favor" but rather, "a gift of power"—a "charismatic miracle-power" given freely and generously by God.[17] This is the central characteristic of the New Covenant empowering by the Spirit: the revealed, prophetic "word" of faith that teaches (Torah) and gives life, truth, and power (Isa 59:21; Jer 31:33). Denial of the "Spirit of grace" is denial of God's gracious gift of the prophetic Spirit—the Torah (teaching) written in the heart, or the "[prophetic] words in the mouth of [God's] children, forever."

Again, the summary and "punch line" of the message of Hebrews is chapter 12 with its defining verse 25: "See to it that you do not refuse him who speaks. If they did not escape when they refused him who warned them on earth, how much less will we, if we turn away from him who warns us from heaven?" This warning is not just from the Bible that posts the warning, rather the signpost points us to him who "warns" (present tense) "from heaven"![18]

This Hebrews chapter has been discussed previously at some length in Chapter 7: The Goal of the Bible—The New Covenant, yet it's crucial to emphasize here that refusing "him who speaks" is the same as refusing the promised New Covenant that was (and is) the essence of Jesus' mission. Since the central process of the New Covenant is the Holy Spirit revelation of God's Torah directly into the heart—our innermost being, leading to the ultimate goal of intimacy with God—we don't want to miss this!

Sadly, traditional, human religion seems to do everything in its power to avoid this climactic command in Hebrews: it explicitly does "refuse him who speaks" in its theologies and practices. Could it be that, like the Gospel of John, the Epistle to the Hebrews was addressed to Christians who had been steeped in the tradition of the scribes, who had denied the voice of God as a factor in their religion? The point of this book is that as an antithesis to "religion," the message of the God of the Bible is intimacy with our Triune God by means of hearing his direct and immediate voice in our hearts.

The central theme of the Bible is that the word of God is revealed directly to the human heart resulting in a testing in confrontations with evil—all with the goal toward intimacy with God. The emphasis of this "directly revealed word" theme is explicit in the above samples of New Testament literature.

CONCLUSION

This chapter surveyed four key New Testament books to demonstrate that the core nature of the biblical message is the powerful, creative voice of God and its testing. Specifically, it shows that the gospel of the New Testament is more than traditional Protestant ideas about "salvation." Rather, the "gospel is the [miracle] power of God unto salvation—so much more than being good and going to heaven! The next chapter examines the central mission of Jesus to show that his mission emphasized the revelation and power of God (working through love) that is a chief characteristic of the New Covenant Spirit. In this, his mission was to . . .

- introduce the New Covenant Spirit
- model the New Covenant Spirit for his disciples
- ratify (sign in blood) the New Covenant Spirit
- vindicate the New Covenant Spirit in his resurrection
- commission and bestow the New Covenant Spirit, and
- *become* the New Covenant Spirit to indwell our life and mission.

We shall now examine each of these actions in turn.

---

1. John 3:8; 5:24–25, 30, 37; 7:40; 8:26, 38, 40–47; 10:3–5, 16, 27; 11:42; 12:28, 49; 14:24; 16:13.
2. E.g., 1:5, 10–11; 3:20, 36; 5:40; 5:16; 7:7; 12:25, 48; 15:18–25; 17:14.
3. 85 times, almost always in the verb form, from the same root word as "faith" (*pistis*), hearing God's word and obeying.
4. For the story, see p. 139, note 9. Rabbi Eliezer ben Hyrcanus (ca. ad 40–118) was the main figure in the story of The Oven of Akhnai, an event which seems to have occurred close to the time John was recording his Gospel, or at least when the "not in heaven" doctrine was widespread.
5. That is emphasis! John actually mentions the process of hearing 54 times, mostly about Jesus. This theme occurs also in Revelation, where words from the root *akouō* appear about 40% more frequently ("He who has an ear to hear, let him hear").
6. The dispute among the scribes and Christians over the voice of God (or *bat kol*) as confirmation of divine truth emerges in the reactions to God's voice in John 12:28–30. "Father, glorify your name!' Then a voice came from heaven, "I have glorified it, and will glorify it again." The crowd that was there and heard it said it had thundered; others said an angel had spoken to him. Jesus said, "This voice was for your benefit, not mine."
7. This thesis is worked out in my two-part article, "'This is My Covenant with Them': Isaiah 59.19–21 as the Programmatic Prophecy of the New Covenant in the Acts of the Apostles." Part 1. *Journal of Pentecostal Theology* 17:1 (2008), 32–47 and Part 2. 17:2 (2008), 219–37. It also appears, slightly revised, as Appendix IV in *On the Cessation of the Charismata*, rev. ed. (Tulsa: Word & Spirit Press, 2010).
8. Chris Thomas, in "The Charismatic Structure of Acts" (*JPT, 10:1 [2004], 19–30)*, argues that the structure of Acts is determined by "literary markers" e.g., Acts 6:7;

[8:3]; 9:[28–]31; 12:24; 16:5[–6]; 19:20, in each case summarizing the "spread of the gospel and growth of the church." One might also note that each of these literary markers—summary statements—involve the spread, specifically, of "the word" (prophetic power) of God [my supplemental passages added in brackets]. He shows that there is a tight correlation between these markers and the content of each related panel: charismatic anointing by the Holy Spirit on key individuals ("children"? 2:39), spreading geographically (from Jerusalem to Rome—the two foci of Isa 59:19, east and west!).

9. The theme of unjust imprisonment and vindication of the prisoner is substantial in Acts, as in the case of the imprisonments of Peter: 4:1–31 (and John); 5:17–41; 12:1–19; and imprisonments of Paul: 8:3; 9:1–20; 16:19–39 (the most direct allusion to Isa 24:14–23); 22:4—27:44; 28:31. The last seven chapters of Acts report Paul's imprisonment and repeated vindications. An important contribution to the combined themes of power and suffering in Acts is a PhD dissertation by Martin Mittelstadt, "The Spirit and Suffering in Luke-Acts: Implications for a Pentecostal Pneumatology." PhD diss., Marquette University, 2002. This combination expresses the *central emphasis* of the Bible, that the life of faith consists in "hearing" the voice of God and obeying it, against often extreme testing. This, of course, expresses the very goal of Paul's life: Phil 3:10.

10. For indirect support of the notion that Paul is arguing in Romans for the readers' participation in the New Covenant of the Spirit in which one's sins "are remembered no more," see John A. Bertone, *"The Law of the Spirit": Experience of the Spirit and Displacement of the Law in Romans 8:1–16* (New York: Peter Lang, 2005); and Peder Borgen, "The Contrite Wrongdoer," in *Holy **Spirit** and Christian Origins* (Grand Rapids: Eerdmans, 2004), 181–92.

    "'But now we have been released from the Law, having died to that which held us captive, so we now serve in the newness of the Spirit and no longer under the old written code.' If Rom 7:7–25 was the explication of the first sentence of this pair, Rom 8:1–17 will unpack the second, in which the Spirit's newness is nothing less than the new creation in Christ proclaimed at 2 Cor 5:17." Richard Dillon, "The Spirit as Taskmaster and Troublemaker in Romans 8," *The Catholic Biblical Quarterly* 60, no. 4 (Oct. 1998): 682–702.

11. 1 Cor 14:1—second on the list, and the *characteristic gift* of the New Covenant (Acts 2:39 > Isa 59:21; also 2 Cor 3 > Jer 31:31–34), echoing the desire of Moses (Num 11:29).

12. Also pertinent, 1 Thes 1:5–8: ". . . our gospel came to you not only in word, but also in power and in the Holy Spirit and with full conviction You know what kind of men we proved to be among you for your sake. And you became imitators of us and of the Lord, for you received the word in much affliction, with the joy of the Holy Spirit, so that you became an example to all the believers in Macedonia and in Achaia. For not only has the word of the Lord sounded forth from you in Macedonia and Achaia, but your faith in God has gone forth everywhere. . . ."

    And 2 Tim 1:7–11: ". . . for God gave us a spirit not of fear but of power and love and self-control. Therefore do not be ashamed of the testimony about our Lord, nor of me his prisoner, but share in suffering for the gospel by the power of God, who saved us and called us to a holy calling, not because of our works but because of his own purpose and grace, which he gave us in Christ Jesus before the ages began, and which now has been manifested through the appearing of our Savior Christ Jesus, who abolished death and brought life and immortality to light through the gospel, for which I was appointed a preacher and apostle and teacher."

13. Something like this proposition appears in Todd A. Wilson, "The Leading of the Spirit and the Curse of the Law: Reassessing Paul's Response to the Galatian Crisis," *Tyndale Bulletin*, 57:1 (2006), 157–160. "The thesis of this study is that Paul intended his four references to the Law in 5:13—6:10 as an affirmation of the sufficiency of the Spirit to enable the Galatians to fulfill the Law and thereby avoid its curse." p. 157. I would clarify the process of "fulfilling the Law": the experience of the Spirit was not to introduce a new list of New Testament "rules" or laws to obey, or a kind of motivation to keep the laws of the Old Testament, but rather to "walk in the Spirit"—a life of "faith" as hearing and obedience to the immediate voice of God to "fulfill" his New Covenant.
14. For a discussion on how God continues to "confirm" or bear testimony via the revelation of spiritual gifts, see Ruthven, *On the Cessation of the Charismata* (rev. ed.), pp. 109–113. In this context Heb 2:4 also uses the word, "confirm" (*bebaiōsis*) for the same charismatic revelation of His word. 1 Cor 1:4–9 shows how this charismatic confirmation pattern moves from the demonstration (in power) of the gospel by Paul (v 6), to the charismata given to the church (v 5), to the future when the Church will continue to receive charismatic confirmation "to the end" (vv 7–9).

    I always thank God for you because of his grace given you in Christ Jesus. 5 For in him you have been enriched in *every* way [including charismata]—in all your speaking and in all your knowledge [spiritual gifts]— 6 because our testimony about Christ was *confirmed* in you. 7 Therefore you do not lack any spiritual gift as you eagerly wait for our Lord Jesus Christ to be revealed. 8 He will *keep you strong* [lit: "will *confirm*" by the charismata as in v 6] *to the end,* so that you will be blameless on the day of our Lord Jesus Christ. 9 God, who has called you into fellowship with his Son Jesus Christ our Lord, is faithful.
15. Note that "baptisms" is the only plural in the list. This cannot refer to the baptism of different people, because the others (repentance, faith, laying on of hands, resurrection, and eternal judgment) are all singular and applied to the same people.
16. Christopher Andersen, *Citizen Jane* (NYC: Henry Holt & Co.), 266.
17. On the charismatic emphasis in the New Testament on grace (*charis*) see J. Noland, "Grace as Power," *NovTest* 28 (Oct. 1986), 31, "a tangible [charismatic] power in the believer." So also, J. D. G. Dunn, *Jesus and the Spirit* (Philadelphia: Westminster, 1975), 202–205. G. Wetter, *Charis: Ein Beitrag zur Geschichte des altesten Christentums* (Leipzig: Hinrichs, 1913).
18. Cessationists make much of the past tense of Heb 2:4 "God also *testified* to it by signs, wonders and various miracles, and gifts of the Holy Spirit distributed according to his will." The rejoinder to this is that a pattern is being set here: that God *typically* "testifies" with miraculous charismata (see p. 137, note 5). Based on this pattern (2:4) of how God typically reveals himself, Hebrews clearly affirms that God not only spoke in the past, but *also continues* to speak "today" (3:7, 15; 4:7; 12:25)—the whole point of Heb 12. This element of God's speaking today appears to be an important, repeated theme in Hebrews.

PART FOUR
WHERE IS JESUS IN ALL OF THIS?

11

THE MISSION OF JESUS: THE SPIRIT COVENANT

Protestant theology has been criticized for being *about* Jesus rather than *from* Jesus. In other words, traditional Protestantism froze around the debate with Romanists over the cost of going to heaven and failed to take seriously the emphases of the New Testament about Jesus' stated mission that fell outside their theology.

For example, traditional Protestantism really does not understand the role of the kingdom of God (the central theme in Jesus' mission) with its signs and wonders in Jesus' ministry and how they are related to his overall goal and mission of introducing and bestowing the Spirit. Accordingly, the traditional creeds describing Jesus that become the basis for traditional theology are selective, fragmentary, and lack the coherent, transparent flow toward the objective of Jesus' mission stated so clearly in the New Testament.

This chapter will show that if we read the New Testament consistently and allow it to speak with its own voice, then Jesus' mission comes into much greater coherence. Focusing on the kingdom/New Covenant Spirit, Jesus came to . . .

1. introduce the kingdom/New Covenant Spirit (Matt 3:11 || Mark 1:8 || Luke 3:16; John 1:26,33; Luke 4:18; Rom 15:8);

2. model a perfect example of how to live out that kingdom, New Covenant Spirit in a ministry of revelation and power. “I have given you an example that you also should do as I have done” (John 13:15); Isa 61:1–2 > Acts 10:38; 1 Cor 11:1; 2 Cor 4:8–16; Phil 3:17; 1 Tim 3:16; 1 Pet 2:21–24; 3:18;
3. ratify (place his signature on) the kingdom/New Covenant Spirit in his blood (Matt 26:28–29 || Mark 14:24–25 || Luke 22:20, 1 Cor 11:25; Gal 3:10–16; Heb 9:15; 10:10; 12:24; 13:20–21;
4. vindicate the kingdom/New Covenant in the power of his resurrection (Rom 1:4–5; Phil 3:10-14; Rom 8:11–14; 1 Tim 3:16);
5. bestow the kingdom/New Covenant Spirit from Heaven (John 14:16–18, 26; 16:7; Acts 2:33; Eph 4:7–11); and, ultimately . . .
6. *become* the New Covenant (John 14:18; 14:26; 1 Cor 15:45; 2 Cor 3:17).

Here is where emphasis comes in. If we can agree that summary statements represent a core emphasis of a document, then look at these New Testament statements concentrating a mass of material about Jesus into a sentence or two. Particularly important is to answer the question: What does the New Testament explicitly say about why Jesus came?

1. JESUS’ MISSION WAS TO BAPTIZE PEOPLE INTO THE NEW COVENANT HOLY SPIRIT OF PROPHECY

Jesus is introduced by John the Baptist in all four Gospels as having the mission of baptizing people into the Holy Spirit (two witnesses add “and fire”—purifying). John came to “prepare” for the “mightier” and more important Jesus. The preparation consisted of repentance and sealing that repentance with water baptism as a sign of washing away sins or death to the old life, being raised into a new life. The importance of this is that repentance and baptism anticipated the removal of the penalties of the Old Covenant (punishment, death) in preparation for the New Covenant. Baptism is a sign of preparation for the New Covenant at which time the Spirit is to come. Henceforth in the New Covenant the Law would be revealed into one's heart (Jer 31:33; Isa 59:21) by the ongoing action of the prophetic Spirit of the New Covenant (Acts 2:38–39; Gal 3; 2 Cor 3). In the Gospel of John, this New Covenant Spirit is experienced as "believing"; in Acts it is the "word" as utterance; in Hebrews it is the "voice of God" (Heb 3:7, 15; 4:7; 12:26).

The biggest single emphasis about Jesus' mission is recorded in all four Gospels—at the beginning of Jesus' ministry (emphasis, again). Here John the Baptist outlines his own mission and that of Jesus:

> "I baptize you with water for repentance. But after me will come one who is more powerful than I, whose sandals I am not fit to carry. He will baptize you with the Holy Spirit and with fire. His winnowing fork is in his hand, and he will clear his threshing floor, gathering his wheat into the barn and burning up the chaff with unquenchable fire." (Matthew 3:11–12 NIV).

> And he preached, saying, "After me comes he who is mightier than I, the strap of whose sandals I am not worthy to stoop down and untie. [8] I have baptized you with water, but he will baptize you with the Holy Spirit" (Mark 1:7–8 ESV).

> John answered them all, saying, "I baptize you with water, but he who is mightier than I is coming, the strap of whose sandals I am not worthy to untie. He will baptize you with the Holy Spirit and fire" (Luke 3:16 ESV).

> John answered them, "I baptize with water, but among you stands one you do not know. . . . [31] I myself did not know him, but for this purpose I came baptizing with water, that he might be revealed to Israel." [32] And John bore witness: "I saw the Spirit descend from heaven like a dove, and it remained on him. [33] I myself did not know him, but he who sent me to baptize with water said to me, 'He on whom you see the Spirit descend

and remain, this is he who baptizes with the Holy Spirit'" (John 1:26, 31–33 ESV).

The central message is clear: John came to "prepare" (Matt 3:3; 11:10; Mark 1:3–4; Luke 3:4; 11:27). This gospel of preparation is shown most clearly in Mark's Gospel summarizing John's mission: "And so John came, baptizing in the desert region and preaching a baptism of repentance for the forgiveness of sins."

It is important to stress that John does not place his service on the same level as Jesus; obviously both ministries were ordered by God, but what Jesus is sent to do is the goal—the most important mission—to baptize in the Spirit! You certainly don't get that impression from traditional Protestantism!

Instead, John's message of preparation is the emphasis of traditional Protestantism: repentance and baptism in water for the forgiveness of sins. Since this was the issue of the Protestant conflict with Catholics, there was no pressure to explore what the Bible actually had to say about Jesus' mission to "baptize in the Holy Spirit." Hence, the role of the Holy Spirit is confined to the Protestant *ordo salutis*—the sequence of salvation (that ends up in heaven). This sequence can run something like this: Foreknowledge, Predestination, Calling, Regeneration, Faith, Repentance, Justification, Adoption, Perseverance, Mortification, Sanctification, and Glorification.[1]

Trouble is, when one studies the mention of God's Spirit in the Bible statistically, the term overwhelmingly correlates (where the context is clear) with prophetic revelation or power—actions that traditional Protestant theology claims to have ceased. Here again, the consistent emphasis of the Bible itself is denied by the Protestant version of the ancient, failed doctrine of the scribes and Pharisees: cessationism. (I plan to deal with this Protestant problem with the Spirit in a sequel titled, tentatively, *How Protestants Rewrote the Bible)*.

So while the mission of John the Baptist was preparation for Jesus and the Spirit by repentance and baptism, the clearly-stated mission of Jesus included John's mission, but focused on the "baptism in the Holy Spirit"—the New Covenant gift of the Spirit of prophecy and intimacy with the Father. After all, Jesus tells us: ". . . this is eternal life, that they know [have intimacy with] thee the only true God, and Jesus Christ whom thou hast sent" (John 17:3).

This mission of Jesus plays out in the book of Acts, as we have seen, when Peter responds to the final question of his audience: "Brothers, what shall we do?" The first part of the answer is the Baptist's: "Peter replied, 'Repent and be baptized, every one of you, in the name of Jesus Christ for the forgiveness of your sins'" (Acts 2:38). And this is where traditional Protestantism puts the period. It's over. If the Spirit is mentioned at all, it is to work only in the *ordo salutis* and nothing more. John's stage of preparation is the essence of Protestantism—not Peter's (or the Bible's).

But Peter goes on: "and you will receive the gift of the Holy Spirit, for this promise/covenant is for you and for your children and for those who are afar off—even as many as the Lord your God shall call" (Acts 2:38). Since it is placed as the action point, or climax of the most important speech in all of Christianity, Luke emphasizes this quotation from Isaiah 59:21. Peter (and Luke) are here emphasizing the explicit, stated mission of Jesus that John had foretold as witnessed in all four Gospels.

The mission of Jesus was to immerse people into the Holy Spirit—the Spirit of revelation and prophecy—according to the goal statements of the New Testament Covenant: Isaiah 59:21 and Jeremiah 31:33. This charismatic mission of Jesus is further illustrated by the explicit purpose statements that we find in the New Testament. Luke introduces Jesus' mission via the prophecy of Simeon:

> "for my eyes have seen your salvation 31 that you have prepared in the presence of all peoples" (Luke 2:30–31 ESV).

Jesus is to provide revelation to the Gentiles and glory (God's presence) to Israel (actually it is both to both) but this is poetic construction here. This revelation and presence is characteristic of the New Covenant of the Spirit (2 Cor 3). The next passage is universally regarded as Jesus' programmatic statement about his mission. Note the prophetic, healing, and deliverance elements in this mission:

And the scroll of the prophet Isaiah was given to him. He unrolled the scroll and found the place where it was written, [18] "The Spirit of the Lord is upon me, because he has anointed me to proclaim good news to the poor. He has sent me to proclaim liberty to the captives and recovering of sight to the blind, to set at liberty those who are oppressed, [19] to proclaim the year of the Lord's favor." [20] And he rolled up the scroll and gave it back to the attendant and sat down. And the eyes of all in the synagogue were fixed on him. [21] And he began to say to them, "Today this Scripture has been fulfilled in your hearing." (Luke 4:17–21 ESV)

This agenda statement of Jesus—his statement of purpose—has its counterpoint and continuation in Acts 2:39, which cites Isaiah 59:21, where the

> "And as for me, this is my covenant with them," says the LORD: "My Spirit that is upon you, and my words that I have put in your mouth, shall not depart out of your mouth, or out of the mouth of your offspring, or out of the mouth of your children's offspring," says the LORD, "from this time forth and forevermore" (ESV).

In this way, Jesus' promise, or covenant, of the Spirit continues in his children, or disciples, forever. Unlike traditional Protestantism, Jesus did not intend his prophetic and miracle agenda to stop with him or even with his immediate apostles, but the charismata were to continue until "the end" (1 Cor 13:10). The scriptural principle is clear: "it is the same God who empowers them all [all the charismata] in everyone (1 Cor 12:6).[2] Thus a continuous experiencing of the ministry of apostles and prophets is to continue until we all attain to the whole measure of the fullness of Christ" (Eph 4:13).

Two of the stated reasons Jesus came was to "testify to the truth" (John 18:37) and to "destroy the works of the devil" (1 John 3:8). The testifying to the truth did not end during his trial (John 18) but continued as part of the New Covenant witness of the Spirit or "teaching" into the heart (John 14:16, 26; 15:26). Destroying the works of the devil involved not only dealing with sin (the context of 1 John 1:8), but also with the physical damage he did as we see in another key summary statement:

> . . . how God anointed Jesus of Nazareth with the Holy Spirit and with power. He went about doing good and healing all who were oppressed by the devil, for God was with him (Acts 10:38 ESV).

As we shall see, this summary agrees with most of the summaries of Jesus' earthly ministry in the Gospels which were written later than the epistles to provide a more complete record and emphasis of Jesus's mission.

The foregoing section shows that Jesus introduces his mission as primarily one of baptizing in the Holy Spirit—the prophetic and miracle power that is the essence of the Christian experience on the way toward intimacy with God. The following section shows the next phase of Jesus' mission: to provide a perfect example of how to live out that New Covenant Spirit in a ministry of miracle power and revelation—"a prophet mighty in deed and word before God and all the people" (Luke 24:19).

2. JESUS MODELED HIS MISSION PERFECTLY FOR HIS TRAINEES TO FOLLOW

The mission of Jesus involved a sizable emphasis on discipleship. Discipleship in the New Testament is quite different in goals and method than contemporary Protestant seminary education. Rather, it involved intensive field experience, all the while replicating as exactly as possible the charismatic mission of Jesus. Proof of this is that Jesus does not reject the term "rabbi" to describe himself some 13 times. A rabbi of that time expected that his disciples would copy not only his words but his deeds. Accordingly, at one point, Jesus offered a generalization that appears to move beyond the immediate context of foot washing: "I have given you an example that you also should do as I have done" (John 13:15).

Jesus begins his ministry—and modeling of it for his disciples—with baptism (Matt 3:13–17 || Mark 1:9–11 || Luke 3:21–22 || John 1:28–33) in order to "fulfill all righteousness" (Matt 3:15). This establishes the pattern of the act of cleansing the sin of the Old Covenant (symbolized by death, burial, and resurrection) to be raised into Christ (Rom 3:6–13; Gal 3:26–29; esp. Col 2:10–15). First Peter 3:21–22 notes that baptism provides "a pledge of a good conscience toward God" and "saves" by the resurrection of Jesus. We know that a "good conscience" is "written on the heart" by God (Rom 2:15), just as the Spirit writes the instructions of God on the heart in the New Covenant (Jer 31:33 > 2 Cor 3; Heb 8:10–11). So, to "follow Jesus in baptism" means that, in this act, He prepares us for the coming of the prophetic, revealing Spirit who raises us into a new life in the Spirit by the power of his resurrection (Rom 8:9b–17).

Moreover, Jesus models faith—hearing and obeying—as the ideal for ministry and even the conduct of life itself: "I tell you the truth, the Son can do nothing by himself; he can do only what he sees his Father doing, because whatever the Father does, the Son does also. For the Father loves the Son and shows him all he does. . . . By myself I can do nothing: I judge only as I hear, and my judgment is just, for I seek not my own will, but the will of the one who sent me, the Father" (John 5:19–20, 30).

With regard to Jesus' miracle power it is clear that his intention was for his disciples to imitate him. For example, in the story of the fig tree withering (Mark 11:12–14, 18–24), Jesus did not indulge in a theological discourse on Israel's rejection of the gospel (as is a common theme in traditional Protestantism), but rather, as is typical of him, he cut to the heart of the matter—faith (hearing God and obeying). The lesson he chooses is the power of faith to uproot mountains ("Have faith in God," Jesus answered, "I tell you the truth, if anyone says to this mountain, 'Go, throw yourself into the sea,' and does not doubt in his heart but believes that what he says will happen, it will be done for him"). Could it be that the "he" in "what he says will happen" refers to what God "says" in the experience: "Have faith in God"? Thus, "faith is the assurance of things hoped for" (Heb 11:1), that is assurance from God—a substance, the thing itself, a prophetic experience of a future event. A clear example of this faith-assurance is seen in the Old Testament when Elijah heard from God that there would be rain. He immediately spoke this word of prophetic faith to Ahab, then he bowed down with his face between his knees as he prayed for rain, trusting God that it would come (1 Kng 18:1–45). Here we see that faith is generated and sustained through the intimate relationship Elijah had with God, the same kind of relationship that Jesus expects to be normal for his disciples.

The New Covenant Spirit mission of Jesus is clear in his explicit charismatic instructions to his disciples: to spread the kingdom of God as normatively expressed (Matt 11:4–5) in healings and deliverance. Both of these actions are indicators that the disciples represent the Messiah. It was for that reason, "He called his twelve disciples to him and gave them authority to drive out evil spirits and to heal every disease and sickness" (Matt 10:1). "As you go, announce this message: 'The kingdom of heaven is near.' Heal the sick, raise the dead, cleanse those who have leprosy, drive out demons. Freely you have received, freely give'" (vv 7–8).

Similarly, he chose 72 others[3] to do essentially the same thing: "Heal the sick who are there and tell them, 'The kingdom of God is near you'" (Luke 10:9). In each case, it is clear that Jesus desired to have his kingdom ministry replicated in his (now) 84 disciples—and, by extension, to the readers of this story. Notice that this large number of "sent out" ones does not conform to the traditional rigid and limited number of twelve apostles that Jesus chose, since in Luke 10:1 alone, there are 72 who were "apostled"—"sent out" (Gk: *apesteilen*).

Traditional Protestantism doubts that the commissions to the 12 and the 72 have anything to do with Christians today. In this old tradition, all this healing and deliverance, along with writing Scripture, is relegated to apostles alone to help corroborate that maybe 3 of these 84 wrote Scripture![4] Remember the Protestant argument against the Catholic position that the so-called last apostle (the pope) alone had binding authority to write new doctrine in the form of encyclicals, that is, writings circulated throughout the church. Protestants responded by claiming that this papal function (writing authoritative doctrine, or Scripture) was limited to the true apostles in the first century. Hence, the apostles' main job (as first-century popes) was to write Scripture (encyclicals).

What traditional Protestants do believe is that Jesus commissioned everybody in another passage: Matthew 28:19–20. It is claimed that this Great Commission is quite different from the earlier commissioning accounts (Matt 10; Mark 6; Luke 9 and 10) because it merely involves teaching all nations and there is no mention of miracles in this commission. Besides the problem that the so-called Great Commission is really no different in substance from the other commissionings because it replicates their essential charismatic themes and message, there are several other problems in confining Jesus's mission to this Matthew passage:

1. Jesus's preface to the commission notes that "all power [authority: *exousia*] is given to me in heaven and on earth." This is the same power word that is used for authority/power of casting out demons, which also appears in the preface to the commissions of the 12 and the 72 (Luke 9:1; 10:1).
2. This preface is connected by a "therefore," meaning a causal connection with the commission to come: because Jesus has demon-casting authority (". . . all authority in heaven and on earth . . ." Matt 28:18), "therefore" the disciples are to make other disciples with this kind of authority. To guarantee the presence of this authority, Jesus promises to be "with them to the end of the age." Recall the simple curriculum in Mark 3:14–15: "that they might be with him and that he might send them out to preach and to have authority to drive out demons." These same elements are the essence of the "Great Commission."
3. As we have seen, baptism is a sign of entering the New Covenant of the Spirit. This passage specifies that they are to be baptized—not in some ritualized formula—but in the

"name" (authority and character) of the Father (who sent Jesus on his mission of power), the Son (who came to baptize in the Spirit and commission disciples to do the same), and the Spirit (the New Covenant Spirit of prophecy and power).

4. Above all, the commission here is to make disciples (that is, to replicate the teachers' life and mission). Recall an important principle in the New Testament: "imitate me as I imitate Christ" (1 Cor 11:1; 1 Thes 1:6; Heb 6:12, cf. 1 Cor 4:16). And what are they to imitate? "Teaching them to obey everything I have commanded you."[5] "Everything"? Certainly this includes what Jesus commanded them in the other similar-sounding commissioning accounts, where he "gave them authority to drive out evil spirits and to heal every disease and sickness" (Matt 10:1)! And it includes the activity of the 72 who "returned with joy and said, 'Lord, even the demons submit to us in your name'" (Luke 10:17). What name is that? The name of Jesus, the one who has "all authority in heaven and on earth"!

These four points against confining Jesus' mission to the Matthew Great Commission are consistent with the themes in the commission of Jesus in Acts, as well:

> And while staying with them he ordered them not to depart from Jerusalem, but to wait for the promise of the Father, which, he said, "you heard from me; [5] for John baptized with water, but you will be baptized with the Holy Spirit not many days from now." [6] So when they had come together, they asked him, "LORD, will you at this time restore the kingdom to Israel?" [7] He said to them, "It is not for you to know times or seasons that the Father has fixed by his own authority. [8] But you will receive power when the Holy Spirit has come upon you, and you will be my witnesses in Jerusalem and in all Judea and Samaria, and to the end of the earth." (Acts 1:4–8 ESV)

The pattern here is very similar to the other commissioning

accounts: the disciples receive the kingdom (actually, the Spirit, based on the authority of the Father). They will then be witnesses (tell what they actually saw) to the world. All very similar to the Great Commission—power from the Father in Acts 1:8 corresponds to "all authority is given to me" in Matthew 28:19; and baptism with the Spirit enables disciples to be "my witnesses" to the end of the earth.

Given the parallels with the other highly charismatic commissioning accounts, it is clear that the Matthean commission means what it says, that is, it encompasses and conveys the same essential charismatic themes of the New Covenant Spirit. This is confirmed in the Pentecost sermon—the charter, founding address of Christianity, especially its "punch line" in Acts 2:38–39, which is the fulfillment of Isaiah 59:21. The prophecy of Isaiah 59:19–21 actually provides the entire thematic structure of Acts, especially chapter 2[6]—so this prophecy is not some incidental, throw-away quote. The Isaiah prophecy is the crucial, climactic goal for the Bible as a whole and for the mission of Jesus, specifically. This is why Paul paraphrases it when he generalizes (a statement of emphasis): "The charismata and [prophetic] calling of God are not withdrawn" (Rom 11:29). This is a response to the problem of the Jews' rejecting the gospel (Rom 9—11) when Paul quotes Isaiah 59:20 and paraphrases the next verse, 21:

> "And as for me, this is my covenant with them," says the Lord: "My [prophetic] Spirit that is upon you [singular > Luke 4:18], and my words that I have put in your mouth, shall not depart out of your mouth [Jesus still speaks today], or out of the mouth of your offspring [disciples], or out of the mouth of your children's offspring," says the Lord, "from this time forth and forevermore." (Isa 59:21 ESV)

Isaiah 59:21 is the central programmatic prophecy of Acts, just as Isaiah 61:1–2 (> Luke 4:18) is to the first volume of Luke's work, his Gospel. It shows that Jesus in Luke's Gospel is the bearer and example of the New Covenant Spirit; in Acts he is the bestower of the New Covenant Spirit.

In his role in the New Covenant, then, Jesus' earthly ministry is essentially a training program for all his disciples "from [his] time on and forever." Jesus modeled to disciples everywhere and forever how to live and serve as they are guided and empowered by the New Covenant Spirit.

The next section shows that Jesus not only introduced and modeled the New Covenant Spirit, but, and this is crucial, he also ratified that New Covenant in his blood

3. JESUS CAME TO RATIFY THE NEW COVENANT IN HIS DEATH

Traditional Christianity rightly focuses on the Cross as its symbol and its crucial (that is, "cross-like") center of its theology. It has also been rightly pointed out that the trial and crucifixion narratives show emphasis by consuming a substantial part, even the climax, of the Gospel narrative—yet this is not nearly as much as the kingdom ministry modeling section. Acts and the remainder of the New Testament, emphasize even more frequently Jesus' resurrection and exaltation with its bestowal of the Spirit.

Historically, in spite of emphasis on the bestowal of the Spirit, Church theology and liturgy continued to emphasize the Eucharist (the "New Covenant in my blood" and broken body) which pointed to the "body" of charismatic ministries. As Paul pointed out as early as the Corinthian correspondence: the church failed to "discern the body" (and the purpose of Jesus' blood, which ratified the New Covenant Spirit), that is, the charismatic operations of the New Covenant. In this way the Corinthians "ate and drank judgment" on themselves in the form of sickness and death, because they ignored the poor, key functions of the body, those with gifts of revelation and healing who could have saved them. Recall that God's judgment for covenant breakers was sickness and death as per Deuteronomy 28. It was in this pattern of failure that the church historically opted for a metaphysical understanding, focusing instead on the relation of Christ to the sacramental bread and wine. This is another case of "looking at the finger" rather than that to which it was pointing. (See the discussion below, "A Note on How We 'Discern' the Body of Christ," 218–223).

The trial and crucifixion is traditionally understood with the purpose of saving sinners. But what is meant by "sinners"? In keeping with the thesis of this book, Paul says that "everything that does not come from faith is sin" (Rom 14:23). What he is saying is that in the New Covenant, the Law is revealed into the heart (Jer 31:33), prophetically (Isa 59:21)—this is the action of faith! It is this faith, the New Covenant Spirit, that guides toward the will of God. Sin, then, is simply not hearing and obeying the voice of God in one's heart. Accordingly, living in the New Covenant is living in the state of perceiving the teaching from God directly into the heart, or living in the Spirit expressed by prophetic "words in the mouth."

Jesus said the words of one's mouth express the condition of the heart (Matt 12:34; 15:18; Luke 6:45, cf. James 3:10). As Paul says when he corrected the scribes of his time (who were using Deuteronomy 30:11–14 to claim their exclusive right to know the will of God only by their interpretation of Scripture): "The word is near you; it is in your mouth and in your heart, that is, the word of faith" (Rom 10:8; Isa 59:21; Jer 31:33). The times Jesus most frequently expressed anger and frustration is precisely when he confronts his disciples' lack of faith! It was this fundamental sin—refusing the voice of God (Heb 12:25) or expressing no faith—against which the New Testament strives and is the basic problem for which Christ died.

Certainly, the summary statements of Jesus' mission in the New Testament suggest the importance of dealing with sin, such as these:

> "even as the Son of Man came not to be served but to serve, and to give his life as a ransom for many" (Matt 20:28 ESV).

> The next day he saw Jesus coming toward him, and said, "Behold, the Lamb of God, who takes away the sin of the world" (John 1:29 ESV).

> Whoever makes a practice of sinning is of the devil, for the devil has been sinning from the beginning. The reason the Son of God appeared was to destroy the works of the devil (1 John 3:8 ESV).

> The saying is trustworthy and deserving of full acceptance, that Christ Jesus came into the world to save sinners, of whom I am the foremost (1 Tim 1:15 ESV).

To anyone raised in the traditional Protestant environment, these verses are familiar because they support its central focus on the problem of sin and how to attain salvation (as is also evident in the great 16th century debate with the Roman Catholics). But by drawing attention to the alternative emphasis of Scripture in this section, are we trying to relativize the importance of the death of Christ? Absolutely not! The crucifixion of Christ is of central importance in the mission of Jesus because it is the great transition event in world history from a life under the death-dealing requirements of the Law to the life-giving benefits of the Law written in our hearts by the Spirit.

It was on the cross and in his death that the judgment of a righteous God against us, under the terms of the Law (Deut 28), was paid and satisfied. In traditional thinking our acceptance of Christ's payment for our sin causes us to stand before God, fully righteous (1 Cor 1:30; 2 Cor 5:21). Indeed, there are many passages that talk about moving from the Law to a "righteousness" which is by "faith" (Rom 1:17; 3:22,25; ch.4; 9:30; 10:6; Gal 5:5; Phil 3:9; Heb 11:4,7). In fact, Romans 8:1–5 seems to make sense of all this in that it is a paraphrase of the New Covenant (Jer 31:33). Walking " . . . after the Spirit" here describes the process of the Law (teaching or will of God) as it is written in the heart.

> There is therefore now no condemnation to them which are in Christ Jesus, who walk not after the flesh, but after the Spirit. 2 For the law of the Spirit of life in Christ Jesus hath made me free from the law of sin and death. 3 For what the law could not do, in that it was weak through the flesh, God sending his own Son in the likeness of sinful flesh, and for sin, condemned sin in the flesh: 4 That the righteousness of the law might be fulfilled in us, who walk not after the flesh, but after the Spirit. 5 For they that are after the flesh do mind the things of the flesh; but they that are after the Spirit the things of the Spirit (Rom 8:1–5 KJV).

Here is the great transition that Jesus made possible in his death. He delivered or translated us from a hopeless, failed, and sinful life because of our human weakness (flesh) to a new kind of "righteousness" (right way of living) because the Spirit reveals God's presence and power in us to live in faith (hearing God and obeying). This passage shows that the "righteousness of the law" is fulfilled in those who walk not in the flesh/Law but who hear and heed the Spirit—as Jesus modeled for us in his earthly life. This is the righteousness of faith (hearing and heeding God), which replaces the old Law which we hopelessly try to read, interpret, apply, and live out—all in the flesh (human abilities). This Law trip is the temptation that confronted Eve and Adam, Jesus, and all of us down through history—to try to understand and follow God without the Spirit guiding and empowering us.

Jesus in his death took the punishment for our failure to keep the Law. Failure to keep this Old Covenant meant death (the domain, dominion, or power of darkness, Col 1:13). He died instead of us, and in so doing, we were sprung from this sentence of death into a new life in the New Covenant Spirit.

The ninth chapter of describes this process:

> [Jesus] entered the Most Holy Place once for all by his own blood, having obtained eternal redemption. [13] The blood of goats and bulls and the ashes of a heifer sprinkled on those who are ceremonially unclean sanctify them so that they are outwardly clean. [14] How much more, then, will the blood of Christ, who through the eternal Spirit offered himself unblemished to God, cleanse our consciences from acts that lead to death, so that we may serve the living God! [15] For this reason Christ is the *mediator* of a new covenant, that those who are called may receive the promised eternal inheritance–now that he has died as a ransom to set them free from the sins committed under the first covenant. [16] In the case of a will [covenant], it is necessary to prove the death of the one who made it, [17] because a will is in force only when somebody has died; it never takes effect while the one who made it is living (Hebrews 9:12–17 KJV EMPHASIS MINE).

. . .

> And by that will [covenant], we have been made holy (set apart for charismatic-priestly/prophetic-ministry) *through the sacrifice of the body of Jesus Christ* once for all (Hebrews 10:10).

Hebrews makes our point that Jesus' death was another crucial link in the chain of his actions to bring us into the New Covenant of the Spirit. Without his cleansing death and blood, we are still under the old death-contract of the Law—totally unqualified to enter the New Covenant of the Spirit expressed by his guidance, gifts, and power. In legal terms, Jesus' death ratified (signed in his blood) the New Covenant for us.

Now we can see a context broader than the traditional Protestant understanding of the death of Christ: it becomes clear that Jesus did not die only to take away our sins so we could be good and go to heaven. Rather, he introduced and modeled a powerful charismatic ministry of grace that included signs, wonders, and casting out demons; and then he died to give us the right to enter into that charismatic covenant of the Spirit!

Proof of this New Covenant transaction is expressed in what Jesus said during the Last Supper, alluding to the blood of the Passover lamb painted on the doorposts as a sign for the death angel to pass over them in Egypt. The Last Supper was a kind of ceremony commemorating the Old Covenant that had been given in Sinai (this is the current Jewish tradition), but also looks forward to the New Covenant "in my blood" (Matt 26:28 || Mark 14:24 || Luke 22:20, cf. 1 Cor 11:25). Jesus additionally said he would not drink again from the "fruit of the vine until the kingdom of God comes" (Luke 22:18 || Matt 26:29 || Mark 14:25). Could this kingdom that comes be a reference to the coming of the Spirit at Pentecost and beyond and to the presence of Jesus at the subsequent Eucharistic meals?[7]

His death also showed us that "If we died with him, we will also live with him; if we endure, we will also reign with him" (2 Tim 2:11–12). As Christians walking by the Spirit, our job will now include imitating

Paul, who was imitating Christ (not an outward mimicking, but an inward living by faith): "I fill up in my flesh what is still lacking in regard to Christ's afflictions, for the sake of his body, which is the church" (Col 1:24). This is not to say that the death of Christ is not sufficient to redeem sinners, but we should expect that confronting the satanic system of darkness with the power of God will invite counter-attacks that could even be deadly to the flesh.

To enter into the New Covenant Spirit is not only to see testing, opposition from Satan, and suffering as a kind of annoying inconvenience and failure on our part to have faith, but as part of the New Covenant package that includes miraculous victories over the evil one: "The things that mark an apostle—signs, wonders and miracles–were done among you with *great perseverance*" (2 Cor 12:12). One who is sent out by God (i.e., an apostle) will normatively be a suffering charismatic, whose faith is continually tested against the domain of darkness.

For Jesus himself, ratification of the New Covenant Spirit involved ultimate suffering. Traditional religion, especially Catholicism, tends to dwell on this stage of Christ's work, particularly as it is constantly repeated in the mass. Similarly, Protestants tend to see the Lord's Supper in church as a commemoration of the "Lord's death until he comes," without seeing its connection with the outpouring of the Spirit.

A NOTE ON HOW WE DISCERN THE BODY OF CHRIST

Central to the experience of most Christians is participation in the Eucharist, also known as The Lord's Supper or Communion. Perhaps because it is so prominent in church ritual, this common experience has caused much ink to be used up speculating about its significance. Predictably, traditional theology has led us into ruminating about the metaphysical nature of the body of Christ more than it has about the emphasis of Scripture on this subject.[8] A common theme in traditional views is their liturgical requirement to repent of sin (generally) lest one take communion "in an unworthy manner" by not "recognizing the body." Yet their identification of "the body" is based not on the scriptural text but on speculative metaphysics—specifically, whether or not the bread and wine . . .

- become the actual body and blood of Christ (transubstantiation), a position held by the Roman Catholic, Orthodox, and some Anglican traditions; or
- are the presence of Jesus "in, with, and under" the forms of bread and wine (consubstantiation) as in Lutheranism; or
- are, as in the Reformed tradition, the elements as the immaterial, "pneumatic" (spiritual) presence of Christ perceived by faith; or
- are merely symbols reminding us of Christ's atonement, hence, a requirement to repent of sins before taking communion.

Since the Eucharist is the central feature of the Mass in Roman Catholicism, debate among Protestants over how to distance their theology from the "papists" by reframing this metaphysical speculation has been intense. Today, we need to seek harmony despite being divided over these strongly-held positions. Certainly, there is nothing wrong in believing that we meet Jesus in the Eucharist, often in very moving and edifying ways. Randy Clark, who heads an effective international program of charismatic impartation, has quite reasonably pointed out that if the Spirit of God could be imparted via "handkerchiefs and aprons" sent out from the apostle Paul (Acts 19:12), why could we not encounter Christ in the more traditional expressions of the body and blood of Jesus? In any case, we are not to wound the body of Christ by fighting over exactly how we meet Jesus in the Eucharist, which is a profound and bitter irony—like fighting over how best to love one another!

At the same time, Scripture itself appears to share little interest in such metaphysics. Rather Scripture takes us to a view of the body and blood that embraces the central theme of the Eucharist passages—recognizing the body of Christ and the New Covenant "in my [Jesus'] blood." Is it possible that by focusing on the metaphysical/theological substance of the communion elements (bread and wine) that the theologians were distracted from the teaching of Scripture in its own context? The relevant passage is found in the eleventh chapter of 1 Corinthians:

> When you come together, it is not the Lord's Supper you eat, 21 for as you eat, each of you goes ahead without waiting for anybody else. One remains hungry, another gets drunk. 22 Don't you have homes to eat and drink in? Or do you despise the church of God and humiliate those who have nothing? What shall I say to you? Shall I praise you for this? Certainly not! 23 For I received from the Lord what I also passed on to you: The Lord Jesus, on the night he was betrayed, took bread, 24 and when he had given thanks, he broke it and said, "This is my body, which is for you; do this in remembrance of me." 25 In the same way, after supper he took the cup, saying, "This cup is the new covenant in my blood; do this, whenever you drink it, in remembrance of me." 26 For whenever you eat this bread and drink this cup, you proclaim the Lord's death until he comes. 27 Therefore, whoever eats the bread or drinks the cup of the Lord in an unworthy manner will be guilty of sinning against the body and blood of the Lord. 28 A man ought to examine himself before he eats of the bread and drinks of the cup. 29 For anyone who eats and drinks without recognizing the body of the Lord eats and drinks judgment on himself. 30 That is why many among you are weak and sick, and a number of you have fallen asleep. 31 But if we judged ourselves, we would not come under judgment (1 Corinthians 11:20–31 NIV).

If we look carefully at Paul's argument here, he is saying, "When you meet for the 'Lord's Supper,' it is not the *Lord's* Supper because you despise the church of God and humiliate those who have nothing." Paul is very upset about this! Why? By contrast, Paul demands that we are to imitate the real Lord's Supper, which shows that Jesus not simply gave people food (Matt 14:14–21 and pars.), as the Corinthians were *not* doing, but he even gave his own body, "which is for you," and his cup, which is "the New Covenant in my blood" (cf. John 6:53–56). Unlike the selfish, elitist Corinthians, Paul shows that Jesus shared his life in order to offer us a New Covenant. This reaction of Paul shows that he has something much more specific in mind than traditional Protestantism about regarding the "body and blood" in "an unworthy manner."

This is crucial! Twice we are told "do this in remembrance of me" and not "in an unworthy manner"; in other words, remember how and why we recognize and apply the Lord's Supper. The Lord's Supper has two clear-cut purposes: 1) to remember the body and 2) to remember the blood that ratified the New Covenant of the Spirit.

We must now ask: How do we know what to remember about the body and the blood of the New Covenant? It's simple—keep reading!

We already have seen how this book gives prominence to the New Covenant of the Spirit. How then does the context of the body and blood affirm this covenant? The answer is in the very next chapter, 1 Corinthians 12, which talks about the working of the New Covenant Spirit in the body of Christ. Is it merely coincidental that this chapter and topic appear next? Apparently Protestant proponents thought so—since from the view of traditional theology certain spiritual gifts had ceased, they found it pointless to connect the Eucharist in 1 Corinthians 11 with the manifestations of the Spirit in the next three chapters. They fail to see how in chapter 12 Paul is talking about the presence of Jesus in his body (in the charismatic members of the church). Paul goes on in chapters 13 and 14 to expound how to manifest the Spirit in these ways in love and inclusively. Chapter 15 finishes off the "body" discussion to talk about how Christ's body has been, and the church's ultimately will be, transformed (cf. John 6:54).

Now let's examine the context of 1 Corinthians 12 that immediately follows the Lord's Supper passage:

> Now concerning spiritual gifts, brothers, I do not want you to be uninformed. 2 You know that when you were pagans you were led astray to mute idols, however you were led. 3 Therefore I want you to understand that no one speaking in the Spirit of God ever says "Jesus is accursed!" and no one can say "Jesus is Lord" except in the Holy Spirit. 4 Now there are varieties of gifts, but the same Spirit; 5 and there are varieties of service, but the same Lord; 6 and there are varieties of

> activities, but it is the same God who empowers them all in everyone. [7] To each is given the manifestation of the Spirit for the common good (1 Cor 12:1–7 ESV).

Notice that Paul shows how to remember the body and blood of the Lord Jesus: don't be "ignorant" or "pagan" or "led astray to mute [non-prophetic] idols" just as you're doing in your so-called "Lord's Supper." Rather, if you are doing the Lord's Supper right, the Spirit will be there and you will recognize Jesus as Lord! Yes, there are differences among you: some rich, some poor; some prominent, some ignored (1 Cor 1:26), but "each one" has a "manifestation of the [New Covenant] Spirit [that] is given for the common good."

But how about recognizing the "body" of Jesus? The same chapter has the answer to this question (1 Cor 12:12–14).

> For just as the body is one and has many members, and all the members of the body, though many, are one body, so it is with Christ. [13] For in one Spirit we were all baptized into one body—Jews or Greeks, slaves or free—and all were made to drink of one [charismatic] Spirit. [14] For the body does not consist of one member but of many (ESV).

All of the members of Christ's body are simply people with spiritual gifts. So it makes perfect sense for Paul to emphasize the sin against the body, the members of which were "all baptized by one Spirit into one body"! Here you have Paul's point: "if you don't recognize and acknowledge in your midst the body, which is very diverse of many kinds of people and spiritual gifts, the 'body' which has been baptized in the New Covenant Spirit, then there is a consequence."

The consequence that Paul describes is this: "That is why many among you are weak and sick, and a number of you have fallen asleep" (1 Cor 11:30). The snubbing of the poor, including possibly slaves, who were Spirit-filled Christians in 1 Cor 11 paralleled the denigration of certain gifts and exaltation of others in chapter 12. Certainly, the same people were involved. It appears that some socially high status tongue speakers showed little concern that their spiritual "blessing trip" was not helping others, while the mutually-edifying gifts that others had were being ignored. The elitists at Corinth were not violating the covenant simply because they were ignoring the poor but because they were violating the spirit and letter of the New Covenant of the Spirit, ratified in Christ's blood and expressed in his broken body, which explicitly and generously *included* the poor and empowered them with his gifts.

Judgment comes upon a church that suppresses Spirit-gifted persons who have charismata of healings and miracles, gifts of prophecy, and words of knowledge (not "discerning the body"). Spiritual gifts express the power of the kingdom of God intended to displace the sickness, sin, and death of the kingdom of darkness. To denigrate and snub the New Covenant Spirit and His manifestations is to deny the central reason for the Lord's Supper: to "remember," "discern," and activate the New Covenant life in the prophetic Spirit—in *all* of God's people! To deny that Jesus' blood ratified the New Covenant of the Spirit for all classes of people is to bring "judgment on oneself." This is why Hebrews 6:4–6 takes such denial very seriously.

> For it is impossible, in the case of those who have once been enlightened, who have tasted the heavenly gift, and have shared in the Holy Spirit, 5 and have tasted the goodness of the word of God and the powers of the age to come, 6 and then have fallen away, to restore them again to repentance, since they are crucifying once again the Son of God to their own harm and holding him up to contempt (ESV).

Denying the charismata, especially denying the first *charism*, the witness of the Spirit prompting one to confess Jesus as Lord—a revelatory process ratified in the body and blood of Christ—is the same thing as "crucifying the Son of God all over again and subjecting him to public disgrace." How so? Because if one falls away, he is outside the covenant. To get back into a covenant, its penalties must be paid, and a new covenant must be ratified in blood. This is not going to happen: Christ is not going to be crucified again (Heb 9:12, 26, 28; 10:10)! Once the Holy Spirit's voice and power have been experienced and then rejected, it's over. This is "blasphemy against the Holy Spirit" (Matt 12:31 || Mark 3:29 || Luke 12:10). In this case, the consequence is worse than "sickness, weakness, and death." Traditional Protestants agree that, in the *ordo salutis*, Christ is *revealed*—a charismatic (gracious) act of the Spirit (Matt 16:17), characterized by hearing God's voice (John 10:3–5, 27; Rom 8:14). Even in traditional theology, denial of this revelation of Christ is fatal.

THE ORIGINAL AND FINAL MEANING OF THE LORD'S SUPPER

Let's backtrack to the historical source of the Lord's Supper and what it means to us. The new covenant meal, that is, the Lord's Supper, originally commemorated the Exodus events—Israel's deliverance with Moses from Egyptian bondage. As a way of recognizing the personal significance of the last miraculous plague on Egypt, the Israelites were to kill a lamb and smear its blood on the doorpost as a defense against the judgment of death. As a result of this covenant they would also experience blessings: "The Lord will keep you free from every disease. He will not inflict on you the horrible diseases you knew in Egypt" (Deut 7:15, cf. 1 Cor 11:30). The Israelites entered into this covenant meal with God in anticipation of their deliverance and the forthcoming covenant at Mt Sinai—they did so by cooking a lamb along with unleavened bread (there wasn't time to wait for it to rise).

Similarly, as the underlying reality that the Passover meal signified, Jesus himself became the Passover/New Covenant meal (John 6:53–58): his body (bread) was broken on the cross for us. His "New Covenant in [his] blood" became our defense against the judgment (the penalties of breaking the Old Covenant) that included sin, sickness, and death. Accordingly, because we discern the body of Jesus, just as the Israelites discerned the significance of the slain lamb and the blood on the doorposts, we have the protection of the New Covenant of the Spirit provided by His gifts—prophecy, words of wisdom and knowledge, healing and miracles. That is why Paul is so insistent that Christians recognize the meaning of the New Covenant so they will employ the protective gifts of the New Covenant Spirit! He is saying that one cannot shun anyone in the New Covenant Spirit community, regardless of their social status, and at the same time accurately "discern" the body and blood of Christ that mediated the New Covenant of the Spirit. To deny the New Covenant community of the Spirit by rejecting the poor, is essentially, in my view, also denying the very essence of why Jesus died: to inaugurate the New Covenant of the Spirit (spelled out in principle in ch 12). Logically, one cannot deny the outworking, manifestation and expression of the New Covenant Spirit (the poor in the New Covenant) and not at the same time deny the blood and broken body of Jesus on the cross which *mediated and ratified* this New Covenant of the Spirit—the very reason for the body and blood. One is the other. As the climax of the Pentecost message clearly affirms, the "promise/covenant" that Jesus provided through his body and blood was not simply "salvation," but the Spirit of prophecy ("words in the mouth"). In Romans 11:29, Paul apparently paraphrases this Pentecost citation, Isaiah 59:21, by identifying the New Covenant with the charismata and calling of God that is not withdrawn.

Similarly, by focusing on the physical Eucharist and speculating on its metaphysical nature, the Protestant traditions also did not fully "discern" the body—members with charismatic giftings, characteristic of the New Covenant—and the blood of Christ that mediated it, as Paul and the writer of Hebrews described. Typical of theologians, Protestant Church Fathers were not asking the right questions and were answering the wrong questions, usually about philosophy and metaphysics! Hence we get a strange scriptural mix—characteristics of sausage once again!

In like manner to Paul's letter to the Corinthians, the Epistle to the Hebrews treats the problem of those who ignored the New Covenant prophetic Spirit. Here the teaching about the New Covenant as associated with Jesus' suffering and death (chs. 8—10) also leads to the New Covenant expressions of faith (hearing God, obeying, and suffering) in chapter 11. Chapter 12, the climax of the book, exhorts us not to "refuse him who speaks" to us from heaven (12:25). Obviously, Jesus' work on the cross was not simply a solution to our sins against the Old Covenant (the stage of John the Baptist) but looked forward to a baptism in the New Covenant Spirit that would relate us to God and our ministry to Him in a radical new Spirit-led, charismatic way.

Put simply, Jesus' death on the cross was not in itself the New Covenant; rather, in the chain of events of his mission, the cross was a crucial link that ratified, mediated, and cleared the way for us to enter that New Covenant. Now we move on to the next indispensable link in Jesus' mission: the vindication of the New Covenant in the resurrection.

The previous section showed Jesus fulfilling the mandate of God for mankind to "guard and serve" his creation (Gen 2), with the understanding that great testing (the crucifixion) would follow that "hearing of faith." Suffering is the test of all people of faith (Heb 11), so it is no surprise that it falls supremely on Jesus, "the author and finisher of our faith" (Heb 12:2). In preparation to sitting down at the right hand of the Father to bestow the charismata to us (Acts 2:33; Eph 4:8–11), he had to endure the cross and the grave so he could experience and unveil the great vindication of the resurrection.

4. JESUS' RESURRECTION VINDICATES HIS MISSION OF BAPTIZING IN THE NEW COVENANT SPIRIT

On the way toward his present role of baptizer in the Holy Spirit, Jesus introduced and presented his kingdom in power. He did so, all the while training disciples to imitate him in every way—particularly in expressing the New Covenant/kingdom Spirit in the power of signs, wonders, and spiritual gifts.

Following the plot line of all the great figures of the Bible, Jesus' Spirit-empowered ministry to "guard and serve" God's creation—thereby unveiling the kingdom of God—inevitably precipitated testing and persecution, and resulted in humiliation before the world, and finally in a shameful death as a cursed criminal (Gal 3:13).

However, in the charter message of Christianity—the keynote address at Pentecost—Peter hammered this issue home (Acts 2:23–24, 33):

> this Jesus, delivered up according to the definite plan and foreknowledge of God, you crucified and killed by the hands of lawless men. [24] God raised him up, loosing the pangs of death, because it was not possible for him to be held by it. . . . [33] Being therefore exalted at the right hand of God, and having received from the Father the promise of the Holy Spirit, he has poured out this that you yourselves are seeing and hearing (ESV).

The crowd becomes fearful (particularly those who had a hand in Jesus' crucifixion) because after the "mighty, rushing wind" (Acts 2:2), they probably recall the prophecy of the thunderous sound of God, "behold he comes like a mighty, rushing torrent, driven by the Spirit of the Lord" (Isa 59:19).[9] The crowd also sees, as Peter points out, the fire distributed on the heads of the 120 (a symbolic number of the new Israel of God) and the gift of prophetic utterance to each (fulfilling Joel 2:28–29 and Isa 59:21 > Acts 2:39). This was proof that the Messiah, the bringer of the Spirit (Matt 3:11 || Mark 1:8 || Luke 3:16 || John 1:33), was inaugurating his kingdom.

So the resurrection of Jesus, the mighty miracle, expressed, restored and vindicated his mission, not by merely restoring him to life, but placing him at the right hand of the Father in heaven where Jesus now bestows the Spirit in "that which you see and hear." This was a time of great apocalyptic expectation (messiahs were popping up all over the place to lead Israel into a revolt against Rome) and along with that, Pentecost brought a keen awareness that the old age was passing away into the age of the Messiah and his Spirit. The problem was, they had just crucified Jesus, which brought with it many ominous cosmic phenomena (Matt 27:45, 51–54; Mark 15:33, 38; Luke 23:44–45). A number of Old Testament judgment passages would likely be swirling around in the consciences of pious Jews who had memorized or otherwise recalled many apocalyptic warnings from the Hebrew Bible.

> And the Spirit of the LORD shall rest upon him, the Spirit of wisdom and understanding, the Spirit of counsel and might, the Spirit of knowledge and the fear of the LORD. [3] And his delight shall be in the fear of the LORD. He shall not judge by what his eyes see, or decide

disputes by what his ears hear, [4] but with righteousness he shall judge the poor, and decide with equity for the meek of the earth; and he shall strike the earth with the rod of his mouth, and with the breath of his lips he shall kill the wicked. [5] Righteousness shall be the belt of his waist, and faithfulness the belt of his loins (Isaiah 11:2–5 ESV).

Behold my servant, whom I uphold, my chosen, in whom my soul delights; I have put my Spirit upon him; he will bring forth justice to the nations. [2] He will not cry aloud or lift up his voice, or make it heard in the street; [3] a bruised reed he will not break, and a faintly burning wick he will not quench; he will faithfully bring forth justice. [4] He will not grow faint or be discouraged till he has established justice in the earth; and the coastlands wait for his law. [5] Thus says God, the LORD, who created the heavens and stretched them out, who spread out the earth and what comes from it, who gives breath to the people on it and spirit to those who walk in it: [6] "I am the LORD; I have called you in righteousness; I will take you by the hand and keep you; I will give you as a covenant for the people, a light for the nations, [7] to open the eyes that are blind, to bring out the prisoners from the dungeon, from the prison those who sit in darkness" (Isaiah 42:1–7 ESV).

Then they shall know that I am the Lord their God, because I sent them into exile among the nations and then assembled them into their own land. I will leave none of them remaining among the nations anymore. [29] And I will not hide my face anymore from them, when I pour out my Spirit upon the house of Israel, declares the Lord God (Ezekiel 39:28–29 ESV).

And I will pour out on the house of David and the inhabitants of Jerusalem a spirit of grace and pleas for mercy, so that, when they look on me, on him whom they have pierced, they shall mourn for him, as one mourns for an only child, and weep bitterly over him, as one weeps over a firstborn (Zechariah 12:10 ESV).

> "I waste away, I waste away. Woe is me! For the traitors have betrayed, with betrayal the traitors have betrayed." [17] Terror and the pit and the snare are upon you, O inhabitant of the earth! [18] He who flees at the sound of the terror shall fall into the pit, and he who climbs out of the pit shall be caught in the snare. For the windows of heaven are opened, and the foundations of the earth tremble. [19] The earth is utterly broken, the earth is split apart, the earth is violently shaken. [20] The earth staggers like a drunken man; it sways like a hut; its transgression lies heavy upon it, and it falls, and will not rise again. [21] On that day the Lord will punish the host of heaven, in heaven, and the kings of the earth, on the earth. [22] They will be gathered together as prisoners in a pit; they will be shut up in a prison, and after many days they will be punished. [23] Then the moon will be confounded and the sun ashamed, for the Lord of hosts reigns on Mount Zion and in Jerusalem, and his glory will be before his elders (Isaiah 24:16–23 ESV).
>
> Certainly, the crowd, standing on Mt. Zion (the temple area) as they saw the outpouring of the Spirit of prophecy, remembered the darkness (eclipse?) and the earthquake when Jesus died—"At that moment the curtain of the temple was torn in two from top to bottom.[10] The earth shook and the rocks split. The tombs broke open and the bodies of many holy people who had died were raised to life" (Matt 27:51–52, 54). At Jesus' resurrection, there was still another earthquake (28:2). Peter's sermon has just reminded them of Joel's prophecy that the "the sun will be turned to darkness and the moon to blood before the coming of the great and glorious day of the Lord" (Acts 2:20).[11] They could remember that darkness also occurred during Jesus' crucifixion. If this were not enough, the "mighty, rushing wind" and other phenomena of the Pentecost event seriously got their attention (Acts 2:2, 6).

All of these elements together evoked fear to the Bible-believing Jewish gathering, especially when they heard Peter sum up: "The Lord said to my Lord: 'Sit at my right hand until I make your enemies a footstool for your feet.' Therefore let all Israel be assured of this: God has made this Jesus, whom you crucified, both Lord and Christ" (Acts

2:34–36). The Jerusalem Jews rightly understood themselves to be enemies of God for their crucifixion of Jesus. Now the whole cosmos was turning against them in judgment for their failed coup attempt.

It is only reasonable at this point that they would cry out: "Brothers [they're "brothers" now!], what shall we do?" (Acts 2:37). Peter's answer is repentance, baptism, and the New Covenant Spirit. Yet he goes on to vehemently warn the crowd, "Save yourselves from this corrupt generation."

The point of all this was that Jesus was vindicated by the Spirit— "who through the Spirit of holiness was declared with power to be the Son of God by his resurrection from the dead: Jesus Christ our Lord" (Romans 1:4).

Again, as a reminder and matter of emphasis, the goal of Paul's life is to replicate the experience of Jesus' vindication by the resurrection:

> . . . and be found in him, not having a righteousness of my own that comes from the law, but that which comes through faith in Christ], the righteousness from God that depends on faith [that is, the New Covenant Spirit]— 10 that I may know [= "experience firsthand"] him and the power of his resurrection, and may share his sufferings, becoming like him in his death . . . . I press on to make it my own, because Christ Jesus has made me his own. 13 Brothers, I do not consider that I have made it my own. But one thing I do: forgetting what lies behind and straining forward to what lies ahead, 14 I press on toward the goal for the prize of the upward call of God in Christ Jesus. 15 Let those of us who are mature think this way, and if in anything you think otherwise, God will reveal that also to you (Philippians 3:9–15 ESV).

Here again, the emphasis is on the replication and imitation of Jesus' mission that begins and continues with faith (hearing God's voice and obeying) and entering into the New Covenant "righteousness" ("I will remember their sins no more") where God's guidance is revealed directly into the heart. The New Covenant experience will lead us into the classic "power and suffering" mission of Jesus, Paul, and all who truly follow Jesus. But it doesn't stop there: we become "like him in his death" in order to "attain to the resurrection from the dead." We therefore "press on toward the goal to win the prize for which God has called [us] heavenward in Christ Jesus." The passage concludes with the clear command that all this is a pattern for all of us: "the power of his resurrection" doesn't mean waiting around till we die and then get resurrected. Because it comes before the suffering, it is clear that this refers to employing the power of the New Covenant Spirit for ministry, which will then precipitate suffering. Every true Christian will see his or her life vindicated by the Spirit of Christ.

> You, however, are not in the flesh but in the Spirit, if in fact the Spirit of God dwells in you. Anyone who does not have the Spirit of Christ does not belong to him. [10] But if Christ is in you, although the body is dead because of sin, the Spirit is life because of righteousness. [11] If the Spirit of him who raised Jesus from the dead dwells in you, he who raised Christ Jesus from the dead will also give life to your mortal bodies through his Spirit who dwells in you (Romans 8:9–11 ESV).

The point of all this is that the resurrection served as the great turnaround that vindicated Jesus and his mission to bring us the Spirit of God, so that we could imitate him and his apostles through a living and active faith in "the power of his resurrection." The resurrection essentially said to the world: "See! This really works!" Paul said, "I am not ashamed of the gospel for it is the power of God unto salvation." What Paul was demonstrably saying was that—in every healing, deliverance from demonic oppression, in every repentance and turning to Jesus Christ in faith—this gospel is both expressed and vindicated in God's power, just as the mission of Jesus was expressed and vindicated in the power of the Spirit in the resurrection.

The next sections describe the goal of Jesus' mission: to bring his elect into the New Covenant Spirit.

5. JESUS' MISSION NOW IS TO BESTOW THE NEW COVENANT SPIRIT FROM HEAVEN

If one of the stated purposes of Jesus was to "save sinners" (1 Tim 1:15) then we might ask, "Save them from what?" The traditional answer is: from their sins! But Scripture demonstrates a broader scope: Jesus saves his sheep from being outside the New Covenant of the Spirit and his gifts. Proof of this is the saving of Paul in a specific context: "The grace of our Lord was poured out on me abundantly, along with the faith and love that are in Christ Jesus" (1 Tim: 1:14). The key words of the glorious gift Paul was given begin with the "grace of our Lord . . . poured out on me abundantly." Again, grace is not simply unmerited favor, as traditional Protestantism reconstructed it, but rather Spirit empowering, or spiritual gifting. Note the metaphor of how this gifting comes: "poured out on me abundantly." The "pouring out" metaphor often describes the bestowal of the Spirit (Isa 44:3; Ezek 39:29; Joel 2:28–39; Zech 12:10; Acts 10:45; Rom 5:5; Tit 3:5–6). Similarly the Spirit at Pentecost was also poured out (Act 2:17, 18, 33), in the same way that the Gospel of John ties the pouring out metaphor specifically to the Spirit bestowed by Jesus (John 7:38–39).

> "Whoever believes in me, as the Scripture has said, 'Out of his heart will flow rivers of living water.'" 39 Now this he said about the Spirit, whom those who believed in him were to receive, for as yet the Spirit had not been given, because Jesus was not yet glorified (John 7:38–39 ESV).

Note that the New Covenant believers' heart was the locus of both the Torah/teaching and of the Spirit, represented by flowing water—a welcome symbol of life and cleansing in a fairly dry climate, desperately dependent on springs and rainfall.

Let's look now at the next two words, faith and love, "that are in Christ Jesus." With a background of the New Covenant passages, we see that faith is the "Law written in the heart"—direct revelation of the will of God; and love is the resulting intimacy with the father, knowing Him, so that He will be our God and we will be his people (Isa 59:21; Jer

31:33–34; Rev 21:3—the goal of the Bible). Notice this outpouring of the Spirit, along with faith and love, are "in Christ Jesus"—the exalted Messiah, the bestower of the Spirit (John 3:34; 14:16–18, 26; 15:26; 16:7; Acts 2:33; Acts 9:17; Gal 4:6; 4:7–11; 1 Pet 1:12; 1 John 3:24). The Spirit is described as "the Spirit of the Son/Christ/Jesus Christ" (Rom 8:9; Gal 4:6; Phil 1:19). Alternatively, we see that God also bestows the Spirit, though this distinction is not practically significant (Gal 3:5; Eph 1:17; 2 Tim 1:7).[12]

The Gospel of John spends a considerable amount of space (emphasis) discussing the bestowal of the Spirit (= Paraclete/Comforter) from Jesus. For example, in John 14, Jesus is modeling the New Covenant since he has the Law/teaching in his heart from the Father:

> Whoever does not love me does not keep my words. And the word that you hear is not mine but the Father's who sent me. [25] These things I have spoken to you while I am still with you. [26] But the Helper, the Holy Spirit, whom the Father will send in my name, he will teach you all things and bring to your remembrance all that I have said to you (John 14:24–26 ESV).

Jesus constantly alludes to the "words in the mouth" spoken of by Isaiah 59:21—the words given him by the Father. In this way, Jesus is modeling the New Covenant experience that he clearly is expecting to transfer to his disciples, and to the reader of this Gospel: "the words I put in your mouth, I will put in the mouth of your children and your children's children forever."

Another key passage that deals with the biblical goal of Jesus for the Spirit coming upon God's people is Ephesians 4:4–13:

> There is one body and one Spirit—just as you were called to the one hope that belongs to your call— [5] one LORD, one faith, one baptism, [6] one God and Father of all, who is over all and through all and in all. [7] But grace was given to each one of us according to the measure of Christ's gift. [8] Therefore it says, "When he ascended on high he led a

> host of captives, and he gave gifts to men." [9] (In saying, "He ascended," what does it mean but that he had also descended into the lower regions, the earth? [10] He who descended is the one who also ascended far above all the heavens, that he might fill all things.) [11] And he gave the apostles, the prophets, the evangelists, the shepherds and teachers, [12] to equip the saints for the work of ministry, for building up the body of Christ, [13] until we all attain to the unity of the faith and of the knowledge of the Son of God, to mature manhood, to the measure of the stature of the fullness of Christ (Ephesians 4:4–13 ESV).

This passage is perhaps the most thorough in the New Testament for describing the present mission of Jesus as baptizer in the Holy Spirit. Paul begins the passage by outlining the common experience of the body of Christ—in the Spirit. The common hope is in "one Lord" (the exalted Jesus), one faith, that is, the common ability to hear and obey the Spirit. The one baptism, in this sequence emphasizes the coming of the Spirit in baptism, or, perhaps more simply, "the baptism in the Holy Spirit." The emphasis on unity continues with the focus (as in the pattern of the New Covenant) on God the Father who is the totality of all reality.

The focus in verse 7 shifts to "each one of us" who receives grace as Christ apportions it. Remember that grace primarily means "generous charismatic empowerment," as is clear from the grace gifts specified in verse 11. The phrase "each one of us" echoes the Pentecost narrative when the Spirit came down on "each of them" (Acts 2:3). The point here is that grace (a gift of the Spirit) is normative for "each one" of Paul's readers (if the universality of the scriptural canon means anything at all!). But for our point, it is Christ who apportions (deals out) these gifts. Jesus' central mission is described here! This is what he was intended to do from the moment he was introduced by John the Baptist.

This next discussion is a little strange to moderns unfamiliar with a specific practice common in Bible times when kings attacked and looted their neighboring kingdoms. If successful, the most prized loot was people, who would then be brought back to be distributed as slaves for the king's supporters. Often these slaves would be quite educated and skilled and therefore very useful to the new owners—and the conquering kingdom. The Roman Empire existed primarily because of this very practice: looting conquered kingdoms by heavy taxation and slavery. It is estimated that most of Rome's population was composed of slaves.

With this understanding we can recognize that Ephesians 4:8–12 (based on Psalm 68:12–18) portrays Jesus as such a king who invades the "lower, earthly" kingdom and loots it of captives whom he leads in a kind of victory parade "on high" (to his kingdom in heaven). From there, he distributes these slaves (gifted as apostles, prophets, evangelists, pastors, and teachers) to his own kingdom, the church. Recall that even the apostle Paul refers to himself as a slave or servant (*doulos*), both to Christ, his church or the gospel (Rom 1:1; Phil 1:1; Col 1:23; Tit 1:1). Apostles are last in the victory parade as captives condemned to die in the arena (1 Cor 4:9).

So if we can picture it: we have been "looted" from the kingdom of darkness (Col 1:13–14, cf. Matt 12:29 || Mark 3:27 || Luke 11:21) and given as a slave to everyone else, and everyone else as a slave to us. (Some church boards at least partly understand this, but only apply it one way to their pastor!)

Today Jesus continues to give[13] these gifts to the church as he persists in looting potential apostles, prophets, evangelists, etc., from Satan's kingdom. How do we know apostles and prophets continue until today? We see it through the following ways:

1. We are commanded in Scripture to "eagerly desire the greater gifts" (1 Cor 12:31)—and we see that "apostles" is a gift as appointed first in the list of spiritual gifts, with prophecy second. So when we are commanded to "desire the greater gifts" it seems reasonable that we should aspire, according to God's written word, to become apostles and prophets! Traditional Protestantism reads this clear command of Scripture as irrelevant today, applying only to a time before the last New Testament document was written—since apostles and prophets were essentially popes and, therefore, Scripture writers.

2. Our Ephesians 4 passage explicitly gives us the expiration date on these gifts.

The reason these gifts appear is "to prepare God's people for works of service so that the body of Christ might be built up" (v 12). Apostles and prophets, then, have a job: to equip the saints for service. Has this job been completed by these gifts? No. Just because a New Testament is written does not mean the tasks of apostles and prophets have been completed—as defined by Scripture itself!

According to Scripture, these five gifts expire when the following events have been completed:

> "until we all reach unity in the faith."

Have we all reached "unity in the faith"—at the same perfect level of hearing and obeying God along with harmony in the church? Um, I don't think so.

> "until we all reach . . . the knowledge of the Son of God and become mature."

Well, maybe, but is everybody "mature"? Conceivable, until we ask, how mature?

> "until we all . . . mature, attaining to the whole measure of the fullness of Christ."

We are all as completely mature as Christ? Not even the apostle Paul would claim that (Phil 3:12)!

So these "until" conditions can only be reached in heaven. Period. What this means is that the five gifts are bestowed by the exalted Christ until the church is in heaven, and not a moment before.

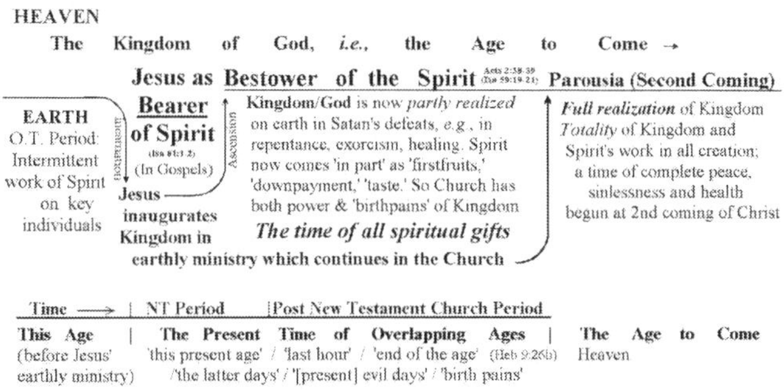

This also means that Jesus is continuously active in bestowing his gifts to all of us throughout this present age. This chart might be helpful in understanding this period of time.

This chart shows on the top lines that the kingdom of God is already the "Age to Come" in the "eternal now" in heaven. But the kingdom is intermittent in the experiences of the Old Testament. Then Jesus comes to bring the kingdom/Spirit as its introducer, bearer, modeler, commissioner, and ratifier in his earthly life. His mission was vindicated in the resurrection. Now Jesus moves from simply the bearer of the Spirit/kingdom to its bestower in this present age. This is "the time of all spiritual gifts" which will no longer be needed after Jesus' second coming (Gk. *parousia)*. In heaven all spiritual gifts (that are "in part" or "taste of the powers of the age to come") will be replaced by the fullness of what they represent: total knowledge, power, love, etc. Karl Barth said it succinctly, "Because the sun is rising, all the lights go out."[14]

Acts 1:1 says that its predecessor, the Gospel of Luke, describes only what Jesus "began to do and teach," while Acts shows what Jesus continues to do and teach through the Spirit (Acts 1:5). In restating what John the Baptist proclaimed, Jesus clearly states his mission: "John baptized with water, but in a few days you will be baptized with the Holy Spirit." Throughout this present age, Jesus, who is "exalted to the right hand of God . . . has received from the Father the promised Holy Spirit and has poured out what you now see and hear" (Acts 2:33). Jesus makes this same point in John 16:12–13: "I have yet many things to say to you, but you cannot bear them now. When the Spirit of truth comes, he will guide you into all the truth." This is the fullness of Jesus' teaching that will take place at a time when the disciples will be able to bear it, that is, when the New Covenant Spirit dwells in their hearts according to the promises of the Old Testament, especially Jeremiah 31:34. Disciples cannot receive what Jesus has to say by the Spirit until he is glorified (John 7:39).

This pattern of what Jesus began and continues to do is seen in the so-called programmatic statements, or prophecies, of Luke's first and second volumes. In the Gospel of Luke it is "The Spirit of the Lord is upon me to proclaim . . ." (Luke 4:18 > Isa 61:1–2). The programmatic prophecy for the Book of Acts is "This is my covenant with them: the Spirit that I put upon you [Jesus] and the words [of prophecy] I have put in your mouth will not depart from your mouth, or from the mouths of your children or the mouths of your children's children forever" (Isa 59:21). It is cited in Acts 2:39, "This promise [or covenant] *(epangelia)* is for you and your children and to those who are afar off, for all whom the Lord your God shall call."[15]

Jesus continues his unique, defined role as the bestower of the Spirit throughout this present age. There is however an important development in this role—not only is Jesus the bestower of the Spirit, he becomes the Spirit!

6. JESUS IS THE NEW COVENANT SPIRIT

As if Jesus' involvement in bringing the baptism in the New Covenant Spirit to us weren't enough with inaugurating it, modeling it, ratifying it, vindicating it, commissioning it, and bestowing it during this age of the church, Jesus actually *becomes* the New Covenant Spirit. This is foreshadowed in a so-called servant passage in Isaiah 42:6, "I have given you as a covenant to the people. . . ." Where traditional Trinitarian theology stresses the differences between the Son and the Spirit, the New Testament stresses the identity between the two. For example, the New Testament frequently uses the term "Spirit of Christ" (Rom 8:9; Phil 1:19; 1 Pet 1:11) or a clear linkage (Rom 8:11; 2 Cor 3:3; 13:14; 1 Pet 4:14). In these cases, one could argue that "Spirit of Christ" simply means "Spirit from Christ."

We also have cases of explicit identification of Christ and the Spirit. In the lengthy discourses to the disciples in the Gospel of John, Jesus promises "the Comforter, which is the Holy Ghost, whom the Father will send in my name, he shall teach you all things, and bring all things to your remembrance, whatsoever I have said unto you" (John 14:26, so also 15:26; 16:7). Additionally, the Comforter (Paraclete) promise that "he shall teach you all things" echoes the New Covenant promise of the Spirit from Jeremiah 31:34 (cf. 2 Cor 3). Jesus said, "I have many more things to say to you, but you cannot bear them now" (John 16:12). This strongly implies that a time will come when Jesus will finish this conversation. Indeed, this is the case, for he states, "I will not leave you as orphans; I will come to you" (John 14:18); and he is identified as "Christ who lives in you" (Gal 2:20). Since Jesus died and ascended into heaven, the only way he could come back to us—apart from his second physical coming—is as the New Covenant Spirit (Matt 28:20; John 14:16–20, 28; 16:7–33) who will "teach all things" (John 14:26 > Jer 31:34; Isa 59:21): one is the other.

In fact, this is exactly what Paul says in 2 Corinthians 3:17–18.

> Now the Lord is the Spirit, and where the Spirit of the Lord is, there is freedom. [18] And we all, with unveiled face, beholding the glory of the Lord, are being transformed into the same image from one degree of glory to another. For this comes from the Lord who is the Spirit. (2 Cor 3:17–18 ESV)

This passage comes in the context of a discussion about the superiority of the New Covenant of the Spirit over the Old Covenant of a written document. The New Covenant restores the ideal of man "in the image of God" from the Genesis creation of mankind, in that through the Spirit we are being "transformed into his likeness," that is, we are being brought into the ideal relationship with God—"made in his image and likeness" (Gen 1:26–27; 5:1). This is the goal of the New Covenant: "I will be their God and they will be my people" (Jer 31:33).

The apostle Paul compares Adam and Christ by saying, "The first man Adam became a living being; the last Adam, a life-giving Spirit" (1

Cor 15:45). So Jesus Christ, then, is identified with the Holy Spirit. Not exactly traditional, creedal theology, but this is what the Bible says.[16]

THE "FIRST POPE" SUMMARIZES A NEW TESTAMENT THEOLOGY OF JESUS' MISSION

In the following sample passage, 1 Peter 3:18—4:11, the apostle Peter outlines the themes of Jesus' New Covenant mission described in the preceding section, though not in the same sequence. This is presented here to show that the outline of Jesus' mission is not alien to the New Testament, nor to the later epistles which are thought by traditionalists to convey doctrine and not mere accounts of "confirming miracles" as the Gospels do. This passage, frequently cited as a proof text for traditional Protestant theology, is here offered as a refutation of that theology in that it supports our foregoing claims.

> 18 For Christ also suffered once for sins, the righteous for the
> unrighteous, that he might bring us to God, being put to death in the
> flesh but made alive in the spirit, 19 in which he went and proclaimed to
> the spirits in prison, 20 because they formerly did not obey, when God's
> patience waited in the days of Noah, while the ark was being prepared, in
> which a few, that is, eight persons, were brought safely through water. 21
> Baptism, which corresponds to this, now saves you, not as a removal of
> dirt from the body but as an appeal to God for a good conscience,
> through the resurrection of Jesus Christ, 22 who has gone into heaven
> and is at the right hand of God, with angels, authorities, and powers
> having been subjected to him. 4:1 Since therefore Christ suffered in the
> flesh, arm yourselves with the same way of thinking, for whoever has
> suffered in the flesh has ceased from sin, 2 so as to live for the rest of the
> time in the flesh no longer for human passions but for the will of God. 3
> For the time that is past suffices for doing what the Gentiles want to do,
> living in sensuality, passions, drunkenness, orgies, drinking parties, and
> lawless idolatry. 4 With respect to this they are surprised when you do
> not join them in the same flood of debauchery, and they malign you; 5
> but they will give account to him who is ready to judge the living and the

> dead. [6] For this is why the gospel was preached even to those who are dead, that though judged in the flesh the way people are, they might live in the spirit the way God does. [7] The end of all things is at hand; therefore be self-controlled and sober-minded for the sake of your prayers.[8] Above all, keep loving one another earnestly, since love covers a multitude of sins. [9] Show hospitality to one another without grumbling. [10] As each has received a gift, use it to serve one another, as good stewards of God's varied grace: [11] whoever speaks, as one who speaks oracles of God; whoever serves, as one who serves by the strength that God supplies—in order that in everything God may be glorified through Jesus Christ. To him belong glory and dominion forever and ever. Amen (1 Peter 3:18—4:11 ESV).

The themes in this passage regarding the New Covenant Spirit are clarified briefly:

1. Jesus inaugurates the New Covenant Spirit (1 Pet 3:18b; 4:6). Through the Spirit he announces [salvation] to the spirits in prison. In 4:6 Jesus preaches toward the goal that we might "live according to God in regard to the Spirit." That is, to live by "faith"—hearing and obeying as prophets, all the time on every issue.
2. Jesus models the New Covenant Spirit for his disciples in that he was "made alive by the Spirit, through whom" he was able to carry out his mission (4:19).[17] Peter here has the "preaching" of Jesus in the timeless dimension between Jesus' death and resurrected body, but the principle of his being empowered by the Spirit at his baptism (expressing death, burial, resurrection, and the reception of the Spirit/resurrected life) is the same for Jesus and for us (3:21). In all this Jesus serves as a teaching example to anyone who will follow and do the same things.
3. Jesus ratifies the New Covenant Spirit by his death (4:1–4) that forgives sins in preparation for ministry in the Spirit (4:7–11). In this suffering Jesus continues the modeling

process in the redemptive value of suffering that aids us in overcoming sin: "arm yourselves also with the same attitude, because he who has suffered in his body is done with sin. As a result, he does not live the rest of his earthly life for evil human desires, but rather for the will of God."

4. Jesus' resurrection vindicates and makes possible the next stage of Jesus' mission: "this water symbolizes baptism that now saves you also, not the removal of dirt from the body but the pledge of a good conscience toward God. It saves you by the resurrection of Jesus Christ."
5. Jesus' exaltation at God's "right hand" is the occasion for the submission of all creation to him (3:22). How? By the sending of the Spirit.
6. Jesus continually bestows the Spirit as he commissions his disciples at the end of this passage: "The end of all things is at hand" gives the time frame for the commissioning, that is, to continue until the end (1 Cor 1:6; 13:10; Eph 4:7–13 and many other passages).[18] The commissioning itself involves not only ministry prayer, but love, hospitality, and "whatever gift (*charisma*) he has received to serve others, faithfully administering God's grace (*charitas* "generous empowering") in its various forms (*poikilas*)."[19] Specifically, Peter lists, among these gifts, prophecy: "words of God" and prophetic empowerment "as from the power that God provides" (4:9–11).[20]

This passage, then (along with Eph 4:7–13 and others), spells out the main themes of the mission of Jesus, and therefore the core doctrine of Christianity. From here, we move on to Part V, which lays out the ideal response to the mission of Jesus Christ (Part IV) by the ideal human believer. Our tack again will be to unveil this theme by determining the emphases of the New Testament and the Bible as a whole.

---

1. What these terms mean may be unclear to those without a background in theology. Much of this sequence is found in Rom 8:29–30. Foreknowledge (God knows beforehand who will be saved – Rom 8:29), Predestination (God not only foreknows, but actually chooses ones to be saved), Calling (to "salvation," but originally had the overtone of being called to be a prophet), Regeneration ("born again"), Faith, Repentance, Justification (deemed righteous before God on the basis of Christ's sacrifice for sin), Adoption, Perseverance (hanging in there in faith), Mortification (putting to death the "old man," Eph 4:2; Col 3:9), Sanctification (made "holy," but originally "set apart" for priestly or prophetic mission), and, Glorification (see Matt 17:2 and parallels). The important thing here is that in this *ordo salutis*, traditional Protestants tended to see the Holy Spirit *limited to this sequence*. Benjamin Warfield, for example, when criticized for not accepting recent research on the charismatic dimension in pneumatology (doctrine of the Spirit), said, when responding to criticism that the Westminster Confession lacked a chapter specifically devoted to "The Holy Spirit and His Work" Warfield retorted, "The sole reason why it does not give *a* chapter to this subject . . . is because it prefers to give *nine* chapters to it." Those chapters appear to be 10 through 18 which treat a Calvinistic *ordo salutis*. It is only with this specific application to the Reformed stages of salvation in the post-biblical period of Christian history that Warfield can appreciate the working of the Holy Spirit. Only within this context then can we understand Warfield's praise for Calvin as "preeminently the theologian of the Holy Spirit." From Warfield's "Introductory Note" to Abraham Kuyper's *The Work of the Holy Spirit*, trans. Henri De Vries (New York: Funk and Wagnalls, 1900, repr., Grand Rapids: Eerdmans Pub. Co., 1979), xxvii.
2. This generalization by Paul is obviously not saying that henceforth all the gifts of the Spirit will be actually expressed in every single person throughout history (1 Cor 12:30). Rather, he seems to be affirming that all spiritual gifts will be empowered "among everyone" (*en pasin*), much as we would say "there is money in that crowd": some might have no money, others, plenty.
3. Replicating the total of 72 newly-commissioned elders of Israel who received the Spirit (Num 11:24–30)?
4. Yes, 3. Remember that Paul was not in these groups of 12 and 72. Fifty-four percent of the New Testament was written by non-apostles, which further strains the connection between miracles and the writing of Scripture. This doesn't count the Gospel of Matthew who shows no evidence, as John and Mark, of someone close to an eyewitness. He uses Mark and a common source with Luke (the infamous Q), and very little that is original with him. The text of the New Testament itself, not even the Gospel bearing his name, does not state that Matthew was the author. Attaching the Gospel to him is based on fairly late church tradition. I would believe Matthew, the disciple of Jesus, was the author if it were in the Bible, but it isn't. But even if Matthew did write the Gospel with his name on it, a huge proportion of the New Testament was written by non-apostles, and only 3 or 4 wrote anything, of the 90 or so apostles. Against the criteria of Acts 1:21–26 even Paul, and probably other apostles mentioned in the New Testament, would not have qualified as an apostle. Could it be that, even as the Twelve hurried to consolidate their position by casting lots, the sovereign Spirit instead broadened his commission by anointing the 120 with his Spirit?

5. Certainly, "everything" could include commands other than healings and deliverances. It has been pointed out that the earlier commissions in the Gospels included commands that were consistent with limited objectives (no purse, not to Gentiles, etc.), indicating that these earlier, charismatic commissions were unique and non-repeatable. The problem with this view is that, while some commands indicated a limited scope in a specific historical setting, the commands to announce the kingdom through healings and deliverances represented the very core of Jesus' own ministry that the disciples, as disciples, were replicating. This Spirit-centered charismatic mission was also commanded in Acts 1, and what was demonstrated throughout the rest of Acts and the epistles.
6. See Ruthven, "'This Is My Covenant with Them': Isaiah 59.19–21 as the Programmatic Prophecy of the New Covenant in the Acts of the Apostles." *JPT* 17 (2008), 32–47 and 219–237.
7. For a thorough comparison (almost identification) of the concepts of Spirit and Kingdom in the New Testament, see James D. G. Dunn, "Spirit and Kingdom," *Expository Times* 82 (1970–71): 36–40.
8. Because a major point of this book is to understand that life in the New Covenant means living in the Spirit with his normative charismata and that the mission of Jesus is to get us into this life, we need to read freshly some of the most familiar Scripture. 1 Cor 11, regarding the Lord's Supper, effectively provides the theological and practical grounding for the three subsequent chapters (12, 13, and 14). The Lord's Supper celebrates "The New Covenant in [Jesus'] blood," key features of which are expressed in Isa 59:21 and Jer 32:33. The New Covenant expressed in these and other Scriptures shapes the significance of chapter 11 and its context. As we will see, the rejection of the poor or lower classes within the Corinthian house church(es) as part of their taking the Lord's Supper violated the essence of the New Covenant of the Spirit, which was poured out on "*all* flesh," irrespective of social distinctions (Joel 2:28–29 > Acts 2:17–18, a passage paraphrased in Gal 3:26–29—*all* "heirs according to the promise/covenant"). The Eucharist, eating and drinking the body and blood of Jesus, was a covenant renewal ritual (based on the Passover) celebrating Jesus' ultimate sacrifice to bring us *all* into the New Covenant of the Spirit and his power. This social snubbing of these New Covenant, Spirit-filled "men servants and maid servants" effectively also snubbed the blood of Jesus, which had ratified this New Covenant of the charismatic Spirit, and His broken body distributed "for you" (composed of the charismatically-gifted "members" 12:7).

   Hence, failure to "discern the body" or to eat and drink "unworthily" by dishonoring the low-status members of the body (1 Cor 11:20–22) contradicted the sacrifice of Jesus, the "signing-in-blood" of the New Covenant, for a large part of the Christian community as New Covenant bearers of the Spirit. By this rejection, the elite failed to follow Jesus' own precedent of giving everything and thereby broke the New Covenant. As a result, they suffered its penalties: "That is why many of you are weak and ill, and some have died" (1 Cor 11:30 ESV, cf. Deut 28). Ironically, the low-status, yet very gifted, people who could have prayed for healing and even for rising from the dead were ignored by the elite, who thought they were enhancing their own status by uttering incomprehensible divine oracles (tongues) which edified no one else in the gathering. Against 1 Cor 13, these elites practiced gifts with no love. In this action, they thwarted the whole generous mission of Jesus to inaugurate the New Covenant of the charismatic Spirit. (For a study of the relationship between social status and speaking in tongues in 1 Cor, see Dale Martin, "Tongues of Angels and Other Status Indicators," *Journal of the American Academy of Religion* 59, no 3 [Fall 1991] 547–589.)

9. Isa 59:19 is a favorite verse among charismatics: "When **the enemy** shall **come** in **like** a **flood**, the Spirit of the Lord shall lift up a standard against him." Unfortunately, this King James translation is so far off, it isn't even *wrong!*
10. This event that opened the Holy of Holies, dramatically demonstrated that the death of Christ successfully ratified a New Covenant that allowed believers to do the unthinkable: to enter boldly into the very presence of God at the holiest place on earth, where only the High Priest could enter, and then only once a year. "Therefore, brothers, since we have confidence to enter the Most Holy Place by the blood of Jesus, by a new and living way opened for us through the curtain, that is, his body, and since we have a great priest over the house of God, let us draw near to God with a sincere heart in full assurance of faith" (Heb 10:19–22).
11. Colin Humphreys and W. G. Waddington, "The Jewish Calendar, a Lunar Eclipse and the Date of Christ's Crucifixion." *Tyndale Bulletin,* 43:2 (Nov 1992): 331–351.
12. Although this was a big enough deal to split the Church into what became Roman Catholicism and Orthodoxy in ad 1054—a triumph of religion over the *unity* of the Spirit; ironically, it was the very issue over which they were *fighting!*
13. Traditional theology sees apostles and prophets essentially as Scripture-writing popes, inconsistently limiting the first two gifts to the apostolic age, while allowing evangelists and pastor-teachers to continue. On this see Ruthven, *On the Cessation of the Charismata,* rev. ed. (2011), 133–140.
14. Karl Barth, *The Resurrection of the Dead,* trans. H. J. Stenning (New York: Arno Press, 1977), 81.
15. This whole program is mapped out in my article, "This Is My Covenant with Them: Isaiah 59.19–21 as the Programmatic Prophecy of the New Covenant in the Acts of the Apostles," *JPT* 17:1–2 (2008), (Part I) 32–47; (Part II) 219–237; also available as Appendix IV in *On the Cessation of the Charismata,* rev. and expanded ed. (Tulsa, Okla.: Word & Spirit Press, 2011).
16. For a thorough summary of scholarship on the relation of Christ and the Spirit, see G. Fee, *God's Empowering Presence: The Holy Spirit in the Letters of Paul* (Peabody, Mass.: Hendrickson, 1994), 831-34. Larry W. Hurtado, however, effectively pushes past the more traditionalist views of the persons of the Trinity toward a strictly biblical understanding his *God in New Testament Theology.* Library of Biblical Theology (Nashville, Tenn.: Abingdon, 2010).
17. The "spirits in prison" have presented a problem to interpreters for generations with the resulting summary of conclusions:

    When Noah was building the ark, Christ 'in spirit' was in Noah preaching repentance and righteousness through him to unbelievers who were on the earth then but are now "spirits in prison" (people in hell).

    After Christ died and before his resurrection, he went and preached to people in hell, offering them a second chance of salvation.

    After Christ died, he went and preached to people in hell, proclaiming to them that he had triumphed over them and their condemnation was final.

    After Christ died, he proclaimed release to people who had repented just before they died in the flood, and led them out of their imprisonment (in Purgatory) into heaven.

After Christ died (or: after he rose but before he ascended into heaven), he travelled to hell and proclaimed triumph over the fallen angels who had sinned by marrying human women before the flood.

I owe this summary to Wayne Grudem *The First Epistle of Peter: An Introduction and Commentary* (Grand Rapids: Eerdmans, 1988), 206–225.

Whatever is true about the "earlier" preaching, the point of the passage is that Jesus' proclamation applies also to us as we partake in his ministry, death, resurrection, and his commissioning to us to use the charismata so that God be praised "through him" (through Jesus' mission of bestowing the Spirit?). "To him [Jesus Christ] be the glory and the power for ever and ever. Amen." The terms "glory" and "power" are closely associated with the *charismata* that are his forever (not withdrawn—Rom 11:29).

18. See *On the Cessation of the Charismata,* rev. and expanded ed. (Tulsa, Okla.: Word & Spirit Press, 2011): 107–68.
19. The same Greek word is used in the term "various miracles" in Heb 2:4, showing how God "bears witness" or reveals himself.
20. We are commanded to use that divine power (*ischuos*) in Eph 1:19 and 6:10, which appears in the context to be the normative, characteristic miracle power of the Spirit-filled Christian.

PART FIVE
HOW PROTESTANTS MESSED UP DISCIPLESHIP

The final part of this book focuses on the central message of the Bible (hearing God's voice and obeying through testing) in the same context Jesus conducted his earthly ministry and continues it ever after—through discipleship. This seems to me a more relevant conclusion than traditional eschatology takes, which usually appears in textbooks as a somewhat detached, tourist's view of the end times.

Why discipleship? Several reasons:

1. Because transmitting God's message/word is the task of the Bible—a book that is, after all, an instruction manual for all generations. It has a lot to say about discipleship and how to do it.
2. Despite its extreme importance in Scripture, the study of discipleship as a process is seriously neglected in traditional teaching and theology.
3. Moreover, as a rule, discipleship as practiced in churches, and especially formal theological institutions, has drifted very far from the content and method of the New Testament—replacing it with lots of verbal instruction in theology and

> ethics, but very little emphasis about modeling on charismatic ministry and practicing it.

If we are serious about being faithful to God's message in Scripture, then we must "not be ignorant of the devil's devices" in traditional education for ministry. Because of the subtle nature of systemic cultural bias that deflects from God's truth, it is crucial that we closely examine the traditional (Protestant) academic system that poisons all our best efforts to disciple and train our next generation in the ministry of Jesus.

The message of this book is not alarmism, nor is it being needlessly confrontational. There really is a serious problem! Just because we have been raised in this traditional system, being brainwashed into conformity with a system that is explicitly motivated by pride (grades, degrees) and the praise of men (accreditation, academic prestige), it is therefore extremely important to identify and break off these educational yokes that are so deadly to our Christian faith. We are required by God in Scripture to see these traditions and values the same way Jesus sees them, and then follow Him faithfully in His radically different direction (in the sense of going back to the root).

Since we have been soaked from birth in this educational culture and have unconsciously absorbed its values, it is extremely difficult to grasp how pernicious and evil this system is when we adopt it as the medium (which is the message) for training the next generation in knowing God, his voice, and his power. To put it rather impolitely, to teach God's message of the Bible in a traditional educational format is like trying to teach sexual purity in a brothel—we're teaching a double message of conflicting values. As we shall see in this concluding study, in theological education, the academic system that is so alien to the practice of faith (hearing God) actually shapes the message of the Bible even as it does its messengers.

12

THE PROBLEM—THEOLOGY OR MINISTRY TRAINING?

For at least the last millennium of Christian history, if ever there was an example of the confusion of cultural values overwhelming truly Christian values, it is in the area of training for ministry.[1] Over a broad front, Western intellectual values inimical to normative Christian experience and their resulting teaching modalities have metastasized throughout the body of Christ, effectively killing many of its members. That is, whole denominations have virtually perished, spiritually and numerically, as a direct result of certain traditions within theological education done in the wrong spirit, toward wrong goals, using wrong methods. While it is fashionable these days for new PhDs to smile at the older generation for their fear of "theological cemeteries," this section affords us the opportunity to examine the concerns of our fathers[2] with at least the same urgency that we examine other marginal concerns that have occupied our time. The English poet Matthew Arnold, who sensed that he was "wandering between two worlds, one dead, the other powerless to be born," could well serve as a kind of spiritual archetype for today's seminaries or Bible colleges. The quotation appears in "Stanzas from the Grande Chartreuse," a reflection of Arnold's Romantic era zeitgeist: a wistful longing for an ancient faith, both strong and reassuring, but which at the same time he viewed as a naïve relic of a simpler past now sadly inaccessible to the enlightened seeker.

Similarly, we find ourselves trapped in a dilemma of our own making—even of our own spiritual commitment. While on the one hand we clearly see the vitality of our fathers' faith, and that displayed in the Third World, we at the same time find ourselves seduced by a sophisticated though secular worldview of education that is by almost any measure, moribund.

Just as a squid when threatened releases volumes of ink, so let me squirt out some caveats on the nature of this study.

First, even though it may at first sound like it, this section is not a wholesale attack on Pentecostal or charismatic institutions, particularly seminaries. It is banal to say that we live and work at the end of a long evolution (or, perhaps better, devolution) of Christian institutions. When we think of examining the nature of theological education today, we are (or at least, I am) committed to working within traditions and institutions that depart in any significant ways from the forms found in the New Testament. Hence, we expect to accommodate ourselves to the existing order, just as, say, St Paul did with the synagogue system and the religious lifestyles of his day. We must add, however, that institutions are created and preserved by an agenda—either explicit or hidden. In any case, our true motives will ultimately emerge in tangible expressions of tradition and institution.

Second, we would not deny the power and utility of serious biblical and theological scholarship. The point at issue here is not a question of antiintellectualism or denial of academic rigor as it contributes to the edification of the church. Certainly many of us owe much to the labors of the biblical theology movement spawned two generations ago by Neo-orthodoxy. This movement was the source of a radically charismatic understanding of the Spirit, of the Kingdom of God, the meaning of New Testament miracles, discipleship, and the solution of many of our theological problems with the discovery of the New Testament tension of the "already" and "not yet"—just to name a few issues. Indeed, our whole theological vocabulary from one end to the other has been enriched by works like Kittel's *Theological Dictionary.* A few of us "out-of-the-closet" Pentecostals, besieged in cessationist seminaries in the 1960s found great comfort and support in such biblical theologies as those by Alan Richardson (my favorite), Adolf Schlatter, and Joachim Jeremias. Even Bultmann's *New Testament Theology* and Gunkel's *Die Wirkungen des Heligen Geistes*—as long as we stayed in the "descriptive" material—showed us Pentecostals that we could believe our own eyes (against our evangelical instructors') when we read the New Testament![3]

A generation later, we can rejoice in the explosion of more moderate and Pentecostal-friendly literature from evangelicals who collectively today more nearly dominate North American biblical and theological scholarship. Certainly these works reflect the godly excitement of spiritual discovery following the divine mandate to explore and subdue God's good creation. The question this observation raises, however, is how scholarship fits into the mission of the seminary.

Third, even though the intervening years of church history have produced great insights into Christian thought and practice, we prescind from generating a historical survey of these issues to examine applicable biblical teaching as a starting point for further discussion. It is naïve to assume that our biblical hermeneutic is unaffected by our tradition, yet we would submit that the biblical material has not yet had an entirely fair hearing on generating policy for seminaries.[4]

Fourth, we need a word on definitions. For this section, the term, "theological education" represents the traditional seminary approach to developing clergy, with an emphasis upon the acquisition of information rather than the acquisition of effective spiritual and ministry giftings. "Christian discipleship" is more the reverse.

In this section we attempt to move beyond the simple observations about the efficacy of Pentecostal ministerial training, which, at least statistically in terms of outcomes these days, probably is not all that bad.[5] Despite the fairly positive figures, however, there is a continuing unease that traditional seminary education somehow fails to deliver on its promise of producing effective Christian workers[6]—that in fact the seminary experience contributes little to the effectiveness of its graduates. Ian S. Markham, President of Virginia Theological Seminary, notes an inverse relationship between "better" theological education and the growth of the denominations it serves.[7] A premise of this section is that to the extent that Pentecostal/charismatic seminaries participate in the characteristics of traditional theological education (TTE) in the areas outlined below—is the extent to which this criticism applies. This section is not an attempt to impugn the motives or Christian commitment of overworked professors in Pentecostal/charismatic seminaries and Bible colleges. I hope it may serve as a warning to us as to the power of our widely-accepted cultural expressions, particularly academic structures, to vitiate the effectiveness of our Christian ministry.

This project seeks to examine three issues that the New Testament views as foundational to the development of a productive minister/disciple. It contrasts these issues against their expression in traditional theological education (TTE) which has proven inimical to effective Christian ministry training. These are . . .

1. epistemology,
2. goals, and
3. teaching modalities.

Each of these elements will be examined in a dialectic: first from the starting point of the biblical norms, then from elements in theological education that contravene those norms, and finally a statement of how the biblical alternative might be practically and appropriately experienced in discipleship.

Our first area of investigation is central to understanding the internal contradictions characterizing any traditional seminary.

1. EPISTEMOLOGY

Epistemology lies at the very core of what it is to be Christian. The central story of Scripture is the issue of first, how we know something is true, and then second, what one does about it. Placed as prominently as possible in the key narratives of the First and Second Adams is the same temptation: to ignore the direct and immediate voice of God and to act independently according to some other principle.

BIBLICAL GROUNDING

We know the story of Eve's choice: to heed God or to be "like God" by her own knowledge isolated from God. But the temptation of the Second Adam is more variously understood. My understanding is that in typical Semitic style, the three temptations are variations on a single theme: the temptation to mis-apply or pre-apply God's "promises" without the immediate assurance of faith (revealed knowledge) to confirm the principle in the case at hand. The temptations are an exercise in the Old Testament "wisdom" tradition in which the wise person discerns the appropriate application of a principle. In both narratives the contrasting issues are "a hearing of faith" or "works of the law." Is Christian knowledge at its core revelatory or is it the independent human acquisition and processing of information?

The beginning of Paul's theological tractate, Romans, lays out the same alternatives before mankind: will "the just man ... live by his faith" (hearing God with appropriate response) or will he "suppress the truth in his unrighteousness?" "For although they knew God they did not honor him as God or give thanks to him, [so without this orientation and commitment] they became futile in their thinking and their senseless minds/hearts were darkened. Claiming to be wise, they became fools," and it is all downhill from there.

The first three chapters of 1 Corinthians treat the two ways of knowing in some detail. Paul sets the tone of this section around a theme of divisions "in mind and thought" that precipitate around leaders of Christian "schools" (Paul, Apollos, Cephas, Christ). Paul is fearful that the initiatory Christian experience, baptism, would result in a misdirected bonding with a leader-teacher in the Christian community. This bonding of students around a teacher was the standard cultural practice of the time, a culture that prized intellectual competition in philosophy and rhetoric.

This culture included the Jews of Jesus' time—those very intellectuals Jesus accused of self promotion (Matt 23:5–7), of fascination with titles and rank while competing against godly, revelatory knowledge (vv 8–9), of the destruction of kingdom faith in their students (vv 13–14) while at the same time maintaining an aggressive student recruitment program (v 15).

It was only natural then for Paul to tie in this state of affairs (academic pride and factionalism) with the same major theme of our section: the nature of the two "wisdoms" vying for control of the church. He appeals to his mission from Christ to preach the gospel, and then he makes an amazing contrast: "not with words of human wisdom, lest the cross of Christ be emptied of its power" (1 Cor 1:17). This theme is repeated in 2:1–5:

> And I, when I came to you, brothers, did not come proclaiming to you the testimony of God with lofty speech or wisdom. [2] For I decided to know nothing among you except Jesus Christ and him crucified. [3] And I was with you in weakness and in fear and much trembling, [4] and my speech and my message were not in plausible words of wisdom, but in demonstration of the Spirit and of power, [5] so that your faith might not rest in the wisdom of men but in the power of God (ESV).

The clear implication of this passage from what follows is a clash of powers: on the one hand the crucified Jesus, who in the mind of Greeks was an absurd joke. Here they see a young failure from the sticks of a backward country who could not even manage his own survival but yet had the temerity to insist on guiding everyone else! What could this disgusting, ignorant criminal possibly tell us—the culture the whole world emulates? On the other hand, we see the powers lifted up for emulation: the wise man, the scholar, the philosopher of this age, ultimately, the "rulers of this age"—all which possess the "wisdom of the world."

How does Paul characterize this "wisdom"? It is competitive and divisive; it is prideful and boastful; it involves "boasting about men" (teachers); it sees itself as persuasive and powerful; and it also characterizes "this age," "this world" which is "passing away," "coming to nothing," or "futile," because the wisdom of this world will be shamed by the "foolish of this world." Elsewhere, Paul complains about debates over "myths and genealogies which promote speculations rather than the divine training that is in faith" (1 Tim 1:4)—that of hearing and obeying God. Indeed the very essence of the kingdom of God is that it "does not consist in talk, but in power" (1 Cor 4:20). Above all, this wisdom utterly fails to understand God—even to the point of trying to kill Him—simply because it is the kind of wisdom Eve and Adam chose, and Jesus rejected. Paul is emphasizing that God's wisdom is, in its essence, revealed as a function of an intimacy with God.

Finally, we lack space to fully treat the concrete manifestation of these two worlds colliding in the experience of Paul in 2 Corinthians 10-13. Instead we will provide a sketch in the following comments. Let us now see how this kind of "wisdom" and "knowledge" appears in our system of TTE.

TRADITIONAL THEOLOGICAL EDUCATION

There are identifiable characteristics of TTE that display its anti-Christian epistemology as laid out above. One proof of this is the use of language that characterizes the structure, if not the very character, of our academies. We evaluate and rank both students and teachers in clear, invidious hierarchies.[8] We assign rank and value to students, using such terms as, grades, degrees, good or bad student, excellent, outstanding, mediocre, or poor.[9] Soon they advance or progress in their institute of higher learning or graduate school to graduate with a degree —we hope with a graduate, rather than a mere undergraduate, degree, or, heaven forbid, a diploma from a high school!

At this point, TTE assigns further distinctions to graduates:[10] "cum laude" (with praise), "magna cum laude" (with great praise); or, at the peak of glory, "summa cum laude" (with total praise)!

We might assume that because a theological seminary or Bible school is in the business of training effective Christian workers, that it would identify and honor those with say, effectiveness in evangelism or church ministry, prayer, faith, morality, demonstrations of spiritual power, or even religious commitment. Actually, none of these appear on the diploma, on the transcript, or are factored into the laude. Instead, the defining ranking is based wholly on what the graduate has intellectually grasped and verbalized during his theological education.

This system of assigning importance and status based on intellectual knowledge completely bypasses a sense of committed intimacy of a believing relationship with God. Nothing could more clearly communicate the value system of TTE! What is particularly chilling is that someone who is Satan incarnate, who "knows" theology and ministry better than any of us, could receive total praise from our schools!

Lest you think this is an absurd abstraction, let me share with you a true story: A certain Pentecostal/charismatic seminary was in the advanced stages of hiring a fairly distinguished Pentecostal professor for its faculty. A female staff member went house-hunting with this professor. At one house, as they interviewed the owner, the question came up, "Why are you selling?" Tears welled up in the owner's eyes as he mumbled something about a divorce. In this opportune moment, the staff member began to gently approach the hurting man about his need for Jesus. The professor brusquely snapped, "This is not the time and place for this!" When she persisted in the approach to this unsaved man, the professor repeatedly tried to stop her. This vignette reflects a number of similar behaviors of this "distinguished" professor.

The question we ought to confront is this: by what criteria did this professor attain distinguished or prominent status in our community? In other words, what system of knowledge was in force here?

Faculty, we find, receive status, power, and the credibility to convince from the same system of institutionalized detached knowledge.[11] Here again, the ranking is clear and institutionalized: Instructor, Assistant Professor, Associate Professor, Dean, etc. Is this system of status based on divine or human criteria? Is it a harmless, value-neutral convention borrowed from our culture in much the same way church organizational structure in the New Testament was borrowed from the synagogue? Or does it reflect the essence of the Hellenistic *hubris*[12] Paul describes in 2 Corinthians 10:12b? "When they measure themselves by one another, and compare themselves with one another, they are without understanding."

It is interesting that in his conflict with the super-apostles in 2 Corinthians, Paul appears to parody the Hellenistic encomium (dare we say résumé) when he lays out a grotesque comedy of humiliations he suffered from the academic, political, and religious establishment. Lurking beneath these humiliations—the very opposite of the honors, letters of recommendation and status of his opponents, (possibly some of the original apostles of Christ)—there may well have been an appeal to the doctrine of the eschatological woes suffered by true saints. Those same woes, in a prototypical way, conform to the crucified Christ himself. It is just that humiliating experience, not academic status, that Paul suggests characterize the true Christian.

The knowledge of the pagans and even of the super-apostles appears to be talk without power (1 Cor 4:20). In contrast is a true apostle whose actions in divine power exemplify that which is to be ideally true of all Christians whose knowledge was the experience. This true experience would thus replicate both the power and humiliating suffering of Jesus Christ (2 Cor 12:12; Phil 3:9–10).

Earlier, in Matthew 23:5–15, Jesus explicitly forbade his disciples even to use the standard academic terms for teacher (Rabbi for "my great one," "teacher," "master") because this practice lay in clear conflict with the normative indwelling of the teaching/Law/Torah/Spirit of God in one's heart or mouth as the central characteristic of the New Covenant (Jer 31:33; Isa 59:21).[13] Why? This practice of labeling human teachers with high-status terms is forbidden because it gives a false authority to human teaching, which contradicts directly the New Testament way God teaches us (via the New Covenant Spirit). It is toxic because it makes students "twice [as much] a son of hell" as the instructors (23:15)! Students quickly bite the serpent's apple: they rabidly invoke prideful flaunting of knowledge (via academic status labels) as superior to the knowledge of God by the Spirit and the humble sacrifice of Christ.

According to Jesus, this academic labeling consciously pits "rabbi" and "master" against Christian "brothers" (who minister God's revelation to each other); "father" (also a term for teacher or religious leader) against God the Father; and "teacher" against Christ himself as our exclusive teacher (Matt 23:8–10). Whereas in Christian educational institutions we see this academic labeling as in service to the mission of Jesus, Jesus himself sees these academic labels as expressing direct conflict with his mission!

The academic system is also a system based on pride which one day must be humbled (Matt 23:11–12). Needless to say, these commands of Jesus about academic labels and the system they represent are routinely and blithely ignored in our Christian educational institutions! This can only be because we have completely, if semi-consciously, embraced the godless academic system these labels represent.

To sum up this section, theological education has then largely adopted the traditional academic model for training clergy. Its way of knowing is pagan, not biblical. This way of knowing promotes a detached, uncommitted, objective relationship to its subject matter. It has institutionalized competition, pride, and dependence on the praise of men (these days we call it accreditation).[14] Typically, it holds out as an ideal the emulation of institutions of higher learning that have nevertheless devastated or stunted the faith of millions. This educational model is seductive precisely because (at least in the expression of scientific method) it has been so spectacularly successful in understanding and manipulating the physical world. It has put men on the moon, a car in every garage, a chicken in every pot, and polyester on our backs. It empowers us to communicate, to travel, to be entertained, to be healed. Part of the seduction of using scientific knowledge as the basis for TTE is the fact that knowledge is measured by the impressive accumulation of scientific data—doubling every 30 months.[15] Some would even say, wrongly, that this explosion of scientific data represents a fulfillment of Daniel 12:4 "in the last days . . . knowledge will be increased." In identifying the knowledge of God with the accumulation of data, we see that the seduction is successful as a failed model for training Christian workers.

The contrast, however, that plays out so prominently in the New Testament is not around the content of knowledge, but rather around its source, object, and use to which it is put.[16] Accordingly, one's epistemology will lead inevitably to the direction one's activities take.

2. GOALS OF TRAINING FOR MINISTRY

The traditional theological education model for seminaries forces a double-minded view of goals vis-à-vis normative, i.e., New Testament, Christianity. As a result, Christian workers today face different church structures and roles that have evolved into forms far different from those of the New Testament. Nonetheless, few of us would actually disagree that the mission of Jesus and that which he passed on to his disciples involves a strong component of charismatic activity.

BIBLICAL GROUNDING

We know this from Jesus' programmatic statements that not only was Jesus' mission of the kingdom centrally charismatic (summarized in Luke 4:18–21, 43; Acts 2:22; 10:38) but the fact that he specifically repeats the emphases of his own mission in the commissions to his disciples (Matt 10; Luke 9—10[17] and Matt 28:19–20, cf. 24:14, "until the end of the age").

This same charismatic emphasis grounds the whole Book of Acts where the church's commission (1:58) is to present the kingdom in the power of signs and wonders and the preaching of the word. In fact, 27.2 percent of the text of Acts are pericopes of signs, wonders, and other charismatic activity. The repeated summary statements of Paul's mission (Acts 15:12; Rom. 15:18–20; 1 Cor 2:4; 2 Cor 12:12; 1 Thes 1:5) show the continuation of this normative pattern of presenting and living out the gospel of the exalted Christ in "word and deed."[18] In this light, the implications of believers' commissioned, but not yet fully realized, vice-regency with the exalted, gift-bestowing Christ could profitably be explored;[19] for Scripture is clear that after the inauguration of the kingdom, the ongoing church continues in the power of the Spirit, edifying itself via the *charismata* until the end of this age.

A reading of the New Testament unfettered by traditional Protestant theology will show that Jesus spends a great deal of time both modeling and teaching about faith and prayer as derivative goals for the mission described above. Analysis of the *pistis* family of words ("faith/believe") in the New Testament, shows that, where the context is explicit as to the intended result of faith, 93 of 230, or over 40 percent of the passages, refer to healings and other acts of power.[20] Moreover, in the Gospel of Mark, for example, major miracle stories occupy a large amount of the text and point the reader explicitly to an unusual, tradition-breaking, aggressive faith in the quest for wholeness (2:1–12; 5:1–20, 21–43; 6:30–56; 7:21–37; 8:14–29; 10:46–52). This highly charismatic New Testament emphasis on the intended result of faith is scarcely mentioned in traditional systematic texts, which tie faith almost exclusively to the *ordo salutis*.

To the contrary, the themes that Scripture reveals for New Testament discipleship training seem to focus on developing the skills needed to replicate the mission of Jesus. If we are to take the commissions of Jesus seriously, these skills would include prayer, faith (for healings, casting out demons, and freedom from sin), along with ministry within church and aggressive evangelism.

TRADITIONAL THEOLOGICAL EDUCATION

It would follow from the above, that if the emphases of the New Testament are applied evenly, we would need to rethink the goals and curricula of our traditional theological educational institutions. Yet even if we concede that Pentecostal institutions are aware of developing a strong charismatic expression in their graduates, the TTE culture works at what appears to be cross-purposes. Indications of this conflict appear typically in two standard documents of a seminary: the catalog and the faculty handbook.

Usually the catalog speaks in glowing terms about the work of the Holy Spirit in both the school activities and in the graduate's ministry, while sections of the faculty handbook often seem headed in another direction. As one non-tenured seminary professor once told me, "Around here, it's publish or parish," as though pastoral ministry represented failure and loss of status.

In the pressure for self-promotion and the fame game in seminaries, the practical ministry department, including missions, tends to be at the low end of the totem pole. All the while, the subject of ministry is central in most cases, to the published raison d'être for the seminary's existence! In faculty meetings, it may well be that the production of a scholarly monograph from a ranking publisher trumps a missions professor's taking 40 tons of grain and the gospel into North Korea, or a ministry prof holding huge revival meetings in Moscow or New Delhi. John Woodyard notes this phenomenon succinctly.

> Currently, major rewards for the seminary professor are research-based, academically and intellectually-based affirmations from published books and articles. Unless different spiritual, emotional, economic, and social rewards for the professor can be created, little or no change can be expected in seminary operations, relationships with the churches, or instruction for the students.[21]

From the very beginning in North America, shaped apparently by English stratified culture and the Enlightenment, the central goal of seminaries has been the crafting of "learned gentlemen"[22] whose academic credentials would assure status and power within the community.[23] Edward Farley, a former professor of theology at Vanderbilt University Divinity School, shows that this same Hellenistic, anti-Christian drive for academic prestige instead of appropriate ministry training continued in modern seminaries.

> Alumni and their affiliated denominations . . . tend to criticize the schools for being "too academic," straying too far from the canons of denominational belief, or being insufficiently practical. But despite these recurring complaints, *theological schools have more and more tended to make academic quality the central element in their reputations* [emphasis mine]. Accordingly, faculty members are required to have earned the Ph.D. degree, and to be promising scholars who contribute to their fields and meet high standards for tenure and promotion. This commitment to having a first-rate academic faculty draws schools into the ethos of American higher education.[24]

And, we might add, away from biblical goals, as well as from effective traditional ministry. In all seriousness, Jesus himself could not qualify to teach in a traditional theological seminary, though conceivably he might be invited in occasionally as an adjunct resource person. Farley continues that because of specialization and the need to protect its turf, "professors' primary loyalty is likely to be to their fields of study [and their prominence in it!] rather than to the school's general aims." Again we see the conflict of goals between catalog and faculty handbook.

The conflict of goals does not end there. A survey of more than 800 lay people, pastors, and seminary professors showed an astonishing divergence in ranking the qualities of an ideal pastor, here summarized in this table.[25]

QUALITIES DESIRED IN PASTORS, RANKED

Rank	by Laypersons	by Pastors	by Professors
1st	Spirituality	Relational Skills	Theological Knowledge
2nd	Relational Skills	Management Skills	Character
3rd	Character	Communication Skills	Leadership Skills
4th	Communication Skills	Spirituality	Communication Skills
5th	Theological Knowledge	Theological Knowledge	Counseling Skills

Note that the most striking difference between the laity and the seminary professors was "spirituality." Where it was ranked first on the list of desirable pastoral traits by the people in the pew, the seminary professors had no room for it on their list! Conversely, where the professors ranked theological knowledge first, the laity and pastors ranked it last.[26] This gap would likely not occur in Pentecostal seminaries. But the point here is to demonstrate the power of the secular, or pagan, epistemology to set goals for TTE.

This tradition of intellectualized ministerial training is literally forced upon seminaries by accrediting bodies.[27] Very early in the history of the Association of Theological Schools (ATS) it was determined that the standard Bachelor of Divinity degree for pastors (now the MDiv) should represent, not a standard for ministry effectiveness, but rather a "standard of scholarship."[28]

As a consequence, it is no wonder that the Murdock[29] report on seminary effectiveness can conclude . . .

- Pastors are highly educated, but generally feel poorly prepared for the job they hold (p. 7)
- In the pastors' forums, those who were seminary graduates reported that they found 70% to 80% of their seminary education did not apply to the duties they were expected to perform in the churches they served as ministers (p. 24).
- With 50% of seminary graduates leaving professional ministry, seminaries are not doing a good job of training. Seminaries need more "practitioners" as teachers. Professors need hands-on ministry experience (p. 19).

If the goals of effective training for ministry actually conflict with the goals for the curricula and careers of most seminary professors, then necessarily another disturbing disconnect occurs: the ineffective *delivery* of training to the seminary students.

3. TEACHING MODALITIES

The clash between the two worlds expresses itself most clearly in the curriculum and its form of presentation. The format is characterized by the presentation of information rather than training; the information is depersonalized—as easily learned from a video as from a live teacher. The information deals with issues rarely if ever encountered in real ministry, but instead reflects tradition or the academic interests of the instructor. The knowledge tends to intimidate rather than edify; it can be intellectually exciting, but spiritually empty. And the knowledge is powerless when facing serious spiritual need; it evokes a vaguely guilty, uncomfortable feeling in the presence of God.

BIBLICAL GROUNDING

The biblical model of teaching modalities for Christian workers is characterized by (1) a significant New Testament emphasis on the process (2) implementing a highly-charismatic expression of ministry skills or giftings (3) within settings of actual ministry (4) primarily by means of mentoring relationships. Let us briefly review each in turn.

> (1) In contrast to its neglected mention within traditional theology, discipleship and its processes receive a great deal of attention in the New Testament.[30] Louw-Nida lists some 42 words or word groups that appear in the semantic field, "Guide, Discipline, Follow," whereas 26 different expressions appear for "teach" or "instruct," which involve a sizeable number of references to such activities as repeating, following, obeying, or instructing.[31] At crucial points the term, mimesis (imitation), or its family occurs 11 times.

We might suggest in view of this New Testament emphasis, that traditional theology ought to heed what Scripture is saying about how to teach, instead of unconsciously applying culturally-approved modalities borrowed from other disciplines.

It is important not simply that instruction is such a major theme in the New Testament, but also what it is that is being taught that requires appropriate teaching modalities to be effective. The New Testament content of discipleship is implementing a highly-charismatic expression of ministry skills or giftings.

> (2) The previous section on goals showed that the simplest examination of what it is that the New Testament expects of its readers in terms of ministry activity is to obey the commissioning accounts,[32] which is to replicate the charismatic mission of Jesus and his disciples. What is the content of those commissions? It is the very commands that traditional

> Protestantism studiously ignores: "preach as you go, saying, 'The kingdom of heaven is at hand.' Heal the sick, raise the dead, cleanse lepers, cast out demons" (Matt 10:7–8 RSV). "He gave them power and authority over all demons and to cure diseases, and he sent them out to preach the kingdom of God and to heal" (Luke 9:1–2; cf. Mark 6:7; Luke 10:9). This "authority" is certainly the authority over unclean spirits, offered here as an example of broader charismatic ministry that is to be spread by the eleven, and ultimately by the church, to the whole world (Matt 28:19–20).

Traditional theological education on this issue, however, is shaped both by Protestant cessationism and Enlightenment rationalism; hence, the commissions of Jesus devolve into the presentation of an ineffective system of moral precepts (that are "culturally sensitive"), or an intellectually respectable apologetic. Obedience of the commissioning accounts in the New Testament, on the other hand, was based on a teaching modality appropriate to the subject matter. One does not learn to swim, drive, counsel, or perform surgery merely by reading or lectures. Actual physical performance is required. This is especially true for learning the skills and giftings of ministry.

> (3) Christian ministry training occurs best within the actual practice of advancing the kingdom of God.

Robert Banks summarizes the biblical pattern of ministry education with a profound insight. He notes that there were concentric circles of followers around the key figures in the New Testament, ranging from full-time to intermittent associations:

> The purpose of these groups was not increase in knowledge of their basic traditions, progress in moral or spiritual formation, or the development of skills associated with ministry or leadership. It was *active service or mission in furthering the kingdom* [italics mine]. . . . Within that framework, however, spiritual growth and practical development as well as substantial learning, also took place. Such learning was often in-service

> and nonformal in character; at other times it was more extensive and systematic. . . . The point of departure for such instruction was often the life-situations of individual members, the group as a whole, or the context in which they were operating.[33]

Here the explicit goal of actual discipleship (obeying the commissions) shaped the teaching modalities. The cart was not before the horse: since the commission was being obeyed, the learning occurred while ministry occurred.[34] This would be as true for ministry within the New Testament home groups as it would be presenting the Kingdom in power in foreign cities. This teaching modality stands at the most extreme polarity possible from the tendency toward isolation from, and irrelevance to, real ministry that we find in TTE.

> (4) Finally, with this context in mind, New Testament ministry training must be done with experienced and effective practitioners through a process of imitation. Paul can insist that believers "imitate me as I imitate Christ" (1 Cor 11:1). The chain of imitation was to go on for generations.[35] The imitation involved duplicating the principles and activities of the mentor, specifically including the dimension of charismatic ministry and evangelism. In the New Testament, disciples do not have the option of picking and choosing their academic religious majors or areas of specialization. God distributes spiritual gifts "as He wills." One is called and directed by the Spirit into a ministry characterized by a tension of both power and suffering.

Let us examine the contrasting approach of traditional theological education.

TRADITIONAL THEOLOGICAL EDUCATION

In sharp contrast to the four irreducible elements of New Testament ministry training, above, TTE typically displays an opposing agenda.

(1) In contrast to the New Testament emphasis on the discipleship process, beyond the acquisition of specific course information, TTE betrays relatively little interest in a student's performance in the field as an effective Christian worker, let alone his or her moral, spiritual or charismatic ministry. Unless a faculty member specializes in spiritual formation, the scholarly publication of the professors within TTE rarely focuses on the discipleship issues of the seminarian.

(2) In contrast to the emphasis placed on prayer, faith, and charismatic expression in the Gospels and Acts (which, after all, came later than most epistles and served as a corrective to restore emphasis upon the ministry patterns of Jesus and his disciples), TTE leaves that to extra-curricular activities. At the beginning of my own seminary experience, the dean, a well-respected evangelical leader, explicitly told us that we were not to expect the seminary to aid us in our spiritual growth, but only in our intellectual development. To be fair, there has been an increased interest in spiritual formation in seminaries, but the models there tend toward classical exercises in piety and ethics rather than the spiritualities of evangelism and power encounters as emphasized in the New Testament.

(3) In contrast to the New Testament pattern of learning-while-doing in actual situations of ministry, TTE seems based on a monastic model of seclusion. This teaching modality may well communicate that ministry is learned best away from real ministry situations; that ministry learning is, formally, at least, not an ongoing experience; that theory and practice are best separated; and that ministry training is primarily an academic exercise.

This approach violates a fundamental truism of education: that the teaching modality must be appropriate to the subject matter; that if ministry involves a variety of higher order cognitive, spiritual, and physical skills, then appropriate provision must be made for this type of learning to occur. Oddly, however, this academic/monastic arrangement is in fact appropriate for TTE, which requires the substitution by an intellectual grasp of information in place of the effective activities of ministry. The epistemology and goals of TTE have quite clearly determined its own venue and setting! It serves as an effective quarantine of Christian ministry from the surrounding world—at least apart from brief periods of field education.

(4) Again in contrast to the New Testament principle, TTE's agenda of academic pre-eminence conflicts with the notion of mentoring students—particularly in the right direction. Most seminary students are at an age where they are mentally hard-wired for a mentoring experience, rather like Konrad Lorenz's baby ducks. In a seminary, who are the objects of mentoring? Sadly, it is PhDs[36] with their secular epistemology, goals, and teaching modalities.

Kenneth Meyer, while President of Trinity Evangelical Divinity School, lamented,

> The curriculum has called for professionals of the academy, rather than professionals of the church. The truth is, students will model their professors. In our [seminary] some 75% of faculty have never pastored a church longer than an intern[ship] during graduate studies. Is it [any] wonder that graduates come out "heady" and lacking ministry skills?[37]

Yet Trinity Evangelical Divinity School is acknowledged as an outstanding seminary and recommended as an excellent place to seek training for ministry. On what grounds? "Outstanding faculty" who are so because they have published a sizable volume of material. Yet you have just seen the President's concern about the product, and he further noted that no changes were made in twenty years to address this concern! Traditional theological education collides with Christian discipleship training and wins again. The hidden agenda trumps the stated purpose of the seminary.

The mentoring process in the New Testament, however, is in a setting very different from that of a typical seminary professor. Quite simply, if the modeling/mentoring process occurs at all in the seminary setting, it is based on someone in a different formal role than that of a pastor, evangelist, or missionary. Most often it is the epistemology and value-system of the academy rather than of Christ Jesus that is being absorbed by the student.[38]

Even if mentoring were done toward the right goals, if not in the right setting, the conventional seminary professor would have great difficulty following up often enough in a mentoring relationship over the years. The schedule does not permit it. We must note, however, that in many settings within the seminaries, many professors provide wonderful spiritual nurture to students both within and outside the classroom. There is also no denying that academic subjects taught well can influence students spiritually and practically. Most of the readers of this chapter can attest to that. The point of this project, however, is that this godly process is shaped, subverted, and even suppressed by the double message inherent in the academic structures and emphases.

If the conventional TTE model is inadequate, what alternatives could we offer?

ALTERNATE MODELS OF MINISTRY TRAINING

The face of training for ministry is changing. I am told that there are now some 500 church-based Bible institutes or ministry training centers in the American Assemblies of God alone. The Internet and other technologies are making it increasingly possible to study for ministry at home. Accordingly, ATS has increased the percentage of distance education credits that may apply to a seminary degree. The trend toward on-the-job training in general is gaining momentum. A couple of examples would be the highly practical training at Bethel Church School of Supernatural Ministry in Redding, California. Randy Clark has a similar school, but has now launched a totally online program of substantial quality in his Christian Healing Certification Program. He also supports the Wagner Leadership Institute, which is offered at many sites world-wide. Presently, despite the enormous expenditure and facilities in American formal education, most education today in this country occurs in business in the workplace. How should seminary education respond to these changes and to the biblical mandates?

First, encourage denominational leaders and pastors to return to the tradition of training pastors by apprenticeship.[39] Give status and "accreditation" to godly, successful pastors who consistently and effectively mentor others into ministry. Quality control could be maintained by the denominational leadership by requiring practical exams of ministry skills, recommendation of the mentor, as well as evidence of successful ministry before ordination.

Second, train only those who are already involved in some local ministry. This has the salutary effect of making the learning experience relevant for the student on the one hand. Moreover, the student's exposure to the real world of ministry will create a demand for courses that provide meaningful training, rather than irrelevant academics.

Third, decentralize the operation of the seminary so that the contributions of professors to ministry could be packaged into short, intensive blocks of instruction at a variety of meeting centers closer to the pastors being served. This move tends to place control and accountability at the level of the clergy-in-training who are already in touch with the needs of ministry than the provider (as is the case presently). This decentralizing would inspire serious scholars with a heart for ministry to "bring out treasures old and new" like the scribes in the kingdom, that is, to recast many useful insights of biblical and theological scholarship into edifying food for the soul.

Alternatively, the use of the Internet to deliver courses is enjoying considerable interest, though most present methods seem to be labor intensive. Automated teaching of courses is already being developed, potentially offering a great deal of informational teaching at low cost to the local consumer.

It might also be a good idea to derive financial support from the larger local divisions of the denomination for the service to them, on the premise of the Golden Rule: the ones with the gold make the rules. This would have the effect of making the seminaries more accountable to "the hand that feeds them" and to the mission of the church.

Fourth, eliminate the system of grades and degrees that conveys status only for the ability to grasp information and to display that ability in order to gain prestige. Jesus describes the academics in Matthew 23 who were ostentatious in displaying their religious symbols and their teaching positions "to be seen of men." This spirit is alive and well in the very similar symbols and attitudes in contemporary academia.

The Bible, by contrast, lays out criteria for recognizing qualifications for various ministries, such as the characteristics of apostles, elders, and deacons, all of whom must express their life in the New Covenant Spirit and His fruits and gifts. Centrally, the honor for New Testament workers is a recognition and encouragement of their servanthood and gifting for ministry in the church and to the world. We must recognize that the value systems of godly and worldly knowledge are inimical to each other: it does us no good to keep the leaven in our midst.

Fifth, if we employ a site-based training program focused strictly on effectiveness in ministry, then what is to be done with all those out of work seminary professors who would prefer to focus on the theoretical and academic? Christian scholarship is after all a noble vocation. The life of the mind as well as Christian interaction with the issues of the day are indeed part of the gifting of the church. Yet it remains to be proven that the issues that generally absorb the time and interest of academics also meaningfully treat the concerns of the people in the pew or the Christian worker. If one's love, interest, and allocation of time lie with academic pursuits, rather than with the demonstrable application of those pursuits to effective ministry training, how can one with integrity resolve this inherent conflict of interest we find in the seminary or Bible college? If the tension seems unbearable or if one's focus fails to conform honestly with the stated goals of the ministry training institution, then perhaps a university serves as a better venue for our talents and interests—"Each one must be fully convinced in his own mind."

Finally, whether or not seminaries change their spots, we must recognize that change in the outside world, if not the kingdom of God, may be passing us by. Electronic media delivered to homes and local churches is increasingly finding a role in the new Christian ministry training paradigm. More local, traditional churches are creating training centers for their people, usually with a strong practical component for ministry. A most exciting (and biblical) example is training centers modeled on that of Bethel Church in Redding, California, which we shall discuss below.

The next chapter discusses a more comprehensive New Testament answer to the problems raised above.

---

1. This chapter was originally delivered as a plenary address at the March 2001 Annual Meeting of the Society for Pentecostal Studies, hosted by Oral Roberts University, Tulsa, OK. Careful readers may note stylistic differences between this chapter, written for oral delivery at a scholarly meeting, and the others, which were written solely for this book.
2. As described in, e.g., William Menzies, *Anointed to Serve: The Story of the Assemblies of God* (Springfield, Mo.: Gospel Publishing House, 1971), 141.
3. Perhaps the strongest case I have discovered for the intellectual mission of the seminary is by George Marsden, "The Intellectual Task of a Theological Seminary," *Review and Expositor* 92:3 (Summer, 1995), 351–57. Of course, this present section is not arguing against intellectual rigor, but intellectual*ism*—the institutionalized centrality of academics vs. the training of effective Christian workers.
4. See the survey of the problem in Robert Banks, *Reenvisioning Theological Education: Exploring a Missional Alternative to Current Models* (Grand Rapids: Eerdmans, 1999), 73–126. Banks comes closest to a biblical model for training Christian workers that I have seen. My problem with his work is his failure to explore fully enough the charismatic dimension of Christian mission. See also, David H. Kelsey, "Rethinking Theological Education," ATLA 48th Annual Conference, June, 1994. *American Theological Libraries Association Proceedings,* 48 (1994), 123–34. As one who sat in endless seminary faculty meetings on curriculum and policy, I can agree with David J. Seiver's conclusion that seminary curriculum and policy decisions were often based, not on clearly defined "theological constructs, but on tradition, culture or experience". "Needs for Change in Evangelical Theological Education as Perceived by Members of a Faculty," EdD dissertation (Bannockburn, Ill.: Trinity Evangelical Divinity School, 1993), 218.
5. At the turn of the new millennium, the Church of God Theological Seminary (renamed Pentecostal Theological Seminary), Cleveland, Tennessee, reported, informally, that only 4% of its graduates, one year after receiving their degrees were *not* in full time ministry. AGTS in Springfield, reported an astonishing 92.4% in full time ministry at one year. In a larger survey of all 1,948 alumni contacted, 35%, or 682 returned questionnaires. Of those, 84% of respondents were holding credentials. Regent University School of Divinity reported 55% of graduates in full-time ministry one year after graduation.
6. E.g., Eta Linneman, "Why the Pastor Sounds Like an Agnostic: The Theological Academy and the Destruction of Faith" [excerpt from *Historical Criticism of the Bible: Methodology or Ideology?* 1990], *Touchstone: A Journal of Ecumenical Orthodoxy* 7 (Winter 1994), 14–19. Seminary effectiveness is a recurring source of angst among the *cognoscenti* of ATS in their house journal, *Theological Education.* S. Loren Bowman, et al., "Some Contributions to Planning the Future of Theological Education: What Is Needed in and from Theological Schools?" XI/1 (Autumn 1974), and articles under the issue titles, e.g., *The Purpose of a Theological School Twelve Years Later,* XIV:2 (Spring 1978); *Dialogue between Church and Seminary* XV:2 (Spring 1979); *Evaluation in Theological*

Education, XXII:1 (Autumn 1985); *Theological Education as the Formation of Character*, XXIV: Supplement 1, 1988.

7. "Yet one challenge for the leadership of theological education is this: the traditions that spend most on theological education are declining, while those who spend much less are getting stronger. So, for example, the Presbyterian Church (USA) has some of the finest seminaries in the world (Princeton Theological Seminary and Columbia Theological Seminary), but the Presbyterian Church lost two hundred thousand members during 1999–2004, which is more than any other mainline Protestant denomination during that period. Contrast this with Pentecostalism, which as David Martin explains, 'includes about a quarter of a billion people,' and in the United States alone has some ten million members and growing. The training for these pastors is often very limited and informal. Much of the congregational leadership is raised up from within and learning is limited to the Bible college. This comparison seems to suggest that the better the theological education, the less effective the congregational leadership." Ian S. Markham, "Theological Education in the Twenty-First Century," *Anglican Theological Review* 92:1 [Winter 2010], 157. Markham concludes by noting, "Theological education will have to mesh in with the strongest and healthiest trends that support the denomination," 165. Wouldn't that include Pentecostalism, as he earlier identified?
8. Interestingly, when Paul says that "we do not venture to class or compare ourselves" (2 Cor 10:12), he uses the verbs *egkrinai* and *synkrinai*—the latter a common term for a training exercise in Greek rhetoric. George Kennedy, *The Art of Persuasion in Greece* (Princeton, NJ: Princeton Univ. Pr., 1963), 270, cited from Mark E. Roberts, "Weakness and Power: The Contribution of 2 Corinthians 10—13 to a Pentecostal/ Charismatic Spirituality," 8. *Drinking from Our Own Wells: Defining a Pentecostal Charismatic Spirituality*. Collected Papers from the 22nd Annual Meeting of the Society for Pentecostal Studies, Springfield, Mo., 1992; also idem, "Weak Enough to Lead: Paul's Response to Criticism and Rivals in 2 Corinthians 10—13: A Rhetorical Reading," PhD dissertation, Vanderbilt University, 2002: 126–127, 205–216.
9. The dilemma of grading students as a way both of assessing and motivating has plagued educators for generations. The motivational component, many educators argue, can lose its moral opprobrium if the idea of competition is removed and replaced with contract grading—the successful attainment of learning goals, rather than a curve grade based on comparisons with others. On this issue, Parker J. Palmer laments, "How can the places where we learn to know become places where we also learn to love? How can we educate today so that 'the day after' will be a time of compassion rather than combat?" *To Know as We Are Known: A Spirituality of Education* (San Francisco: Harper and Row, 1983), 9-10. See the summary in J. M. Eddy and Wm. H. Zimmerli, "Contract Grading—Traditional Grading: A Comparison," 1974, accessible from ERIC (ED124623). See also, David B. Austin, "Grading Systems," *The Encyclopedia of Education* (New York: MacMillan, 1971) 4:182–184.
10. At commencement ceremonies do we see archetypes of Jesus' words about the academics of his day about long robes and tassels (Matt 23:5–12; Mark 11:38; Luke 20:46)?
11. Though post-modernism seems to oppose this movement, the traditional academic fascination with detachment, distance, and objectivity may actually have a kind of psycho-pathological etiology, much like the epistemology of gnosticism, which sought to escape from the physical into a pure, spiritual, and safe vantage point from which

to view the world. It was a doctrine that simultaneously led to asceticism and license. If the levels of child sexual abuse were as high in Greece and the Hellenistic world as some believe, then the experience of "splitting off" from the body during sexual trauma, and the resulting oscillation between promiscuity and frigidity may have provided a widespread experiential grounding for gnosticism, and ultimately, the Enlightenment notion of "objectivity" in knowledge. This, of course, stands in stark contrast to the biblical "knowing" that involves relationship, direct involvement, and experience.

12. Roberts, "Weakness and Power," 16–18.
13. Matt 23:5–15 esv: "5 They do all their deeds to be seen by others. For they make their phylacteries broad and their fringes long, 6 and they love the place of honor at feasts and the best seats in the synagogues 7 and greetings in the marketplaces and being called rabbi by others. 8 But you are not to be called rabbi, for you have one teacher, and you are all brothers. 9 And call no man your father on earth, for you have one Father, who is in heaven. 10 Neither be called instructors, for you have one instructor, the Christ. 11 The greatest among you shall be your servant. 12 Whoever exalts himself will be humbled, and whoever humbles himself will be exalted. 13 But woe to you, scribes and Pharisees, hypocrites! For you shut the kingdom of heaven in people's faces. For you neither enter yourselves nor allow those who would enter to go in. 15 Woe to you, scribes and Pharisees, hypocrites! For you travel across sea and land to make a single proselyte, and when he becomes a proselyte, you make him twice as much a child of hell as yourselves."
14. To be fair, however, accrediting agencies, at least theoretically, attempt, as much as possible, to allow their educational institutions to define the content of teaching, goals, and outcomes within the accepted conventions of certain degree programs. Seminaries, under the new Association of Theological Schools (ATS) accreditation standards, are to be evaluated as to the "extent they are doing what they claim to be doing and the way in which the school can do that better." Sara Myers, "The New ATS Accreditation Standards," *ATLA Proceedings*, 51:1 (Winter, 1997), 267. In practice, however, the range of options is limited. The cultural and theological agenda of the accreditors inevitably shapes their requirements. For example, a theological stance on women in ministry can affect a seminary's accreditation for academic competence. "Westminster Accreditation," *Christian Century*, 108:19 (Jun 12 and 19, 1991), 615. The accrediting agency in this case was not, however, ATS.
15. For a variety of areas in which knowledge increases see: http://activated.org/books/chapter.php?id=17.10.
16. This last point seems to be that also of 2 Cor 10:5, "take every thought captive to obey Christ." This is not a question of suppressing sinful daydreams. Rather, the context is dealing with competing theological epistemologies. A captive was not incarcerated, but *used* as a *slave*, hence, the "obey," above. Our "knowledge" must not only be pressed into "service" for Christ, but be shaped by His continuing revelation to us. The contrast is between "arguments" and "proud obstacle[s]" vs. the "knowledge of God."
17. See William Kurz, *Following Jesus: A Disciple's Guide to Luke-Acts* (Ann Arbor, MI: Servant Books, 1984), "Chapter Four: Sharing Jesus' Power for Service," 57–67. Kurz implies in the introduction, 5, that these early commissions in Luke 9 and 10 were intended by Luke to apply beyond the early disciples mentioned there to Luke's readers

generally. So also, Don Williams, *Signs, Wonders and the Kingdom of God,* 125; Charles Kraft, *Christianity with Power* (Ann Arbor, MI: Servant, 1989), 136.

18. The miraculous nature of the term "deed" in the above expression is confirmed in contemporary rabbinic materials according to G. Vermes, *Jesus the Jew: A Historian's Reading of the Gospels* (Philadelphia: Fortress Press, 1973), 78–82. Echoes of these summaries of how Paul "preached" the gospel appear also in other writers, e.g., in Acts 26:17–18 and Heb. 2:4, although in this latter case, as in Gal. 3:5 and 1 Cor. 1:58, the "confirmation" of the gospel was God working via a distribution of spiritual gifts in members of the various congregations. F. F. Bruce, "The Spirit in the Letter to the Galatians," *Essays on Apostolic Themes* (Peabody, MA: Hendrickson, 1985), 37–38.
19. D. G. McCartney, "Ecce Homo: The Coming of the Kingdom and the Restoration of Human Viceregency," *WesJTh* 56/1 (1994), 1–21. The exaltation/Spirit theme deserves much greater study from a charismatic point of view. Indeed, a good portion of this section could have profitably been devoted to an analysis of the so-called Spirit Christology, in which *Jesus-as-prototype* derives his power and ministry, not from his status as God, as traditional theology would have it, but from the anointing of the Spirit coming *fully* on him, but in the same sense as, and on a continuum with, his followers, who receive the Spirit as a "guarantee," as "first fruits," or as a "taste of the powers of the age to come." Jesus's own empowering by the Spirit extends in time into his exaltation and into the experience of those replicating his life—his disciples.
20. "In the Synoptic tradition [faith] is used almost exclusively in relation to miracles." R. T. France, "Faith," *Dictionary of Jesus and the Gospels,* 223. This association is by no means limited to the Gospels. W. Bodine, "Power Ministry in the Epistles: A Reply to the Evangelical Cessationist Position," *The Kingdom and the Power,* 197–206. G. Fee, *God's Empowering Presence,* 323–324, 608–610 and *passim* on the "charismatic" function of faith in the epistles.
21. **John M. Woodyard, "A 21st Century Seminary Faculty Model," in *The M. J. Murdock Charitable Trust Review of Graduate Theological Education in the Pacific Northwest*, 7.**
22. "Ministers were to be not only theologians and preachers; they were to be 'learned gentlemen.' . . . Although seminary leaders issued frequent rhetorical appeals for more ministers, they showed scant interest in the average minister or in pastoral practice. The scholarly aspects of theology fascinated the founders of theological schools. . . . The purpose of the seminary's residence requirement was to train students to be 'gentlemen theologians.'" Glenn T. Miller, *Piety and Intellect: The Aims and Purposes of Ante-Bellum Theological Education* (Atlanta, GA: Scholars Press, 1990), 26–27.
23. "Protestantism promoted a well-educated clergy, which quickly became the backbone of the international revolutionary movement. . . . In villages throughout Protestant lands for centuries to come, the clergyman would be the best educated citizen and education would be a key to his authority." George M. Marsden, *The Soul of the American University: From Protestant Establishment to Established Nonbelief* (Oxford, UK: Oxford University Press, 1994), 37–38. Marsden also noted the primal clash of epistemological worlds, or power systems, in the simultaneous establishment of Harvard and the Anne Hutchinson case. For it to have been a case at all indicates the apparent support she received at least at the grass roots level. "1636 was the year not only of the legislation establishing Harvard College but also of the turmoil over the Anne Hutchinson case. These two famous events were related since they dealt with two sides of the question of authority. . . . Anne Hutchinson . . . addressed theological

issues (accusing most of the clergy of preaching works rather than grace) and thus defied the principle that formal university education . . . was the normal prerequisite for exercising theological authority. . . . Most alarming to the authorities, Hutchinson was what we would today call a charismatic Christian who appealed to the direct voice of the Holy Spirit. . . . Had Hutchinson's appeal to a direct voice from God been allowed to stand, the whole Puritan system of hierarchical authority would have collapsed. Anyone, male or female, however unqualified they otherwise might be, would be able to challenge the biblical and theological principles on which the society was being built" (p. 41).

24. E. Farley, "Why Seminaries Don't Change: A Reflection on Faculty Specialization," *The Christian Century,* 114 (Feb. 5–12, 1997), 133–143.
25. Timothy C. Morgan and Thomas S. Giles, "Re-Engineering the Seminary: Crisis of Credibility Forces Change," *Christianity Today* 38 (Oct. 24, 1994), 75.
26. A similar result appeared in an ATS study contrasting seminary graduates' "sense of curricular importance" (what should be stressed in the curriculum) and their "sense of curricular effectiveness" (what the seminary actually produced). Ranked first out of 14 categories in "importance" was "devotional habits" while the seminary "effectiveness" in this area was ranked 9th, just ahead of "ability to administrate." Ellis L. Larsen, "What Does Seminary Education Produce?" *Theological Education* XXXI, Supplement (1995), 51.
27. "Authority for the seminary rests in the control of accreditation associations. Evaluation is built around the shrouds of academic freedom and tenure as defined by their peers in the accreditation process." *The M. J. Murdock Charitable Trust Review of Graduate Theological Education in the Pacific Northwest* (Vancouver, Wash.: M. J. Murdock Charitable Trust, 1994), 90.
28. **David B. Cable, "The Development of the Accrediting Function of the American Association of Theological Schools, 1918–1938" (PhD dissertation, University of Pittsburgh, 1970), 45. "Additional critiques of American theological education appeared during the first quarter of the twentieth century. Of these, the most detailed and influential was a study by Robert L. Kelly, published in 1924 as *Theological Education in America.* Dr. Kelly intimated his hope that through standardization all institutions for the education and training of ministers would someday emulate the relatively few theological schools which were generally recognized for their *academic excellence*" [emphasis mine], 11.**
29. *The M. J. Murdock Charitable Trust Review.*
30. **Jon Mark Ruthven, "The 'Imitation of Christ' in Christian Tradition: Its Missing Charismatic Emphasis," *JPT* 16 (Spring 2000), 60–77.**
31. Louw, Johannes P. and Nida, Eugene A., *Greek-English Lexicon of the New Testament Based on Semantic Domains,* (New York: United Bible Societies, 1988, 1989), sections 27, 33, 36, and 41:44–41:49.
32. Traditionalists, however, feel that the highly-charismatic earlier commissioning accounts in Mark 6 and Luke 9 and 10, with parallels, do not apply to the church today. Moreover, "when we turn to the Great Commission at the end of Matthew, we find no mention at all of miracles or healing. The commission of the risen Christ to go and make disciples of all nations, baptizing them in the name of the Father and of the Son and of the Holy Spirit, teaching them to observe all that Christ has commanded, makes no mention of miracles (Matt 28:19–20)." Colin Brown, "The Other Half of the Gospel?" *CT* 33 (21 April, 1989), 27. Against this see Jon Ruthven, *On the Cessation of*

the Charismata, revised & expanded edition (Tulsa, OK: Word & Spirit Press, 2011), 175; and Gary S. Greig and Kevin N. Springer (eds.), *The Kingdom and the Power* (Ventura, Calif.: Regal Books, 1993), 399–404.

33. Robert Banks, *Reenvisioning Theological Education: Exploring a Missional Alternative to Current Models* (Grand Rapids: Eerdmans, 1999), 123. For an encouraging development in our own circles, see Jay Paul Taylor, "A Spiritual Transformation Program for Resident Students at the Assemblies of God Theological Seminary," D. Min. dissertation, AGTS, Springfield, Missouri, 2001. This work seeks a quantifiable approach to spiritual development in the seminary program.
34. **"To separate those who are to be trained for ministry from normal church life and activity and from the conditions in which their ministry is to be carried on is a serious mistake. One preparing for the ministry of evangelism and church planting needs the church and the evangelistic field just as the medical student needs the Hospital and the clinic." Alexander R. Hay, *The New Testament Order for Church and Missionary* (Audubon, N.J.: New Testament Missionary Union, 1970), 488.**
35. "Discipleship, however, moves to a third, fourth and even a fifth generation in the New Testament. Paul can require of his readers, for example, 'Imitate me even as [*kathōs*–to the same degree and extent that] I imitate Christ' (1 Cor 11:1). Four other times he exhorts churches to imitate him (1 Cor 4:16; Phil 3:17; 2 Thes 3:7, 9, *cf*. Gal 4:12, Phil 4:9; Jas 3.1; 1 Tim 4.16; 2 Tim 3:4). In 1 Cor 4:15–17 Paul says that he became the Corinthians' "'father' through the gospel." This obviously means something more than progenitor, or father, of a new religion, but rather retains the more technical meaning of rabbi/teacher. Proof of this is the remainder of the verse: "I exhort you to become imitators of me. For this reason I have sent to you Timothy, who is my *son* [student] whom I love [an echo of Jesus' baptism?] who will *remind* you *of my ways*." The term "ways" is a Semitism that refers to the whole characteristic pattern of life. Here, then, we implicitly have three generations of imitators described: Jesus, Paul, Timothy/the Corinthians. Similarly, 1 Thes 1:5–6 displays the pattern of imitation, not only to the third generation, but also to the fourth! Not only could the believers observe the type of people Paul and his companions were as they presented the gospel, but the Thessalonians "became imitators of us and of the Lord, so as (*hōste* —"for this reason") to become a pattern to all those in Macedonia and in Achaia." In other words the explicit reason the Thessalonians became imitators of Paul, was that they, themselves, become exemplars for others to imitate in exactly the same way.

    "A further pattern evolves in 2 Tim 2:1–2 where Paul addresses Timothy as "my son" and encourages him to perpetuate the process of replication to the *fifth* generation! "And the things which you have heard me say in the presence of many witnesses, entrust to reliable men who will also be qualified to teach others also." It is important to note that while the "teaching" here is verbal, it is directed toward spiritual empowerment and action, as is suggested from the previous verse." Ruthven, "Imitation of Christ," 70–71.
36. A doctoral level degree is still required by ATS standards (standard number 6.1.1) for all seminary faculty of accredited seminaries.
37. Kenneth Meyer in *The M. J. Murdock Charitable Trust Review of Graduate Theological Education in the Pacific Northwest*, 63.
38. The "heady" knowledge that Kenneth Meyer complains about is analogous to the problem of intellectualization in psychotherapy, in which the patient discovers (often

subconsciously) that it is less painful to construct an elaborate geography of the emotional problem, its sources, expressions, etc., than the discomfort of confronting emotional and moral change. Theology can act as the same distraction for a seminarian.

39. "According to the ATS (the Association of Theological Schools, which accredits most seminaries in North America), evangelicals in the 1990s lay claim to 63 divinity schools and theological seminaries in North America, enrolling more than 30,000 students. . . . Ironically, at the very moment evangelical theological education appears to have come of age, some influential parachurch and megachurch leaders are questioning the whole idea of formal theological education. The observation is made that if men who never spent a day in seminary can build successful ministries like Prison Fellowship, Focus on the Family, and Willow Creek Community Church, why have seminaries at all? In fact, a seminary degree will actually disqualify a candidate from a staff position at some megachurches." Robert W. Patterson, "Why Evangelicals Have the Biggest Seminaries, and Why They Are in Crisis," *Christianity Today,* 42 (Jan. 12, 1998), 50.

13
THE NEW TESTAMENT SOLUTION

The good news is that there is a solution to the serious problems with ministry training outlined above. This chapter suggests general solutions and recommends specific actions.

1. A SURVEY OF TRADITIONAL THEOLOGY

An increasing focus on the spiritual in popular American culture[1] has generated the now declining fad among teenagers. A "WWJD?" ("What would Jesus do?") bracelet, while clinging to the wrists of video game players or entangling the TV remote while clicking to the latest rapper on MTV, seeks to draw its wearers toward an imitation of Christ.

The WWJD bracelet expresses a more or less continuous tradition throughout church history to replicate the life of Christ—the impulse having deep but somewhat selectively attended roots in the New Testament itself. Devotional classics ranging from St. Thomas à Kempis' *Imitatio Christi* to Charles Sheldon's *In His Steps* easily spring to mind as examples. But the notions of following Jesus, discipleship, or today's favorite, spirituality, call up a historically-conditioned set of restrictions on how far that imitation may be applied. Traditionally, aside from minor movements in the radical reformation or from certain restorationist groups, we understand that a replication of Jesus' life is properly restricted to piety and ethics.

Progress in biblical scholarship over two millennia has produced little movement on this front. A recent academic collection of essays, *Patterns of Discipleship in the New Testament,* [2] continues this tradition without any serious consideration of extending discipleship to any other areas of emulating Jesus, especially to the miraculous. Protestant discipleship remains limited to piety and ethics, very much as is our present notion of spiritual formation.

In traditional theology, because Jesus' uniqueness as divine was accredited by miracles, traditionalists felt it was impious, even blasphemous, to aspire to replicate the charismatic in Jesus' ministry. Within this framework, an attempt to perform miracles would be an arrogant attempt to promote oneself as divine—an effort virtually as blasphemous as to claim one's own suffering and death to be redemptive for sin.

This section attempts to show that the elimination of charismatic and miraculous works from the purview of the *imitatio Christi* simply does not derive from Scripture and is not, therefore, normative. Against the traditional, restricted view of imitation, the New Testament contains a strong exhortation for replicating the life and activities of Jesus in all areas, including the ministry of the full range of the charismata.

The recent trend toward a more biblical Spirit Christology strengthens our thesis that a central New Testament theme in Jesus' ministry was that he is presented not only as a unique sacrifice for sin, but is himself a normative exemplar of charismatic ministry for others to replicate. Hence, in this section, after our survey of traditional theology and developments in this area, section 2 examines the New Testament and its contemporary expressions of mimesis (imitation / replication) and its semantic field; while section 3 shows that the New Testament content of mimesis requires a remarkably detailed replication of each stage of Jesus' life and ministry, specifically including his ministry of signs and wonders.

Early on, the doctrine of Christology found much of its shape in Greek philosophical apologetics. Since it was no difficult matter to prove that Jesus was a man, the overwhelming apologetic emphasis focused on establishing His divinity, the importance of this being that only God could redeem from sin.[3] In Christian tradition, then, Jesus came to be seen principally as the divine savior from sin, whose nature and mission was utterly and transcendently unique. To protect this image of Christ, the apologetic impulse tended to recast the New Testament portrayal of his ministry, particularly his miracles, into proofs for divinity—a move that had the effect of distancing the life and actions of Jesus from those of his mortal followers. Of course Christian tradition is far from uniform on this as on most issues, yet St. Cyril of Alexandria (d. 444) expresses some flavor of this discontinuity when he insisted:

> If any man shall say that the one Lord Jesus Christ was glorified by the Holy Ghost so that he used through him a power not his own and from him received power against unclean spirits and power to work miracles before men and shall not rather confess that it was his own spirit through which he worked these divine signs let him be an anathema.[4]

An anonymous commentator on this passage clarifies Cyril's distinction between Christ and the apostles with respect to miracles and the anointing of the Spirit:

> The apostles worked miracles through the Holy Ghost but as by a power external to themselves but not so Christ. When Christ worked wonders through the Holy Ghost he was working by a power that was his own via the Third person of the Holy Trinity, from whom he never was and never could be separated, ever abiding with him and the eternal Father as the divine unity.[5]

Obviously, while it is granted here that the apostles could and did perform miracles through the power of the Spirit, it is clear that Jesus' experience with the Spirit is unique and cannot be replicated precisely, even by his apostles. In fact, Ambrosiastor (d. 384), somewhat earlier, suggested that the experience of the Spirit involves a kind of spiritual entropy, moving from Christ to the apostles, who, in John 14:12 were promised they alone would perform "greater works."

A second, lower level of spiritual power is described by Ambrosiastor in John 20:22. Here it denotes an impartation of the Spirit conferring ecclesiastical power to enable the successive transfer of the Spirit throughout history by the imposition of hands. Finally, a third level appears in Acts 2 in which the Spirit was bestowed on the laity "whence arises the preaching of the church."[6] The specifics of this spiritual power are murky both in terms of the exegesis as well as the specific manifestations of the Spirit intended at the lower levels. Ambrosiastor does seem to intend, however, that spiritual power, over time, diminishes in stages and therefore the layman of today could never aspire to the level of charismatic power of Jesus or even his apostles. Calvin echoes this principle: "How plainly is his deity shown in miracles! Even though I confess that both the prophets and the apostles performed miracles equal to and similar to his, yet in this respect there is the greatest of differences: they distributed the gifts of God by their ministry, but he showed forth his own power."[7]

This impulse to protect the uniqueness of Christ, and by extension, his apostles, nourished the doctrine of cessationism which held that miracles and certain spiritual gifts appeared only to point to the deity of Christ and the significance of his work. These miracles, perforce, ceased when the core of Christian doctrine was established.[8]

It is in this mode that Luther sets the agenda for subsequent Protestantism with respect to our imitation of Christ. He suggests that while Christ's role involves serving as an example, his chief mission, "the *cardinal doctrine* and the *most precious one of the Gospel*" [emphasis mine], is to redeem us from sin through his work on the cross. When we possess Christ through faith as a free gift we should go on and do as he has done for us, and imitate him in our entire life and suffering."[9] From other passages, we know that Luther limited the imitation of Christ to traditional acts of piety, suffering, and ministry, yet he drew the line at miraculous spiritual gifts.[10] Subsequently, scholastic Protestantism and the deistic Enlightenment overwhelmingly expressed Christian praxis as a matter of ethics. Hence, with the restriction of the miraculous to the first century on the one hand, and the emphasis on Christianity-as-morality that developed later, the profile of traditional Christian discipleship was set.

Prominent evangelical scholars follow this traditional Protestant line even today. For example, Colin Brown claims that the programmatic charismatic ministry of Jesus in, say, Luke 4:18, cannot apply beyond Jesus himself; "no one else may claim this anointing and this role." Similarly, Hebrews 2:4[11] "refers to the ministry of Jesus and the founding of the church. The passage is not talking about what happens when the gospel is proclaimed in each and every age."[12] D. A. Carson applies the principle a step further: "The apostles and other writers of the New Testament must be viewed as something other than proto-Christians, models of what more Christians should enjoy and experience."[13]

TOWARD A MORE BIBLICAL EMPHASIS ON THE NATURE AND MISSION OF JESUS

As opposed to the evangelical denials that Jesus (or his apostles) could serve as examples to the rest of us for charismatic ministry, we can appeal to a perfectly biblical portrayal of Jesus as modeling all he did on the basis of his own Spirit empowering, rather than his divinity.[14] The emphasis in the New Testament on the example of Jesus who modeled his entire ministry, including his miracles, is clear, as shown above in Chapter 11.

Do evangelicals reject the clear biblical teaching to imitate and follow Jesus to do even greater works than He because these commands imply that Jesus' followers may then claim to be equal with Jesus in His deity? Since traditional theology had long maintained that Jesus performed miracles "because He was God," it would follow that anyone claiming miracles today was also claiming to be God. This is an intolerable conclusion, but a conclusion to which one is driven if we share an unbiblical view of Jesus and his mission.

However, the New Testament does not say that Jesus did miracles to prove He was God; rather he performed miracles because "God was with him" (Acts 10:38). Miracles were the essential way that God revealed himself, simply because they were beyond human ability. Their purpose was to reverse Satan's ruin in demonization, sickness, and sin. Jesus performed miracles as a way the kingdom of God manifested itself and as a model for us who are called to continue introducing the kingdom. Miracles were not intended for proving doctrines, as signs with no intrinsic value only pointing to something else. Rather, they were an expression of the gospel: miracles really are "good news."

Moreover, miracles and the charismata express God's testimony to the world; in these acts, He is revealing Himself (Heb 2:4). This is why Paul dares not "speak of anything except what Christ has worked through me to win obedience from the Gentiles." And how does he describe the content and process of this working of Christ? In this way: he "filled" or "fulfilled" *(peplērōkenai)* the gospel of Christ "in word and deed [prophecy and miracle], by the power of signs and wonders, by the power of the Holy Spirit" (Rom 15:18–19). Note that there is no warrant in the original Greek text for the translation that Paul "fully preached" the gospel (a Protestant idea); instead, he fulfilled the commission by presenting it in the charismatic power of the Spirit "in word and deed" just as Jesus did (Luke 24:19). Based on the normative model for presenting the gospel (Acts 4:29–30), Paul used words "of generous empowerment" (grace) in conjunction with God's witness via signs and wonders worked by the Lord (Acts 14:3). Paul and Silas could silence their Jerusalem Christian critics by showing that the normative gospel of signs and wonders had been received by the Gentiles (Acts 15:12), since these signs and wonders represented God's testimony about the gospel—not proof of the gospel—but the gospel itself.

So the gospel in the New Testament is not so much a message about Jesus (Protestant theology) as it is an expression of what Jesus himself presented: the kingdom of God in power. Jesus did this explicitly "in the power of the Spirit" (Luke 4:14; Acts 10:38) just as it was to be expressed in his "children" or disciples (Acts 5:12; 6:8; 8:13; Rom 15:13; 1 Cor 2:4; 1 Thes 1:5, etc.). Because Jesus was modeling his ministry for others to replicate, he necessarily needed to do so as a man anointed by the Spirit. He had emptied himself of his divine prerogatives in order to become flesh and thereby to offer a credible example for us to emulate. This view of Jesus is today described as Spirit Christology.

Modern evangelical belief about miracles as proof of Jesus' divinity and about non-transferable apostolic authority is challenged somewhat by the emerging emphasis on Spirit Christology. Traditional Protestants see this doctrine as denying the divine nature of Jesus. But Spirit Christology can be better understood, rather, as a turn toward a scriptural emphasis, as Del Colle argues.[15] It is possible to affirm the central creedal statements about Jesus while at the same time retaining biblical emphases with respect to his Spirit anointing. A variant of this line of Christology may also be described as paradigm Christology, reflecting an emphasis upon human response and replication of Jesus' life and ministry.[16]

Arguably, any discussion of Spirit Christology engages the most attended, developed, and dauntingly complex areas of theology—many areas we must bypass, as outside the focus of our study. The point here is that this theological complexity has not dissuaded countless numbers of Pentecostal preachers from expressing their intuitive (or perhaps simply, biblical) insight that "everything Jesus did we should do, because he was empowered by the same Holy Ghost we have"—in other words, a Christology of mimesis. Indeed, we would argue, something very much like this Christology of mimesis can be demonstrated as a key New Testament theme.

2. IMITATION OF PRACTICE AS A MAJOR NEW TESTAMENT THEME

The mimesis ("imitation") theme is extraordinarily large in the New Testament. While Louw-Nida lists only 5 words in this immediate family, some 42 words or word groups appear in the semantic field: "guide, discipline, follow," 26 expressions for "teach" or "instruct," and comprising a sizeable number of references to such activities as repeating, following, obeying, instructing.[17] Moreover, the extensive field of "knowing" words contains a strong Semitic overtone of "knowing by interaction with someone" as opposed to knowing by detached observation or deriving knowledge from abstract principles.

It is impossible to survey here all of the multitude of variations in the above fields, yet to do so would overwhelmingly make our point that Jesus expressed His clear intention that his followers would replicate His mission exactly, irrespective of their place in succeeding generations. This intention can be shown by examining Jesus' cultural and religious context, particularly his designation, rabbi, the ideas of disciple and follow(er), his explicit statements about the nature of his ministry's continuity in his followers, and the disciples' expectations of those who would follow them.

While examining Jesus' cultural context with respect to the teacher-disciple relationship does not prove the nature of the relationship between Him and His disciples, it is nonetheless instructive to note that in general in the Greek world, the teacher-student relationship "is predominantly characterized by the concept of mimesis. Teachers and students are bound together by a certain teaching and practice of life, and the student is recognizable in his imitation of the teachings and life of the teacher."[18]

Closer to Jesus' experience, Josephus offers a similar goal for all young Jews: "[The Law] orders that they shall be taught to read and shall learn both the laws and the deeds of their forefathers, in order that they may imitate the latter, and being grounded in the former, may neither transgress nor have any excuse for being ignorant of them."[19]

Even more relevant, the Jewish rabbi-student relationship expresses a similar pattern.[20] Ben Sirach (d. ca. 175 BC) says that the goal of a rabbi is to train his student to such an extent that "When his father [teacher] dies, it is as though he is not dead. For he leaves behind him one like himself."[21] To a humorous extreme, Rabbi Akiva (d. 135), followed his mentor, R. Joshua into the privy, during which time Akiva claimed to have "learned three good habits." He defended his action: "I considered everything a part of the Torah and I needed to learn."[22]

In the Gospels and Acts the followers of Jesus are called "disciples" (*mathetai*) some 67 times in Matthew, 44 in Mark, 34 in Luke and 73 times in John. This total does not include numerous references to the disciples of John the Baptist, the Pharisees, and others. In Acts the term, including one feminine form applied to Tabitha (9:36), appears 29 times, generally to believers in Jesus. The verb form (*mathēteuō*—"to become a disciple") appears three times in Matthew and once in Acts.

The word "follow" in its noun and verb forms appear some 14 times in reference to the disciples of Jesus in the Gospels and once as a participle in Revelation 14:4, referring to the 144,000 "who follow the Lamb wherever he goes." It is interesting here that these terms, "disciple" and "follow," apply both to the disciples of the earthly Jesus and to Christians in general.

In the Gospels, Jesus clearly stakes out a claim for his status as teacher/rabbi in the face of potential competing claims among his own followers. For example, in the context of rabbinic pride and intellectualism run amok (Matt 23), Jesus makes a triptych of demands, focusing on his authority as rabbi:

> 8 But you are not to be called rabbi, for you have one teacher, and you are all brothers. 9 And call no man your father on earth, for you have one Father, who is in heaven. 10 Neither be called instructors, for you have one instructor, the Christ. (vv 8–10 ESV).

Jesus is frequently described in the Gospels as "rabbi"—a term ranging in meanings from respect ("Sir") to a more formal term of "teacher/role model."[23] It is clear, however, from a variety of statements that the relationship of Jesus to his disciples rested upon the latter notion. For example, in Luke 6:40 Jesus affirms the traditional rabbinic notion that "a pupil [*mathētēs;* Heb *talmid*] is not above his teacher [rabbi], but everyone [each, in every case, without exception], *after he has been fully trained* [*katertismenos*], will be like his teacher" (emphasis mine). The expression "not above," in view of the contrasting parallel in the second part of the verse, suggests that the pupil normatively does not deviate from anything the teacher does. In the Gospel of John this pattern of rigidity in replicating Jesus' life is repeated in 13:34; 17:18, 23; and 20:21, using the conceptual formula, "As I . . . so you." In 13:15 Jesus states, "For I gave you an example that you also should do as [*kathos*] I did." The continuation and replication of Jesus' mission in his disciples is explicit in John 20:21, "As [*kathos*] the Father has sent me, I also send you." The English translation, "as" for *kathos* implies a sense of rough equivalence, expressing similarity, but necessarily not being the same, as in its synonym, "like." By contrast, the Greek, *kathos* is a word that carries the stronger sense of "exactly as," or, "to the exact same degree and extent."[24] Hence, in both these verses, the specific, exact duplication of Jesus' mission is intended. The significance of all this is that, in Jewish tradition contemporary with Jesus, as well as in the New Testament itself, no detail of a teacher's life is to be either ignored or not replicated.

One could argue, however, that the disciples' relationship with Jesus was unique and not to be replicated in further generations of Christians. Indeed, this is explicit in the cessationist tradition when it comes to replicating Jesus' ministry of signs and wonders. If we put aside the miracle aspect of discipleship, however, it is generally understood in Christendom that the Gospels and Acts seem to present the disciples of Jesus as surrogates for the reader.[25] In fact this is explicit throughout the New Testament: subsequent generations of Christians are normatively to be disciples of the disciples even as Christians are followers of Christ.

When we move into the epistles, the discipleship theme is every bit as strong as in the Gospels and in Acts, only the vocabulary has changed. Outside the narrative documents it appears that the terms "disciple" and "follower" are replaced with specific exhortations to live out the Christian life: to "walk" in the "way" of Christ, or to "put on" or be "in Christ" in some sense. There is a consciousness of the presence of the promised Spirit who is virtually equated with the presence of Jesus, e.g., 2 Corinthians 3:17, cf. John 14:17–18, 28; 16:16. In these examples, discipleship is advanced toward an even more intimate awareness of the rabbi, Jesus, who will empower them and guide them into all truth.

Discipleship, however, moves to a third, fourth, and even a fifth generation in the New Testament. Paul can require that his readers, for example, "Imitate me even as [*kathos*—to the same degree and extent that] I imitate Christ" (1 Cor 11:1). Four other times he exhorts churches to imitate him (1 Cor 4:16; Phil 3:17; 2 Thes 3:7, 9; cf. Gal 4:12 and Phil 4:9).

In 1 Corinthians 4:15–17 Paul says that he became the Corinthians' "father through the gospel." This obviously means something more than progenitor, or father of a new religion, but rather retains the more technical meaning of rabbi/teacher. Proof of this is the remainder of the verse: "I exhort you to become imitators of me. For this reason I have sent to you Timothy, who is my son whom I love [an echo of Jesus' baptism?] . . . who will remind you of my ways [Gk *hodous* = Heb *d^{e}rakim*]." The term "ways" is a Semitism that refers to the whole characteristic pattern of life.[26] Here, then, we implicitly have three generations of imitators described: Jesus, Paul, Timothy/the Corinthians.

Similarly, 1 Thessalonians 1:5–6 displays the pattern of imitation, not only to the third generation, but to the fourth! Not only could the believers observe the type of people Paul and his companions were as they presented the gospel, but the Thessalonians "became imitators of us and of the Lord . . . so as (*hoste,* "for this reason") to become a pattern to all those in Macedonia and in Achaia." In other words, the explicit reason the Thessalonians became imitators of Paul, was that they, themselves, become exemplars for others to imitate in exactly the same way.

A further pattern evolves in 2 Timothy 2:1–2, where Paul addresses Timothy as "my son" and encourages him to perpetuate the process of replication to the fifth generation! "And the things which you have heard me say in the presence of many witnesses, entrust to reliable men who will also be qualified to teach others also." It is important to note that while the teaching here is verbal, it is directed toward spiritual empowerment and action, as is suggested from the previous verse and as we shall see in the next section.

In section 2 we reviewed the nature of discipleship as mimesis in the New Testament setting, let us now in section 3 briefly examine the content of discipleship:[27] What does the New Testament emphasize that a disciple was expected to do when he imitated the life of his teacher/rabbi?

THE CONTENT OF THE IMITATION OF CHRIST

Let us step back for a moment and view the big picture of the content of New Testament discipleship by asking four simple questions: 1) What is it that the New Testament says that Jesus came to do? 2) What does he actually spend his time doing? 3) What does Jesus tell his disciples to do? 4) What is it that they actually spend their time doing? Finally, 5) what is the reader of the New Testament (the disciple of the disciples) expected to do?

(1) Frequently, when the New Testament writers condense Jesus' ministry into a sentence or two, they show him in opposition to the reign of the devil which appeared as demonic possession, sickness, the disruption of nature, or sin—it was "for this purpose that Jesus appeared, to destroy the works of the devil" (1 John 3:8).

(2) Peter spelled out the result of Jesus' baptism and gave a summary of Jesus' mission on earth: "God anointed Jesus of Nazareth with the Holy Spirit and power. . . . he went around doing good and healing all who were under the power of the devil, because God was with him" (Acts 10:38). Both of these verses confirm the programmatic statement about Jesus' mission in Luke 4:18. Summary statements about Jesus' mission abound throughout the text of the Gospels with references to healing and deliverances:

The blind and the lame came to him at the temple, and he healed them (Matt 21:14).

[A]nd Jesus healed many who had various diseases. He also drove out many demons, but he would not let the demons speak because they knew who he was (Mark 1:34 NIV).

And he taught in their synagogues, being glorified by all (Luke 4:15 ESV).

> In that hour he healed many people of diseases and plagues and evil spirits, and on many who were blind he bestowed sight (Luke 7:21 ESV).

> Nevertheless, I must go on my way today and tomorrow and the day following, for it cannot be that a prophet should perish away from Jerusalem (Luke 13:33 ESV).

> When the crowds learned it, they followed him, and he welcomed them and spoke to them of the kingdom of God and cured those who had need of healing (Luke 9:11 ESV).

> And great crowds came to him, bringing with them the lame, the blind, the crippled, the mute, and many others, and they put them at his feet, and he healed them, [31] so that the crowd wondered, when they saw the mute speaking, the crippled healthy, the lame walking, and the blind seeing. And they glorified the God of Israel (Matt 15:30–31 ESV).

> And large crowds followed him, and he healed them there. (Matt 19:2 ESV).

The preceding passages illustrate the sizable emphasis the Gospel writers place upon the role of healing in Jesus' ministry. Of course, Jesus did many other things besides healing and casting out demons. But the point is, if New Testament discipleship depends upon replicating the life of the exemplar, then miracles represent a significant part of "imitating Christ." Indeed, if the amount of space a writer devotes to a subject is any index to its importance, then the healings, exorcisms, and other extraordinary charismata must be extremely important. To show its emphasis—as a percentage of the text describing the public ministry of Jesus as recorded in the four gospels—the space devoted to the accounts of miracles amounts to 44 percent of Matthew, 65 percent of Mark, 29 percent of Luke, and 30 percent of John.[28] This percentage is continued in the ministry of the early church as recorded in the Book of Acts, if not actually expanded! Of the total text of Acts, 27.2 percent is devoted to signs and wonders. That represents more text than that of all the speeches of Acts combined.[29] If you add in the prophetic messages (22.5 percent), then you have almost one-half of the text of Acts recording charismatic activity![30] Bottom line? Jesus' public ministry in inaugurating the kingdom of God consisted to a sizeable degree in healings, exorcisms, and miracles and other charismata, not as a way of proving the kingdom but of expressing it.[31]

(3) Now we look briefly at what Jesus tells his disciples to do. At the outset, it is important to note the explicit reason Mark gives for Jesus selecting disciples in the first place: "He appointed twelve—designating them apostles—that they might be with him and that he might send them out to announce[32] [to prophesy] and to have authority to drive out demons" (Mark 3:14–15). It is only natural, then, in view of our previous discussion, that after being with him, Jesus would then send them out to replicate his own mission: "He sent them out two by two and gave them authority over evil spirits" (Mark 6:7). Both Matthew (10:1, 7, 8) and Luke (9:1, 2, 6) echo this commission in some detail. Luke includes a similar commission to 72 others: "Heal the sick [wherever you visit] and tell them, 'The kingdom of God is near you" (Luke 10:9). The numbers 12 and 72 could represent the "new Israel" the church, which is here commissioned to perform the same works.[33]

The Great Commission similarly commands the disciples' continuation of the miraculous (though some would wish to deny this[34]). This pattern is not limited to the Synoptics. The command to do "greater works" than Jesus is understood as a command to replicate Jesus' ministry in miraculous signs.[35]

(4) Now we ask, what did the disciples actually do? The only extensive historical account of the disciples' activities after the ascension of Jesus is the Book of the Acts of the Apostles. This work records, we assume, with an appropriate emphasis, the results of Jesus' training of the disciples: in short, what does Acts emphasize about discipleship? True, the disciples exhibited the virtues of the traditional notion of Christian discipleship in morality and piety. Recall that a conservative 49.7% of the text of Acts is comprised of charismatic expression: miracles and prophecies.Moreover, this high percentage of charismata

accounts does not occur without an apparent consciousness by the author. Several studies[36] note the deliberate parallel composition of the Lukan miracle stories in the careers of Jesus, Peter, and Paul and have drawn various conclusions as to the reasons these parallels were framed. Susan Praeder[37] points out that there are a variety of unreliable criteria, e.g., coincidental events or language, which indicate only spurious parallels, hence her caution that mere similarities do not demand an author's conscious motive to draw comparisons of the persons or points described. Nevertheless she notes that for Luke, parallel composition is the "surest evidence" that the miracle-working activity of Jesus, Peter, and Paul was intended to be understood as sharing parallel roles, that is, as prophets, healers, and exorcists. Some of the parallels Praeder examined appear in the following table:

Jesus	Peter	Paul
----	Acts 5:1–11	Acts 13:6–12
Luke 5:17–26	3:1–10	14:8–18
8:26–39	----	16:16–24
6:17–19	5:12–16	19:8–12
8:42, 49–56	9:36–42	20:7–12
4:38–41	9:32–35	28:7–10

(5) Even without the clearest similarities in content, verbal composition, or position in relation to the surrounding periscopes, the charismatic-mission activities of Jesus' followers in Acts (at least in broad scope) closely replicate those in the ministry of Jesus and those resulting from the first commissions of the twelve and seventy-two.[38]

(6) Finally, what is the reader of the New Testament (the disciple of the disciples) expected to do? Let us assume as before that the New Testament instructions to the disciples or apostles are in general also instructions to the reader. From this perspective we see that it frequently commands the reader/disciple to replicate the charismatic ministry of the apostles, e.g., to "seek," "desire earnestly," "rekindle," and "employ" certain miraculous charismata (1 Cor 12:31; 14:1, 4, 5, 39; 2 Tim 1:6; 1

> Pet 4:10, cf. John 14:12–14; 15:7; 16:23–24[39]; 1 John 3:22). The implication is clear that appearance of the charismata can be suppressed simply by neglecting to imitate faithfully the New Testament exemplars (Rom 12:6; 1 Cor 14:39; 1 Thes 5:19–20; 1 Tim 4:14; 2 Tim 1:6).[40]

Of particular interest is that the very verses that command a replication of Paul's ministry are verses that are explicit about the charismatic content of that replication. For example, 1 Thessalonians 1:5 is a summary of Paul's pattern of presenting the Gospel "not in word only (as in traditional Protestantism), but also in power (*en dunamei*—the most frequent word for "miracle/mighty work" in the New Testament) and in the Holy Ghost (*en pneumati hagiō*—carrying a strong overtone of prophetic anointing) and in much assurance (that is, in strong confirmation)." The Thessalonians are reminded that they came to know by experience and interaction (*oidate*) what sort of messengers Paul and the others proved to be. This reference is not primarily to character or ethics. At this point, Paul notes that the Thessalonians then, "became imitators of us and of the Lord"! The context demands that the Thessalonians were both imitating and modeling for others (v 7) Paul's miraculous/ charismatic gospel presentation, mentioning specifically among other things, their faith in God—a charismatic gift of the Spirit.A second example of the "imitation" pattern being integrally bound up with charismatic expression is 1 Corinthians 1:4–8, which shows Paul's presentation of the miraculous/charismatic gospel to the Corinthians—who then replicate the pattern "exactly as (*kathōs*) the testimony of Christ was confirmed among you, with the result that you do not lack any spiritual gift." This replication is to continue among believers until the parousia.[41]A third example derives from another main "imitation" passage, above: "be strong in the grace that is in Christ Jesus" (2 Tim 2:1–2). Traditional Protestantism might understand this as an exhortation to "be encouraged to receive the unmerited favor of Christ for forgiveness of sin and for promoting sanctification." A more biblical understanding would not only include this, but have a much stronger emphasis on availing oneself of the miraculous charismatic power indicated by the use of *endunamou en tē chariti* (be strengthened in the grace) of the Messiah, who bears the Spirit of prophecy in this, the end of the age (cf. 2 Tim 1:6). This exhortation, then, is the normative content of the teaching that is to flow from generation to generation of Christian disciples.

CONCLUSION

This section should not be construed as an attempt to deny that what we have demonstrated as normative New Testament discipleship contains none of the elements traditionally associated with the term "discipleship." Certainly, piety, meditation, self-sacrifice, and moral behavior are all essential expressions of an *imitatio Christi*. Nevertheless, the forgoing clearly indicates that a thorough review of the New Testament will confirm that our somewhat docetic[42] traditional Christology as well as our unbiblical evidentialist view of miracles has contributed to an understanding of Christian discipleship decidedly shorn of its intended spiritual depth and power. By now it should be evident that the high percentage of space devoted to Jesus' miracles in the New Testament follows the emphasis in the Old Testament on the way that God causes people to know him: that is, by acts of mighty power. Today, nothing is more crucial for the church to "stand mature and fully assured in all the will of God" (Col 4:12) and to be able to proclaim the gospel "in demonstration of the Spirit and of power" (1 Cor 2:4) than our understanding of the central charismatic mission of Christ Jesus and our relation to it.

---

1. In a December, 2008 Gallup survey, two thirds (65%) of survey respondents said "that religion was important in their daily lives." http://www.gallup.com/poll/114022/State-States-Importance-Religion.aspx
2. Edited by R. N. Longenecker (Grand Rapids: Eerdmans, 1996).
3. See the surveys by F. W. Norris, "Christ, Christology," *Encyclopedia of Early Christianity*, ed. E. Ferguson (New York: Garland, 1990), 197–206; M. Simonetti, "Christology," *Encyclopedia of the Early Church*, ed. A. DiBerardino (New York: Oxford, 1992), I:163–165; W. Pannenberg, "Christologie II, Dogmengeschichtlich," *RGG3* I:1763–1777.
4. Anathema IX: Against Nestorius, *PNF* 2nd ser., XIV:540.
5. Ibid., 541.
6. *PL* 35, cols. 2289–2291.

7. *Institutes* (trans. Battles) I.XII.13.
8. Or, alternatively, miracles served as scaffolding for the church: that when the church was established, the scaffolding (accrediting miracles) were no longer required, and so were removed. Ruthven, *On the Cessation of the Charismata,* rev. & exp. ed., 1–28.
9. "On Christ Crucified," *Luthers Werke,* Weimar ed. 12:372. "Christ is [secondarily] an example and pattern which we are to follow."
10. For a popular summary on miracles see E. M. Plass (ed.), *What Luther Says: An Anthology* (St. Louis: Concordia, 1959), II: 953–957.
11. "[God] bore witness by signs and wonders and various miracles and by gifts of the Holy Spirit distributed by His own will."
12. C. Brown, "The Other Half of the Gospel," *Christianity Today* 33 (April 21, 1989), 27. L. Smedes (ed.), *Ministry and the Miraculous: A Case Study at Fuller Theological Seminary* (Pasadena: Fuller Theological Seminary, 1987), *passim.*
13. "The Purpose of Signs and Wonders in the New Testament," *Power Religion,* ed. M. S. Horton (Chicago: Moody, 1992), 102.
14. J. D. G. Dunn, "The Spirit of Christ," in *Christology in the Making* (Philadelphia: Westminster, 1980), 136–149. C. Pinnock, "Spirit and Christology" [Ch. 3], in his *Flame of Love: A Theology of the Holy Spirit* (Downers Grove, Ill.: IVP, 1996), 79–111. M. E. O'Keeffe, "Contemporary Spirit Christologies: An Examination of G. W. H. Lampe, Walter Kasper, and Piet Schoonenberg," PhD dissertation, Notre Dame University, 1994.
15. "[We have] concluded that a dogmatic Spirit-christology may be developed from New Testament sources in a manner that maintains and affirms hypostatic differentiation in God." R. Del Colle, *Christ and the Spirit: Spirit-Christology in Trinitarian Perspective* (New York: Oxford, 1994), 184.
16. B. Ramm, *An Evangelical Christology* (Nashville: Th. Nelson, 1985), 179–81.
17. Johannes P. Louw and Eugene A. Nida, *Greek-English Lexicon of the New Testament Based on Semantic Domains* (New York: United Bible Societies, 1988, 1989), sections 27, 33, 36, and 41:44–41:49.
18. H. Weder, "Disciple, Discipleship," *ABD* II:209.
19. *Contra Apion* II.204.
20. For examples see: *y Ber.* I.8.3d; III.5.6d, cf. *y Ber.* 24a-b; *Shab.* 12b and 41a. N. Drazin, *History of Jewish Education from 515 bce to 220 ce* (New York: Arno Pr., 1979), 12. Having used these examples, we must avoid the temptation of forcing onto the New Testament later associations of the term "rabbi" from the second century CE and beyond, where the term has assumed a more rigid and professional cast. In this connection, John Christopher Thomas lists a dozen important differences between Jesus as a teacher and the roles of the rabbis contemporary with him. Thomas's paper anticipated many of the points made here. The overall point, however, is that the demand for *mimesis* in the New Testament does not rest on these later rabbinic models, which are only illustrative. We are seeking here to emphasize the clear patterns of discipleship found in the New Testament itself. John C. Thomas, "Discipleship in Mark's Gospel," in Paul Ebert (ed.), *Faces of Renewal: Studies in Honor of Stanley M. Horton* (Peabody Mass.: Hendrickson, 1988), 65–67.
21. *Wisdom of Ben-Sira,* 30:4.
22. *B Ber.* 62a and *y Ber.* 9.8, 14c. Typically, a rabbi's disciple was so intent on mastering the "rules of proper behavior that he followed every action of his teachers with the closest scrutiny and recorded their slightest habits." L. Finkelstein, *Akiba* (New York:

Covici, Friede, 1936), 181. So also, B. Gerhardsson *Memory and Manuscript* (Lund: C.W.K. Gleerup, 1961), 182–183.

23. E. Lohse, *"rabbi," TDNT,* VI:964–965. H. Lapin, "Rabbi," *ABD,* V:600–602. Some German scholars, *e.g..,* R. Bultmann in his *Theology of the New Testament* (New York: Scribners, 1951), 3, and M. Hengel, *The Charismatic Leader and His Followers* (New York: Crossroad, 1981), 50–57, attempt to distance Jesus' rabbinic pattern of *mimesis* from that of his Jewish contemporaries. This move may have been safe politically at a time in Nazi Germany when Jews and Judaism were being extirpated from Christianity. Hence, Bultmann offers the dubious claim that any characteristic of rabbinicism would necessarily be an inauthentic tradition about Jesus. Similarly, Hengel slides into a logical pitfall when he says, "it is singular what a small part basically is played in the Gospels by the 'example' or 'imitation' of Jesus: he seems to have directed his disciples' gaze not towards his everyday behaviour but towards the dawning *basileia* [kingdom] and the realization of the will of God in its particular and specific requirements" (p. 53), that is, not to "follow" Jesus in the sense of carrying on a tradition, but "to prepare for the service of the approaching rule of God."

    The problem of this observation lies in the fact that Jesus' "everyday behaviour" consists in acts inaugurating the kingdom of God—the very mission for which Hengel sees the disciples preparing! Hengel confuses Jesus' partial duplication of the rabbinic *pedagogical method* with a duplication of rabbinic *religious content.* Hengel's major contribution, however, is his emphasis on the charismatic dimension of Jesus' mission and discipleship, though his use of "charismatic" seems nebulous compared with more concrete expressions of the *charismata* in Paul's writings. Moreover, Hengel seems focused on what Jesus the charismatic leader is *not,* while this present study is more concerned with spelling out the *content* of the charismatic leader's mission and the *process* of its commission. Also see, B. Viviano, "Study as Worship," in *Studies in Judaism in Late Antiquity,* v. 26 (Leiden: E. J. Brill, 1978), 159. C. Blendinger, *"akoloutheo," NIDNTT,* I:482.

24. See *BAG, ad loc.,* 391. See especially, Klaus Issler, "Jesus' Example: A Prototype of the Dependent, Spirit-filled Life" in F. Sanders and K. Issler (eds.) *Jesus in Trinitarian Perspective* (Nashville, Tenn.: B & H Academic, 2007), 189–225.

25. E.g., Longenecker, "Introduction," *Patterns of Discipleship in the New Testament,* 5–6. L. Hurtado, "Following Jesus in the Gospel of Mark—and Beyond," ibid., 13, 15, 22, 28, 37. T. L. Donaldson, "Guiding Readers—Making Disciples: Discipleship in Matthew's Narrative Strategy," *Patterns of Discipleship.,* 40, 42, 44, esp. 47–48, *et al.* On discipleship in Luke-Acts, Longenecker affirms that all the lessons for the disciples "Luke meant to teach his readers, whether of his day or ours" in "Taking up the Cross Daily: Luke-Acts," *Patterns of Discipleship,* 75. Similarly in John: M. R. Hillmer: "at all times and in all places. . . . to be a disciple of Jesus . . . is to do what Jesus calls his followers to do" *Patterns of Discipleship,* 93. See also, W. Kurz, "Chapter Four: Sharing Jesus' Power for Service" in *Following Jesus: A Disciple's Guide to Luke-Acts* (Ann Arbor: Mich.: Servant Books, 1984), 57–67.

26. H. Wolf, *"derek," TWOT* (Harris, Archer, Waltke), I:197. E. Merrill, *"derek," NIDOTE* (VanGemeren), I:989–993. W. Michaelis, *"hodos," TDNT* (One-vol. ed.), 670.

27. Certainly, one could show that the New Testament exhorts its readers to view every aspect of Jesus' life as a pattern for the believer: spiritual birth, deliverance from bondage, baptism (with water and spirit), temptation, moral purity, prayer, ministry, rejection, suffering, trial before judges, death, resurrection, exaltation, and rule.

28. See, for example, Richardson's figures on Mark (*Miracle Stories of the Gospels,* 36–37). He counts the number of verses dealing with miracle stories to arrive at a relatively lower, though still significantly large, 47 percent of the Gospel, excluding the passion narrative. But this procedure may result in deceptively lower ratios of miracles to the total book. The present approach is to measure the complete miracle pericope, usually a paragraph unit, which dealt specifically and clearly with a miracle. Summaries of miracle activity in Jesus' public ministry were also included. Although Jesus performed miracles while alone with his disciples, e.g., the stilling of the storms, the resurrection appearances, the ascension, etc., these cases were eliminated from the count, since they were not part of Jesus' public proclamation of the kingdom of God.
29. Colin Hemer notes that the total text of its speeches fill about 22.5 percent of the Book of Acts. Appendix 1: "Speeches and Miracles in Acts" in his *The Book of Acts in the Setting of Hellenistic History,* ed. C. Gemph (Tubingen: J.C.B. Mohr [Paul Siebeck], 1989), 415–443. When you add the prophetic sermons to the charismata of signs and wonders in Acts, the total comes to almost one-half of the text of Acts (49.7%)!
30. One might object that these sermons in Acts are not prophecies. The rejoinder would be that these messages fulfill Jesus' prediction and instruction: "do not worry beforehand about what to say. Just say whatever is given you at the time, for it is not you speaking, but the Holy Spirit" (Luke 12:11–12; Mark 13:11).
31. Although it is also a kind of proving, in the same way race-car drivers demonstrate the fitness of a vehicle for the rigors of racing by putting it through the paces on a proving ground. Such is a correct way of viewing the temptation of Jesus: a demonstrating (to himself and, through his witness of the event to his disciples, to others) of his fitness to enter the ministry of the kingdom of God. But this sense of proving is not what cessationists mean, as long as "signs" merely identify a phenomenon (the presence of the kingdom) but do not express, or instantiate, the phenomenon to which they point.
32. The usual rendering, "preach," in most English translations is an unfortunate one, since the Greek *kerussein* in the New Testament suggests "to announce" or verbally to point out or introduce something with an overtone of prophecy, rather than the formal process and structure of preaching (three points and a poem) that we see in churches today.
33. F. F. Bruce, *The Book of Acts,* NICNT, 54.
34. D. A. Carson and M. Horton (eds.), *Power Religion,* 103. C. Brown, "Other Half of the Gospel," 28. For a rebuttal: G. Greig, "Matthew 28:18–20—The Great Commission and Jesus' Commands to Preach and Heal," Appendix 3 in *The Kingdom and the Power* (Ventura, Ca: Regal, 1993), 399–403.
35. G. Greig, "John 14:12—The Commission to All Believers to Do the Miraculous Works of Jesus," in *The Kingdom and the Power,* 393–397. J. Ruthven, *On the Cessation of the Charismata,* rev. & exp. ed., 92–93, 104–105.
36. E.g., see the review of proposed parallels in C. Talbert, *Literary Patterns, Theological Themes, and the Genre of Luke-Acts,* SBL Monograph Series 20 (Missoula, MT: Scholars Press, 1974), 55–65. W. Radl, *Paulus und Jesus im lukanischen Doppelwerk: Untersuchungen zu Parallelmotiven im Lukasevangelium und in der Apostelgeschichte,* Europisch Hochschulschriften 23/49 (Frankfurt: Lang, 1975), 346–351 and F. Neirynck, "The Miracle Stories in the Acts of the Apostles: An Introduction," *Les Actes des Apôtres: Traditions, rédaction, théologie,* ed., J. Kremer, B.E.T.L. 48 (Gembloux: Duculot, 1979), 169–173. See especially the extended parallels between the miracles of Jesus and

those of the church in Acts in G.W.H. Lampe, "The Holy Spirit in the Writings of St. Luke," *Studies in the Gospels: Essays in Memory of R.H. Lightfoot*, D.E. Nineham, ed. (Oxford: Basil Blackwell, 1955), 194–196.

In view of scholarly emphasis on the miracles of Jesus (see the bibliographies in Loos, *Miracles of Jesus*, 707–726 and L. Sabourin, *The Divine Miracles Discussed and Defended* [Rome: Catholic Book Agency, 1977], 237–271), the dearth of scholarship on what is truly a huge emphasis in Acts; i.e., 27 percent of the text dealing with miracle accounts, is astonishing. Besides the above and scattered references in the commentaries: J. Fenton, "The Order of Miracles Performed by Peter and Paul in Acts," *The Expository Times* 77 (1966): 381–383; J. Ferguson, "Thoughts on Acts," *Congregational Quarterly* 35 (1957): 117–133; J. Hardon, "The Miracle Narratives in the Acts of the Apostles," *CBQ* 16 (1954): 303–18; Th. Crafer, *The Healing Miracles in the Book of Acts* (London: SPCK, 1939). On the charismata generally, see James D. G. Dunn, *Jesus and the Spirit* (Philadelphia: Westminster Press, 1975), 146–196.

37. Susan Marie Praeder, *Miracle Worker and Missionary: Paul in the Acts of the Apostles*, S.B.L. Seminar Paper, No. 22 (Missoula, MT: Scholars Press, 1983), 115–116. The table (modified) is from p. 115.
38. See the numerous references in Acts, above. "The fact that the same Spirit which worked in Jesus is now given by him as the exalted Messiah to his followers renders the subsequent history of his Church and its mission parallel, in certain respects, to that of his own life and work. The ministry of the apostles and of other disciples resembles that of Jesus at many points." G.W.H. Lampe, "The Holy Spirit in the Writings of St. Luke," 194; Minear, *To Heal and Reveal*, 122–47.
39. John 16:23–24 as prayer for "anything" in the context of the Spirit's descent to the disciples.
40. On 2 Tim 1:6, J.N.D. Kelly affirms that "the idea that this grace operates automatically is excluded." *The Pastoral Epistles*, HNTC (New York: Harper & Row, 1963), 159. He compares the point of this passage with the "quenching" of the Spirit of prophecy in 1 Thes 5:19.
41. On this passage see Gordon Fee, *God's Empowering Presence: The Holy Spirit in the Letters of Paul* (Peabody, Mass.: Hendrickson, 1994), 84–90 and Ruthven, *Cessation*, rev. & exp. ed., 88 n197, 103 n11, 107–113.
42. "Docetism" was an early heresy about the nature of Christ, claiming that Jesus only appeared (from Gk *dokeo*, "seem, appear") to be physical and human—traits that would block out the revelation of Christ whom they believed to be pure spirit. This being so, Christ's crucifixion and resurrection were unnecessary. The possible influence of this view was the need in early apologetics to stress the divinity of Christ at the expense of his humanity. The religious tendency to exalt Jesus (and the apostles, and later, the saints) to a status so out of reach of humanity that to try to emulate Him, or even his apostles, is to thwart the clear intent of Scripture. On the other hand, Spirit Christology results from a more biblical grasp of the nature of Jesus (fully man and fully God), especially his claim that he came to be an example for us, and that we *are* in fact to emulate/imitate Him (John 15:13; 1 Cor 11:1; 1 Thes 1:6). Christian fundamentalism and conservative evangelicalism tended to reject the "example theory" of Jesus' atonement (and ministry) because it was the theory associated with modernism/liberalism, in favor of the traditional Protestant theory of the substitutionary atonement, which atonement only a unique, sinless, fully divine Christ could offer.

So traditional evangelicals tended to reject the notion that the followers of Jesus should perform miracles on the grounds that: 1) miracles existed only to accredit Jesus as God or the apostles as writers of Scripture; therefore, 2) Jesus and the apostles were only to be emulated in the area of ethics and piety, not in charismatic ministry. 3) Imitating Jesus could only go so far: just as one could never be sinless like Jesus, so we should not even *think* of trying to do the impossible: perform miracles. Similarly, nor could anyone aspire to the power and status of an apostle, since the gift of apostleship, by Protestant consensus, ceased. See Zane Hodges' comments, above.

14

DISCIPLESHIP GOALS AND METHOD BASED ON NEW TESTAMENT EMPHASES

The distinguishing mark between godly, biblical discipleship and traditional theological education is simply faith: that is, hearing from God and obeying, versus human "wisdom of this world" (1 Cor 1:20–21). Whom we hear and obey is the biggest single issue in the Bible: do we base our life on faith (hearing and obeying God) or on the traditional wisdom of men? Faith is the plot line of all the biblical narratives, including the major temptation narratives (Eve and Jesus), the calling of the prophets, the wisdom of the Wisdom literature, the word/logos of the Gospel of John and Acts, the mission of Jesus, his body and blood, and the goal of the Bible—the New Covenant Spirit.

Godly people down through the ages have, in spite of their cessationist doctrines, lived their lives semi-consciously hearing God's voice as they *de facto* experienced the New Covenant Spirit. In practical terms, they prayed for and received divine guidance, healing, and provision, even as they were forbidden to label these most striking experiences "charismatic" or "miraculous." Indeed, such godly people serve as pastors and seminary teachers, even as they teach that such experiences have ceased.[1]

The thesis of this section is that traditional theological education is founded on an explicit, poisonous doctrine that comes directly from the snake: the choice of the wrong tree. This intellectually exciting and seductive system is based on the false notion that the biblical message is a series of great ideas, information, correct doctrines, a creed—a kind of intellectualized belief that identifies one as a Christian. The controlling goals and methods of traditional theological education is the religion of the scribes and pagan teachers, expressed in competitive, detached, intellectualized, human knowledge: the great chasm between normative Judaism and pagan Hellenism, on the one hand, and New Testament Christianity, on the other.

Ultimately, this intellectualized labeling as a substitute for knowing-by-revelation is the strategy of the demons in the New Testament, who, when confronted, testified (in the most impeccable orthodoxy) as to the nature of their confronters: "We know who you are: the Holy One of God" (Mark 1:23–25; 5:7); "These men are servants of the Most High God, who are telling you the way to be saved" (Acts 16:17; 19:15). The demons, like false apostles, were all talk and no divine power (John 10:21; 1 Cor 4:19–20), "having a form of godliness (theology) but denying its power. . . . always learning but never able to acknowledge the truth" (2 Tim 3:5, 7). The truth is not simply a doctrine, but Jesus revealed and received. Pagan education strategy is all about gaining human control by substituting an intellectual understanding of God (Satan's "knowledge") for a revealed and received relationship, a "hearing of faith."

This intellectualized knowledge is the explicit goal of traditional theology: "Faith seeking understanding." This phrase expresses the human compulsion to conceptualize and articulate religious experience, partly as a way of controlling it. By contrast the Bible requires us to grow "from faith into faith" (Rom 1:17)—in other words, not moving from a religious experience with God to a state of human control-by-labeling, but from one revelation experience to deepening levels of experiencing God's ongoing revelation. Recall that the term "experience" is a naughty word to many traditional Protestants, whose theology is now based substantially on an "Enlightenment" epistemology. It rejects experiences of miracles, spiritual gifts, and personal revelation as a way of knowing—in direct, blatant contradiction of normative biblical teaching.

This traditional religious education primarily involves the study of documents (2 Cor 3:3) rather than "hearing" and modeling on the ministry of Jesus and living out his charismatic commission—the essence of the New Covenant. Put simply, according to the Scriptures, our primal choice is, do we hear and please God or men? Is our goal to receive a diploma or to learn ministry as Jesus modeled it? The disaster of traditional religion's teaching methods is that somehow we can have both: "head and heart" is the way it is deceptively put. Can't be done; the fruit of the two trees cannot be eaten together.

To repeat: the goals of the two systems could not be more opposite. The "faith" of traditional religious education is "persuasive words of wisdom," whereas the foundation of biblical discipleship is Christ revealed and "the [miracle] power of God" (1 Cor 1:24; 2:4–5). The essence of the biblical message relates directly to the goal of New Testament discipleship: "the kingdom of God is not a matter of talk but of power" (1 Cor 4:20). It follows, then, that the central activities of Jesus' commissions would be: "Heal the sick, raise the dead, cleanse those who have leprosy, drive out demons. Freely you have received, freely give" (Matt 10:8). This command, and many others like it continue if we are truly "partakers of the divine nature," and "imitate" Christ, since the very essence of Christ's nature is "Christ, the power of God and the wisdom of God" (1 Cor 1:24). "The testimony of Jesus is the spirit of prophecy" (Rev 19:10)—this Scripture describes our thesis, that we are not to substitute any means of communication (angels, saints, doctrines or documents) in place of one's embracing of the "true words of God," and that embracing is essentially to worship God. To receive the Spirit of prophecy is to receive Jesus himself, and vice versa (Matt 16:17).

All this lies in sharp contrast to the denigration and minimization of the power of God in traditional Protestant academics. In this tradition, miracles were given only for the "weak faith" of ignorant pagans until the real "gospel" took root. That is, when the notion of "creed" (a somewhat arbitrary list of doctrines and the outline of later theologies) replaced its lexical original: *credere*, to "believe/have faith," that is, to hear and obey a revelation.

THE GOAL OF CHRISTIAN DISCIPLESHIP:THE NEW TESTAMENT PROFILE OF A BELIEVER

Traditional Protestant theology emphasized a Christian life that has been saved from sin and hell by the death of Christ on the cross. The next step in the traditional *ordo salutis* is sanctification, that is, living in a state of being "set apart" from sin. Holiness, or sanctification, means primarily that one will now be good and live a moral or ethical life. This process of sanctification, as all of the steps of the Protestant *ordo salutis*, is thought to be empowered by the Holy Spirit, who enables one to avoid sinful behavior.

Certainly, there is nothing wrong with avoiding sinful behavior. In fact it is non-negotiable if one is to live a Christian life in the New Covenant Spirit (Gal 5:22). But if the traditional Protestant emphasis of sanctification is about avoiding sin until we reach heaven, then the concept is muddled when compared with the New Testament message.

SANCTIFICATION IS A CHARISMATIC MISSION

The essential nature of sanctification in the New Testament is to be "set apart" for God's mission, primarily to become a priest or a prophet. Granted, the Old Testament priests or prophets had a higher standard of professional ethics (Lev 21:5, 7; 1 Sam 2:12), but this was not the biblical focus, which was on their Spirit-empowered mission.

The essential roles of the priest and prophet were quite similar. Besides conducting the rituals of sacrifices, which renewed the Old Testament Covenant, the priest, like the prophet, was a discerner of God's will in that he "inquired of the Lord" for those who asked him (Num 27:21; Deut 17:9; 1 Sam 22:10; 30:7–8; 2 Kng 22:12–13; Neh 7:65). An ideal priest, as all the role models in the Bible (patriarchs, leaders, judges, good kings, women, prophets, and yes, priests), was one who received or heard the word of the Lord (1 Sam 3:1–10).

The prophet was not tied to the temple as a priest, but he often was more clearly set apart spiritually by his call from God (Isa 6; Jer 1:5–19; Ezek 1—3). His central function was to reveal the will of God to his constituents in the form of prophetic words or miraculous deeds (cf. Luke 24:19; Rom 15:18; Col 3:17).

Based on what the Bible emphasizes, we can say that the most important commands to a man or woman who wishes to serve God is summarized in the term "sanctified." All of the traits in the list below will appear in the sanctified Christian worker. The list describes the sanctified Christian as first being illuminated and empowered by the Spirit; after that there is no particular sequence in the Christian life as listed below.

Here is a summary of the characteristics that God requires based on New Testament emphases. The implications of this list will be developed more fully after this summary.

1. **Enter the New Covenant**. Repent, be baptized, and receive the Spirit. Every Christian can potentially become a prophet and minister in all spiritual gifts (1 Cor 12:4–7 "He energizes them all in all"). The goal of the Bible is the New Covenant Promise (Jer 31:31–34 > John 14:26; 1 John 2:27; 2 Cor 3 also, Isa 59:21 > Acts 2:39). Entering the New Covenant is the same as having faith. The number one theme in the Bible is faith, that is, hearing God's voice internally and then obeying that word under strong testing (disappointment, failure, persecution, suffering). "Every word of God is tested" (Prov 30:5). Having faith is also a nearly synonymous expression for "entering the kingdom of God," that is, the "area of God's ruling activity," which confronts and expels the kingdom of darkness and the demonic.

2. **Follow Jesus**. Christian disciples are to model on the ministry of Jesus, and all he did. The central purpose of Jesus' coming was to bring the New Covenant Spirit. Accordingly, he:

- introduced it (Matt 3:11 || Mark 1:8 || Luke 3:16; John 1:26, 33; Luke 4:18; Rom 15:8);
- modeled it (John 13:15; 1 Cor 4:16; 11:1; 1 Thes 1:6; 1 Tim 4:12; Heb 13:7);
- ratified it (Matt 26:28–29 || Mark 14:24–25 || Luke 22:20, 1 Cor 11:25; Heb 9:15; Heb 10:10; 12:24; 13:20–21);

- vindicated it by the power of his resurrection (Rom 1:4–5; Phil 3:10–14; Rom 8:11–14); 1 Tim 3:16);
- commissioned it (Matt 10; Mark 6; Luke 9, 10; Matt 28:19-20; Acts 1:8);
- bestows it (John 14:16–18, 26; 16:7; Acts 2:33; Eph 4:7–11);
- and actually becomes the New Covenant Spirit (John 14:18; John 14:26; 1 Cor 15:45; 2 Cor 3:17).

All this New Testament information about Jesus indicates that we are to "imitate" and continue Jesus' Kingdom mission as the commissioning accounts require. We are to be "clothed with Christ" (Rom 13:14; Gal 3:27), or clothed with "the Spirit" (Luke 24:49), or clothed with the "new person" (Eph 4:14; Col 3:10), or clothed with Spirit-given armor of virtues (Rom 13:12; Eph 6:11; Col 3:12; 1 Thes 5:8).

3. **Love God**. The ideal Christian worker will obey the first commandment of Jesus: "you shall love the Lord your God with all your heart, and with all your soul, and with all your mind, and with all your strength" (Mark 12:30). This is made more possible when we realize that we are loved by God simply because we are (John 3:16). Love is a result of the Spirit (Rom 5:5; 15:30; Gal 5:22; Col 1:8; 2 Tim 1:7) or associated with the Spirit (Matt 12:18; Luke 3:22; Phil 2:1–2; 2 Cor 6:6). Scripture is abundantly clear that even great spiritual power is meaningless without divine love (1 Cor 13).

4. **Love Your Neighbor.** "'You shall love your neighbor as yourself.' There is no other commandment greater than these." (Mark 12:31; Matt 5:43–46). Loving God and neighbor necessarily demands that one exhibit a visible and evident life of holiness (being "set apart for ministry") that necessarily entails being led and empowered by the Holy Spirit. Holiness, therefore, is characterized by biblical morality and ethics, a lifestyle of repentance from evil and purity of heart, speech, and mind. Understand and teach others that we are in a multi-dimensional sin-war between the kingdom of God and Satan's kingdom of darkness (Acts 26:18; Eph. 2:1–5; Col. 1:12–14). Walking in holiness and resisting sin and the enemy is

a non-negotiable state, without which no one will see the Lord (Heb 12:14), as well as an essential part of the battle to advance God's Kingdom.

5. **Pray constantly**. (Jer 42:7; 42–44; Dan 10; Luke 18:1; 21:36; 22:41–46; Rom 8:26; 1 Thes 5:17). To hear God's voice and to be empowered to obey it, prayer is absolutely crucial. Twenty-six times in the New Testament Jesus is described as praying, sometimes all night (e.g., Luke 6:12).

6. **Expect "Fire"**—persecution and suffering. The mission of Jesus for us: "baptize you in the Holy Spirit and with fire" (Matt 3:11–12 || Luke 3:16–17; John 15:20–21; 16:1–3; 2 Cor 12:10; Jas 1:2–4; 1 Pet 1:6).

7. **Disciple Others**. Make copies of yourself as above, now. Don't wait until you are perfect. It is a collaborative effort: your disciples will help to disciple you also. We are not called to build big ministries, churches or institutions, but to "disciple all nations" (Matt 28:19–20) as Jesus did to his disciples (Mark 3:14–15; 6:7–13; Luke 9:1–7; 10:1–21); and those disciples to their disciples. Every Christian should be able to say, "imitate [us] exactly as [we] imitate Christ" (1 Cor 11:1; see also, 4:16; 1 Thes 1:6; 2:14; Heb 6:12; 13:16 and John 13:15).

HOW DOES ALL THIS COME TOGETHER?

If we examine the preaching in a typical Protestant church, we will discover a pattern that emphasizes our need for grace ("unmerited favor") and our need to live out that grace by living an ethical life until we die and go to heaven. Occasionally we are encouraged to "evangelize" by inviting our neighbors to church, so that they, too, can receive saving grace from Christ, become regenerated, and continue the cycle above. Imitating the New Testament apostles or Jesus in their exact way of presenting the kingdom of God in power (Matt 10; 28:19-20; Mark 3:14–15; 6:7–13; Luke 9—10; Acts 1:8) is rarely mentioned or, more often is discouraged. That is what's wrong with traditional Protestant theology: it is simply not biblical! It does not follow the core emphasis of the Bible itself. In fact, as often as not, it denies it!

Traditional Protestant theology, then, emphasizes certain aspects of the biblical message and de-emphasizes others. Specifically, much traditional Protestantism emphasizes the New Testament themes of "salvation" from eternal punishment and "sanctification" from sin, even as it denies the central theme, taught and commanded by Scripture. This central theme is the immediate voice of God revealed directly to the human heart—the essence of the New Covenant, which, if obeyed consistently, precipitates the revelation of God in charismata, in signs and wonders. This theme is expressed in such terms as faith, the Kingdom of God, Spirit, dunamis (miracle power), charismata, and New Covenant.

WHAT WOULD A TRULY BIBLICAL DISCIPLESHIP PROGRAM LOOK LIKE TODAY?

First, let's look at the governing principles emphasized in the New Testament.

1. We assume that the emphases of Scripture would be reflected in the emphases of the ideal discipleship program. The thesis of this book is that the miracle-producing word of God revealed directly to our hearts is the central process in the Bible. Obedience to this word results in the mighty acts of God. Study of the "word of God written" (the Scripture) follows immediately from and simultaneously with the experience of hearing God's voice. We cannot designate them "Spirit" and "word" because ultimately they both come from the mouth of God. One qualifies and interprets the other.
2. Specifically, the mission of Jesus is intended as a model for his disciples. This modeling requires that the reception and expression of the gift of the Spirit is normative for all.
3. With the gift of Spirit we have entered into God's New Covenant, which involves the biblical covenant idea that all we have is God's and that all he has is ours. This includes our love. Therefore, just as his love for us is complete, so ours for Him should be also (Mark 10:27; 1 Cor 16:22; 2 Cor 13:14).

Practicing the presence and love of God, then, should be an important emphasis of a discipleship program. As Rolland and Heidi Baker frequently say from their vast experience of seeing God's power revealed, "we do not expect fruitfulness to come out of anything but intimacy with Jesus."[2]

4. Love for God automatically results in love for our neighbor—for any human. This will produce a consistent emphasis on outreach to those in need of a deeper relationship with God.
5. Prayer is crucial to remaining in the presence of God, whence comes all love, cleansing, blessing, and power for ministry. Therefore, prayer will be central to the training program.
6. Discipling others is also a function of being discipled. The church operates as a charismatic body of gifted people, each of whom uses his or her gift to build up, purify, and strengthen others. Practice in using the charismata, both within the body and toward those outside of Christ, is an imperative from the very beginning of the training. Even the most immature Christian can, at very least, offer love and intercessory prayer for others.
7. The method of conducting this discipleship program should avoid the competitive, prideful expressions of pagan educational programs that accredit the quality of instruction on criteria that are utterly alien and opposed to the heart of God. Above all, we should not offer the praise of men for mere intellectual grasp of ideas (no "grades"). One may evaluate the disciple's progress, offering correction and encouragement, but only on biblical criteria, such as growth in faith, power, love, maturity, and effectiveness in mission—all objectives that rarely appear on traditional transcripts.

Discipleship, then, will structure its activities around the goals that Jesus established for his disciples, as seen in the emphases He expressed in his training program outlined in Chapter 13, above. The commissioning accounts best describe his emphasis. Very importantly, it is imperative that the ministry be modeled for the disciples. They have a right to say, "Show me, not just tell me!" Traditional Christian education is centered around the "tell" part, and avoids the "show me," typifying "In the last days . . . [they will] have a form of godliness but denying its power. Have nothing to do with them, always learning but never able to acknowledge the truth" (1 Tim 3:1–7).

What would this look like today? In a nutshell, one may look to the program of Bill Johnson's, the Bethel School of Supernatural Ministry, or the mentoring and impartation practices of Randy Clark and his Global School of Supernatural Ministries (GSSM). More recently, an exciting new program that I have long dreamed of is developing as I write a Christian Healing Certification Program.[3] As far as I am able to discern, these programs seek to follow the biblical, rather than secular, criteria for training Christian workers (no MAs or PhDs teaching unless they are effective "modelers" of the New Testament charismatic commissions). In this, they appear to be exceptionally effective and biblical. In other words, these programs do not blindly follow the notion of a seminary education and its so-called "core courses" consisting of blocks of Bible, Theology, Church History, and Practics. Rather, they focus on the core courses of Jesus: intimacy with God, love, faith (hearing and obeying), and the mission of the kingdom in power, that is, the seven biblical characteristics of the ideal disciple, listed above.

One may object to this biblicistic approach: "Don't we need to contextualize our message? Or become 'incarnational,' or relevant, to our culture before presenting the gospel?" There are two answers to that:

1. "Becoming all things to all men in order to win some" only gets you in the door, at best. In most cases, over time, the ones presenting the gospel in this way end up becoming more like the target culture than the target culture becoming like Christ. Certainly, this is the consistent pattern of seminaries and some missions programs.
2. Nothing is more effective cross-culturally than raising a dead child to life, or healing the blind, deaf, lame, or cleansing lepers. Jesus' method works. Period. Any experienced

missions observer will admit that. Why depart from Jesus' methods just to be "contextualized" and "cool," that is, for the praise of men?

So what's wrong with Protestant theology? The following Epilogue is my attempt to sum it all up and bring it home.

---

1. For a poignant, insightful article treating this problem, see Daniel B. Wallace, "Who's Afraid of the Holy Spirit? The Uneasy Conscience of a Noncharismatic Evangelical," *Christianity Today* (Sept 12, 1994) <http://www.christianitytoday.com/ct/1994/september12/4ta035.html>. Wallace refers to the ideas of Dr Vern Poythress, who later published an article, "Modern Spiritual Gifts as Analogous to Apostolic Gifts: Affirming Extraordinary Works of the Spirit within Cessationist Theology," *JETS* 39:1 (March 1996), 71–101. This article recapitulates the dilemma that the writers of the Westminster Confession of Faith faced (see Milne, p. 8, note 3, above) in that many in their Presbyterian cessationist community, including their founder, John Knox, experienced charismata of revelation and power. Despite this, the writers rejected "experience" and "enthusiasm" in favor of a doctrine (cessationism), a doctrine that purportedly "protected" Scripture, even as it denied its major teaching: normative New Covenant revelation sent by God immediately and permanently into believers' hearts and mouths (Jer 31:33 > 2 Cor 3; Isa 59:21 > Acts 2:39; Rom 11:29). Ironically, in order to defend their doctrine, cessationists necessarily *create a second canon of the New Testament* —one for *after* the apostolic era (for the rest of us) and *another*, earlier canon that included *commands*, such as: "seek," "desire earnestly," "rekindle" and "employ" certain "miraculous" charismata (1 Cor 12:31; 14:1,4,5, and 39; 2 Tim 1:6; 1 Pet 4:10, *cf.* John 14:12–14; 15:7; 16:23–24—ask for "anything" in the context of the Spirit's descent to the disciples, John 3:21–22), which implies that their appearance can be suppressed by simple neglect (Rom 12:6; 1 Cor 14:39; 1 Thes 5:19–20; 1 Tim 4:14; 2 Tim 1:6). See p. 37, note 9, above. This "old canon"/"new canon" notion reminds me of one of my favorite *New Yorker* cartoons. In the old Roman Coliseum a lion and a Christian are standing behind lecterns, debating. One of the bored spectators in the audience comments to another: "Personally, I found the older format much more engaging."
2. Missionaries to Mozambique. www.irismin.org/about
3. Christian Healing Certification Program (CHCP): http://globalawakening.com/schools/christian-healing-certification-program

EPILOGUE

SO WHAT IS WRONG WITH PROTESTANT THEOLOGY?

Let's start with the positive: Protestants did a lot of things right. Protestants challenged the idolatry of greed and the usurpation of power in the traditional church. Protestants initially tried to remove the highly-evolved system of "mediators" or buffers between God and man, ranging from "the Mother of God" (Mary), the pope, the saints, and the "vicars" of Christ representing the pope, that is, the priesthood. Luther introduced the idea of the priesthood of all believers (that is, until his movement started taking it a little too seriously by going charismatic and undermining his academic authority).

This unshackling of the individual believer, however, succeeded in shifting the power to grant "salvation" to God himself in Christ Jesus and away from the manipulation of traditional religion. The power shift also moved authority from papal encyclicals to the Scriptures, and from the pope to the first popes (the apostles). "Saints" became all those who were regenerated by the power and blood of Christ, a sacrifice that released "unmerited favor" (grace) that was given to all who expressed "saving" faith. These were liberating concepts, that historians claim planted the seeds of the scientific and industrial revolutions, as well as the political revolution toward freedom and democracy.

On the other hand, when we examine Reformation theology, hastily forged as it was, in the heat of polemics and persecution, and measure it against the emphases of Scripture (believed to be the prime source of authority for Protestants), then we can see the essential flaws. Again, the emphasis markers of the Bible are the temptation narratives, the common plot line of narratives, central characteristics of biblical role models (Heb 11), conceptual repetitions, space devoted, summary statements, goal statements, and the covenants, etc. All of these emphasis markers point to the primal biblical experience: the New Covenant Spirit that causes us to hear and know God, resulting in our being empowered to fulfill His word of commission. With this in mind, herewith is a list of what's wrong with Protestant theology:

> 1) **Christian Epistemology.** For all the emphasis the Protestants placed upon Scripture as their ultimate doctrinal authority, they tended to use the Bible as a source for proof texts rather than allowing it to speak with its own voice and emphasis. As Protestantism expanded the creeds into their catechisms, theologies, and institutes, it becomes clear that the emphases of Protestantism were not shaped by the emphases of Scripture. I have argued here that even the earliest Protestant academics had been so trained in this "wrong tree" epistemology, that their starting point and thinking is far closer to that of the Jewish scribes of Jesus' time than the epistemology (directly hearing and obeying the Father) of Jesus himself. This starting point spun off into other crucial flaws that substantially clouded the message of Scripture.

Hence, the notion of "word" in Protestantism shaded more toward a collection of ideas—a creed, assent to which conferred the status of "Christian." Motivated by the fear of runaway Spirit movements and by claims to revelation and ultimate authority by the papacy, Protestants refused in practice, if not in theology, the central theme of the Bible: the word of God as directly and normatively revealed in the human heart that demanded obedience. The New Testament idea of "word" included, not only its prophetic verbal nature, but its wondrous power as well. As a consequence . . .

2) **Signs and wonders,** the central way God (and his Son) revealed himself in the Bible, were rejected by Protestants as obsolete devices to "prove" doctrine—as "signs" with no value except as they pointed to an accredited Gospel creed. This misconception resulted in . . .

3) **The loss of the "big picture" of Jesus' mission.** The Protestant alternative to the Mass and the sale of indulgences (which got you sprung from Purgatory), was their emphasis on the free gift of Christ's sacrifice, which paid for our damning sins. By contrast, the New Testament portrays Jesus' kingdom mission as introducing, modeling, ratifying, vindicating, commissioning, and bestowing the New Covenant charismatic Spirit—a synonym for the kingdom of God—a concept traditional theology largely ignored (See Sec. III, above). Within Protestantism, the Reformed tradition ironically failed to grasp the essentially charismatic nature of its own central tenet: the New Covenant!

4) **By denying Jesus' central kingdom mission,** traditional Protestantism seriously messed up New Testament discipleship, by denying the essential work of the Spirit in the life and mission of the believer. The New Testament emphasizes that a disciple necessarily takes the commissioning accounts seriously by imitating the mission of Jesus Christ exactly: that is, to minister in the power of the charismatic Spirit to advance the kingdom of God throughout the world (Luke 24:14; Matt 28:19–20), as well as within the Christian community (Rom 12; 1Cor 12—14; 1 Thes 5:19–21; 1 Pet 4:10–11).

5) Instead, **in traditional theology, the believer's role is essentially that of a consumer:** to receive salvation, meaning a place in heaven, and to "be good" until then. In this, Protestantism, failed to "discern the body," that is, those endowed with charismatic blessing, the New Covenant in the blood of Christ, which ratified this charismatic inheritance/blessing found in the body of Christ (1 Cor 11—14). Crucially, traditional Protestantism fails to grasp the central essence of the biblical message: that "the kingdom of God does not consist of talk but of miracle power"—that "your faith not rest on persuasive words of 'wisdom,' but on God's miracle power" (1 Cor 4:19–20; 2:4–5, cf. Rom 1:16; 1 Thes 1:5; 1 Pet 1:5).

So what is wrong with traditional Protestant theology? It tends to deny the very Scripture it purports to defend, especially as the Bible centrally points away from itself to the experience of God in personal revelation and power. It's a case of "focus on the finger." It fails to appreciate the wider mission and Gospel of Jesus as bearer and bestower of the Spirit. It is enslaved to a pagan educational system that ignores or devalues the core experiences and empowering of a true, New Testament disciple.

What's wrong? Other than this, not much.

In our answer, however, let us offer qualifications. This reframing of the Christian message, like the present expressions of our divine gifts, is partial—"we know in part and we (even) prophesy in part." We gratefully recognize that only in that glorious future "when the perfect comes, these partial things will be done away."

Certainly, the discerning reader will find much that is "in part" in this book, just as I believe we found corresponding incompleteness in the work of those brave, godly, faithful, divinely-guided, but incomplete men who confronted and conquered great darkness during their soul-trying times some 500 years ago. Certainly, we can proclaim further truth in the church only as we build on the insights, wisdom, and sacrifices of these indispensable pioneers of the faith.

I hope, nonetheless, that the overall message of this book will not be discarded because of perceived imprecise characterizations of traditional theology. Clearly I have painted this project with a broad brush. More importantly, I hope that this work will not be received merely as information or ideas. If that is the result, then it has utterly failed. Rather, it is written to encourage us to experience the true knowledge of the word of God, to be immersed in His loving presence, and to accept the charismatic commission that the Spirit of Christ Jesus has revealed to us, even as He empowers us to fulfill it. Jesus, after all, commissioned us to make, not scholars, but disciples.

At this point I feel it is crucial to emphasize that, while the kingdom of God is characterized by charismatic power, it is also characterized by moral, righteous behavior. Jesus is emphatic that there would be those who prophesy, cast out demons, and perform mighty works in the

Lord's name but who do not produce the "fruit" of righteousness. These he called "workers of lawlessness" (Matt 7:15–23). *They will not "enter the kingdom of heaven."* God does not know them.

Similarly, the apostle Paul writes,

> do you not know that *the unrighteous will not inherit the kingdom of God?* Do not be deceived: neither the sexually immoral, nor idolaters, nor adulterers, nor men who practice homosexuality,[10] nor thieves, nor the greedy, nor drunkards, nor revilers, nor swindlers will inherit the kingdom of God.[11] And such were some of you. But you were washed, you were sanctified, you were justified in the name of the Lord Jesus Christ and by the Spirit of our God (1 Corinthians 6:9–11 ESV, emphasis mine).

Just who is "led by the Spirit" (heeds God's voice) or is marching "in step" with the Spirit is spelled out in Galatians 5:18–25.

> But if you are led by the Spirit, you are not under the law. [19] Now the works of the flesh are evident: sexual immorality, impurity, sensuality, [20] idolatry, sorcery, enmity, strife, jealousy, fits of anger, rivalries, dissensions, divisions, [21] envy, drunkenness, orgies, and things like these. *I warn you, as I warned you before,* that *those who do such things will not inherit the kingdom of God.* [22] But the fruit of the Spirit is love, joy, peace, patience, kindness, goodness, faithfulness, [23] gentleness, self-control; against such things there is no law. [24] And those who belong to Christ Jesus have crucified the flesh with its passions and desires. [25] If we live by the Spirit, let us also keep in step with the Spirit. (Galatians 5:18–25 ESV, emphasis mine. See also Eph 5:1–17; 1 Thes 2).

Thus the New Testament teaches that it is perfectly possible to display all kinds of kingdom charismata without dwelling in the kingdom of God. We must recall that in Luke 10 Jesus does not minimize the huge significance of the disciples' mission; they did, after all, exactly what he commissioned them to do: to introduce the kingdom of God, not only in signs, wonders and exorcisms, but in total dependence on God for their physical survival (no money, extra clothes). The "wise and understanding" as well as the great prophets and kings of the past could not perceive the crucial events that were revealed to these disciples—to these "little children"—by the Father. Jesus even identified this mission with nothing less than "Satan falling like lightning from heaven." Jesus, however, emphasizes that the focus is not on the displays of power, or even on the epochal event of the overthrow of Satan, but rather that the focus is on God and their intimacy with Him; that their "names are written in heaven."

Thus Jesus does not deny the crucial charismatic focus of the mission, but neither does He allow for the idolatry of revelation in charismatic power any more than he allows the idolatry of revelation in Scripture: both are *necessary means to an end;* they point beyond themselves: the purpose of charismatic power (and Scripture) is to *reveal the loving God that we may receive and enjoy Him forever.* A true disciple will not only be empowered, but will walk in holiness before the righteous Judge of all the earth, who guides us in righteousness by his Spirit.

The New Testament pattern for receiving the power of the Spirit is necessarily *first* to "repent and be baptized." If Protestantism represents a gospel of preparation (repentance, regeneration, and baptism), then we must acknowledge that this *preparation* for the New Covenant Spirit is *absolutely indispensable,* a preparation to occur before and to *remain effective* during one's Christian life in the Spirit.

So let's hear His word, confirm it within the big picture of Scripture, then get out there and "do the stuff" by literally fulfilling the commission of Jesus Christ, our Lord! And above all, "Do not refuse the One Who Speaks."

ABOUT THE AUTHOR

Jon Mark Ruthven, Ph.D., Professor Emeritus at Regent University School of Divinity, wrote numerous scholarly articles and books including: *On the Cessation of the Charismata: The Protestant Polemic on Postbiblical Miracles (1993)* and *What's Wrong with Protestant Theology? Tradition vs. Biblical Emphasis (2013, 2022)*. Ruthven sought to develop a radically biblical approach to ministry training that replicated the discipling mission of Jesus in both content and method. He emphasized a biblical grounding for a practical ministry of healing, signs and wonders in the power of the Spirit. Although Ruthven passed away on April 11, 2022, his legacy lives on.

Printed in Great Britain
by Amazon

13942470R10212